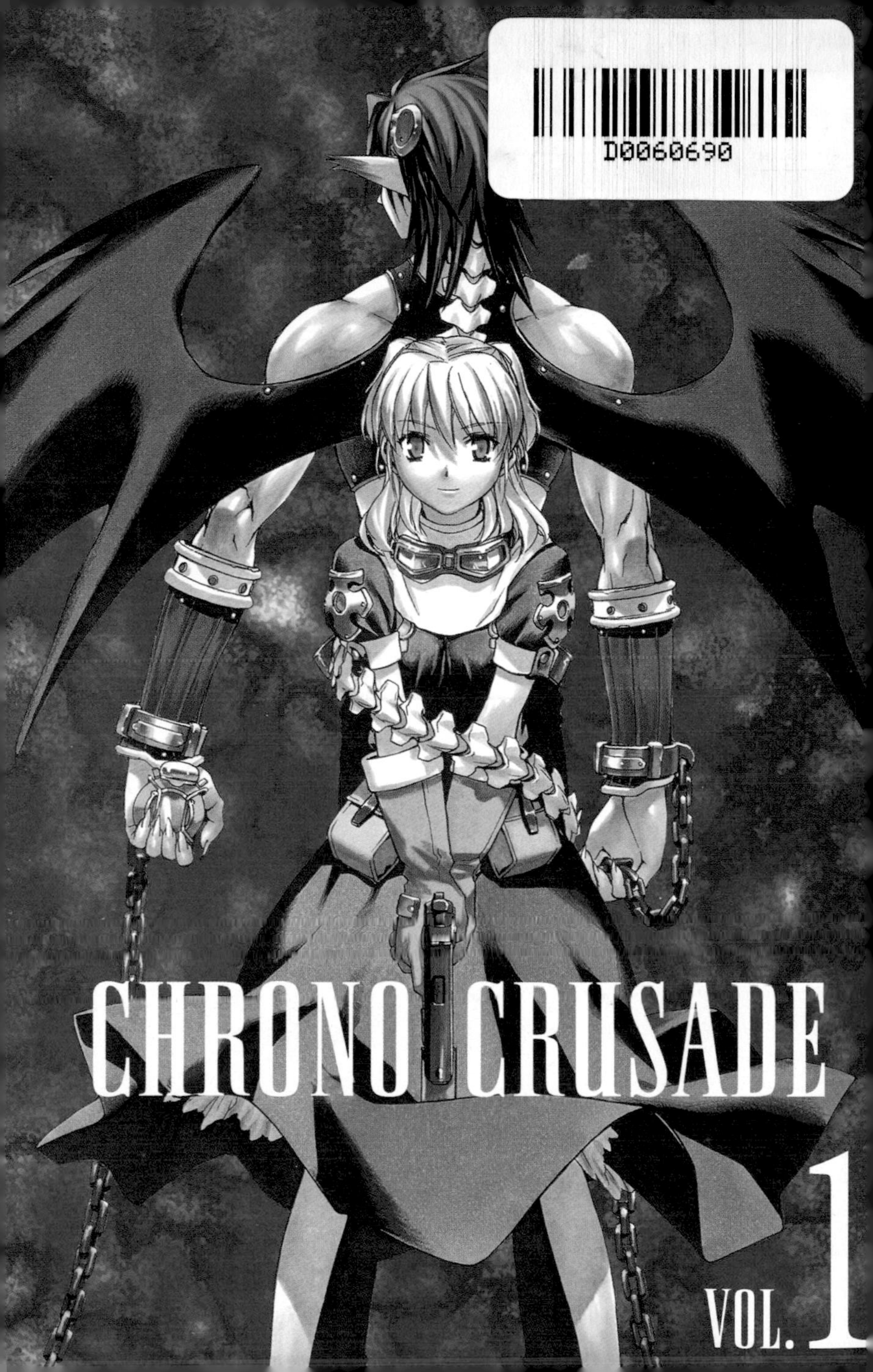
CHRONO CRUSADE
VOL. 1

CONTENTS

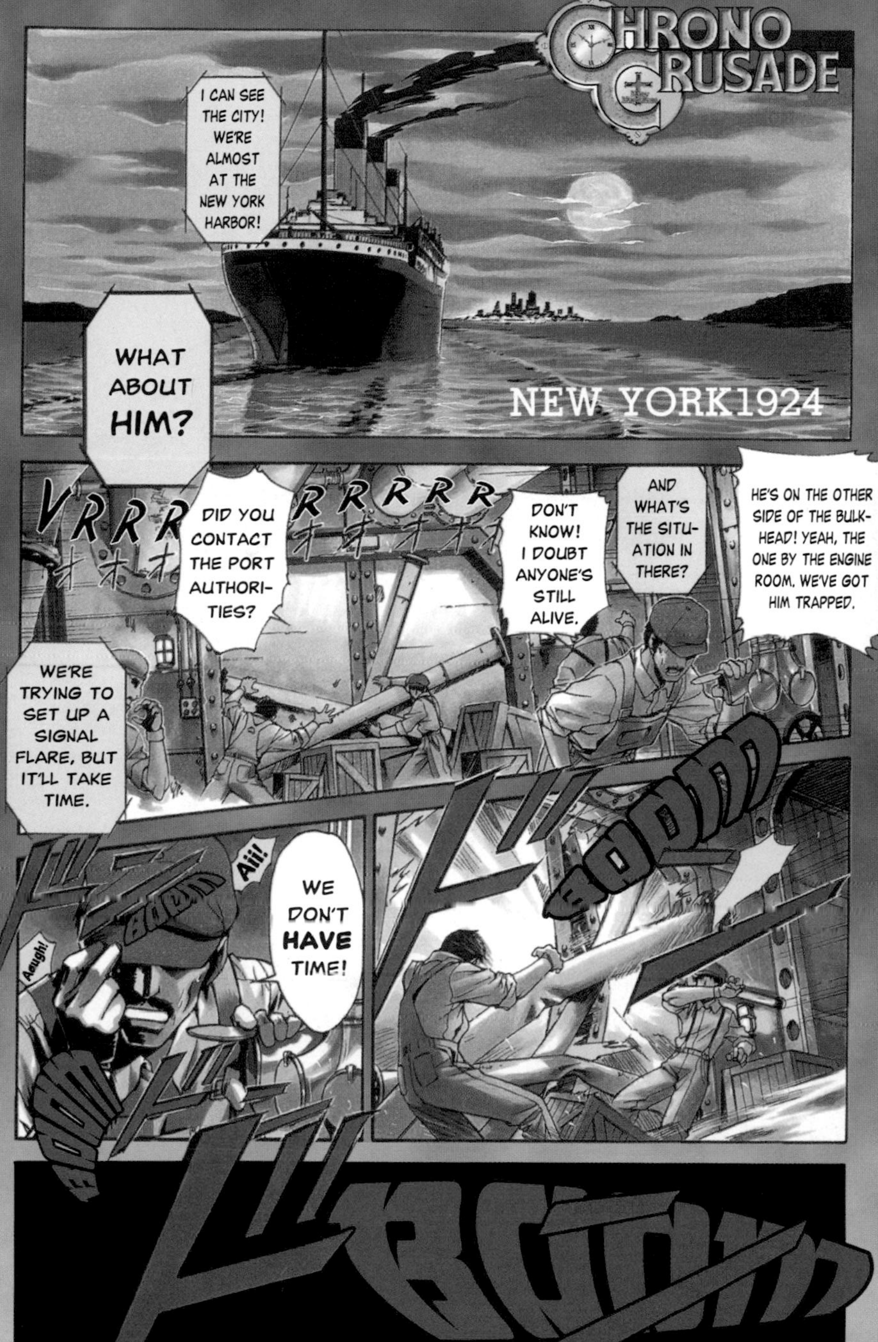
CHRONO CRUSADE
I CAN SEE THE CITY! WE'RE ALMOST AT THE NEW YORK HARBOR!
NEW YORK1924
WHAT ABOUT HIM?
HE'S ON THE OTHER SIDE OF THE BULKHEAD! YEAH, THE ONE BY THE ENGINE ROOM. WE'VE GOT HIM TRAPPED.
AND WHAT'S THE SITUATION IN THERE?
DON'T KNOW! I DOUBT ANYONE'S STILL ALIVE.
RRRRR
DID YOU CONTACT THE PORT AUTHORITIES?
VRRR
WE'RE TRYING TO SET UP A SIGNAL FLARE, BUT IT'LL TAKE TIME.
BOOM
Aii!
WE DON'T HAVE TIME!
Aaugh!
BOOM

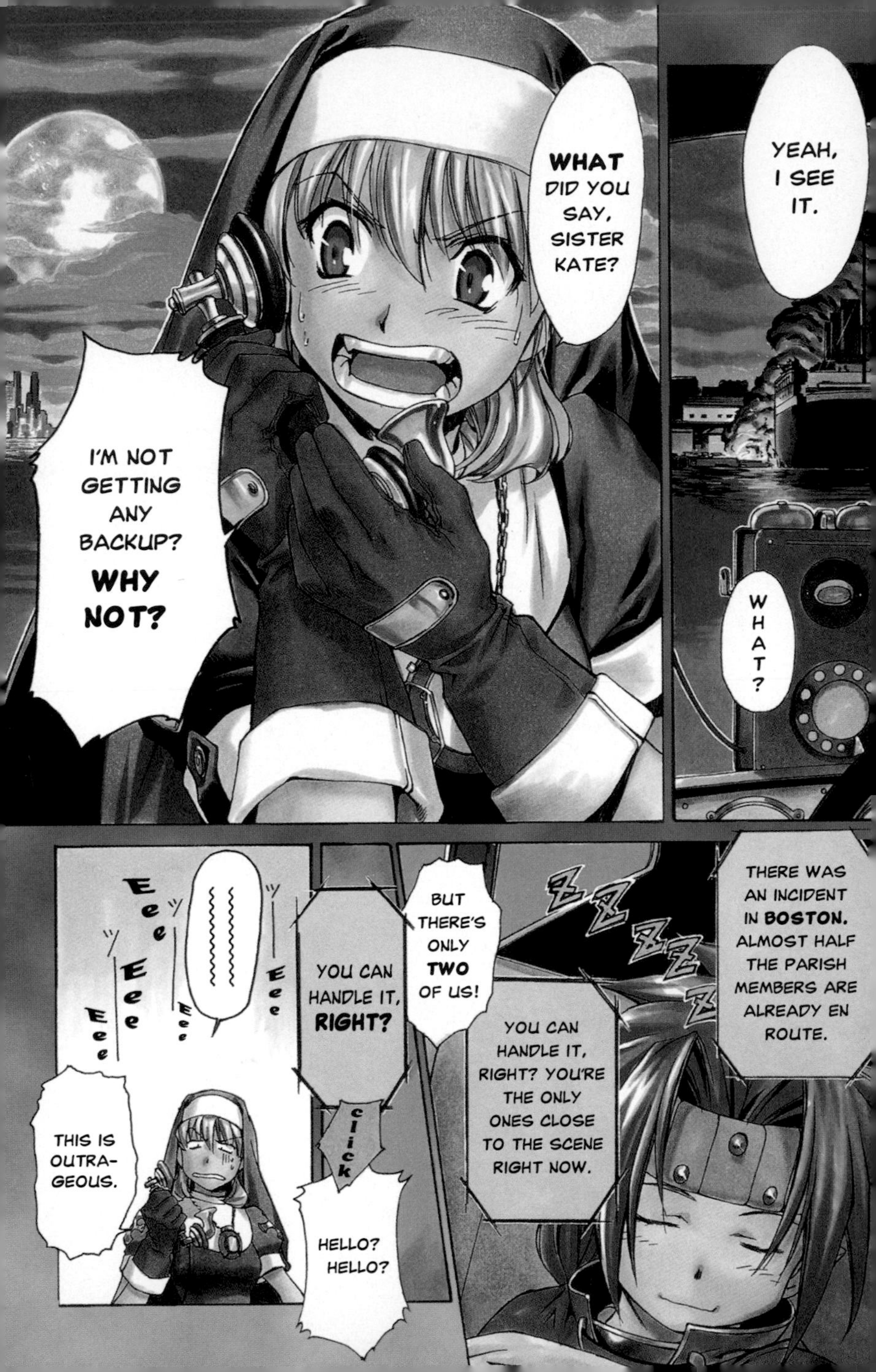
YEAH, I SEE IT.
WHAT?
WHAT DID YOU SAY, SISTER KATE?
I'M NOT GETTING ANY BACKUP? WHY NOT?
THERE WAS AN INCIDENT IN BOSTON. ALMOST HALF THE PARISH MEMBERS ARE ALREADY EN ROUTE.
YOU CAN HANDLE IT, RIGHT? YOU'RE THE ONLY ONES CLOSE TO THE SCENE RIGHT NOW.
BUT THERE'S ONLY TWO OF US!
YOU CAN HANDLE IT, RIGHT?
click
HELLO? HELLO?
Eee
Eee
Eee
Eee
Eee
THIS IS OUTRAGEOUS.

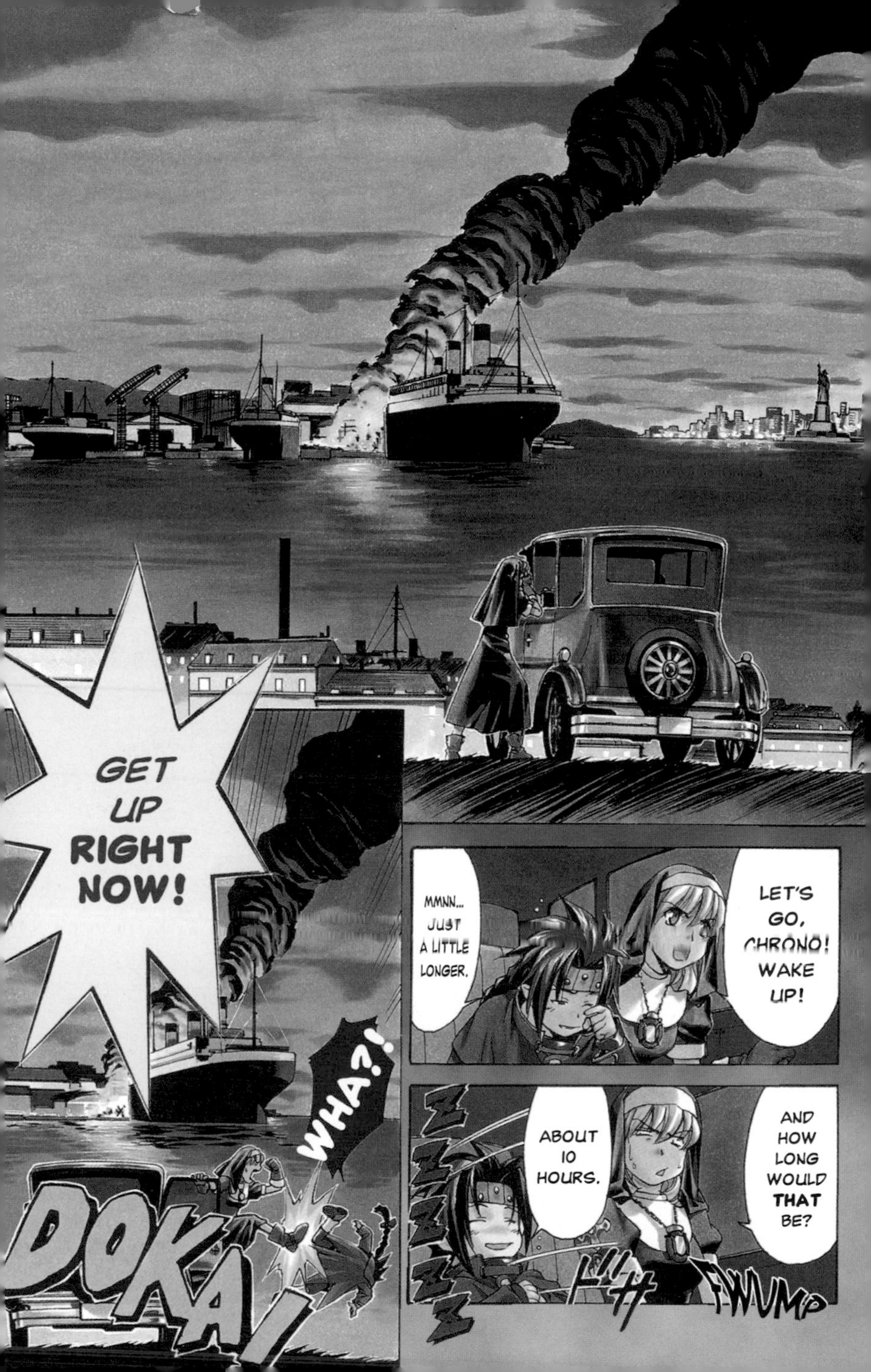
LET'S GO, CHRONO! WAKE UP!
MMNN... JUST A LITTLE LONGER.
AND HOW LONG WOULD THAT BE?
ABOUT 10 HOURS.
FWUMP
GET UP RIGHT NOW!
WHA?!
DOKA!

Created by
DAISUKE MORIYAMA

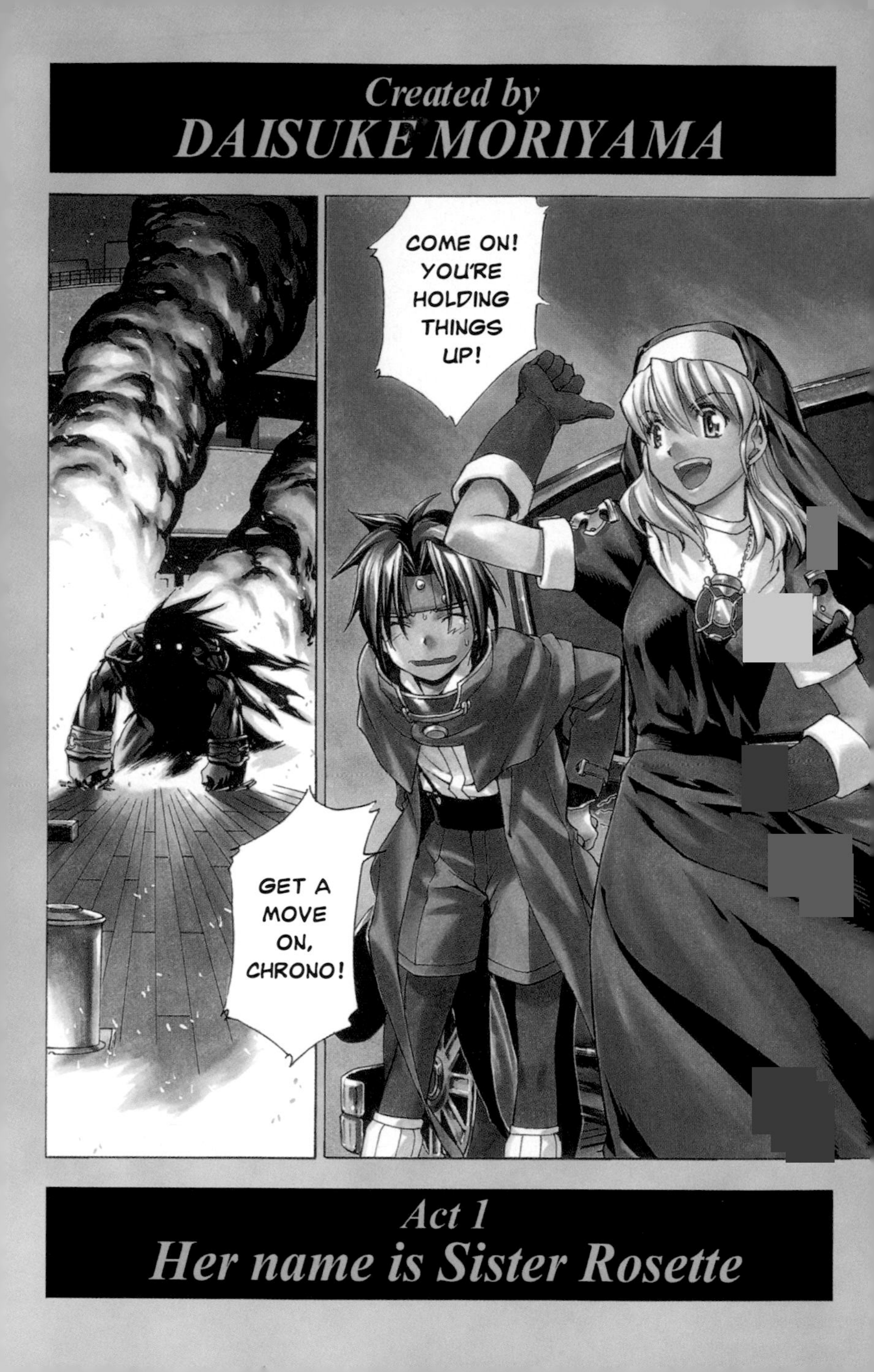
COME ON! YOU'RE HOLDING THINGS UP!
GET A MOVE ON, CHRONO!

Act 1
Her name is Sister Rosette

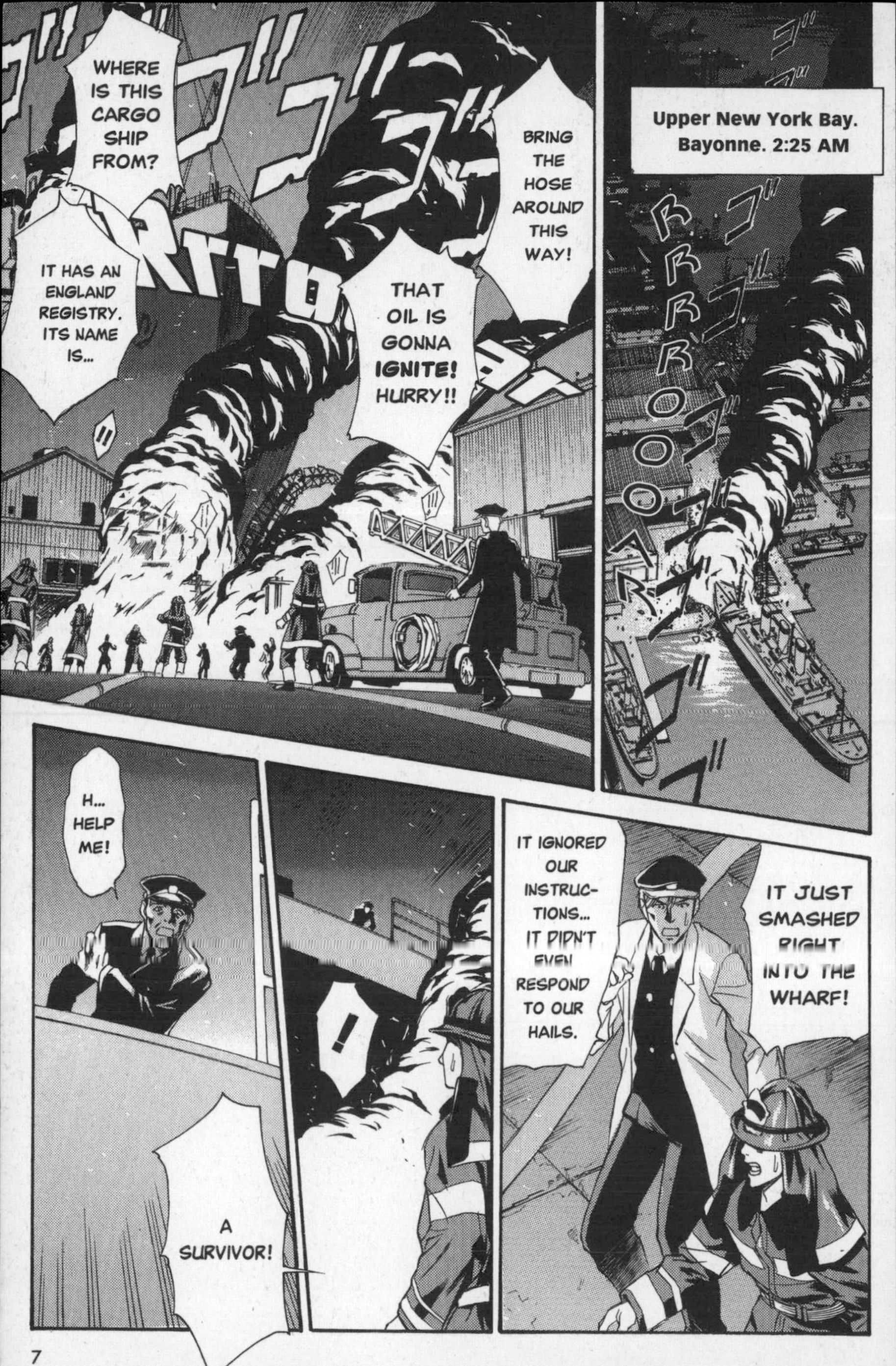
Upper New York Bay.
Bayonne. 2:25 AM
RRRROOOOAR
WHERE IS THIS CARGO SHIP FROM?
BRING THE HOSE AROUND THIS WAY!
Rrro
IT HAS AN ENGLAND REGISTRY. ITS NAME IS...
THAT OIL IS GONNA IGNITE! HURRY!!
!!
IT IGNORED OUR INSTRUC-TIONS... IT DIDN'T EVEN RESPOND TO OUR HAILS.
IT JUST SMASHED RIGHT INTO THE WHARF!
!
H... HELP ME!
A SURVIVOR!

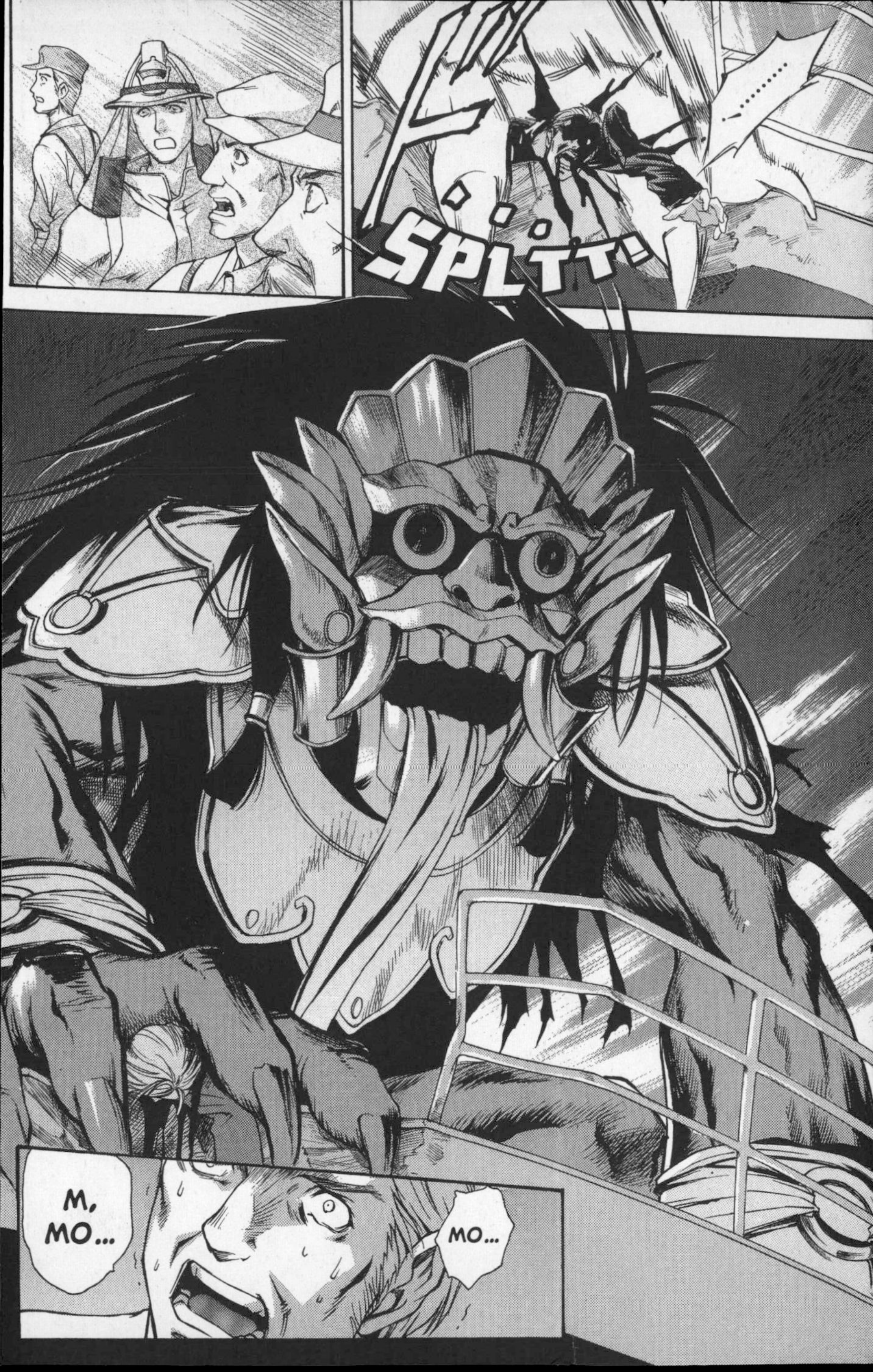
...
SPLITT!
M, MO...
MO...

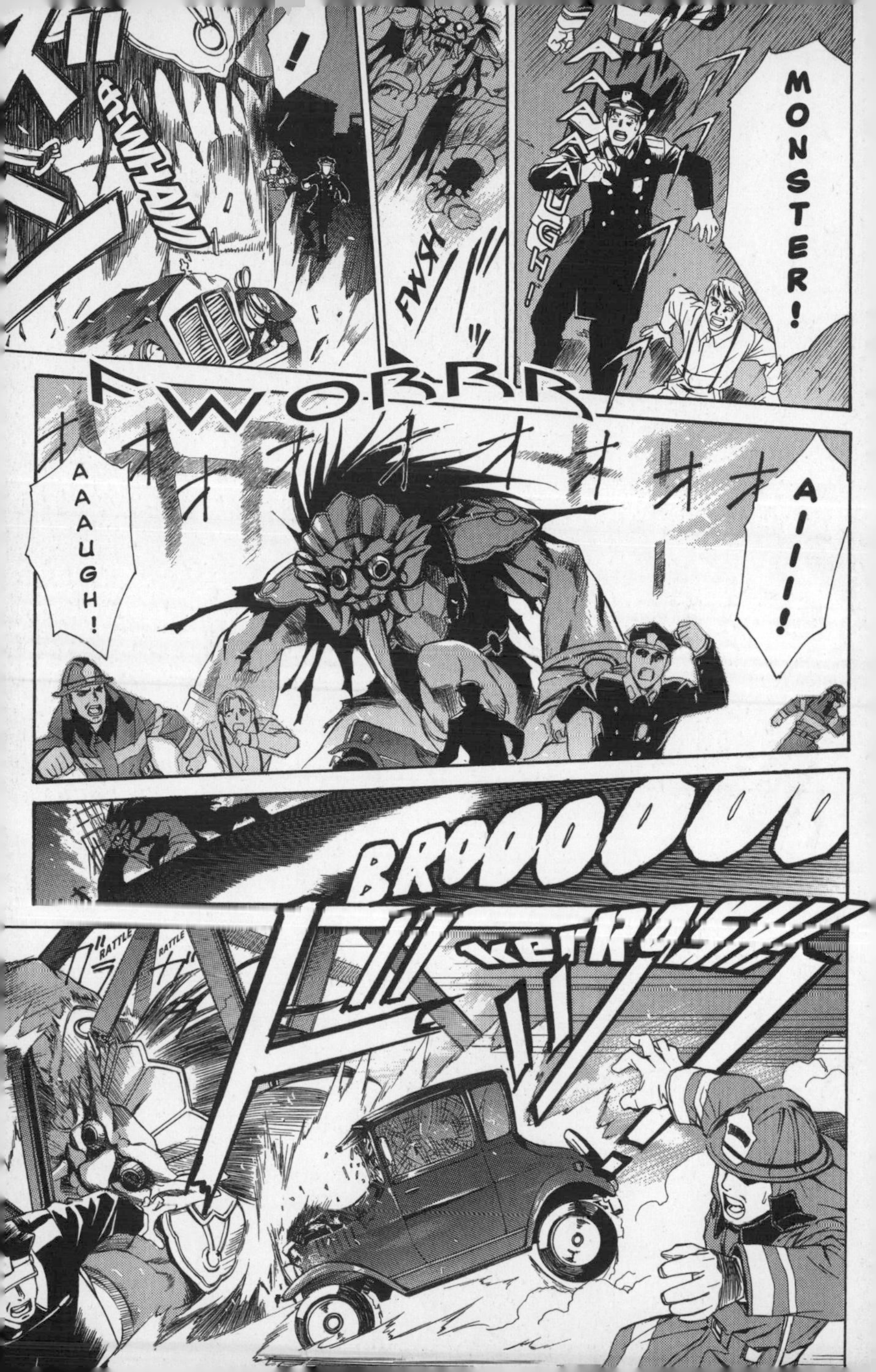
MONSTER!
AAAAAUGH!
FWSH
WHAM
!
FWORRR
AIIII!
AAAUGH!
BROOOOOO
kerRASH!!
RATTLE
RATTLE

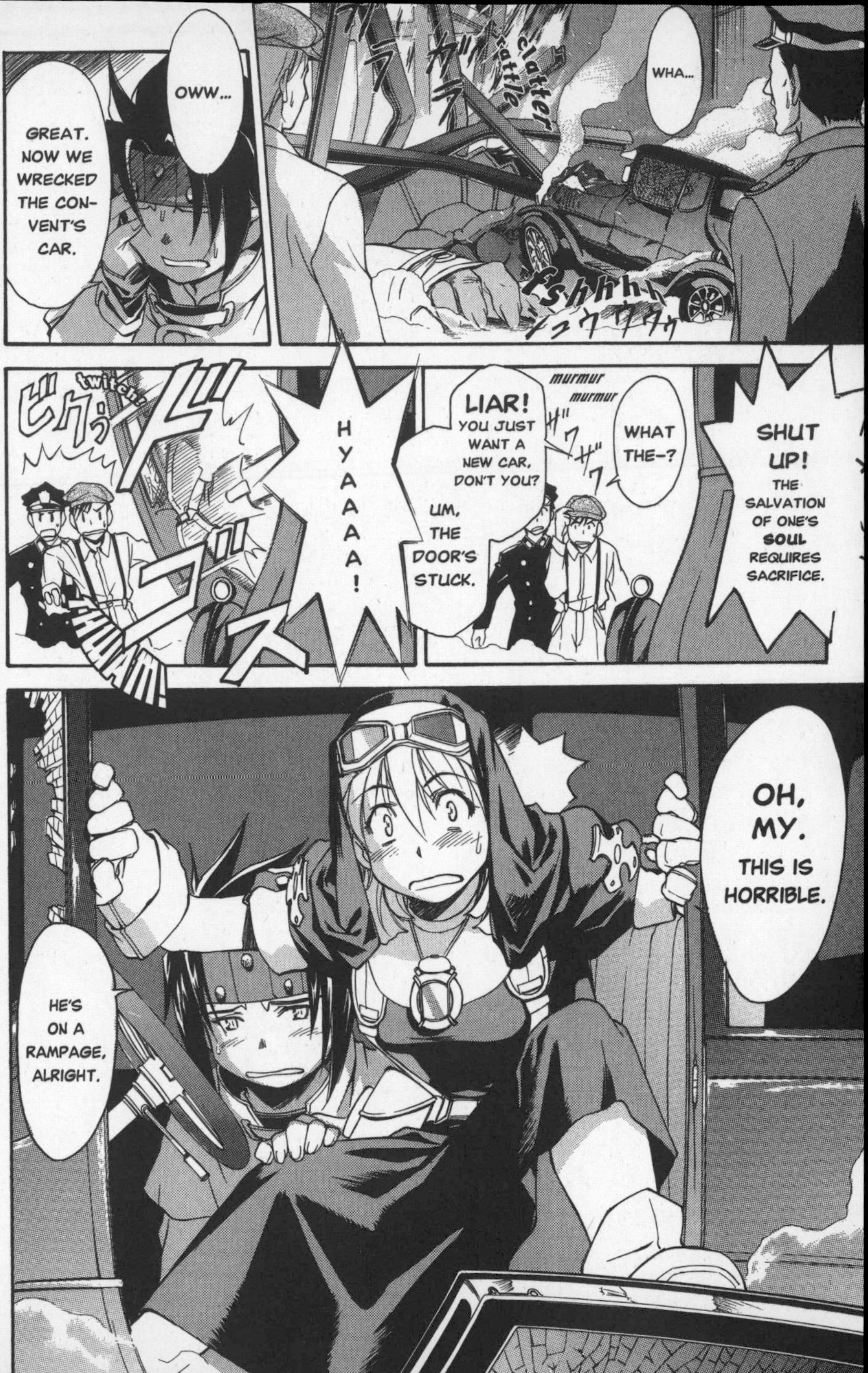
WHA...
clatter rattle
fshhhh
OWW...
GREAT. NOW WE WRECKED THE CONVENT'S CAR.
SHUT UP! THE SALVATION OF ONE'S SOUL REQUIRES SACRIFICE.
murmur murmur
WHAT THE-?
LIAR! YOU JUST WANT A NEW CAR, DON'T YOU?
UM, THE DOOR'S STUCK.
HYAAAAA!
twitch
OH, MY. THIS IS HORRIBLE.
HE'S ON A RAMPAGE, ALRIGHT.

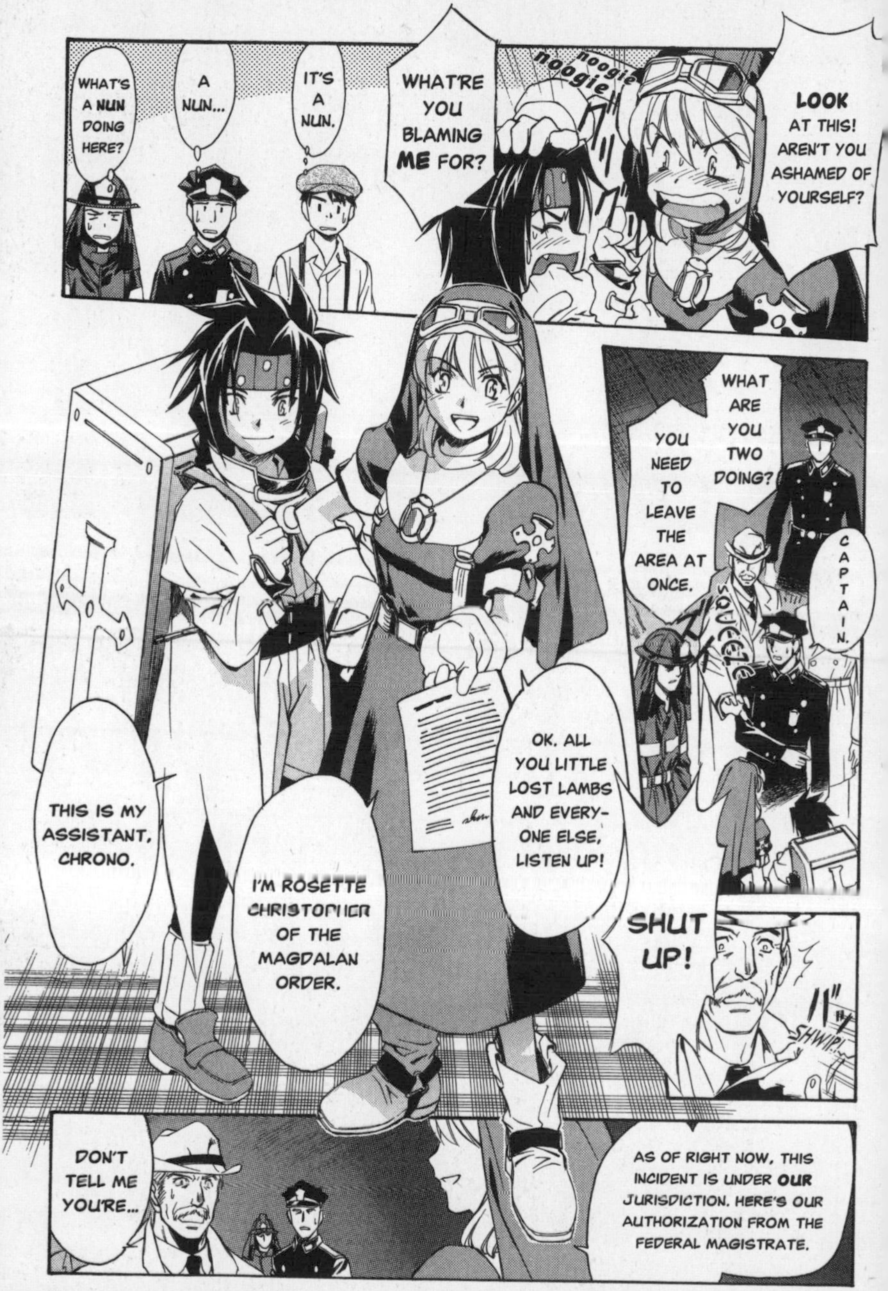
LOOK AT THIS! AREN'T YOU ASHAMED OF YOURSELF?
noogie noogie
WHAT'RE YOU BLAMING ME FOR?
IT'S A NUN.
A NUN...
WHAT'S A NUN DOING HERE?
WHAT ARE YOU TWO DOING?
YOU NEED TO LEAVE THE AREA AT ONCE.
SQUEEZE
CAPTAIN.
SHUT UP!
SHWIP!
OK. ALL YOU LITTLE LOST LAMBS AND EVERY-ONE ELSE, LISTEN UP!
I'M ROSETTE CHRISTOPHER OF THE MAGDALAN ORDER.
THIS IS MY ASSISTANT, CHRONO.
AS OF RIGHT NOW, THIS INCIDENT IS UNDER OUR JURISDICTION. HERE'S OUR AUTHORIZATION FROM THE FEDERAL MAGISTRATE.
DON'T TELL ME YOU'RE...

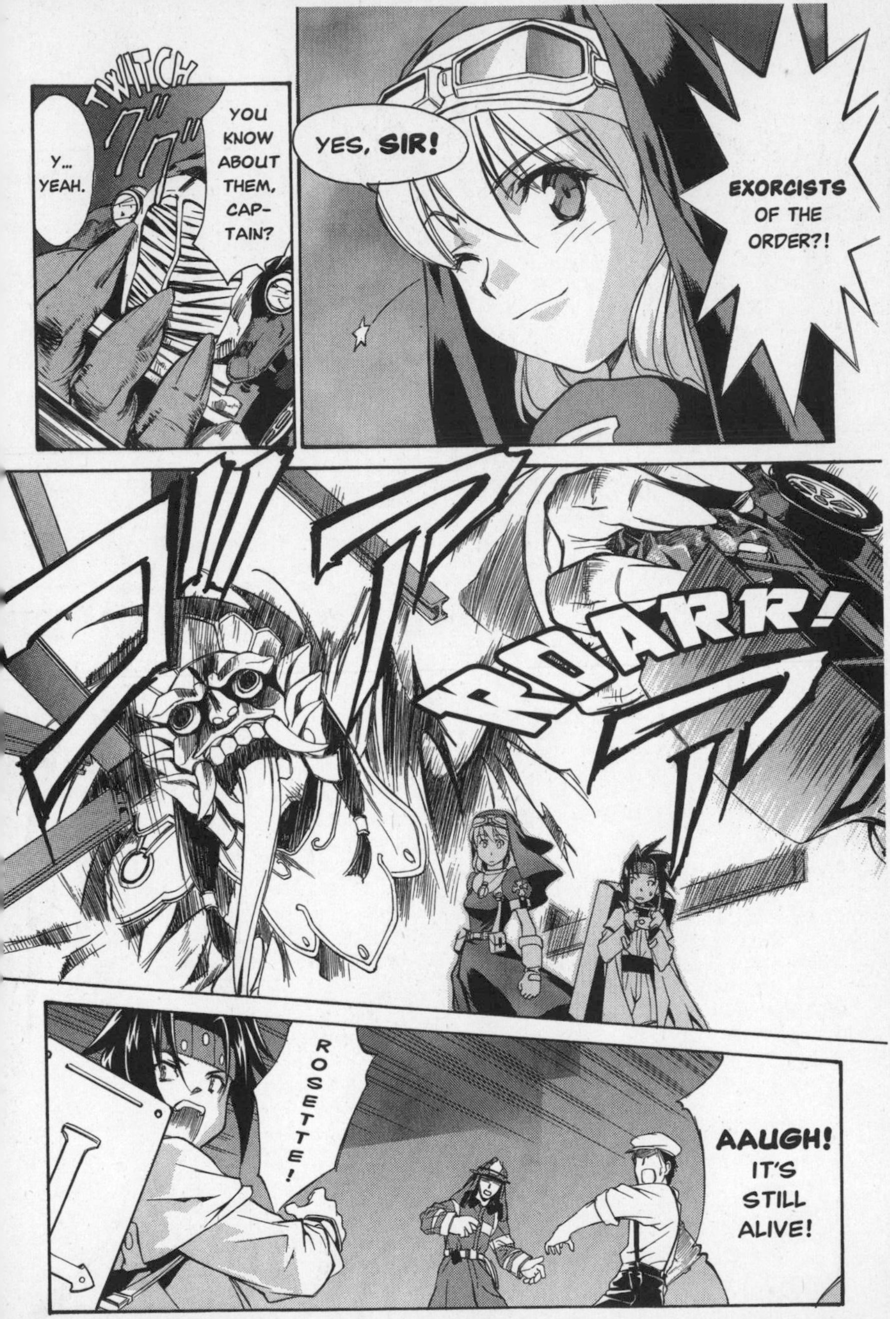
EXORCISTS OF THE ORDER?!
YES, SIR!
YOU KNOW ABOUT THEM, CAP-TAIN?
Y... YEAH.
TWITCH
ROARR!
AAUGH! IT'S STILL ALIVE!
ROSETTE!

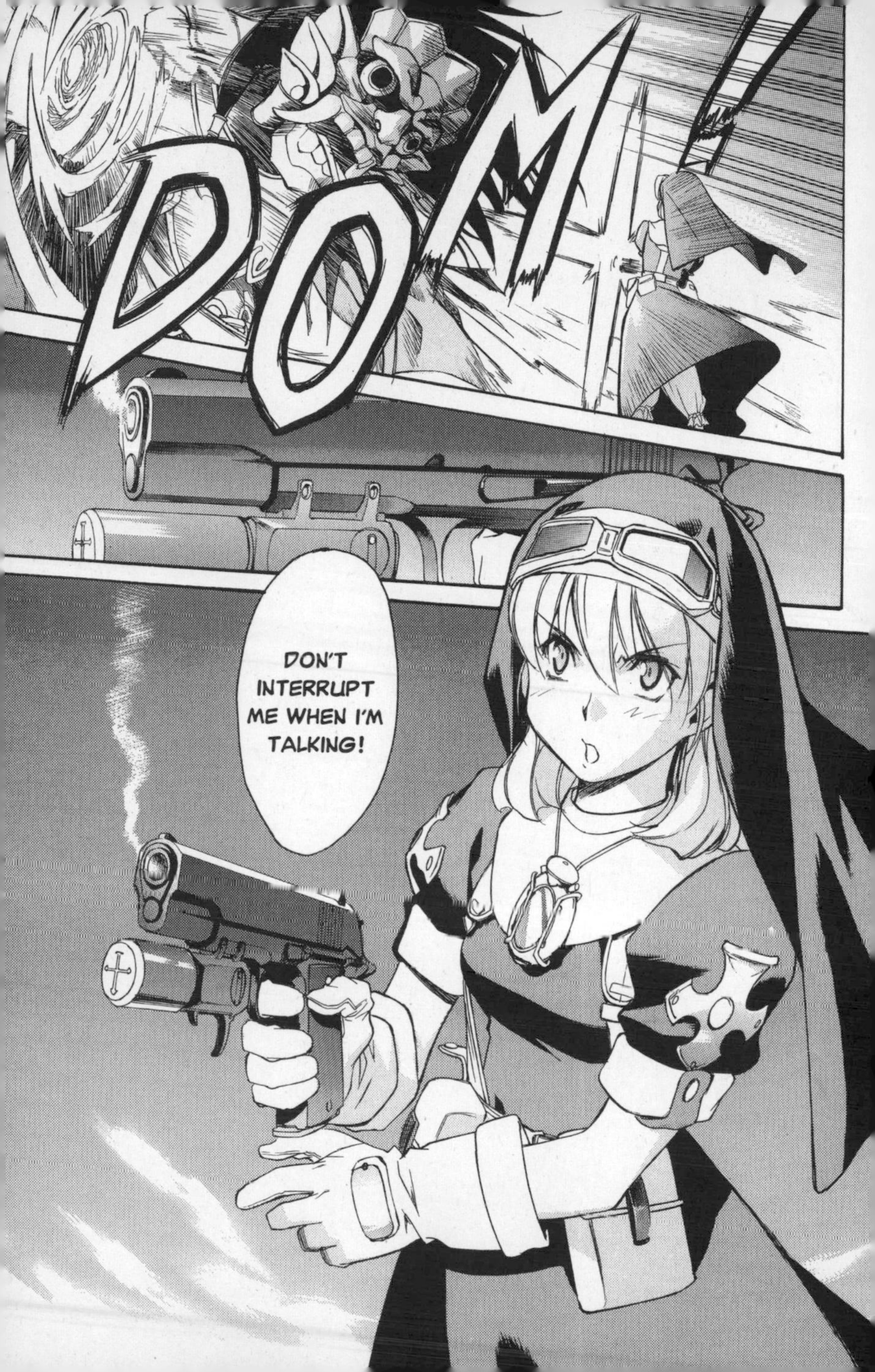
DOM!!
DON'T INTERRUPT ME WHEN I'M TALKING!

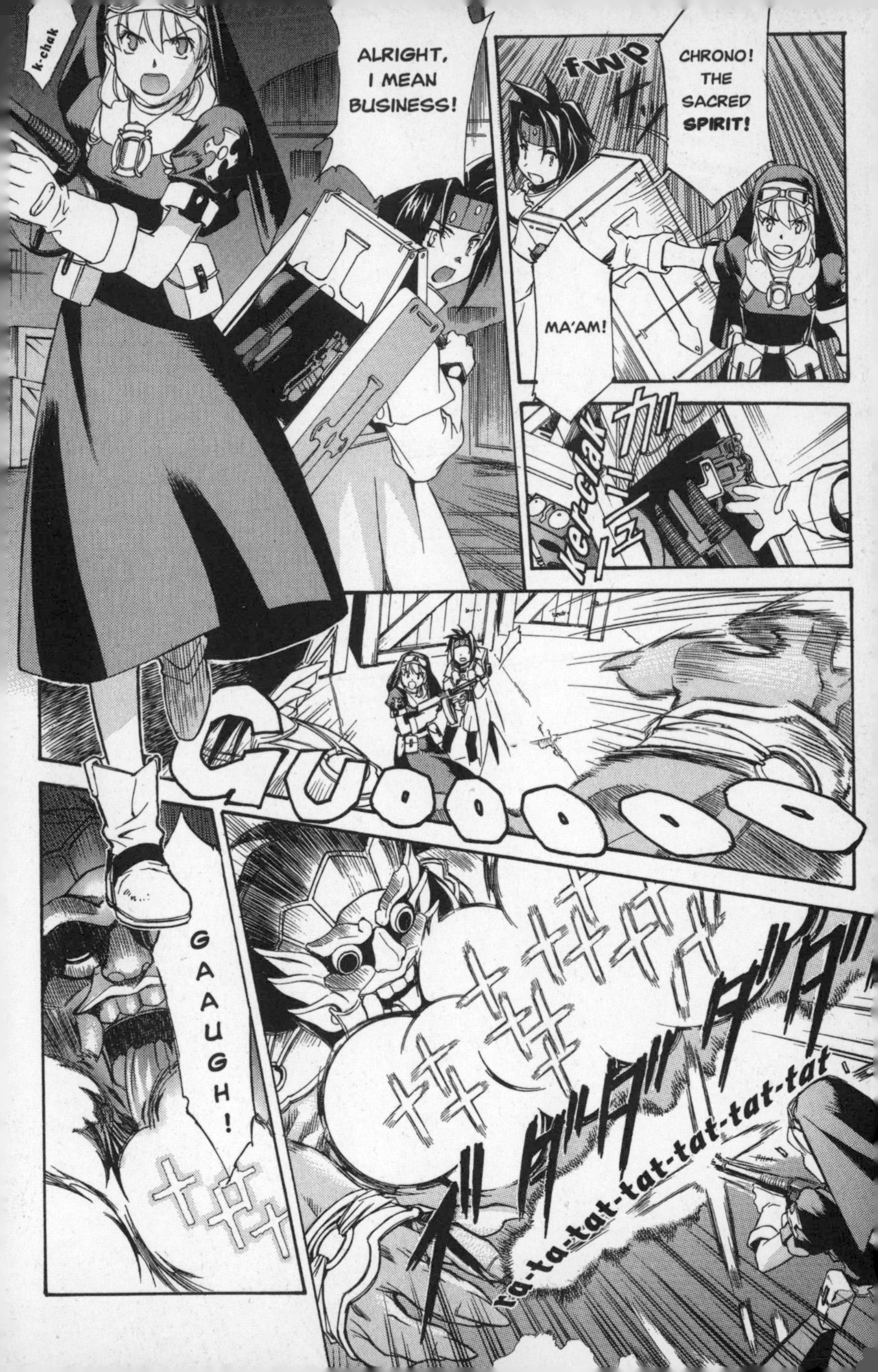
fwp
CHRONO! THE SACRED SPIRIT!
MA'AM!
ker-clak
k-chak
ALRIGHT, I MEAN BUSINESS!
GUOOOOO
ra-ta-tat-tat-tat-tat-tat-tat
GAUGH!

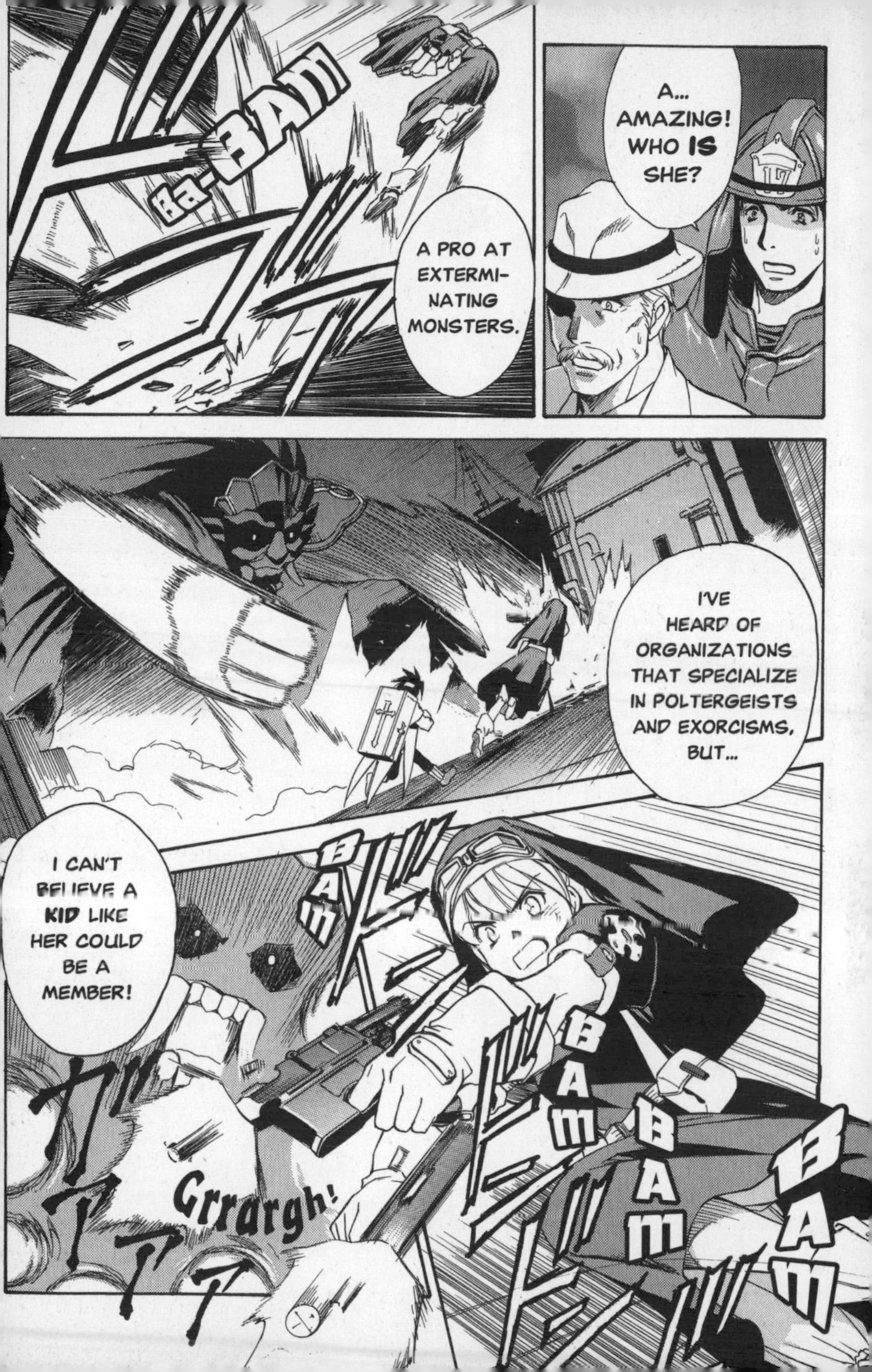
A... AMAZING! WHO IS SHE?
Ba-BAM
A PRO AT EXTERMINATING MONSTERS.
I'VE HEARD OF ORGANIZATIONS THAT SPECIALIZE IN POLTERGEISTS AND EXORCISMS, BUT...
BAM
I CAN'T BELIEVE A KID LIKE HER COULD BE A MEMBER!
BAM
BAM
BAM
Grrrargh!

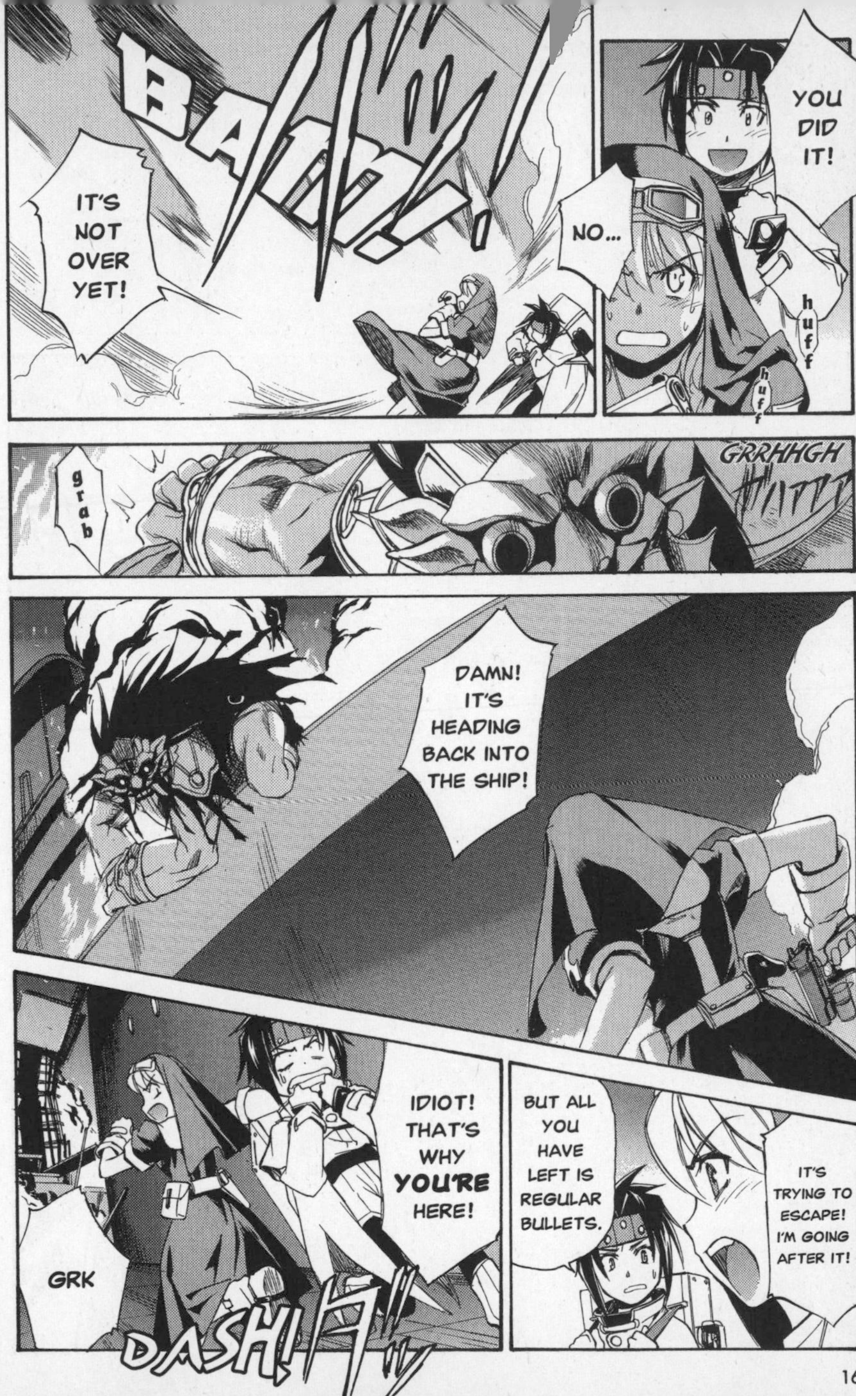
YOU DID IT!
NO...
huff
huff
IT'S NOT OVER YET!
GRRHHGH
grab
DAMN! IT'S HEADING BACK INTO THE SHIP!
IT'S TRYING TO ESCAPE! I'M GOING AFTER IT!
BUT ALL YOU HAVE LEFT IS REGULAR BULLETS.
IDIOT! THAT'S WHY **YOU'RE** HERE!
GRK
DASH!!

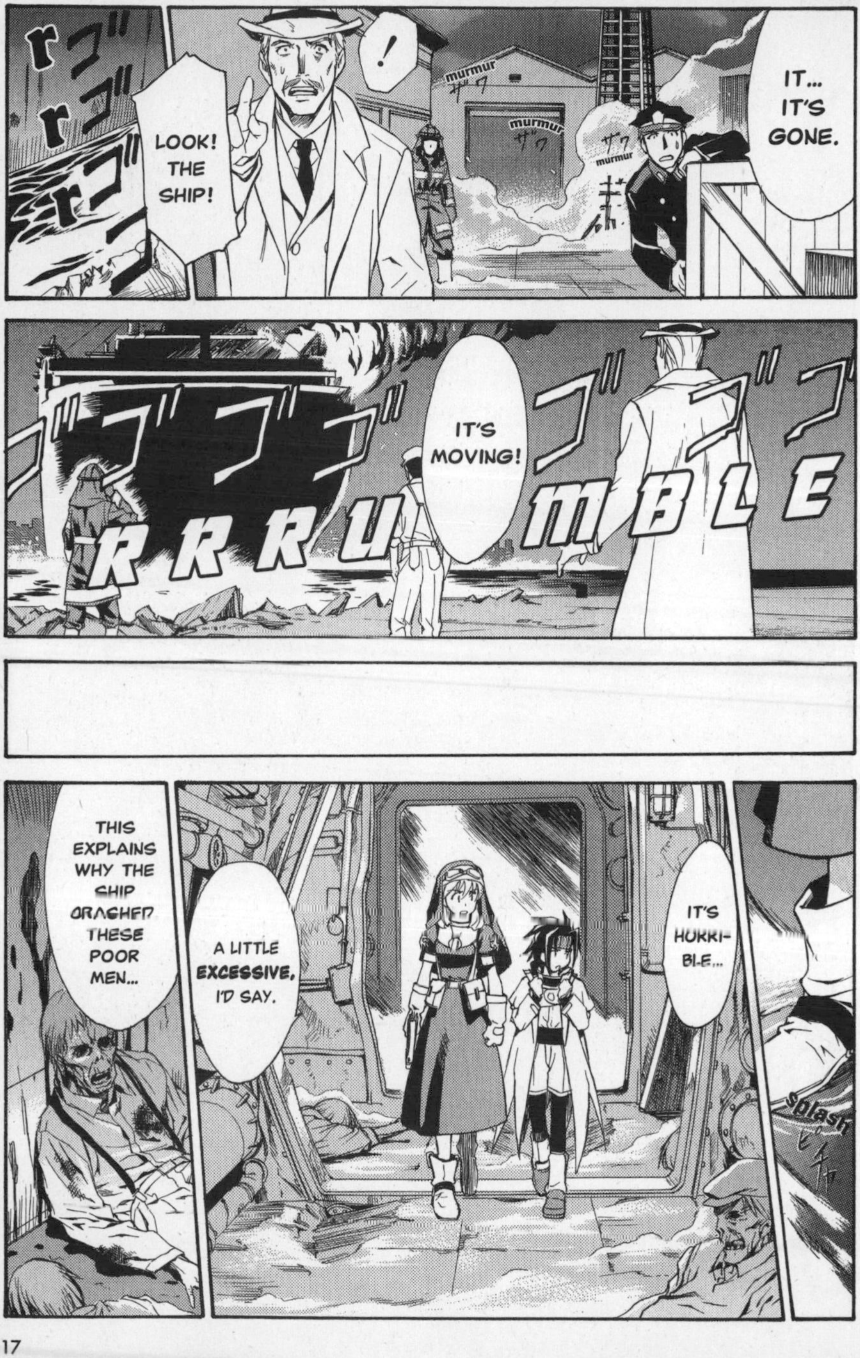
IT... IT'S GONE.
murmur
murmur
murmur
!
LOOK! THE SHIP!
IT'S MOVING!
RRRRUMBLE
splash
IT'S HORRI-BLE...
A LITTLE EXCESSIVE, I'D SAY.
THIS EXPLAINS WHY THE SHIP CRASHED. THESE POOR MEN...

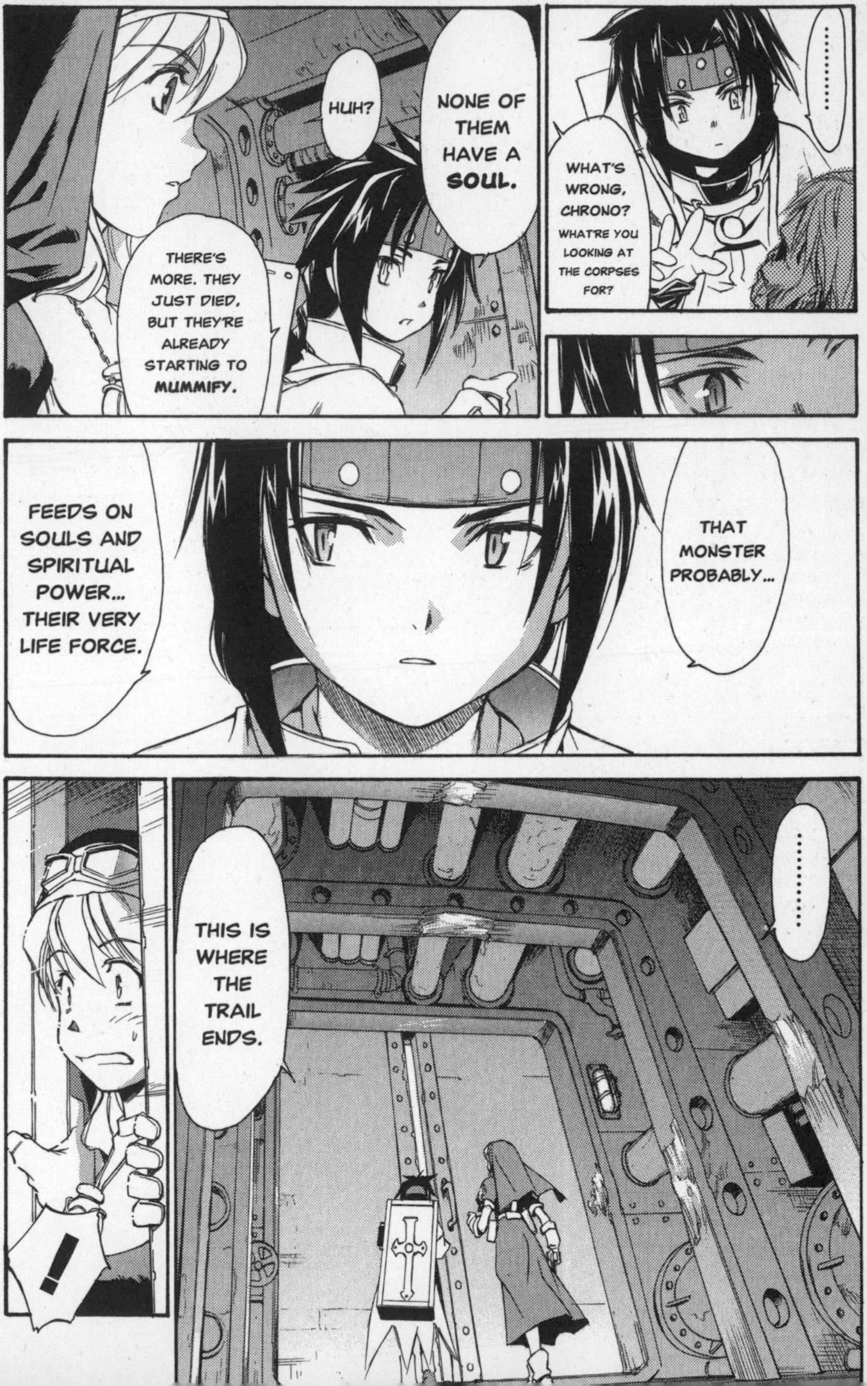
......
WHAT'S WRONG, CHRONO? WHAT'RE YOU LOOKING AT THE CORPSES FOR?
NONE OF THEM HAVE A SOUL.
HUH?
THERE'S MORE. THEY JUST DIED, BUT THEY'RE ALREADY STARTING TO MUMMIFY.
THAT MONSTER PROBABLY...
FEEDS ON SOULS AND SPIRITUAL POWER... THEIR VERY LIFE FORCE.
......
THIS IS WHERE THE TRAIL ENDS.
!

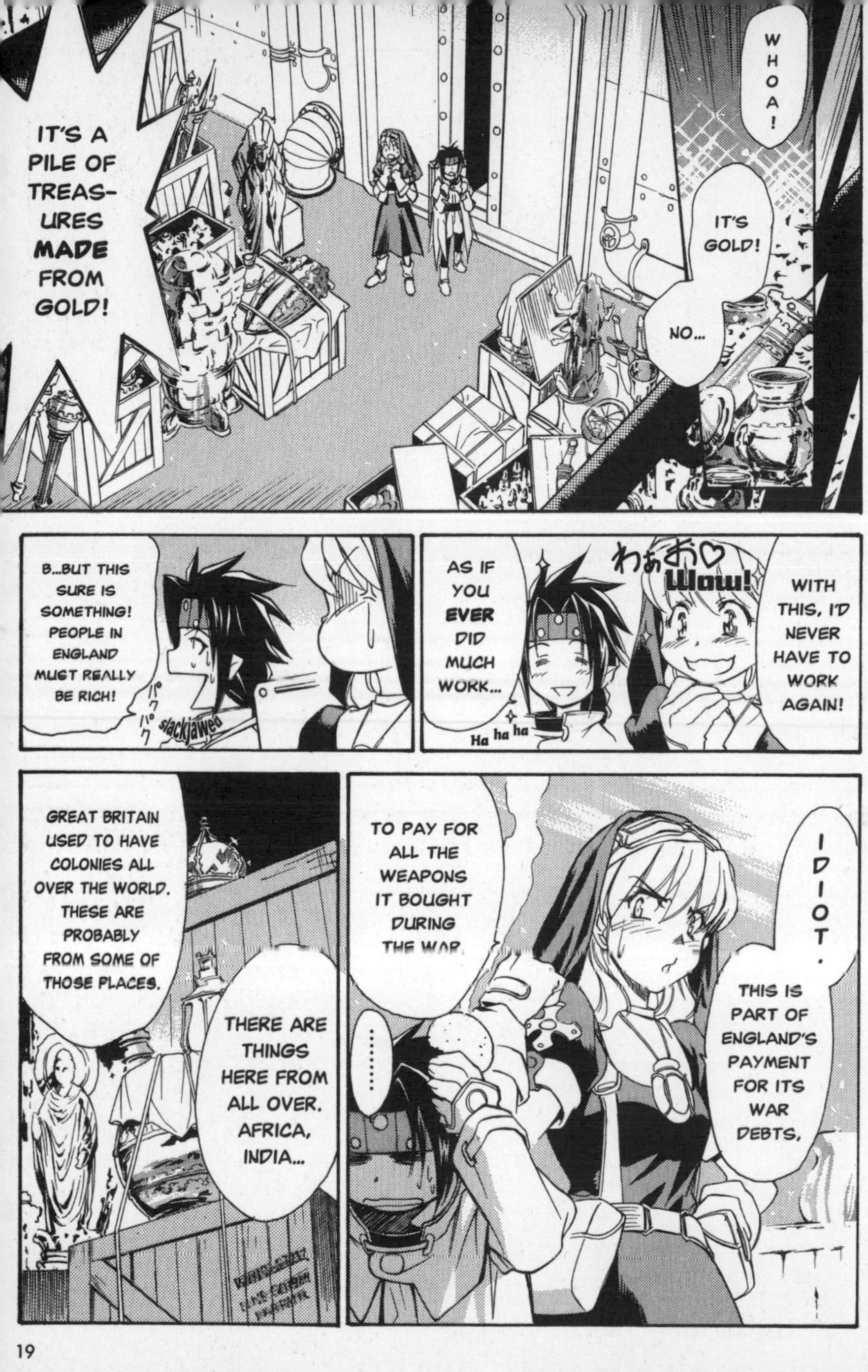
WHOA!
IT'S GOLD!
NO...
IT'S A PILE OF TREASURES MADE FROM GOLD!
わぁお♡ Wow!
WITH THIS, I'D NEVER HAVE TO WORK AGAIN!
AS IF YOU EVER DID MUCH WORK...
Ha ha ha
B...BUT THIS SURE IS SOMETHING! PEOPLE IN ENGLAND MUST REALLY BE RICH!
パクパク slackjawed
IDIOT.
THIS IS PART OF ENGLAND'S PAYMENT FOR ITS WAR DEBTS,
TO PAY FOR ALL THE WEAPONS IT BOUGHT DURING THE WAR.
......
GREAT BRITAIN USED TO HAVE COLONIES ALL OVER THE WORLD. THESE ARE PROBABLY FROM SOME OF THOSE PLACES.
THERE ARE THINGS HERE FROM ALL OVER. AFRICA, INDIA...

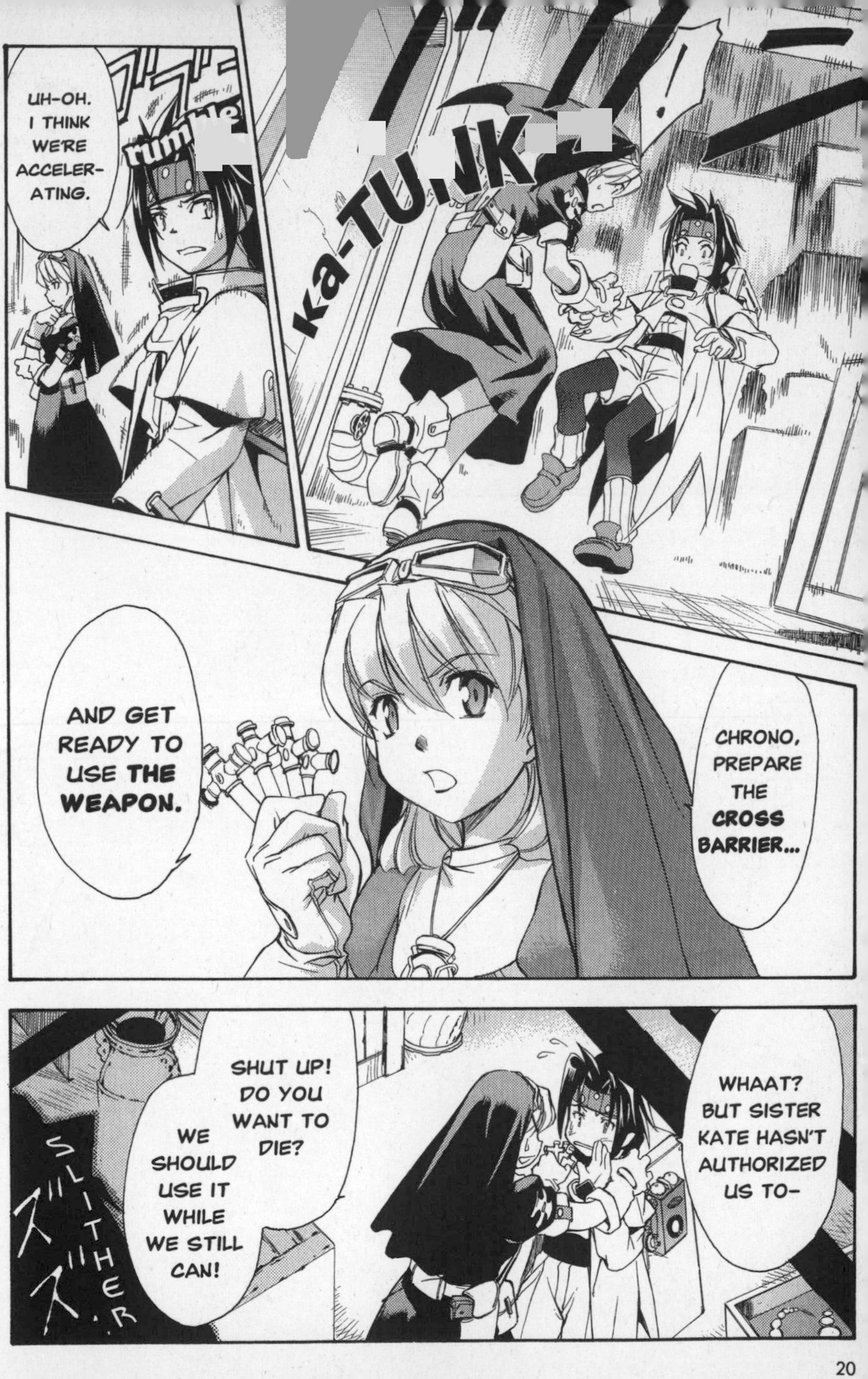
ka-TUNK
UH-OH. I THINK WE'RE ACCELER-ATING.
CHRONO, PREPARE THE **CROSS BARRIER...**
AND GET READY TO USE **THE WEAPON.**
WHAAT? BUT SISTER KATE HASN'T AUTHORIZED US TO–
SHUT UP! DO YOU WANT TO DIE?
WE SHOULD USE IT WHILE WE STILL CAN!
SLITHER

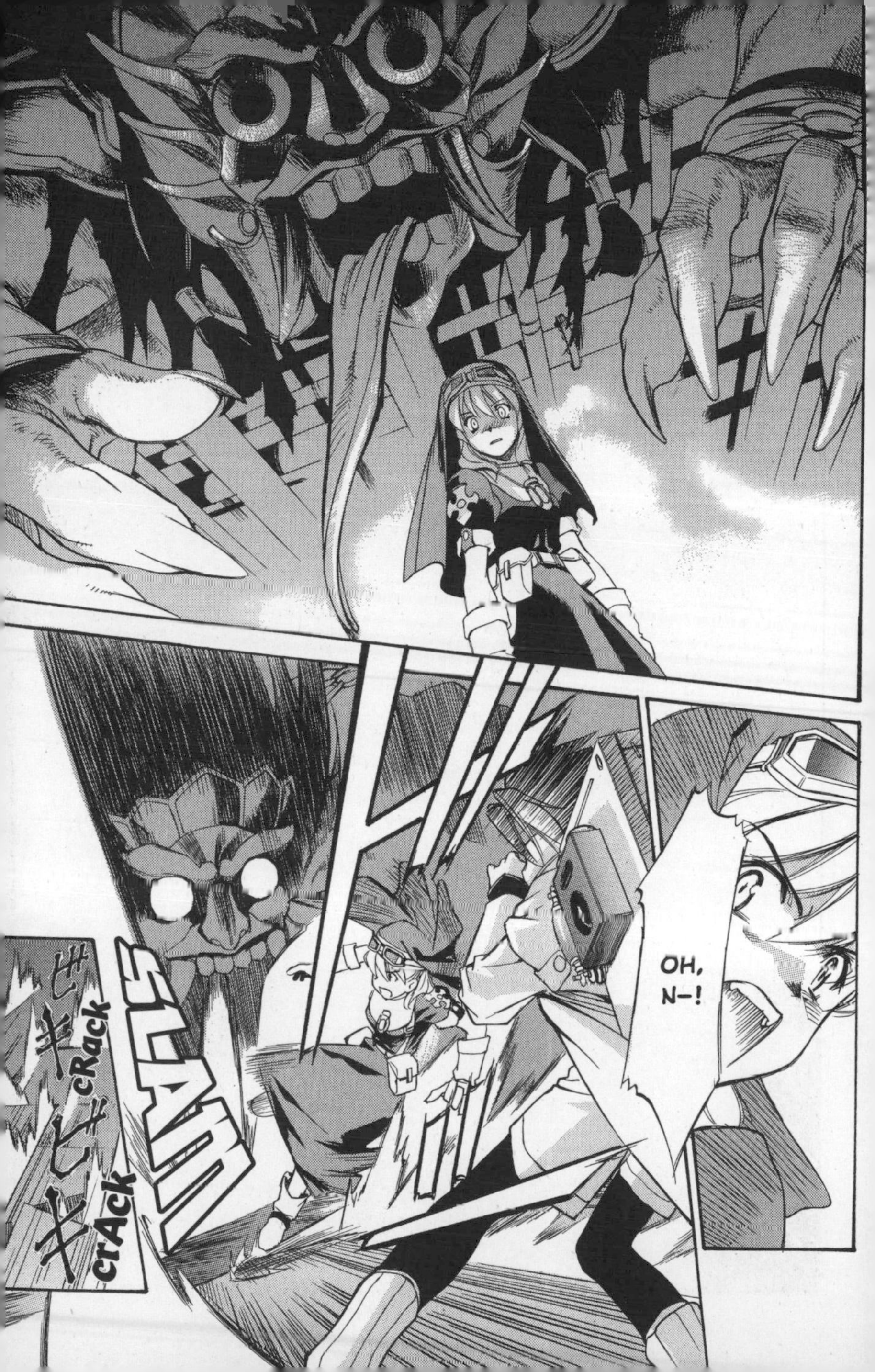
OH,
N–!
SLAM
cRack
crAck

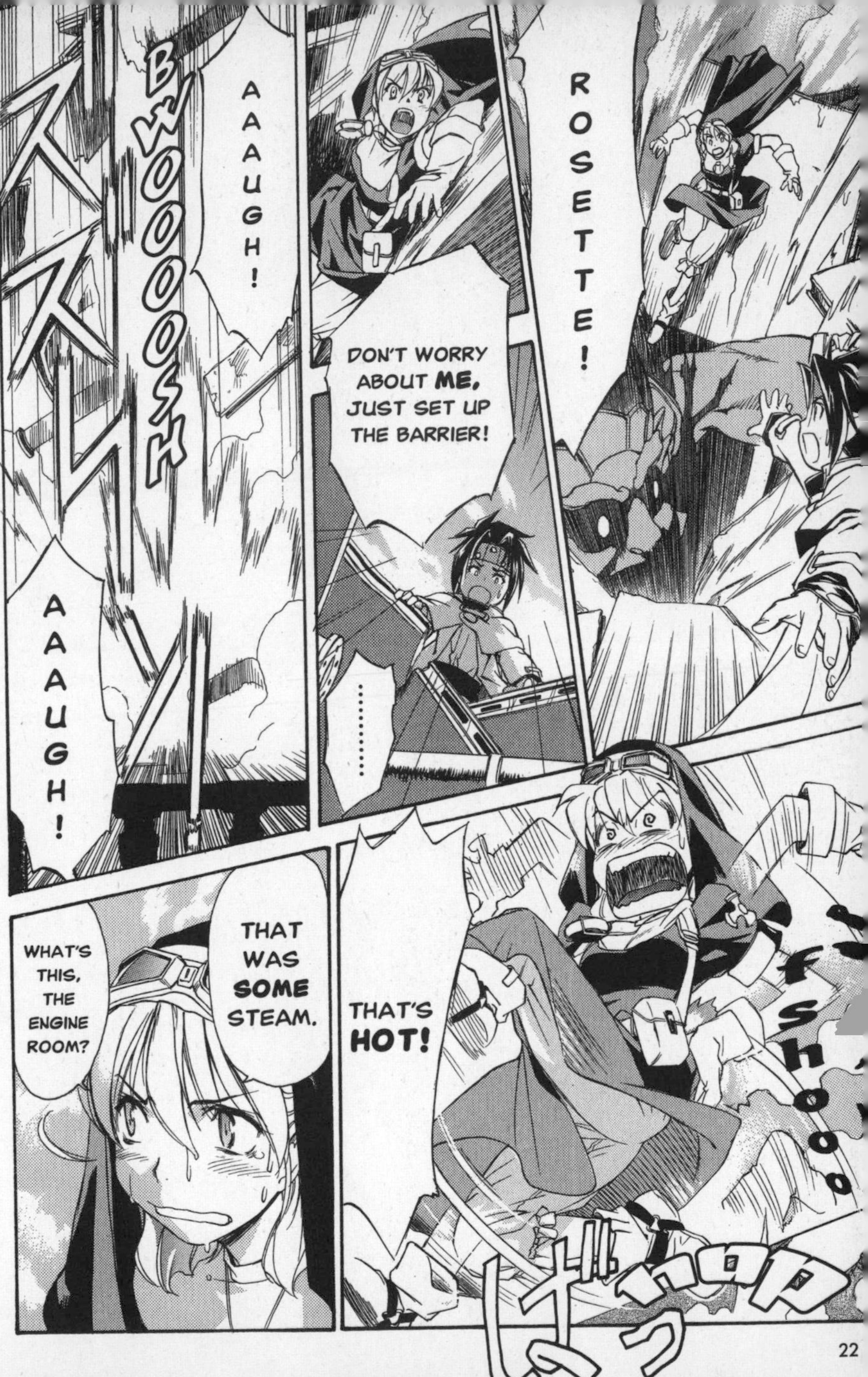
ROSETTE!
AAAUGH!
DON'T WORRY ABOUT ME, JUST SET UP THE BARRIER!
......
BWOOOOSH
AAAAUGH!
THAT'S HOT!
fshooo
hop
THAT WAS SOME STEAM.
WHAT'S THIS, THE ENGINE ROOM?

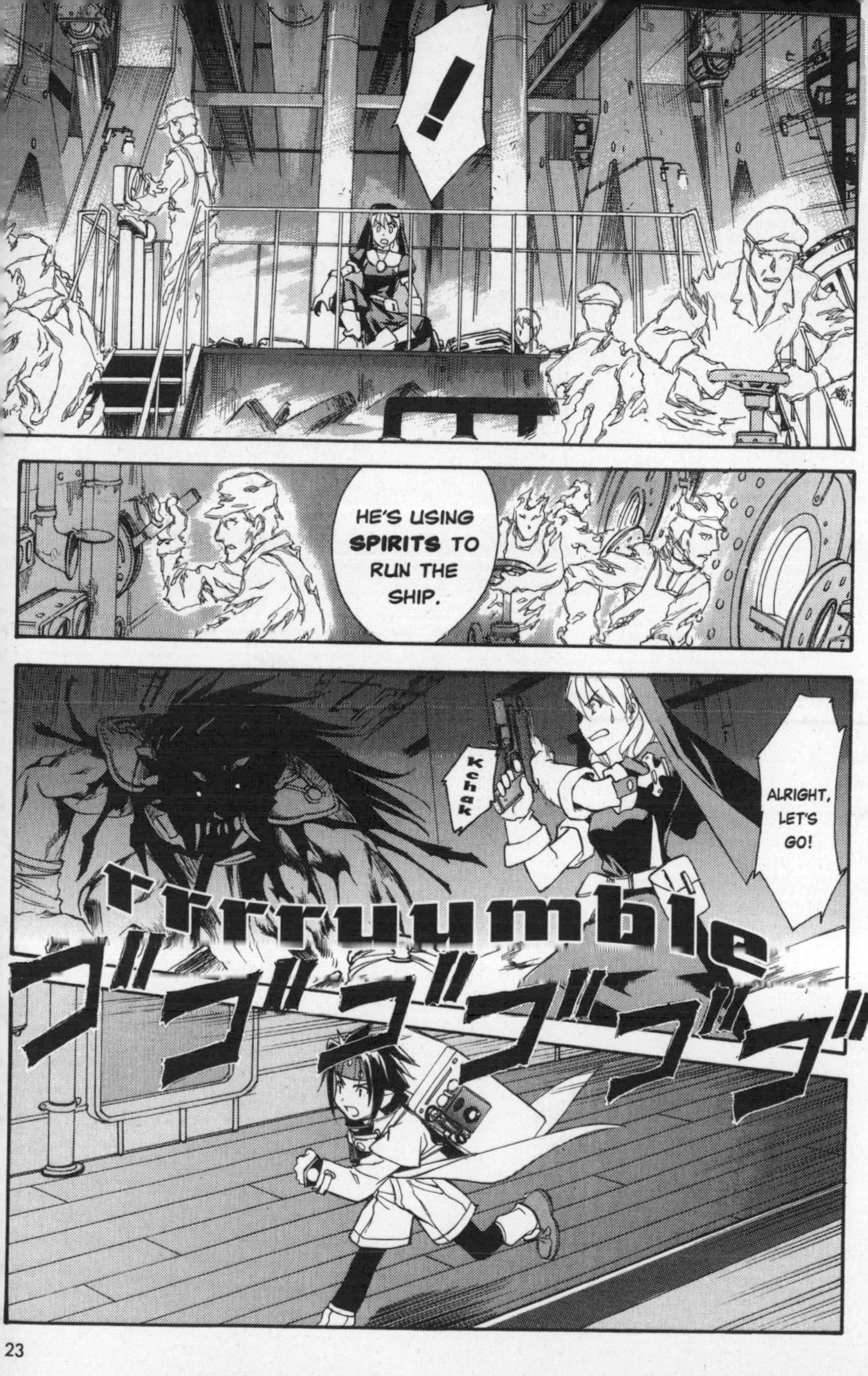
!
HE'S USING SPIRITS TO RUN THE SHIP.
ALRIGHT, LET'S GO!
Kchak
rrruumble
ゴゴゴゴゴゴ

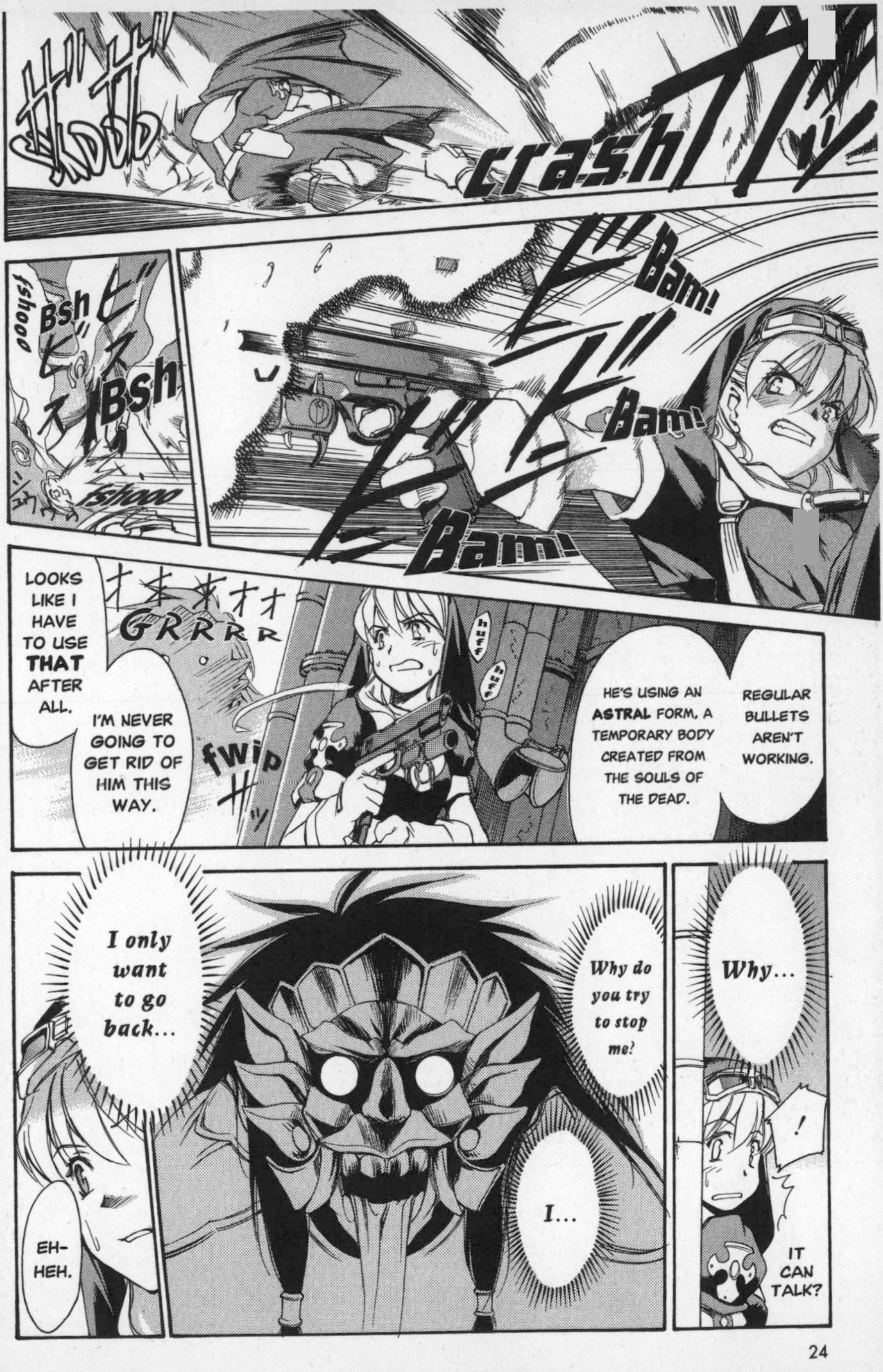
crash
Bam!
Bam!
Bam!
Bsh
Bsh
fshooo
fshooo
REGULAR BULLETS AREN'T WORKING.
HE'S USING AN ASTRAL FORM, A TEMPORARY BODY CREATED FROM THE SOULS OF THE DEAD.
huff
huff
fwip
GRRRRR
I'M NEVER GOING TO GET RID OF HIM THIS WAY.
LOOKS LIKE I HAVE TO USE THAT AFTER ALL.
Why...
!
IT CAN TALK?
Why do you try to stop me?
I only want to go back...
I...
EH-HEH.

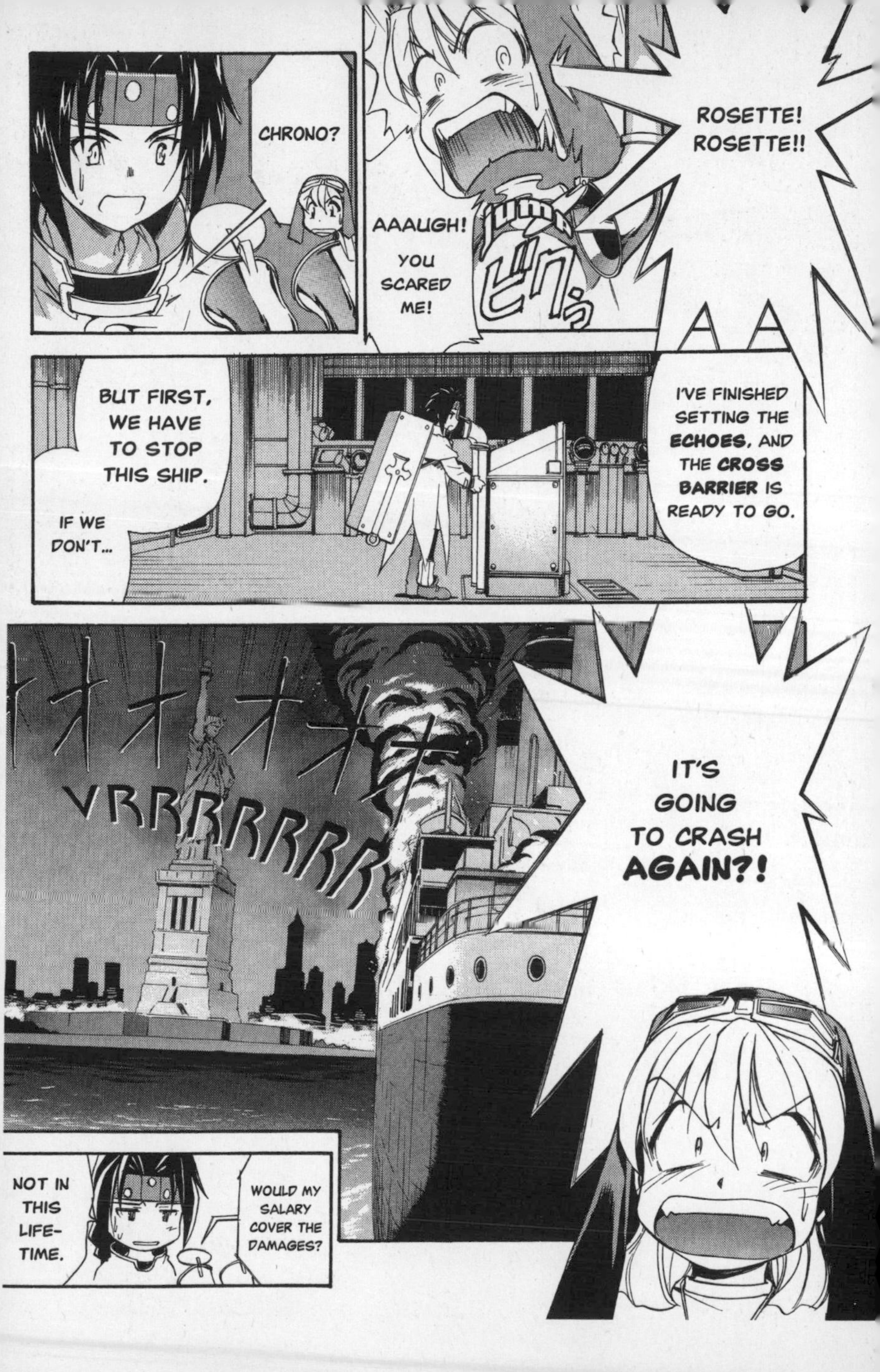
ROSETTE! ROSETTE!!
AAAUGH!
YOU SCARED ME!
CHRONO?
I'VE FINISHED SETTING THE ECHOES, AND THE CROSS BARRIER IS READY TO GO.
BUT FIRST, WE HAVE TO STOP THIS SHIP.
IF WE DON'T...
IT'S GOING TO CRASH AGAIN?!
VRRRRRRRR
WOULD MY SALARY COVER THE DAMAGES?
NOT IN THIS LIFE-TIME.

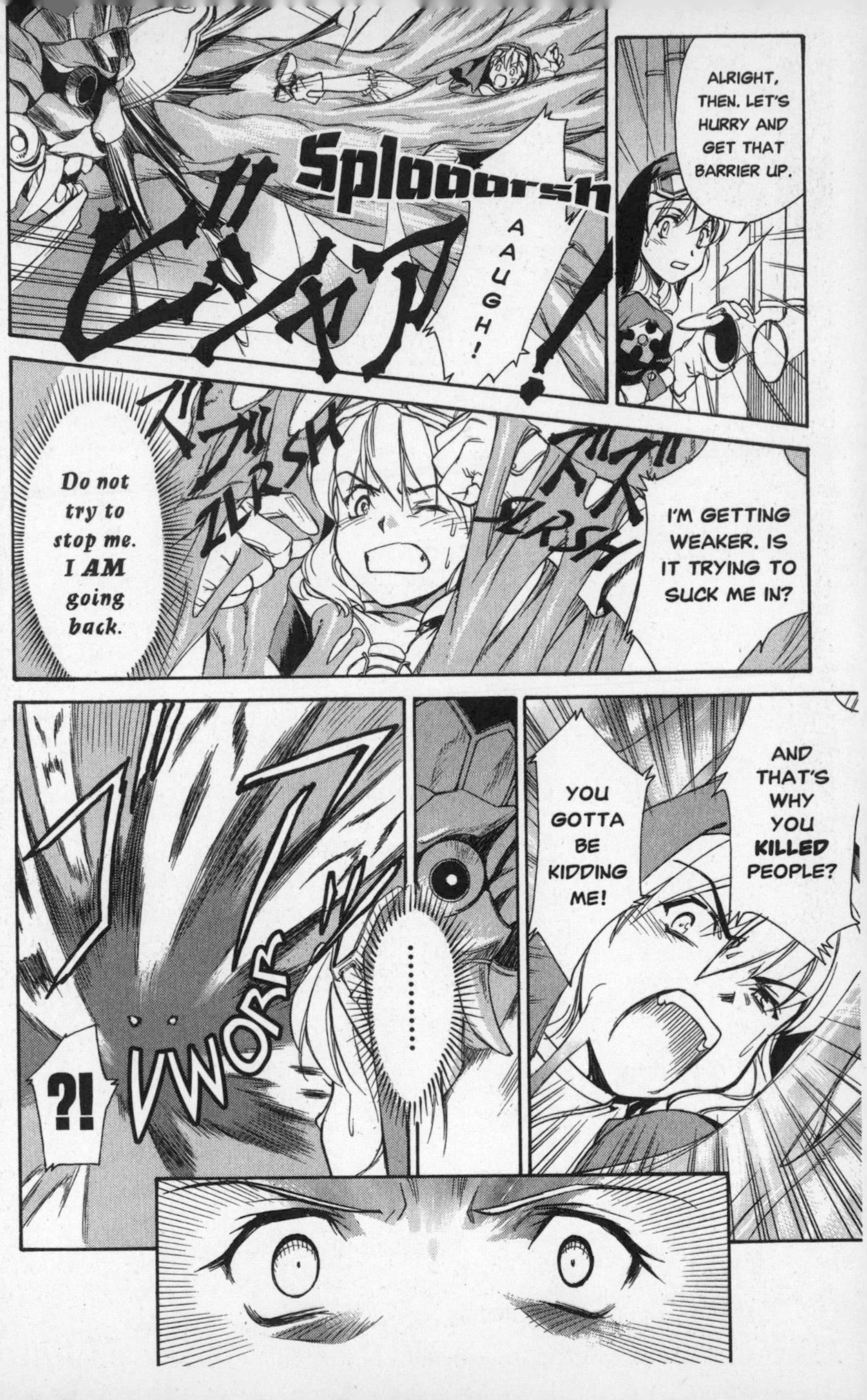
ALRIGHT, THEN. LET'S HURRY AND GET THAT BARRIER UP.
Splooarsh
WAAUGH!
I'M GETTING WEAKER. IS IT TRYING TO SUCK ME IN?
ZLRSH
ZLRSH
Do not try to stop me. I **AM** going back.
AND THAT'S WHY YOU **KILLED** PEOPLE?
YOU GOTTA BE KIDDING ME!
....
VWORR
?!

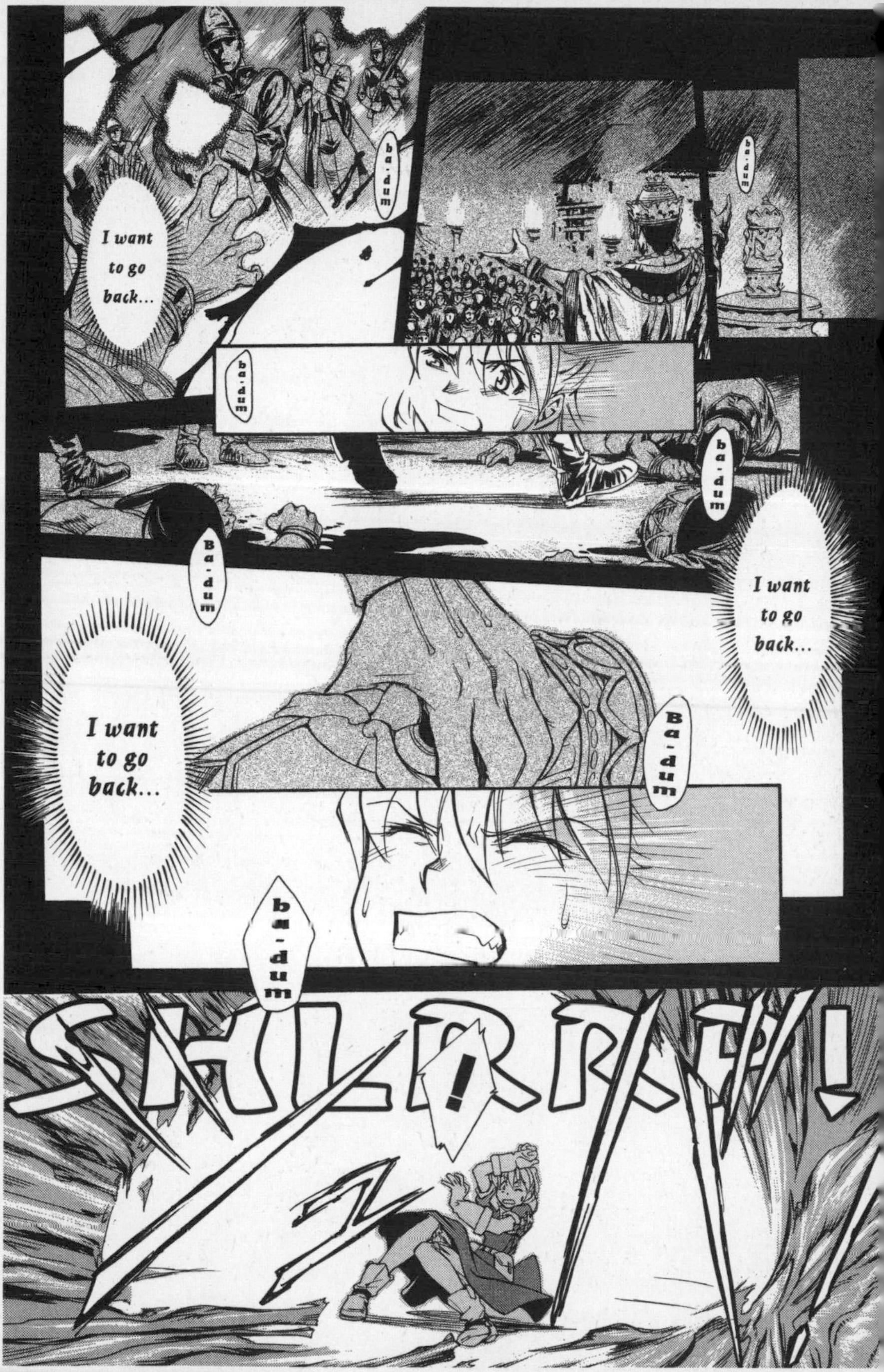
ba-dum
ba-dum
I want to go back...
ba-dum
ba-dum
I want to go back...
Ba-dum
Ba-dum
I want to go back...
ba-dum
SHLRRAK!
!

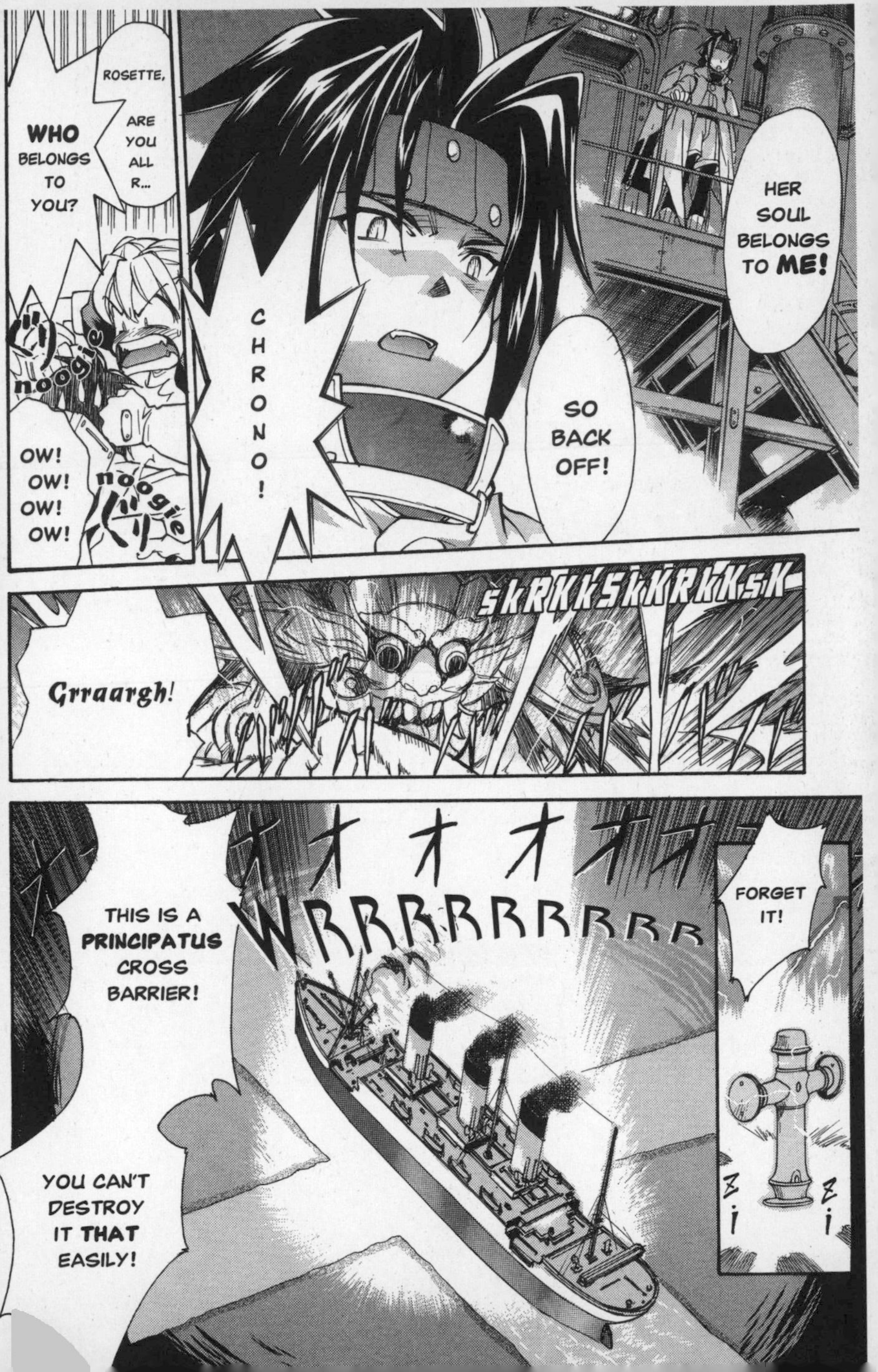
HER SOUL BELONGS TO **ME!**
SO BACK OFF!
CHRONO!
ROSETTE, ARE YOU ALL R...
WHO BELONGS TO YOU?
noogie
OW! OW! OW! OW!
noogie
sKRKK'SKKRKKsK
Grraargh!
FORGET IT!
zi
zi
オオオオオ
WRRRRRRRRR
THIS IS A **PRINCIPATUS** CROSS BARRIER!
YOU CAN'T DESTROY IT **THAT** EASILY!

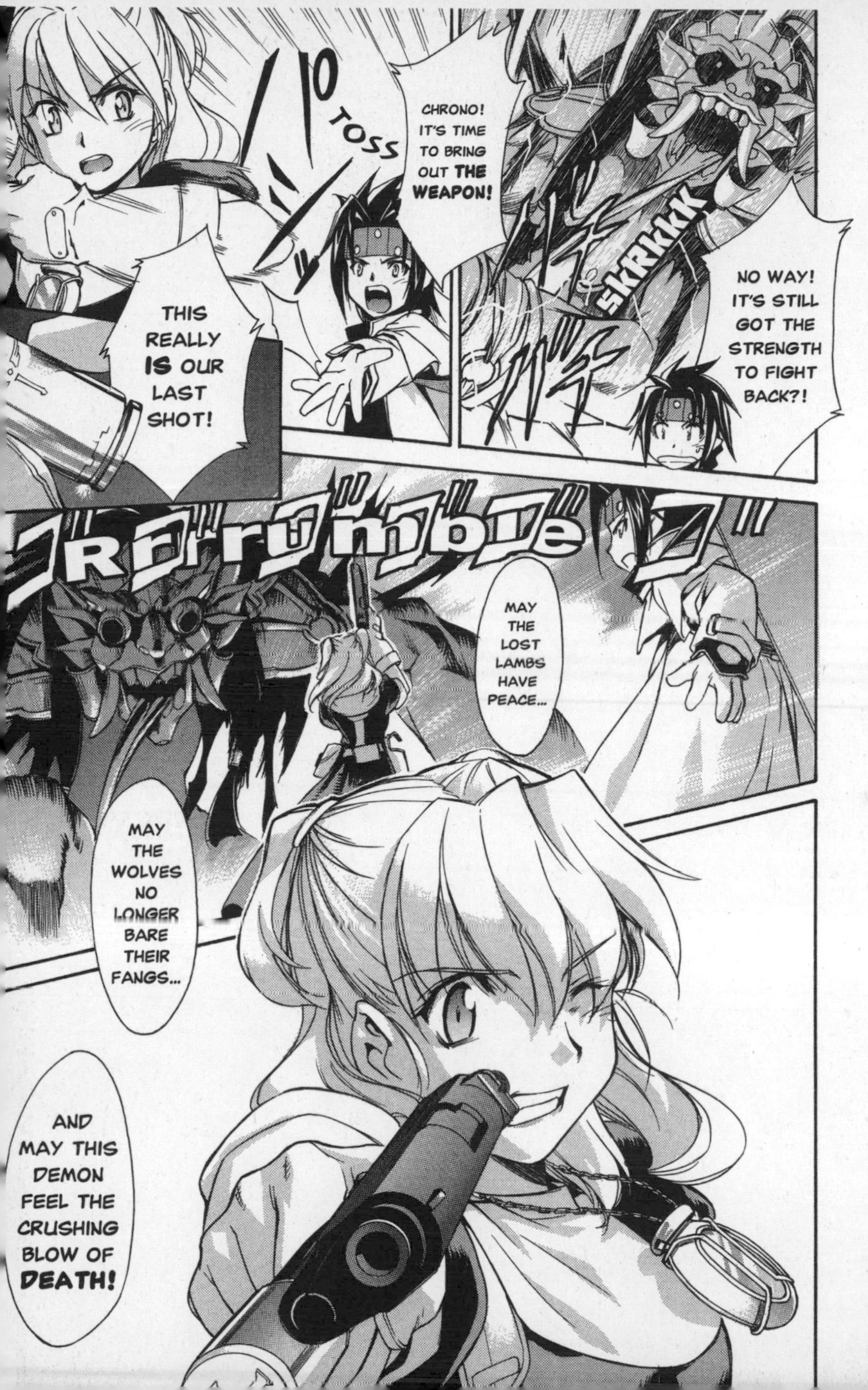
SKRKKK
NO WAY! IT'S STILL GOT THE STRENGTH TO FIGHT BACK?!
CHRONO! IT'S TIME TO BRING OUT THE WEAPON!
TOSS
THIS REALLY IS OUR LAST SHOT!
RRrrrumble
MAY THE LOST LAMBS HAVE PEACE...
MAY THE WOLVES NO LONGER BARE THEIR FANGS...
AND MAY THIS DEMON FEEL THE CRUSHING BLOW OF DEATH!

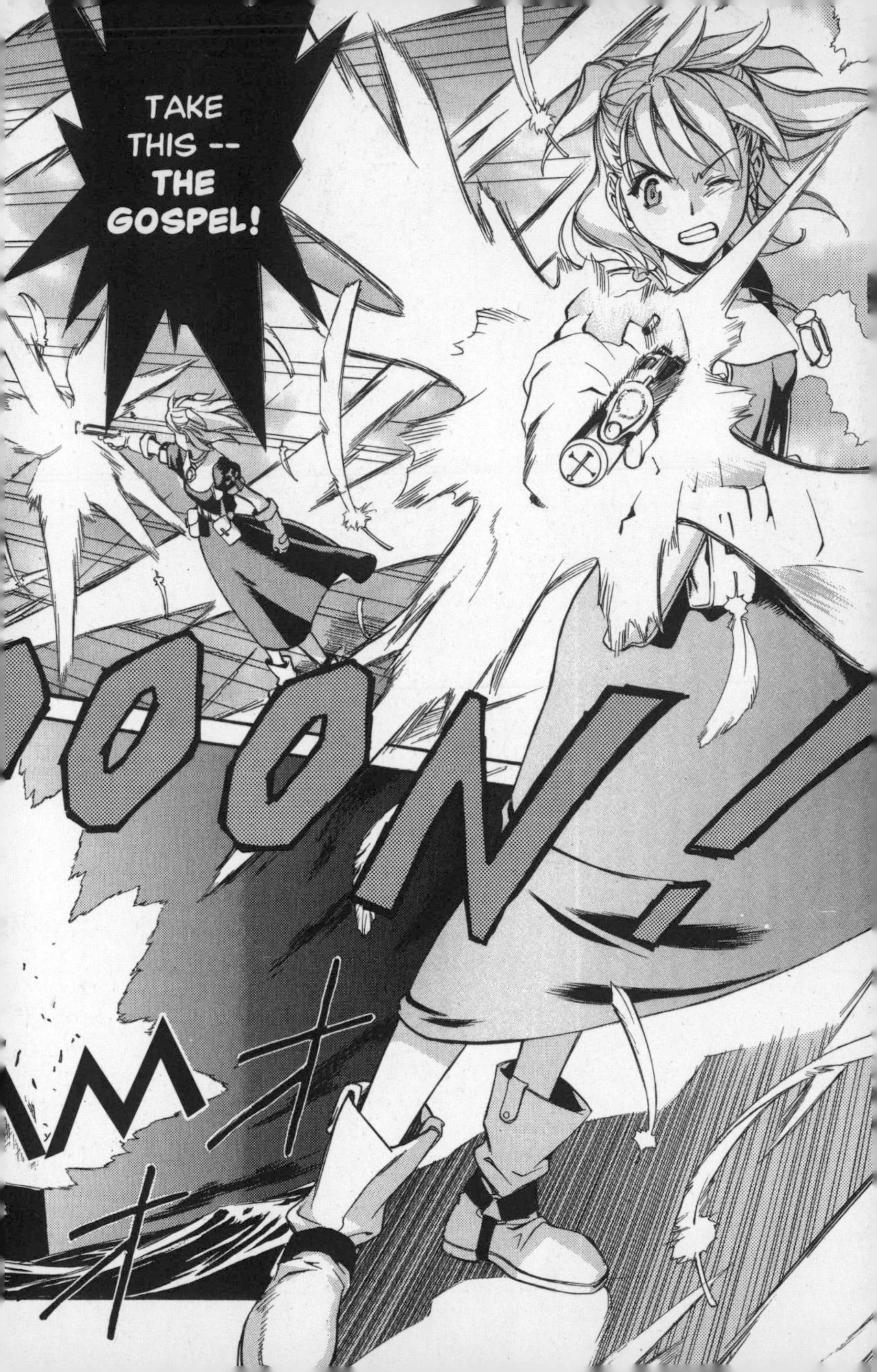
TAKE THIS -- THE GOSPEL!

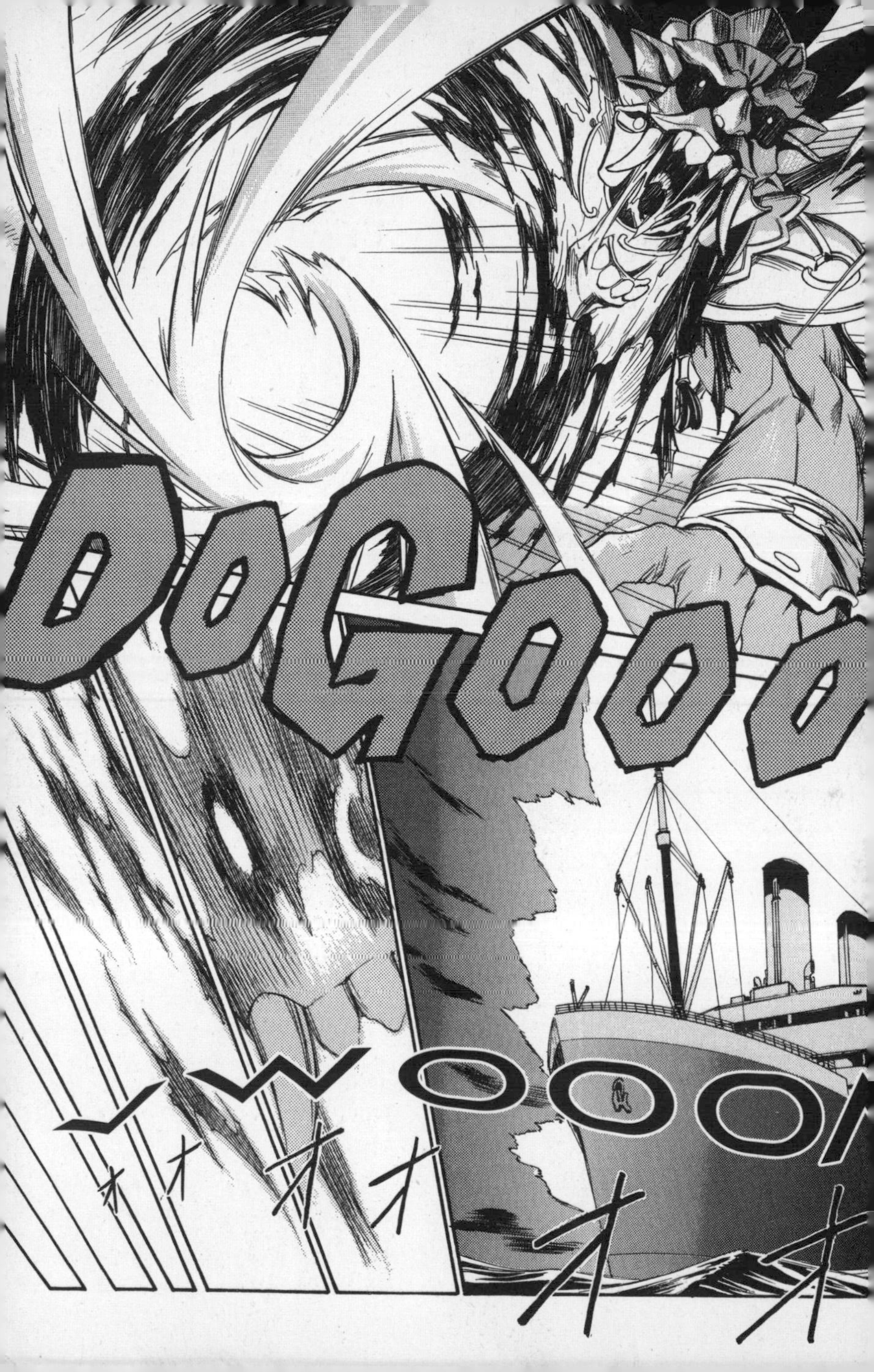

DOGOOOO
VWOOOO
オオオオ
オオ

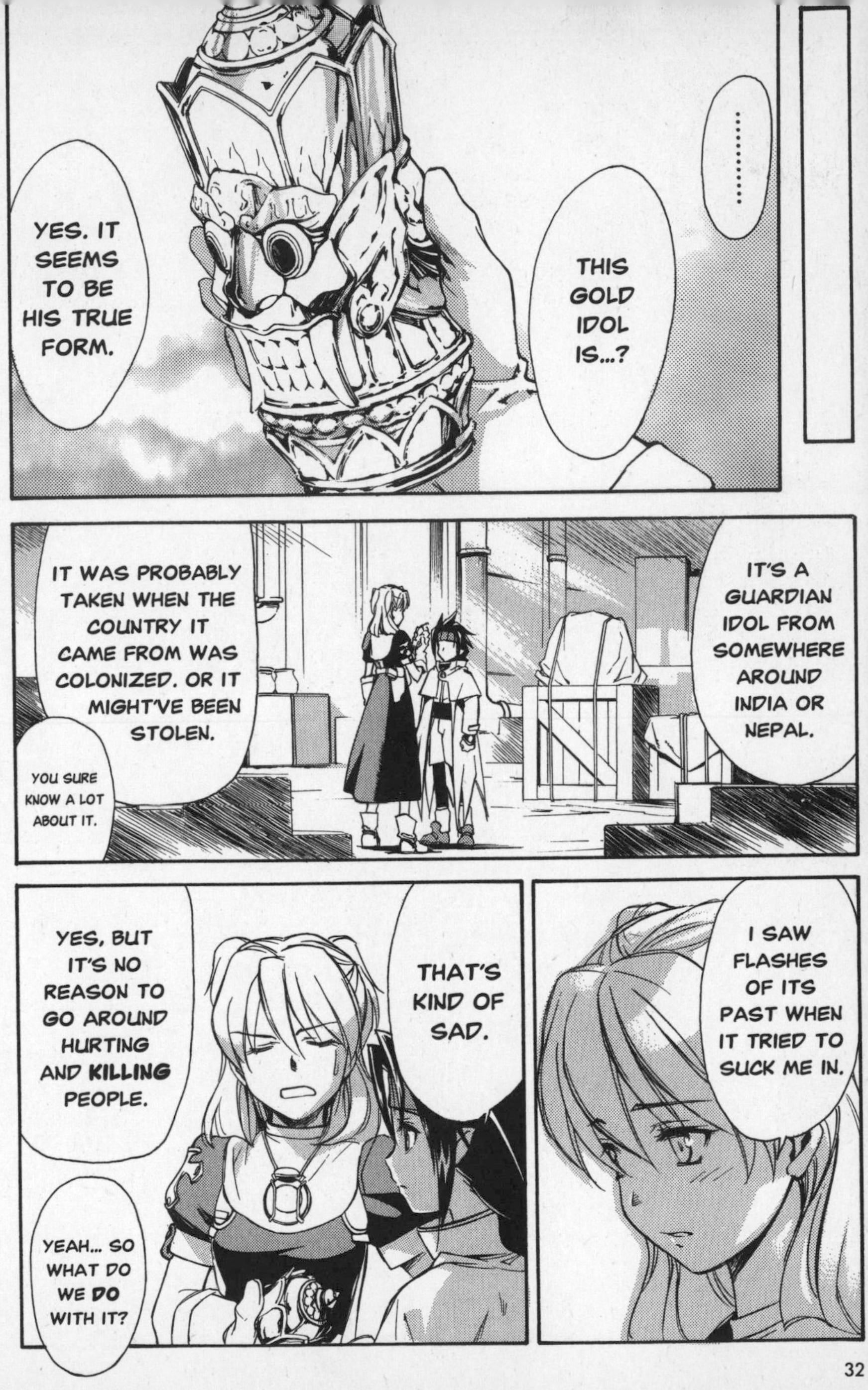
......
THIS GOLD IDOL IS...?
YES. IT SEEMS TO BE HIS TRUE FORM.
IT'S A GUARDIAN IDOL FROM SOMEWHERE AROUND INDIA OR NEPAL.
IT WAS PROBABLY TAKEN WHEN THE COUNTRY IT CAME FROM WAS COLONIZED. OR IT MIGHT'VE BEEN STOLEN.
YOU SURE KNOW A LOT ABOUT IT.
I SAW FLASHES OF ITS PAST WHEN IT TRIED TO SUCK ME IN.
THAT'S KIND OF SAD.
YES, BUT IT'S NO REASON TO GO AROUND HURTING AND **KILLING** PEOPLE.
YEAH... SO WHAT DO WE **DO** WITH IT?

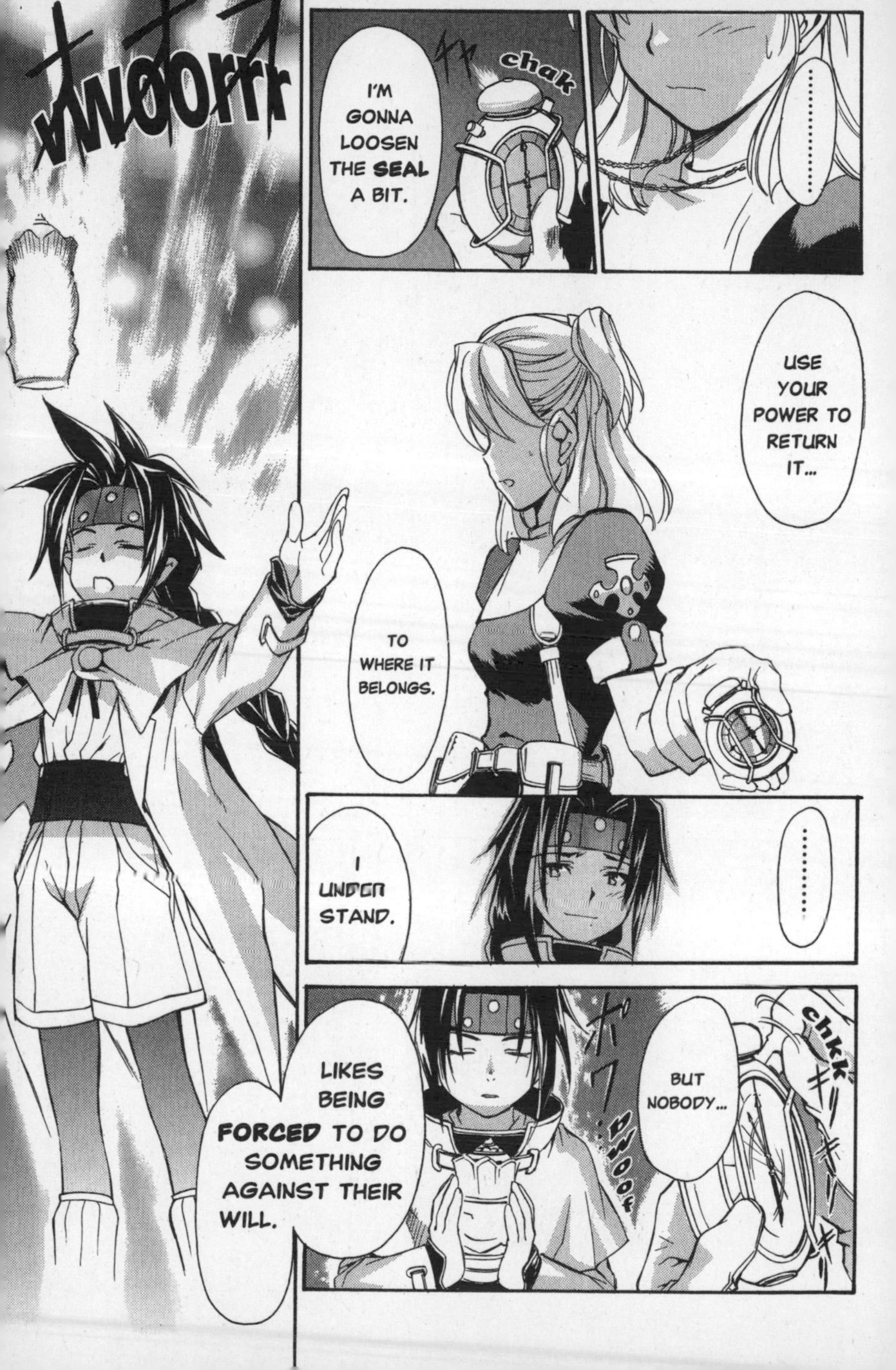
......
chak
I'M GONNA LOOSEN THE SEAL A BIT.
USE YOUR POWER TO RETURN IT...
TO WHERE IT BELONGS.
......
I UNDER STAND.
chkk
BUT NOBODY...
bwoof
LIKES BEING FORCED TO DO SOMETHING AGAINST THEIR WILL.
fwoorrr

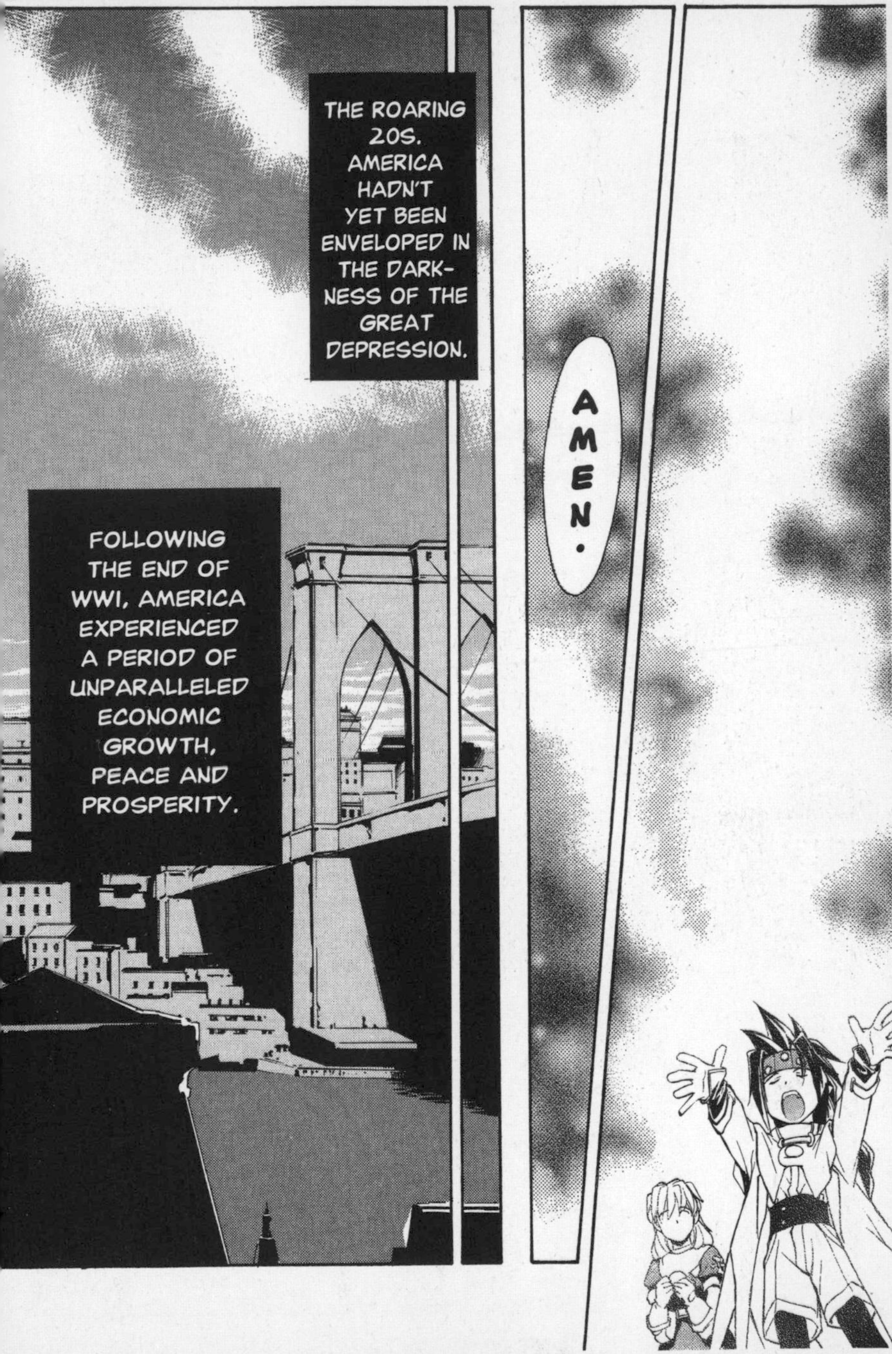
AMEN.
THE ROARING 20S. AMERICA HADN'T YET BEEN ENVELOPED IN THE DARK-NESS OF THE GREAT DEPRESSION.
FOLLOWING THE END OF WWI, AMERICA EXPERIENCED A PERIOD OF UNPARALLELED ECONOMIC GROWTH, PEACE AND PROSPERITY.

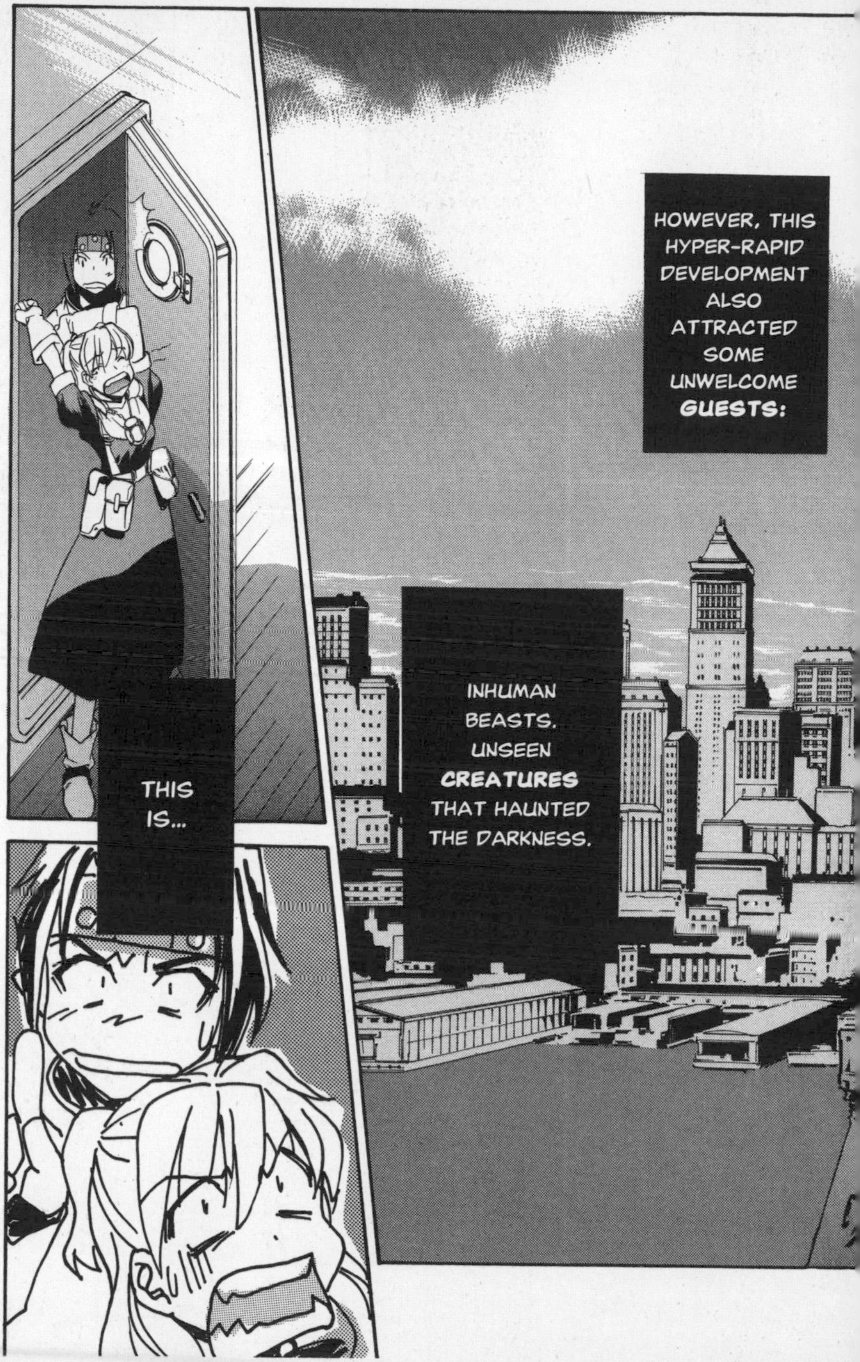
HOWEVER, THIS HYPER-RAPID DEVELOPMENT ALSO ATTRACTED SOME UNWELCOME GUESTS:
INHUMAN BEASTS, UNSEEN CREATURES THAT HAUNTED THE DARKNESS.
THIS IS...

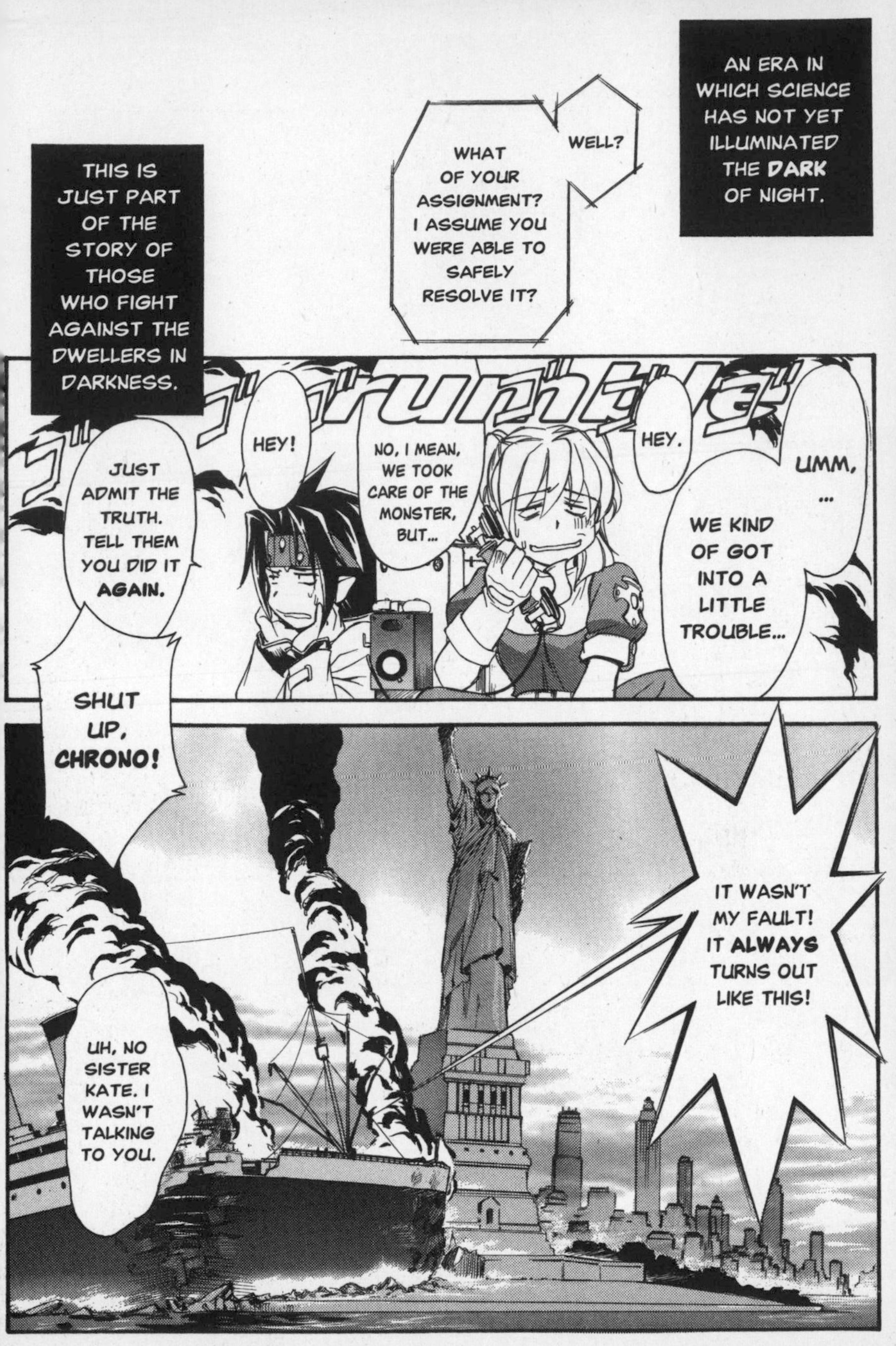
AN ERA IN WHICH SCIENCE HAS NOT YET ILLUMINATED THE **DARK** OF NIGHT.
WELL?
WHAT OF YOUR ASSIGNMENT? I ASSUME YOU WERE ABLE TO SAFELY RESOLVE IT?
THIS IS JUST PART OF THE STORY OF THOSE WHO FIGHT AGAINST THE DWELLERS IN DARKNESS.
UMM, ...
WE KIND OF GOT INTO A LITTLE TROUBLE...
HEY.
NO, I MEAN, WE TOOK CARE OF THE MONSTER, BUT...
HEY!
JUST ADMIT THE TRUTH. TELL THEM YOU DID IT **AGAIN.**
SHUT UP, **CHRONO!**
IT WASN'T MY FAULT! IT **ALWAYS** TURNS OUT LIKE THIS!
UH, NO SISTER KATE. I WASN'T TALKING TO YOU.

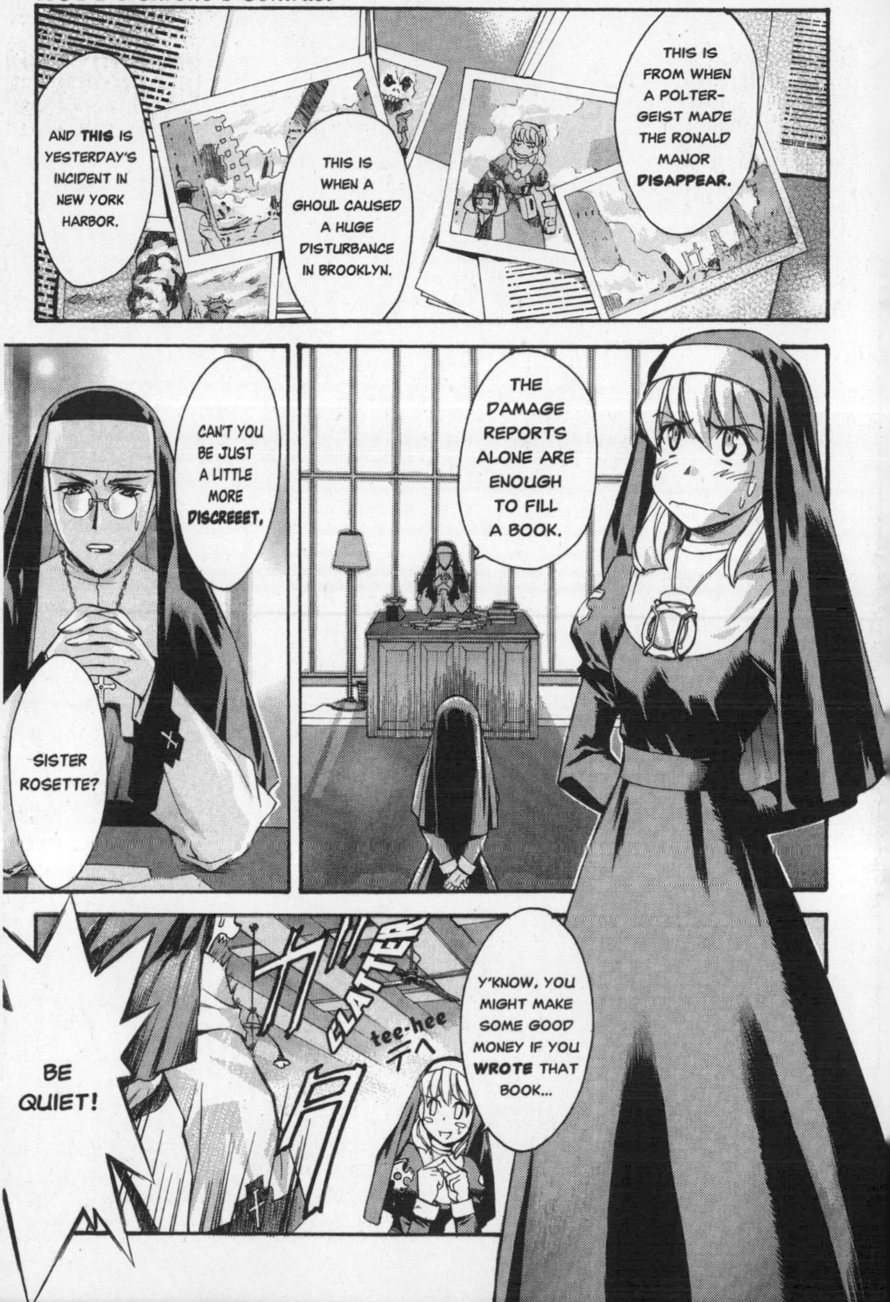
THIS IS FROM WHEN A POLTER-GEIST MADE THE RONALD MANOR **DISAPPEAR.**
THIS IS WHEN A GHOUL CAUSED A HUGE DISTURBANCE IN BROOKLYN.
AND **THIS** IS YESTERDAY'S INCIDENT IN NEW YORK HARBOR.
THE DAMAGE REPORTS ALONE ARE ENOUGH TO FILL A BOOK.
CAN'T YOU BE JUST A LITTLE MORE **DISCREEET,**
SISTER ROSETTE?
Y'KNOW, YOU MIGHT MAKE SOME GOOD MONEY IF YOU **WROTE** THAT BOOK...
tee-hee
CLATTER
BE QUIET!

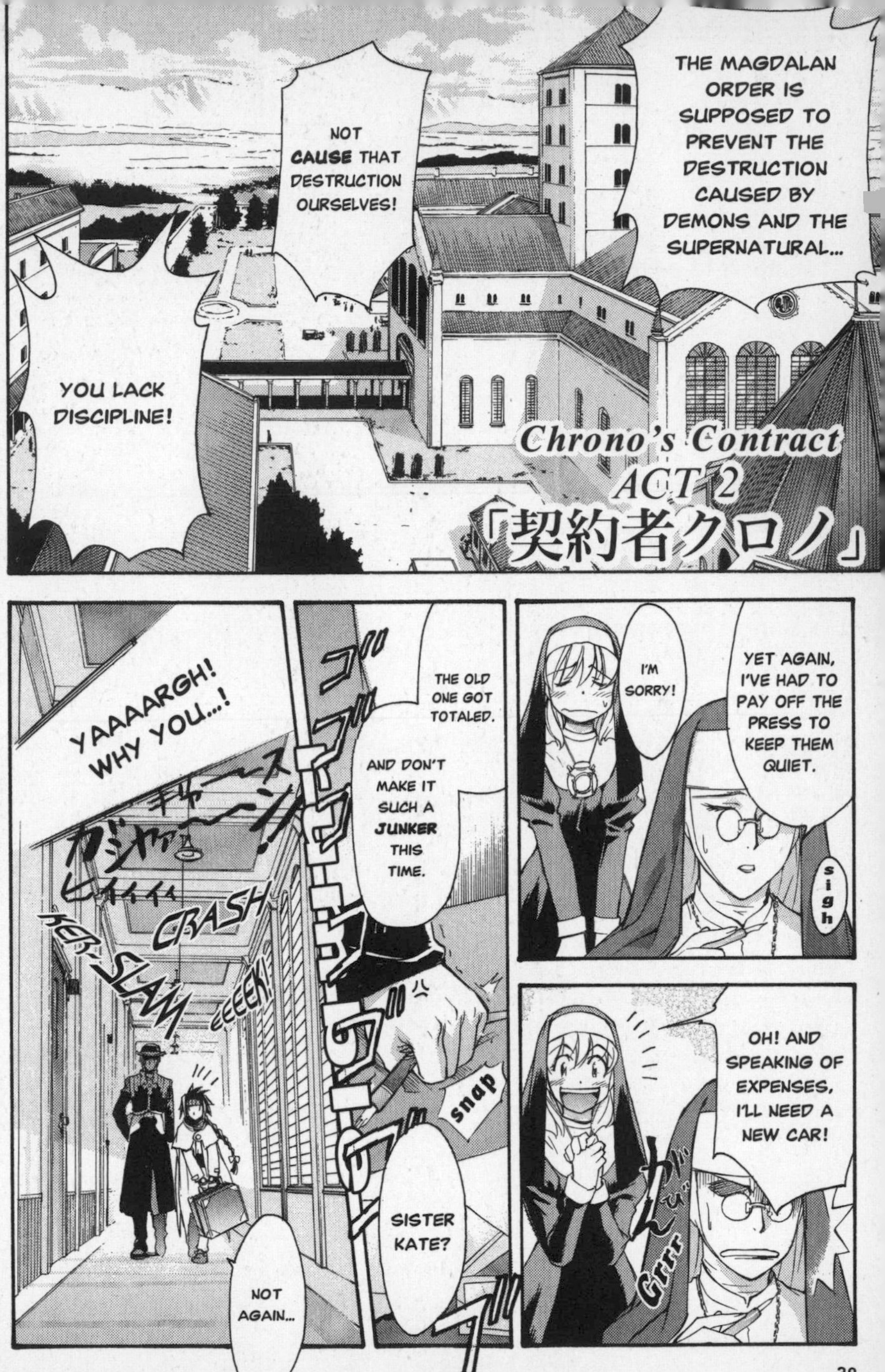
THE MAGDALAN ORDER IS SUPPOSED TO PREVENT THE DESTRUCTION CAUSED BY DEMONS AND THE SUPERNATURAL...
NOT CAUSE THAT DESTRUCTION OURSELVES!
YOU LACK DISCIPLINE!
Chrono's Contract
ACT 2
「契約者クロノ」
I'M SORRY!
YET AGAIN, I'VE HAD TO PAY OFF THE PRESS TO KEEP THEM QUIET.
sigh
OH! AND SPEAKING OF EXPENSES, I'LL NEED A NEW CAR!
Grrr
THE OLD ONE GOT TOTALED.
AND DON'T MAKE IT SUCH A JUNKER THIS TIME.
snap
SISTER KATE?
NOT AGAIN...
YAAAARGH! WHY YOU...!
CRASH
KER-SLAM
EEEEK!

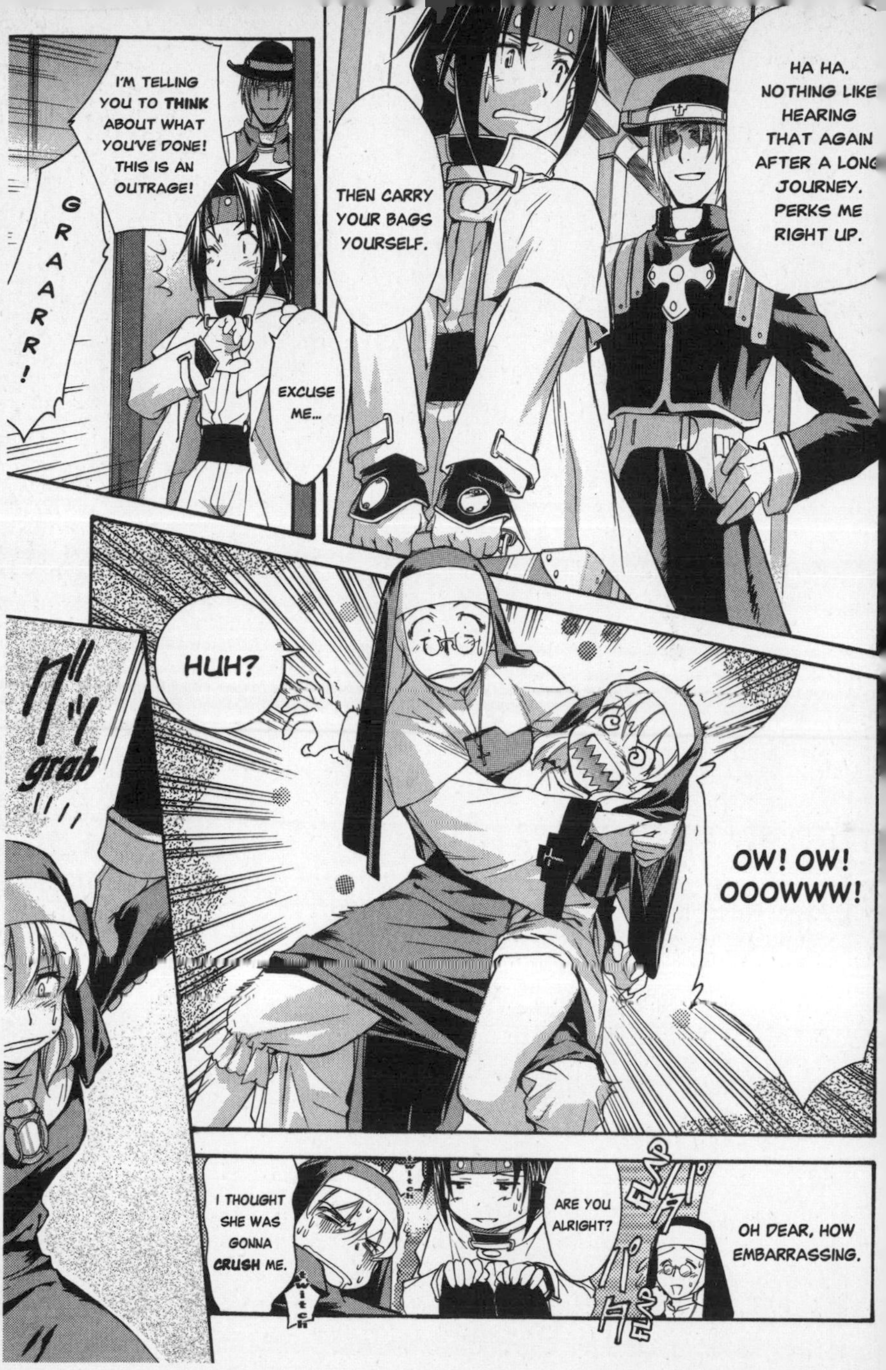
HA HA. NOTHING LIKE HEARING THAT AGAIN AFTER A LONG JOURNEY. PERKS ME RIGHT UP.
THEN CARRY YOUR BAGS YOURSELF.
EXCUSE ME...
I'M TELLING YOU TO **THINK** ABOUT WHAT YOU'VE DONE! THIS IS AN OUTRAGE!
GRAARRR!
HUH?
OW! OW! OOOWWW!
grab
OH DEAR, HOW EMBARRASSING.
FLAP
FLAP
ARE YOU ALRIGHT?
twitch
twitch
I THOUGHT SHE WAS GONNA **CRUSH** ME.

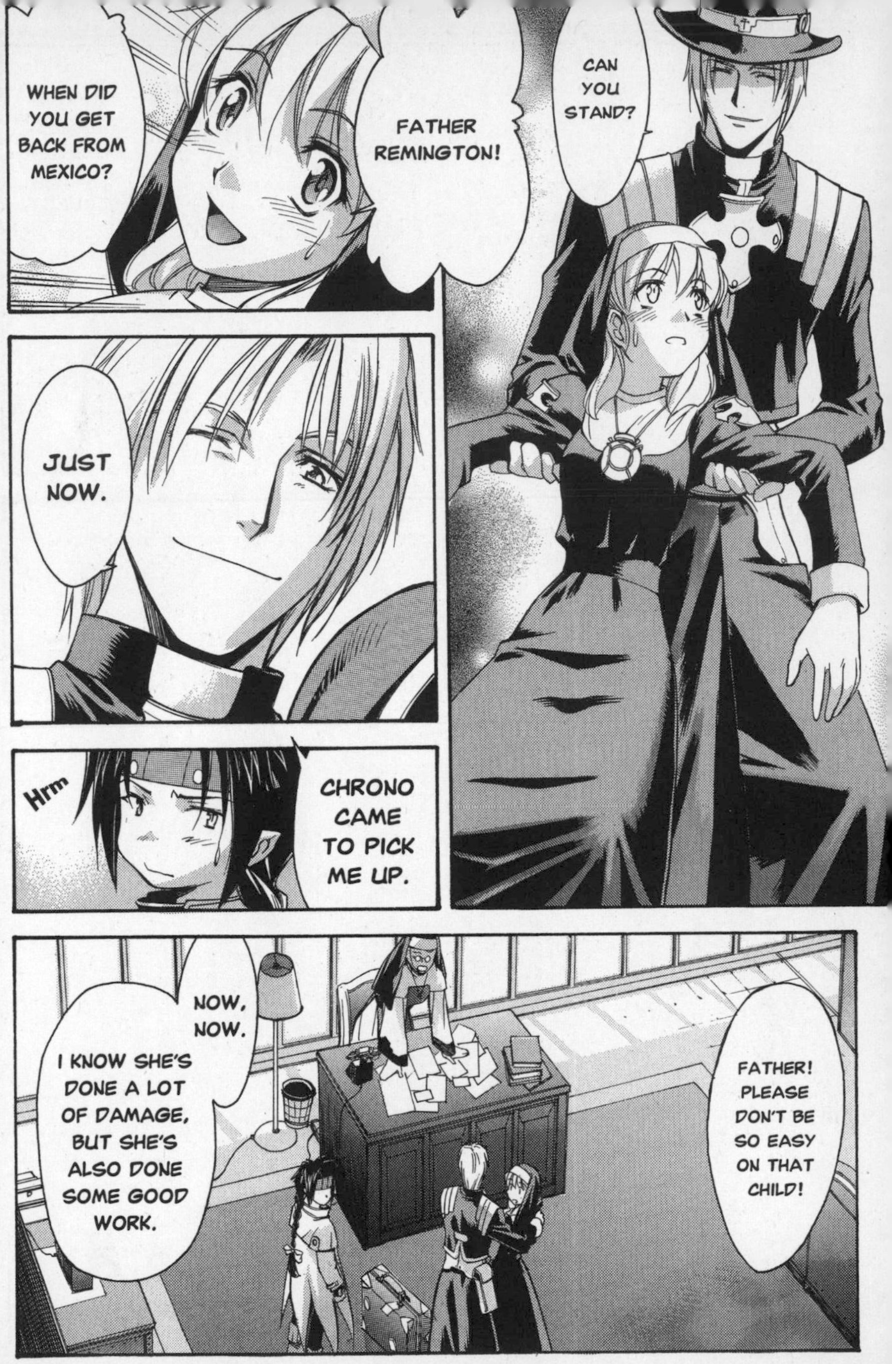
CAN YOU STAND?
FATHER REMINGTON!
WHEN DID YOU GET BACK FROM MEXICO?
JUST NOW.
CHRONO CAME TO PICK ME UP.
Hrm
FATHER! PLEASE DON'T BE SO EASY ON THAT CHILD!
NOW, NOW.
I KNOW SHE'S DONE A LOT OF DAMAGE, BUT SHE'S ALSO DONE SOME GOOD WORK.

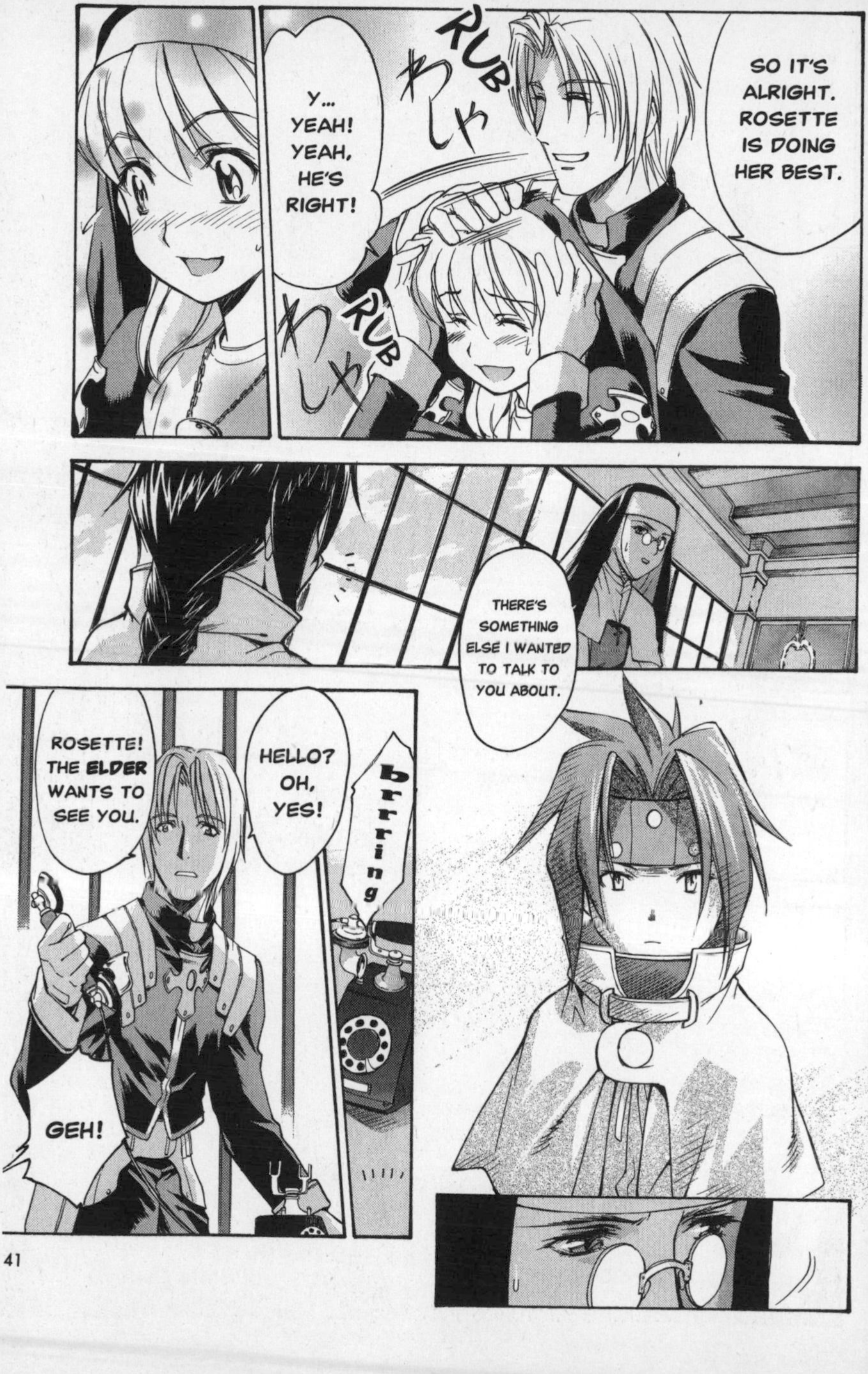
SO IT'S ALRIGHT. ROSETTE IS DOING HER BEST.
RUB
わしゃ
Y... YEAH! YEAH, HE'S RIGHT!
RUB
わしゃ
THERE'S SOMETHING ELSE I WANTED TO TALK TO YOU ABOUT.
brrring
HELLO? OH, YES!
ROSETTE! THE **ELDER** WANTS TO SEE YOU.
GEH!

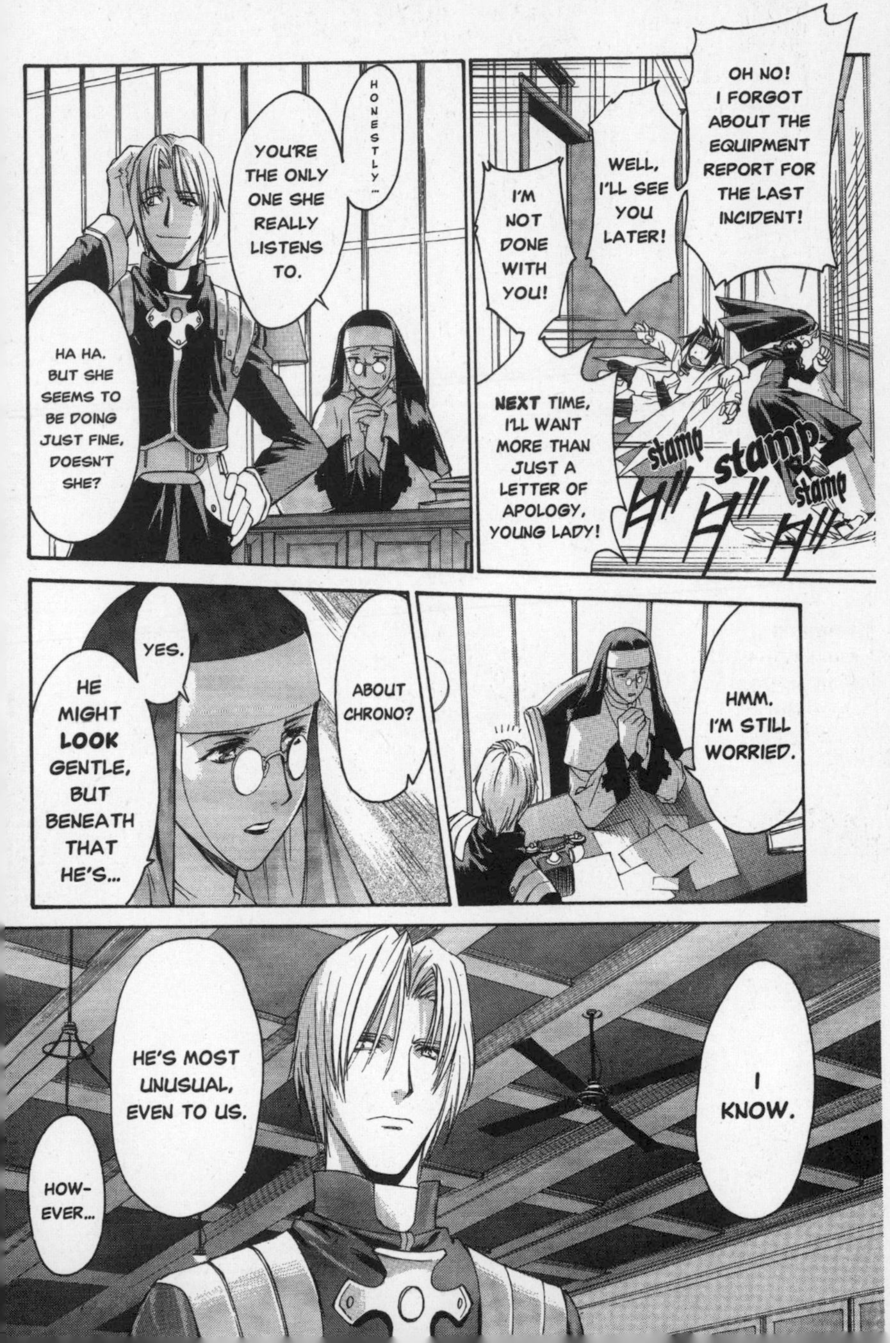
OH NO! I FORGOT ABOUT THE EQUIPMENT REPORT FOR THE LAST INCIDENT!
WELL, I'LL SEE YOU LATER!
I'M NOT DONE WITH YOU!
NEXT TIME, I'LL WANT MORE THAN JUST A LETTER OF APOLOGY, YOUNG LADY!
stamp
stamp
stamp
HONESTLY...
YOU'RE THE ONLY ONE SHE REALLY LISTENS TO.
HA HA. BUT SHE SEEMS TO BE DOING JUST FINE, DOESN'T SHE?
HMM. I'M STILL WORRIED.
ABOUT CHRONO?
YES.
HE MIGHT **LOOK** GENTLE, BUT BENEATH THAT HE'S...
I KNOW.
HE'S MOST UNUSUAL, EVEN TO US.
HOW-EVER...

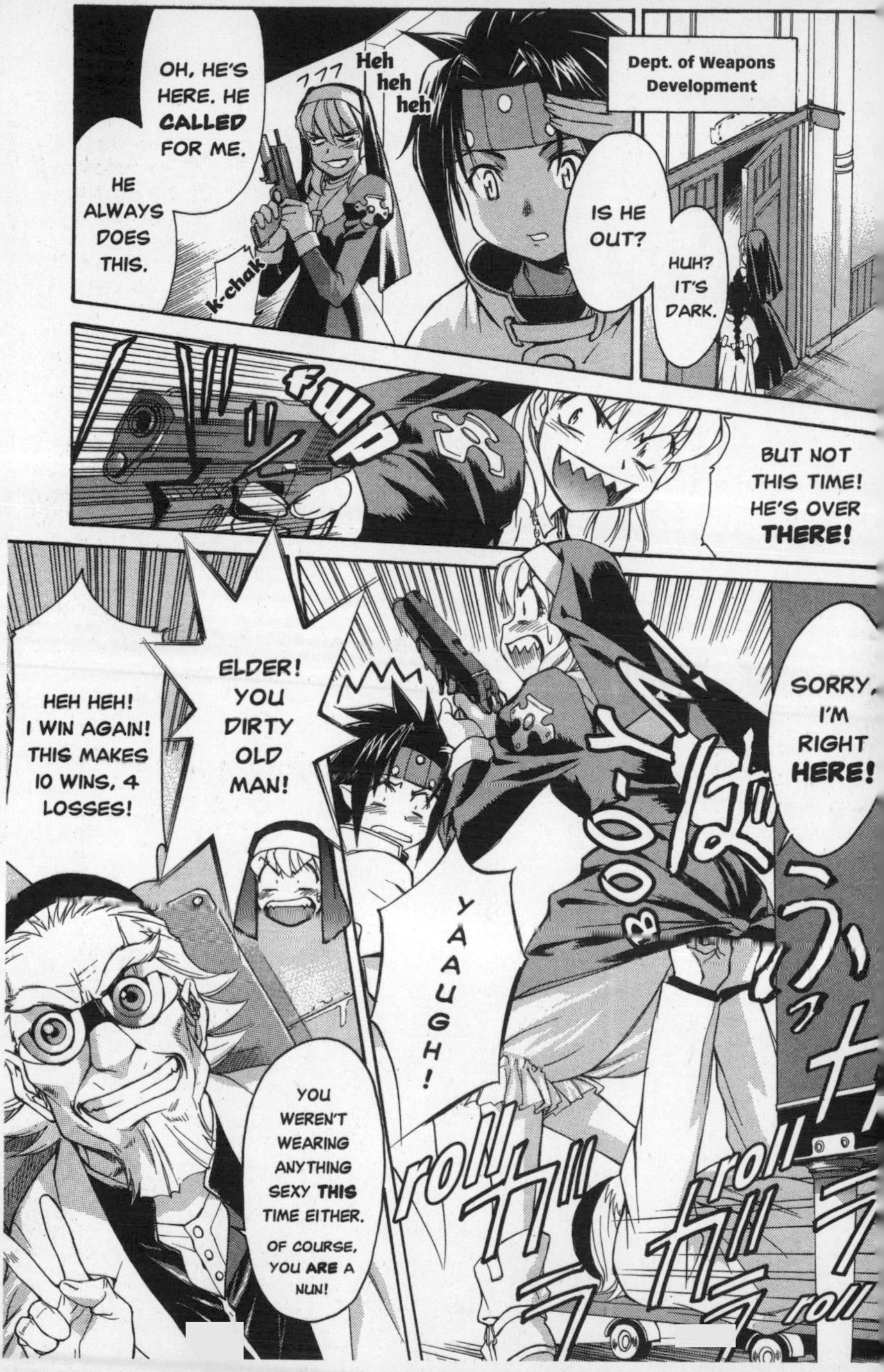
Dept. of Weapons Development
IS HE OUT?
HUH? IT'S DARK.
Heh heh heh
OH, HE'S HERE. HE **CALLED** FOR ME.
HE ALWAYS DOES THIS.
k-chak
fwup
BUT NOT THIS TIME! HE'S OVER **THERE!**
SORRY, I'M RIGHT **HERE!**
YAAUGH!
ELDER! YOU DIRTY OLD MAN!
HEH HEH! I WIN AGAIN! THIS MAKES 10 WINS, 4 LOSSES!
YOU WEREN'T WEARING ANYTHING SEXY **THIS** TIME EITHER.
OF COURSE, YOU **ARE** A NUN!
roll
roll
roll

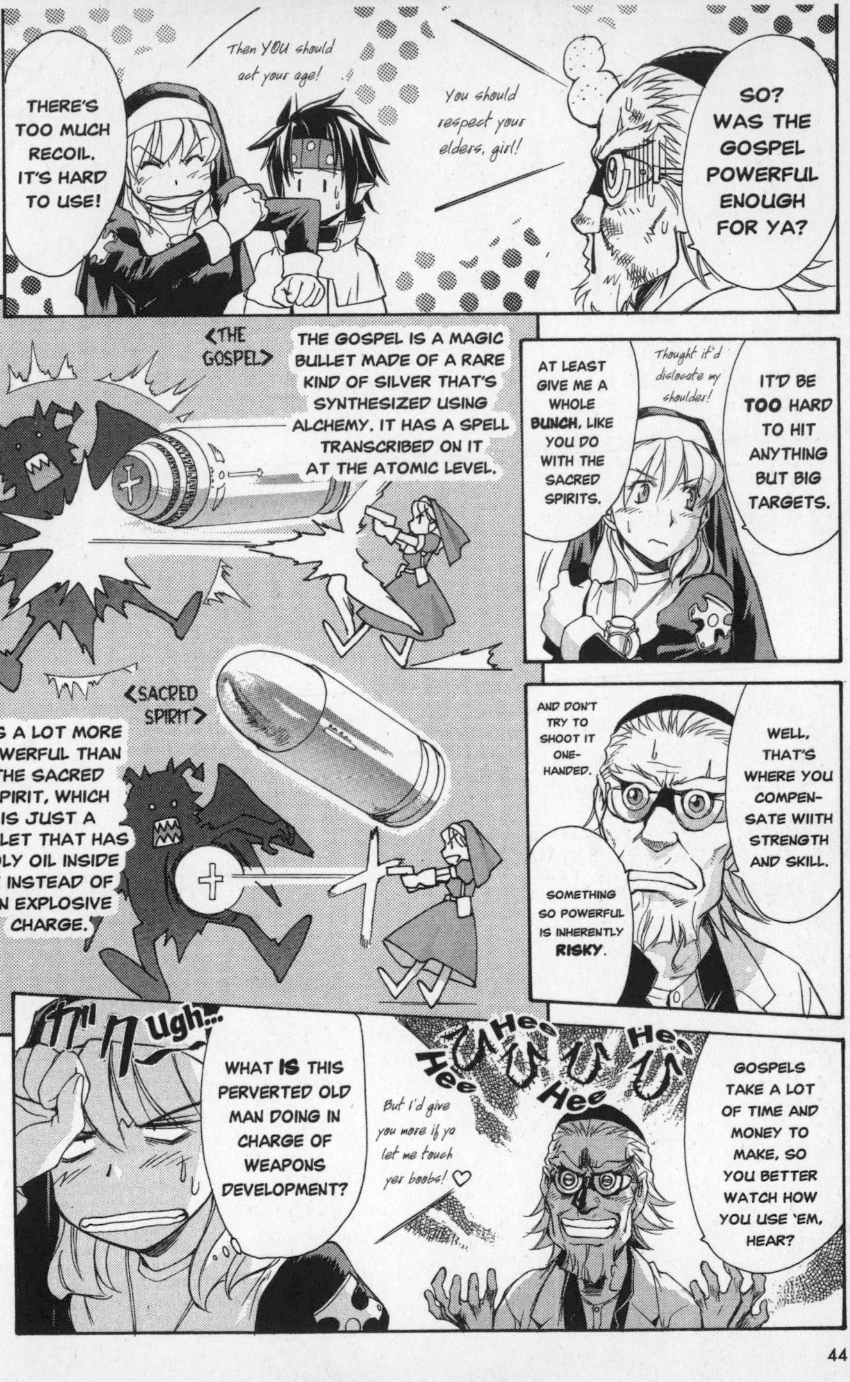
SO? WAS THE GOSPEL POWERFUL ENOUGH FOR YA?
You should respect your elders, girl!
Then YOU should act your age!
THERE'S TOO MUCH RECOIL. IT'S HARD TO USE!
IT'D BE TOO HARD TO HIT ANYTHING BUT BIG TARGETS.
Thought it'd dislocate my shoulder!
AT LEAST GIVE ME A WHOLE BUNCH, LIKE YOU DO WITH THE SACRED SPIRITS.
WELL, THAT'S WHERE YOU COMPENSATE WIITH STRENGTH AND SKILL.
AND DON'T TRY TO SHOOT IT ONE-HANDED.
SOMETHING SO POWERFUL IS INHERENTLY RISKY.
<THE GOSPEL>
THE GOSPEL IS A MAGIC BULLET MADE OF A RARE KIND OF SILVER THAT'S SYNTHESIZED USING ALCHEMY. IT HAS A SPELL TRANSCRIBED ON IT AT THE ATOMIC LEVEL.
<SACRED SPIRIT>
IT'S A LOT MORE POWERFUL THAN THE SACRED SPIRIT, WHICH IS JUST A BULLET THAT HAS HOLY OIL INSIDE IT INSTEAD OF AN EXPLOSIVE CHARGE.
GOSPELS TAKE A LOT OF TIME AND MONEY TO MAKE, SO YOU BETTER WATCH HOW YOU USE 'EM, HEAR?
Hee Hee Hee Hee
But I'd give you more if ya let me touch yer boobs! ♡
WHAT IS THIS PERVERTED OLD MAN DOING IN CHARGE OF WEAPONS DEVELOPMENT?
Ugh...

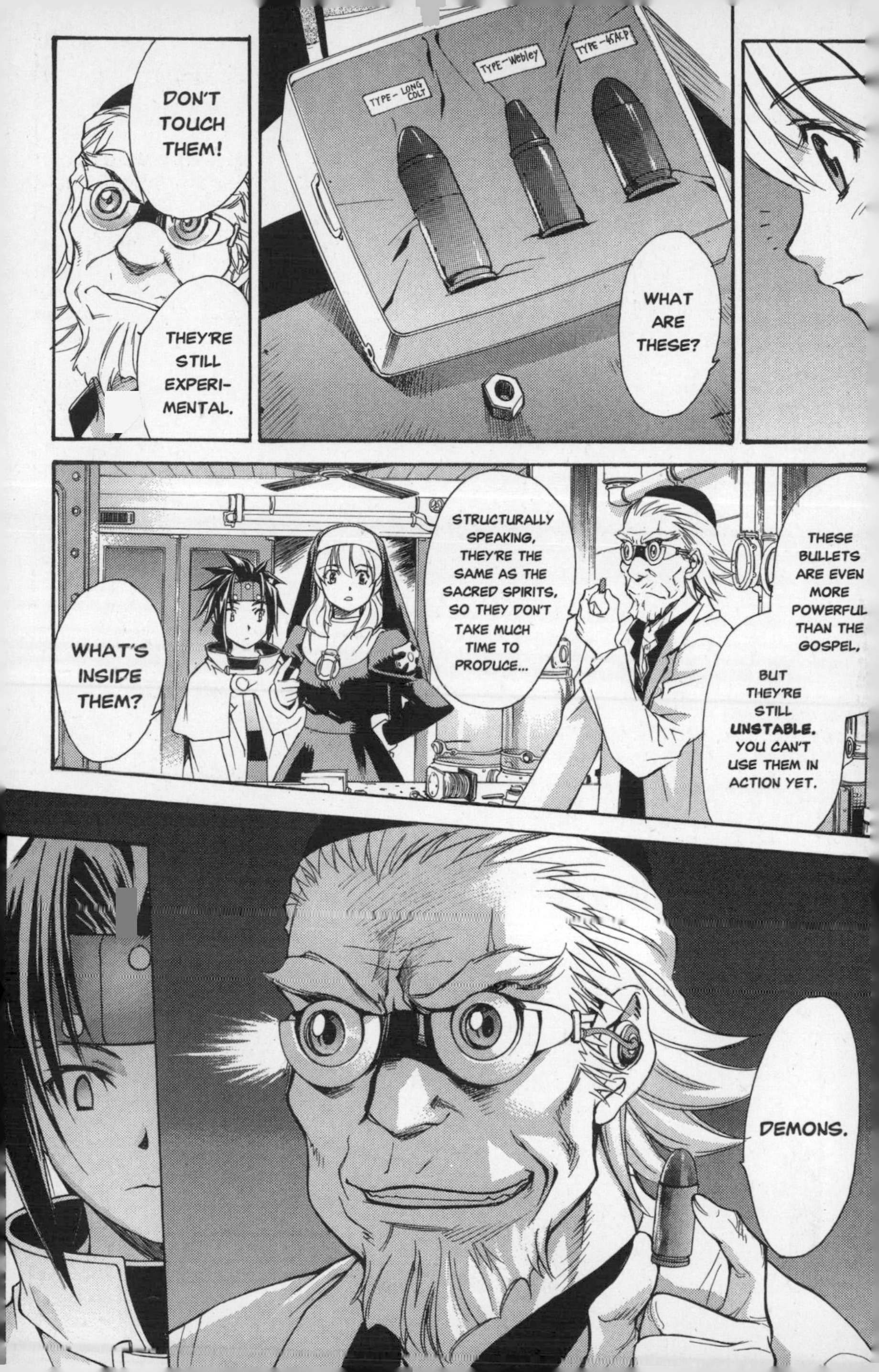
TYPE-45ACP
TYPE-Webley
TYPE-LONG COLT
WHAT ARE THESE?
DON'T TOUCH THEM!
THEY'RE STILL EXPERI-MENTAL.
THESE BULLETS ARE EVEN MORE POWERFUL THAN THE GOSPEL,
BUT THEY'RE STILL **UNSTABLE.** YOU CAN'T USE THEM IN ACTION YET.
STRUCTURALLY SPEAKING, THEY'RE THE SAME AS THE SACRED SPIRITS, SO THEY DON'T TAKE MUCH TIME TO PRODUCE...
WHAT'S INSIDE THEM?
DEMONS.

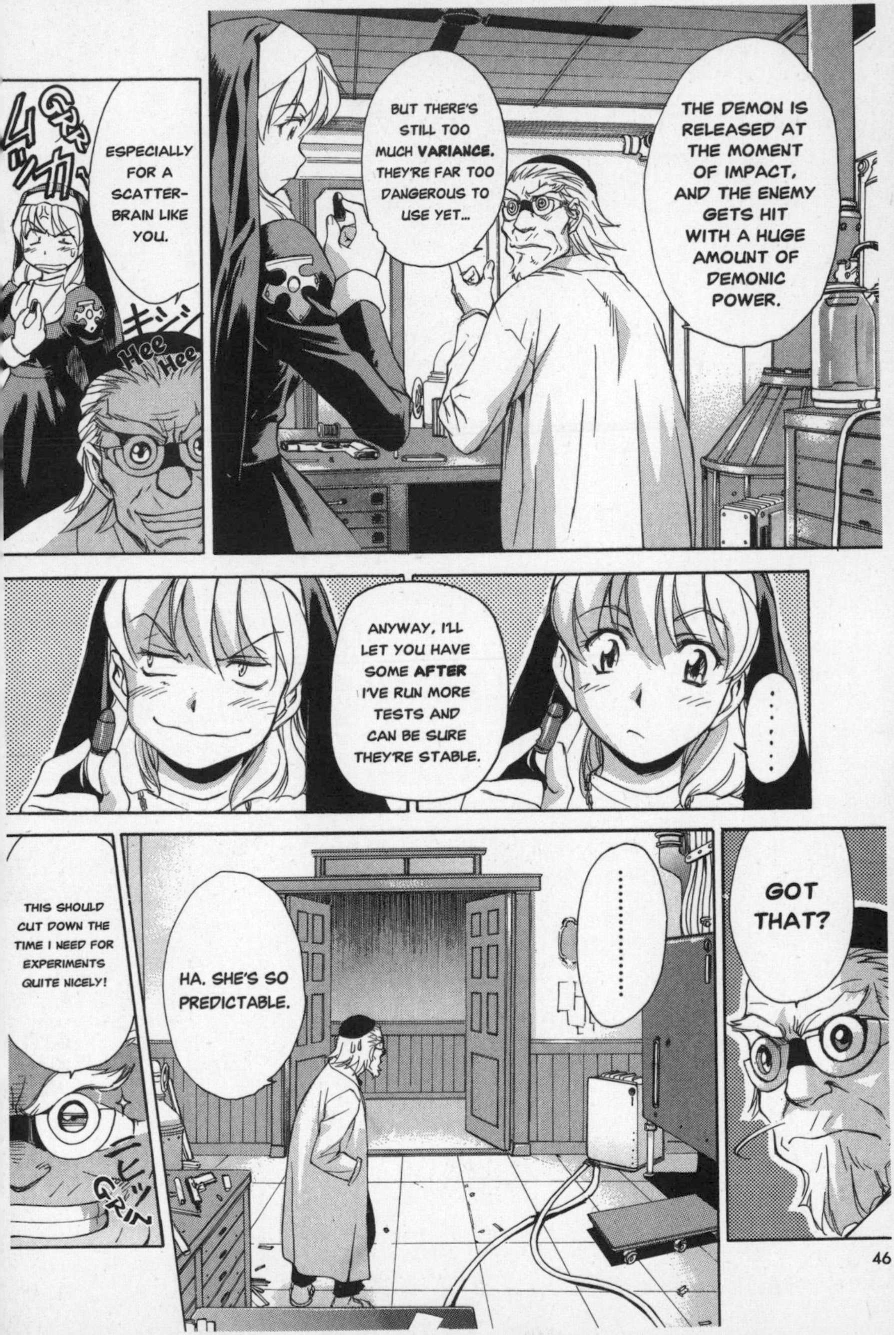
THE DEMON IS RELEASED AT THE MOMENT OF IMPACT, AND THE ENEMY GETS HIT WITH A HUGE AMOUNT OF DEMONIC POWER.
BUT THERE'S STILL TOO MUCH **VARIANCE.** THEY'RE FAR TOO DANGEROUS TO USE YET...
GRR
ESPECIALLY FOR A SCATTER-BRAIN LIKE YOU.
HEE HEE
......
ANYWAY, I'LL LET YOU HAVE SOME **AFTER** I'VE RUN MORE TESTS AND CAN BE SURE THEY'RE STABLE.
GOT THAT?
......
HA. SHE'S SO PREDICTABLE.
THIS SHOULD CUT DOWN THE TIME I NEED FOR EXPERIMENTS QUITE NICELY!
GRIN

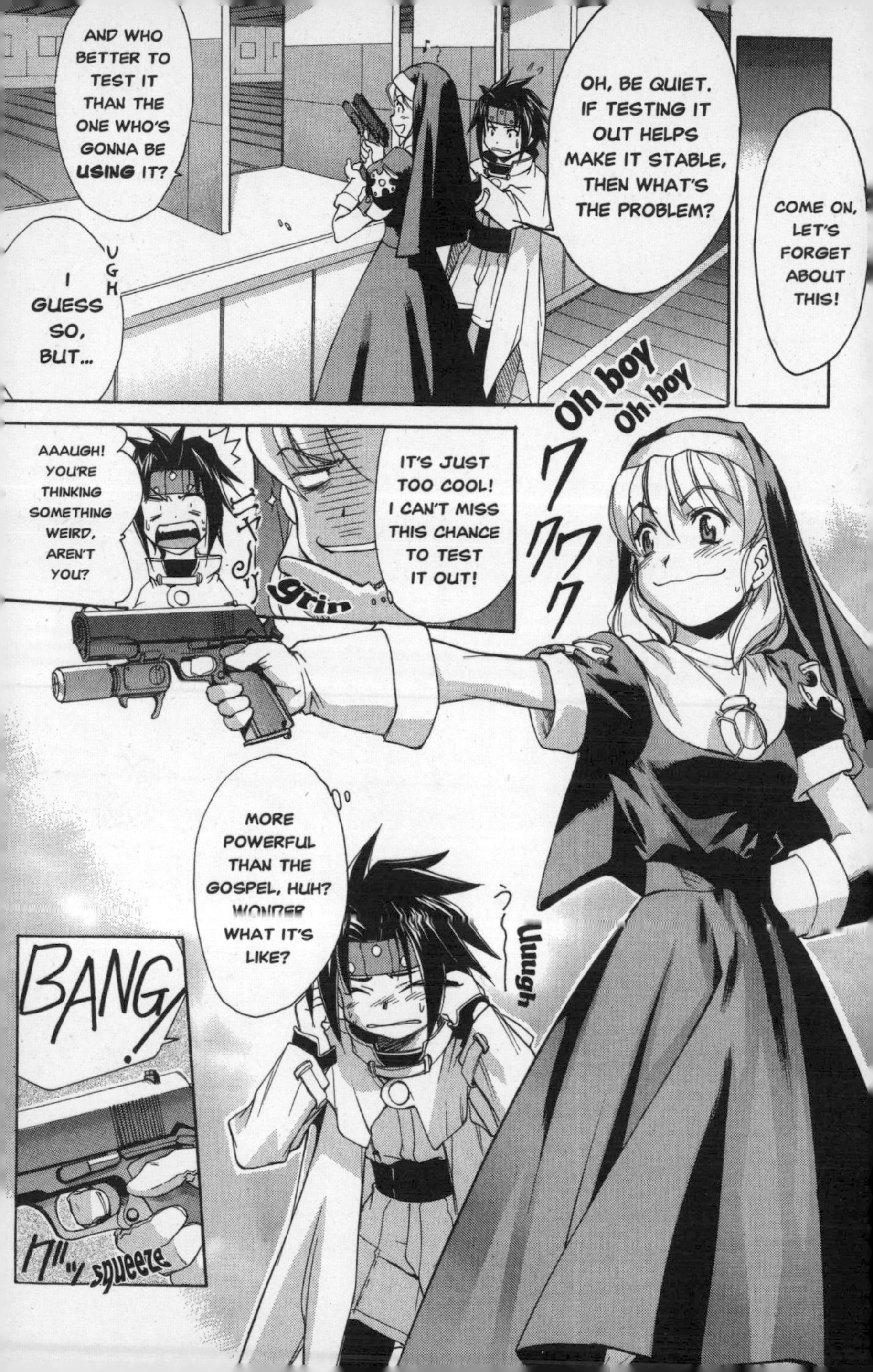
COME ON, LET'S FORGET ABOUT THIS!
OH, BE QUIET. IF TESTING IT OUT HELPS MAKE IT STABLE, THEN WHAT'S THE PROBLEM?
AND WHO BETTER TO TEST IT THAN THE ONE WHO'S GONNA BE **USING** IT?
UGH
I GUESS SO, BUT...
Oh boy Oh boy
ワクワク
IT'S JUST TOO COOL! I CAN'T MISS THIS CHANCE TO TEST IT OUT!
grin
AAAUGH! YOU'RE THINKING SOMETHING WEIRD, AREN'T YOU?
Uuugh
MORE POWERFUL THAN THE GOSPEL, HUH? WONDER WHAT IT'S LIKE?
BANG!
squeeze

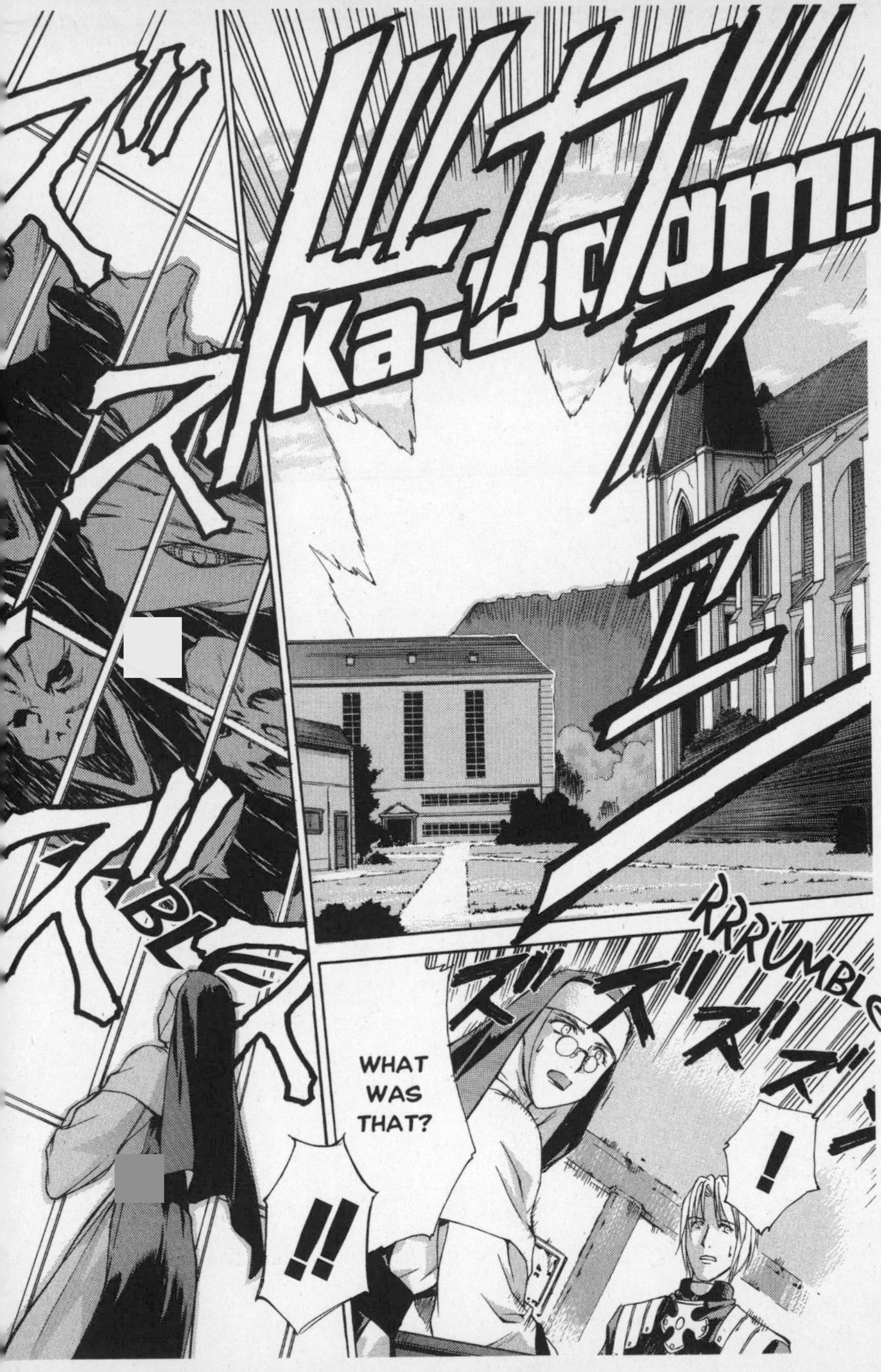
Ka-Baaam!
RRRUMBLE
!
WHAT WAS THAT?
!!

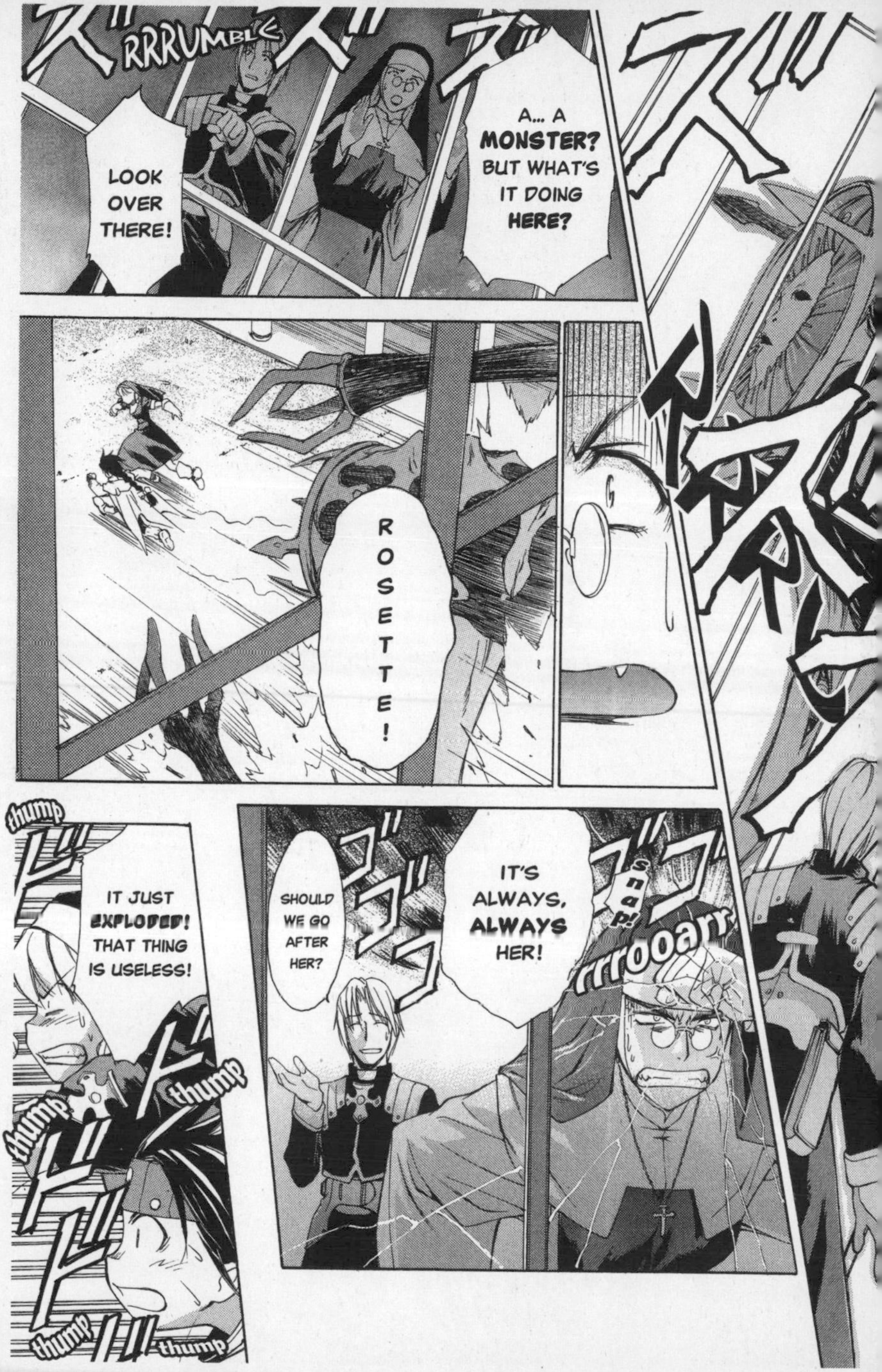
RRRUMBLE
A... A MONSTER? BUT WHAT'S IT DOING HERE?
LOOK OVER THERE!
ROSETTE!
snap!
rrrooarr
IT'S ALWAYS, ALWAYS HER!
SHOULD WE GO AFTER HER?
thump
IT JUST EXPLODED! THAT THING IS USELESS!
thump
thump
thump
thump

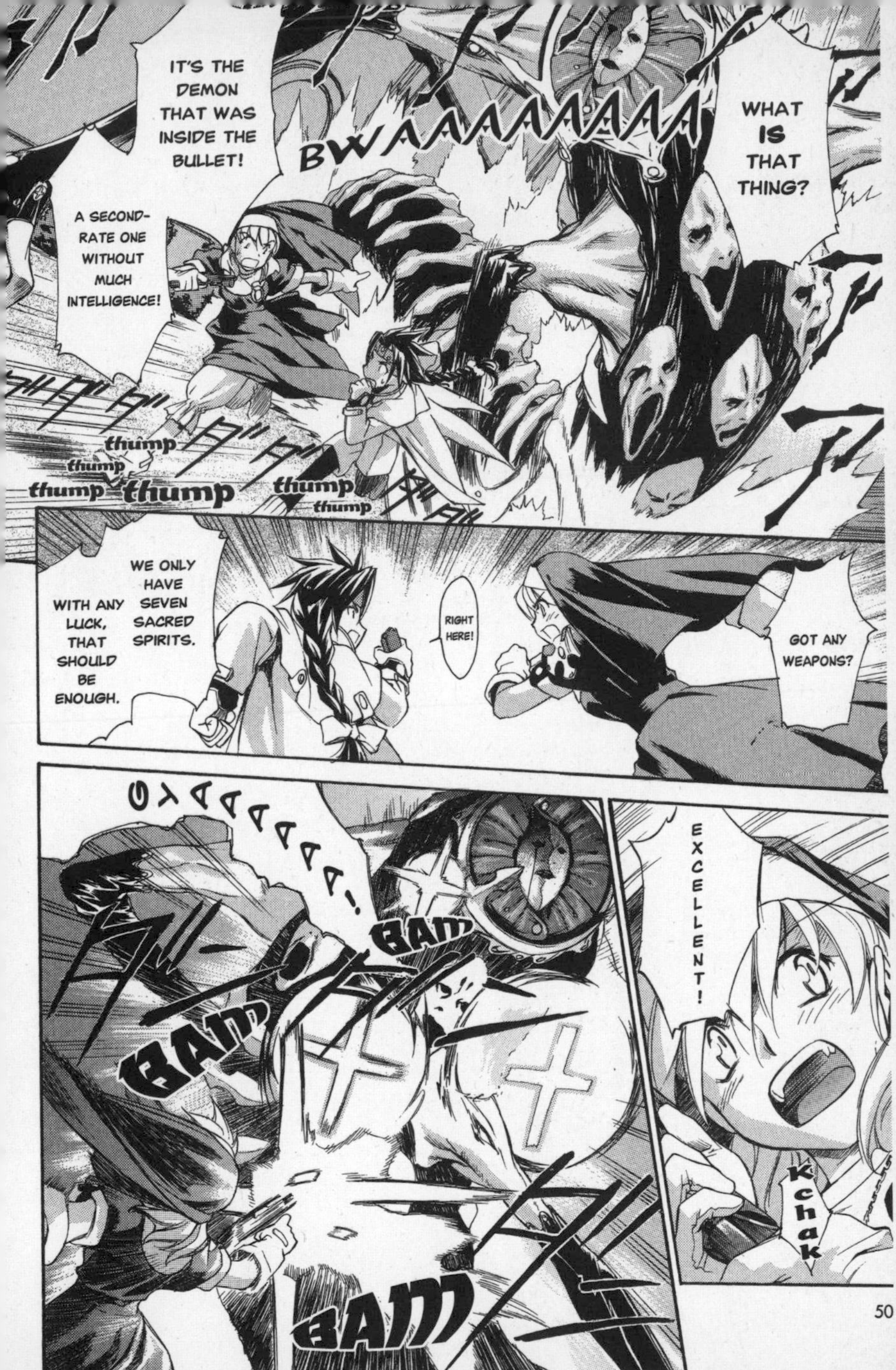
WHAT IS THAT THING?
BWAAAAAAAAA
IT'S THE DEMON THAT WAS INSIDE THE BULLET!
A SECOND-RATE ONE WITHOUT MUCH INTELLIGENCE!
thump thump thump thump thump thump
GOT ANY WEAPONS?
RIGHT HERE!
WE ONLY HAVE SEVEN SACRED SPIRITS.
WITH ANY LUCK, THAT SHOULD BE ENOUGH.
EXCELLENT!
Kchak
GYAAAAAAAAA!
BAM
BAM
BAM

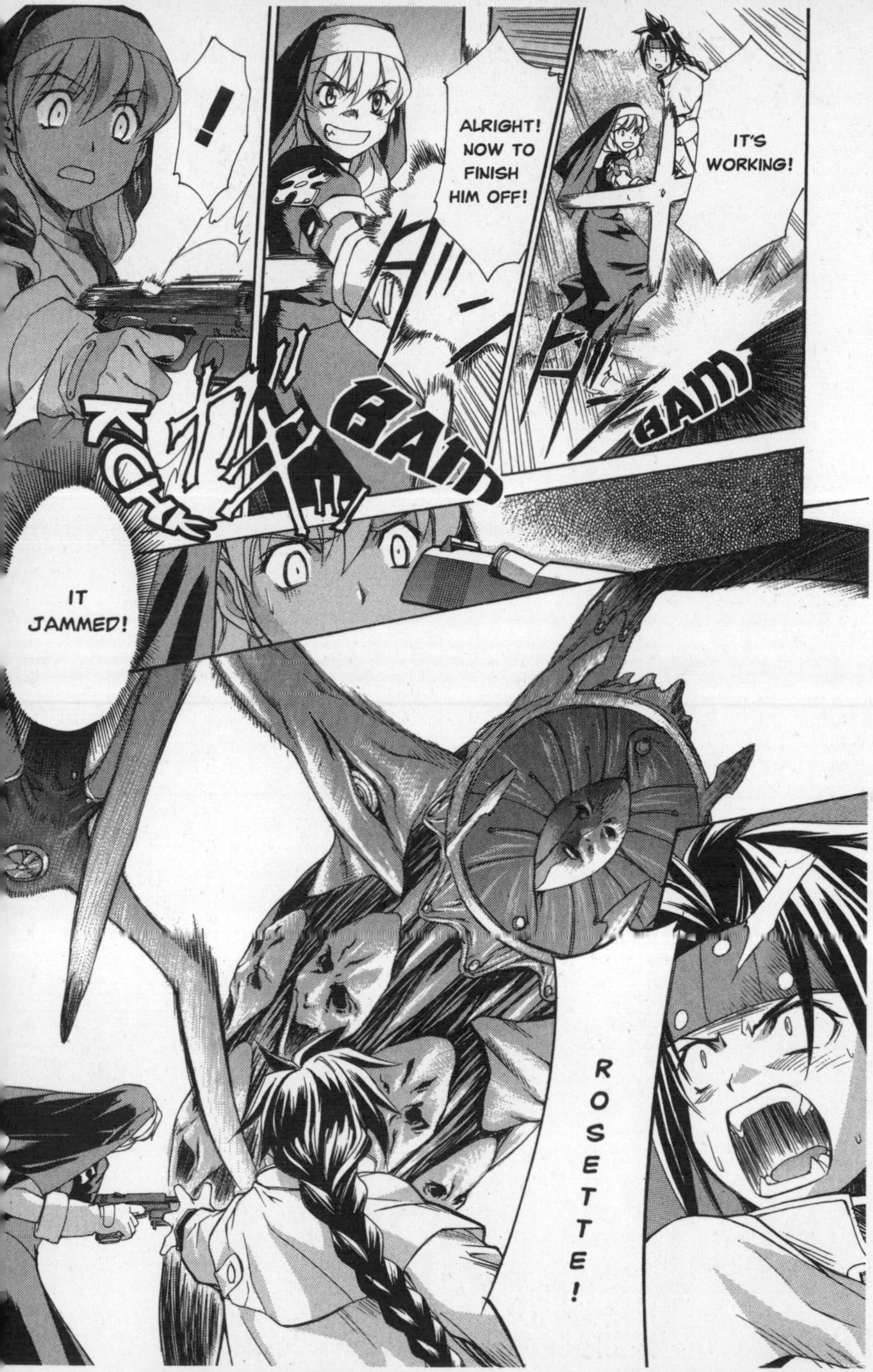
IT'S WORKING!
BAM
ALRIGHT! NOW TO FINISH HIM OFF!
BAM
!
KCHK
IT JAMMED!
ROSETTE!

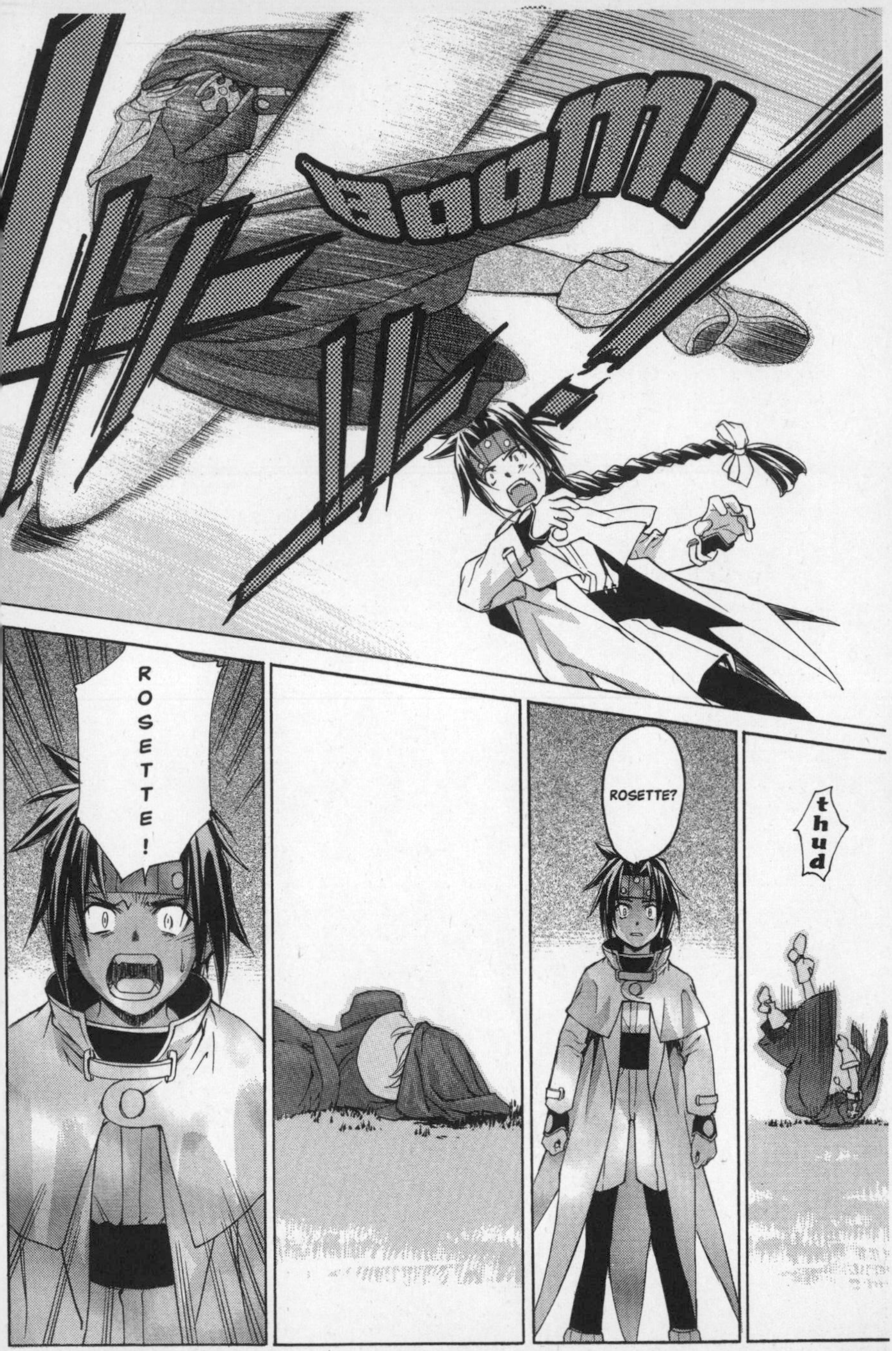
BOOM!
thud
ROSETTE?
ROSETTE!

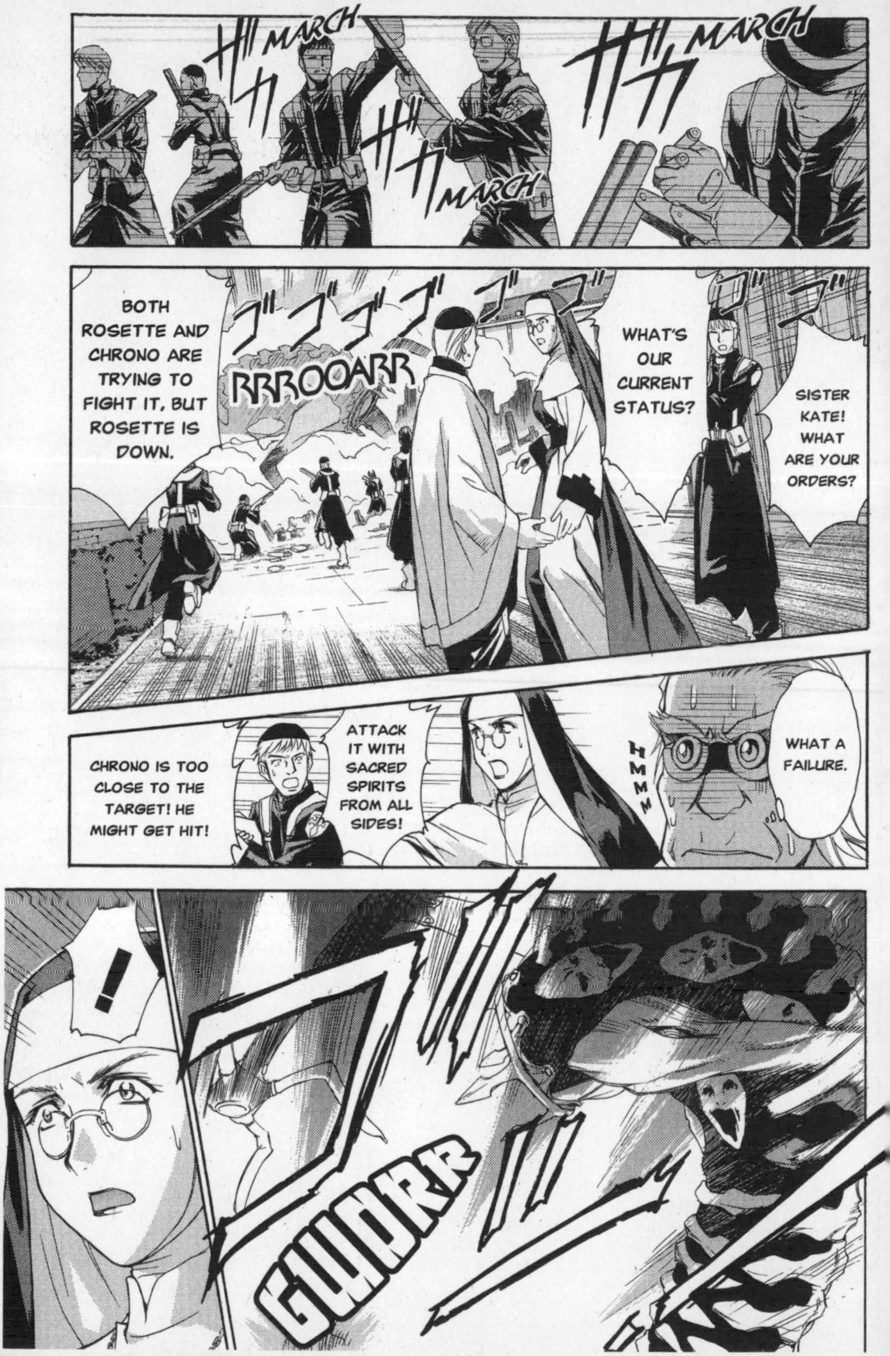
MARCH
MARCH
MARCH
SISTER KATE! WHAT ARE YOUR ORDERS?
WHAT'S OUR CURRENT STATUS?
RRROOARR
BOTH ROSETTE AND CHRONO ARE TRYING TO FIGHT IT, BUT ROSETTE IS DOWN.
WHAT A FAILURE.
HMMM
ATTACK IT WITH SACRED SPIRITS FROM ALL SIDES!
CHRONO IS TOO CLOSE TO THE TARGET! HE MIGHT GET HIT!
GUORR
!

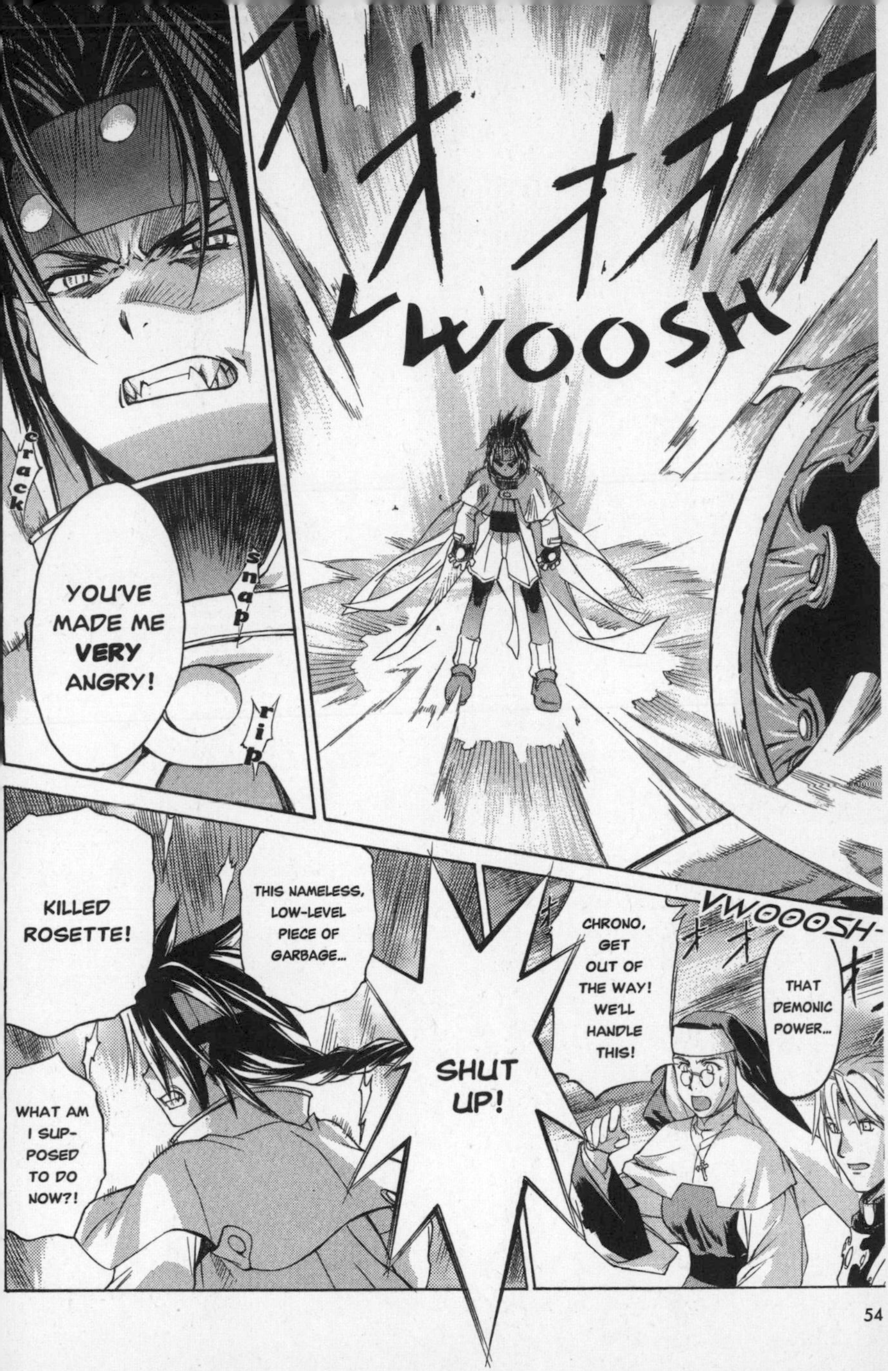
VWOOSH
crack
snap
YOU'VE MADE ME VERY ANGRY!
rip
VWOOOSH
THAT DEMONIC POWER...
CHRONO, GET OUT OF THE WAY! WE'LL HANDLE THIS!
SHUT UP!
THIS NAMELESS, LOW-LEVEL PIECE OF GARBAGE...
KILLED ROSETTE!
WHAT AM I SUP-POSED TO DO NOW?!

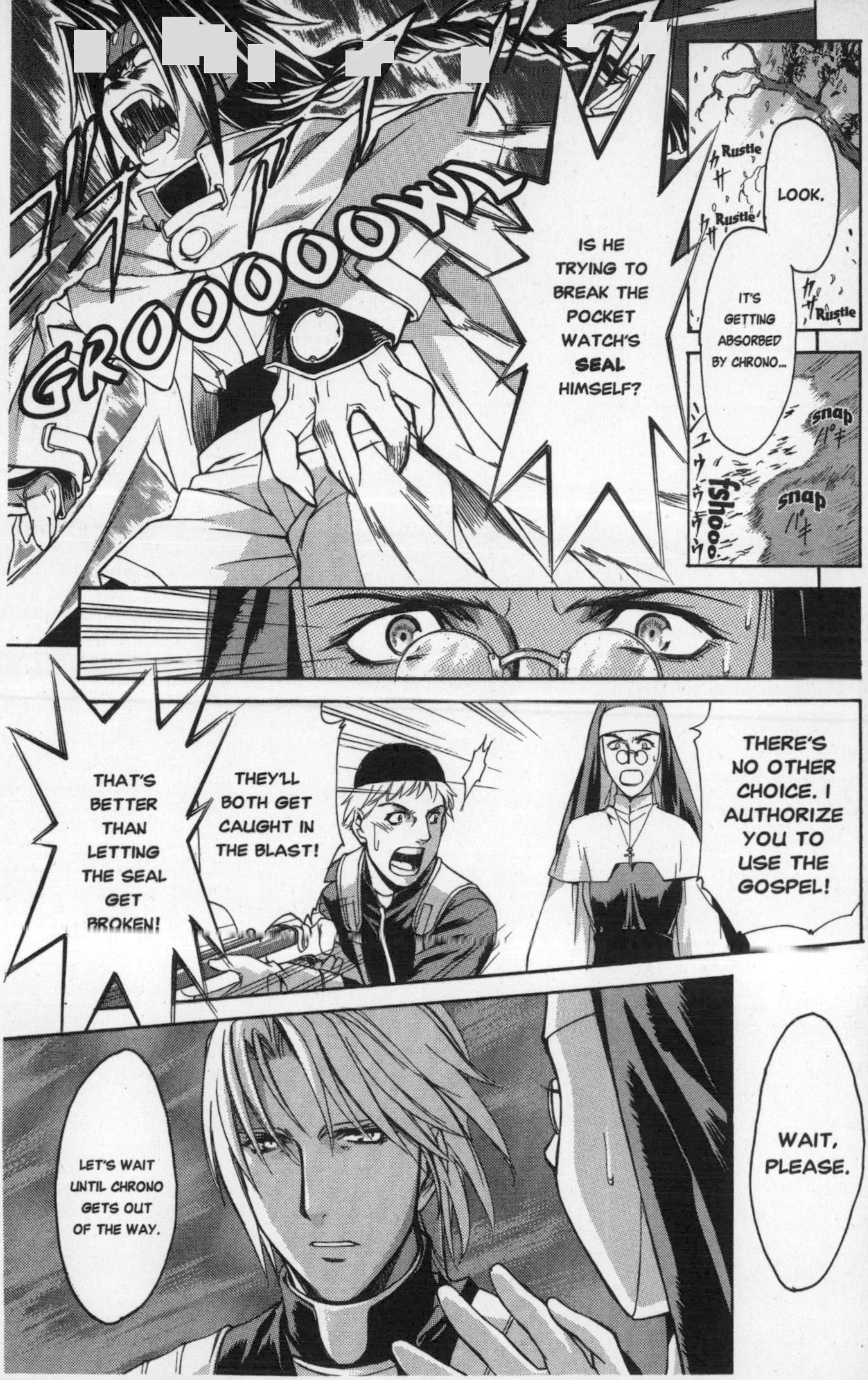
Rustle
Rustle
LOOK.
Rustle
IT'S GETTING ABSORBED BY CHRONO...
snap
snap
fshooo
GROOOOOWL
IS HE TRYING TO BREAK THE POCKET WATCH'S SEAL HIMSELF?
THERE'S NO OTHER CHOICE. I AUTHORIZE YOU TO USE THE GOSPEL!
THEY'LL BOTH GET CAUGHT IN THE BLAST!
THAT'S BETTER THAN LETTING THE SEAL GET BROKEN!
WAIT, PLEASE.
LET'S WAIT UNTIL CHRONO GETS OUT OF THE WAY.

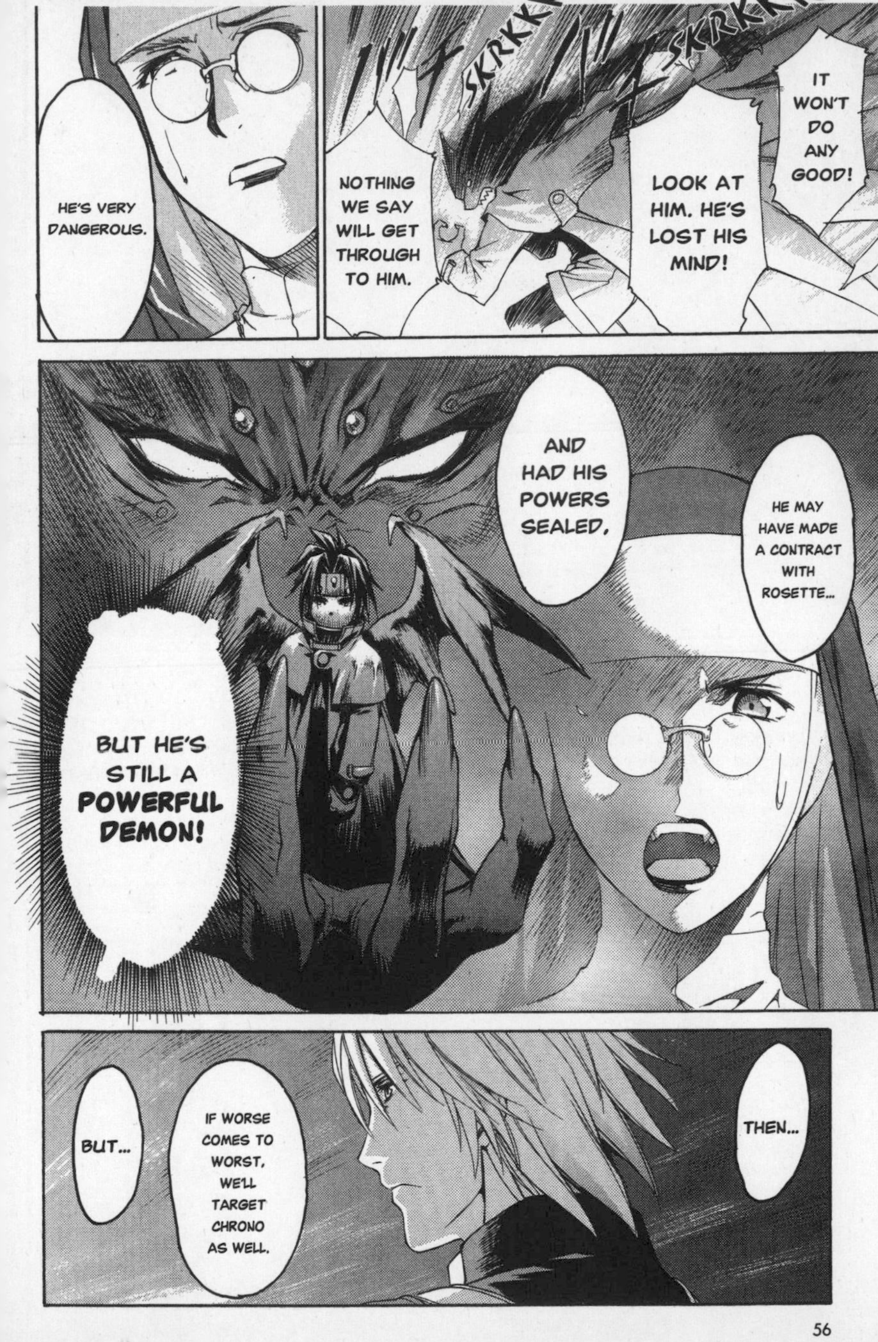
SKRKKK
IT WON'T DO ANY GOOD!
SKRKKK
LOOK AT HIM. HE'S LOST HIS MIND!
NOTHING WE SAY WILL GET THROUGH TO HIM.
HE'S VERY DANGEROUS.
HE MAY HAVE MADE A CONTRACT WITH ROSETTE...
AND HAD HIS POWERS SEALED,
BUT HE'S STILL A POWERFUL DEMON!
THEN...
IF WORSE COMES TO WORST, WE'LL TARGET CHRONO AS WELL.
BUT...

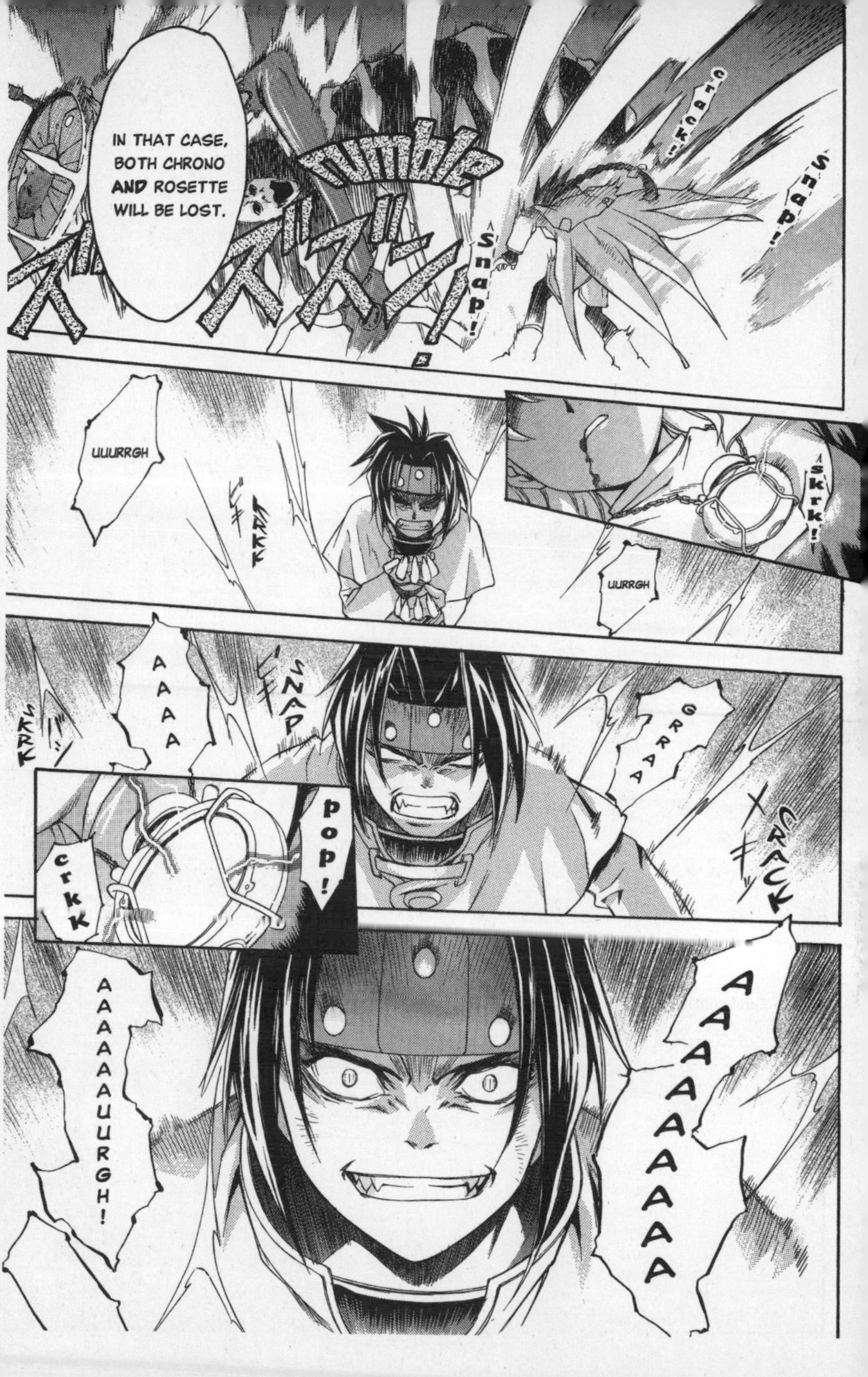
crack!
snap!
snap!
rumble
IN THAT CASE, BOTH CHRONO AND ROSETTE WILL BE LOST.
skrk!
UURRGH
KRKK
UUURRGH
GRRAA
CRACK
SNAP
AAAA
SKRK
pop!
crkk
AAAAAAAAA
AAAAAAUURGH!

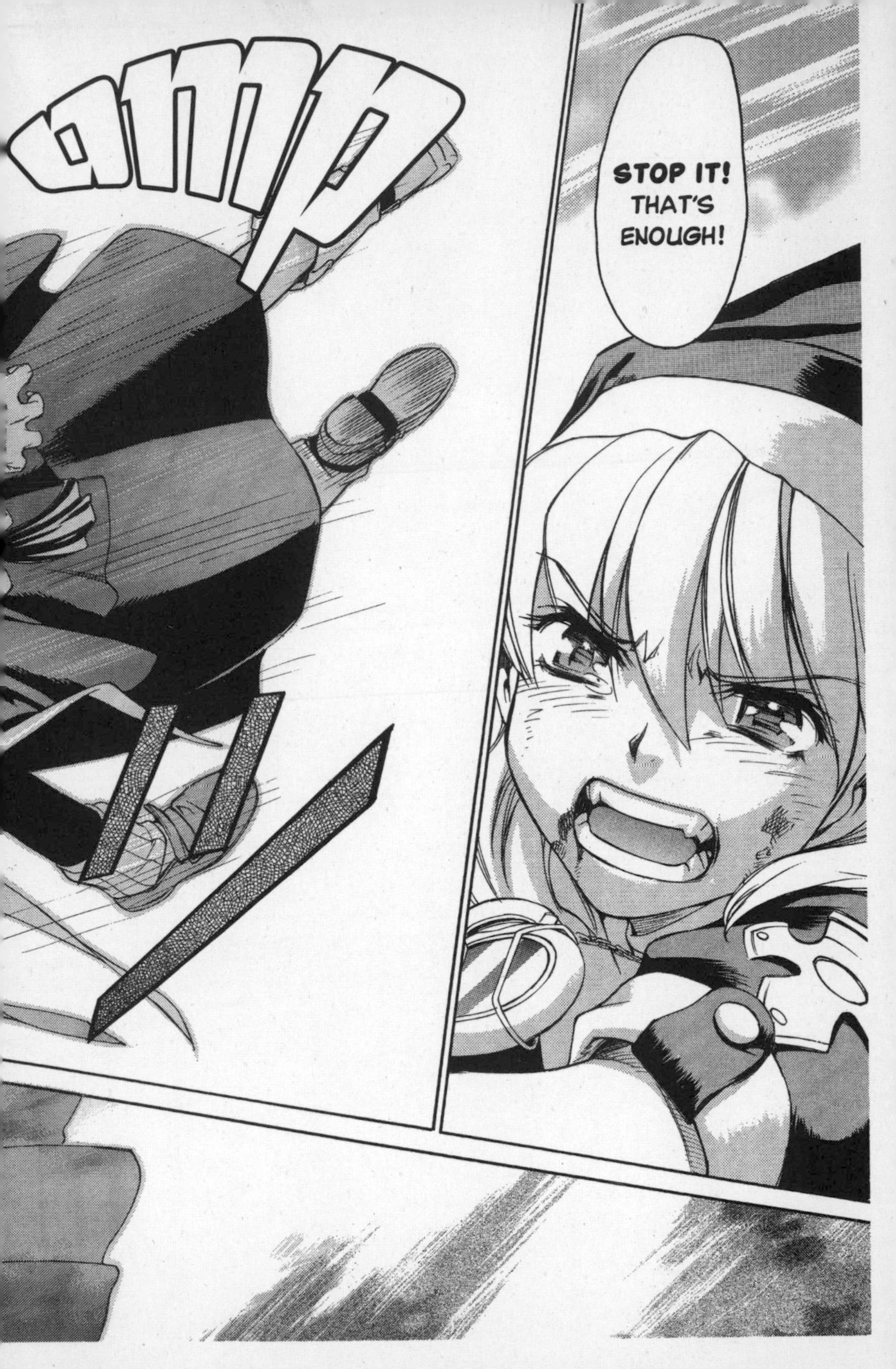
STOP IT! THAT'S ENOUGH!

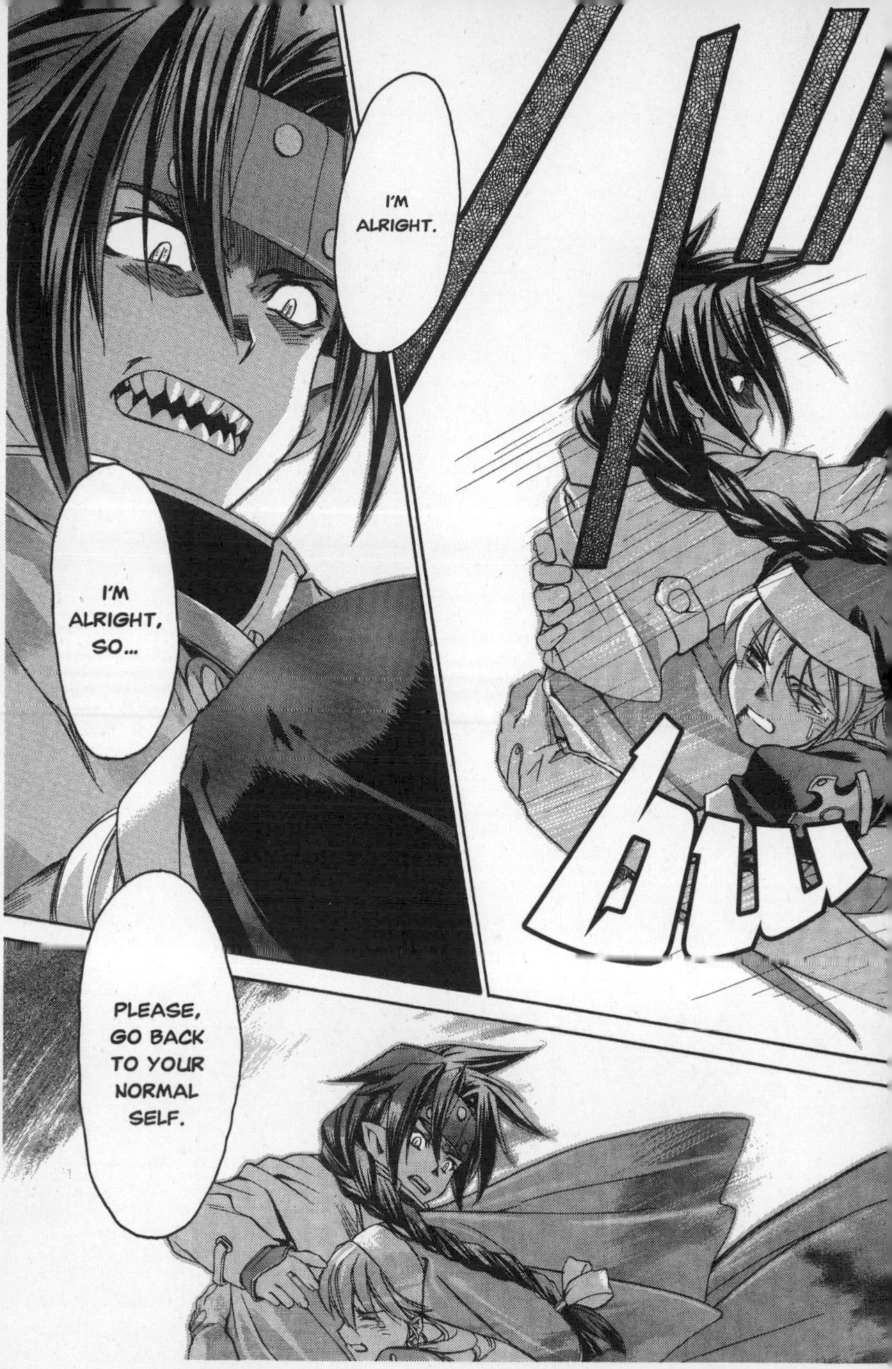
I'M ALRIGHT.
I'M ALRIGHT, SO...
PLEASE, GO BACK TO YOUR NORMAL SELF.

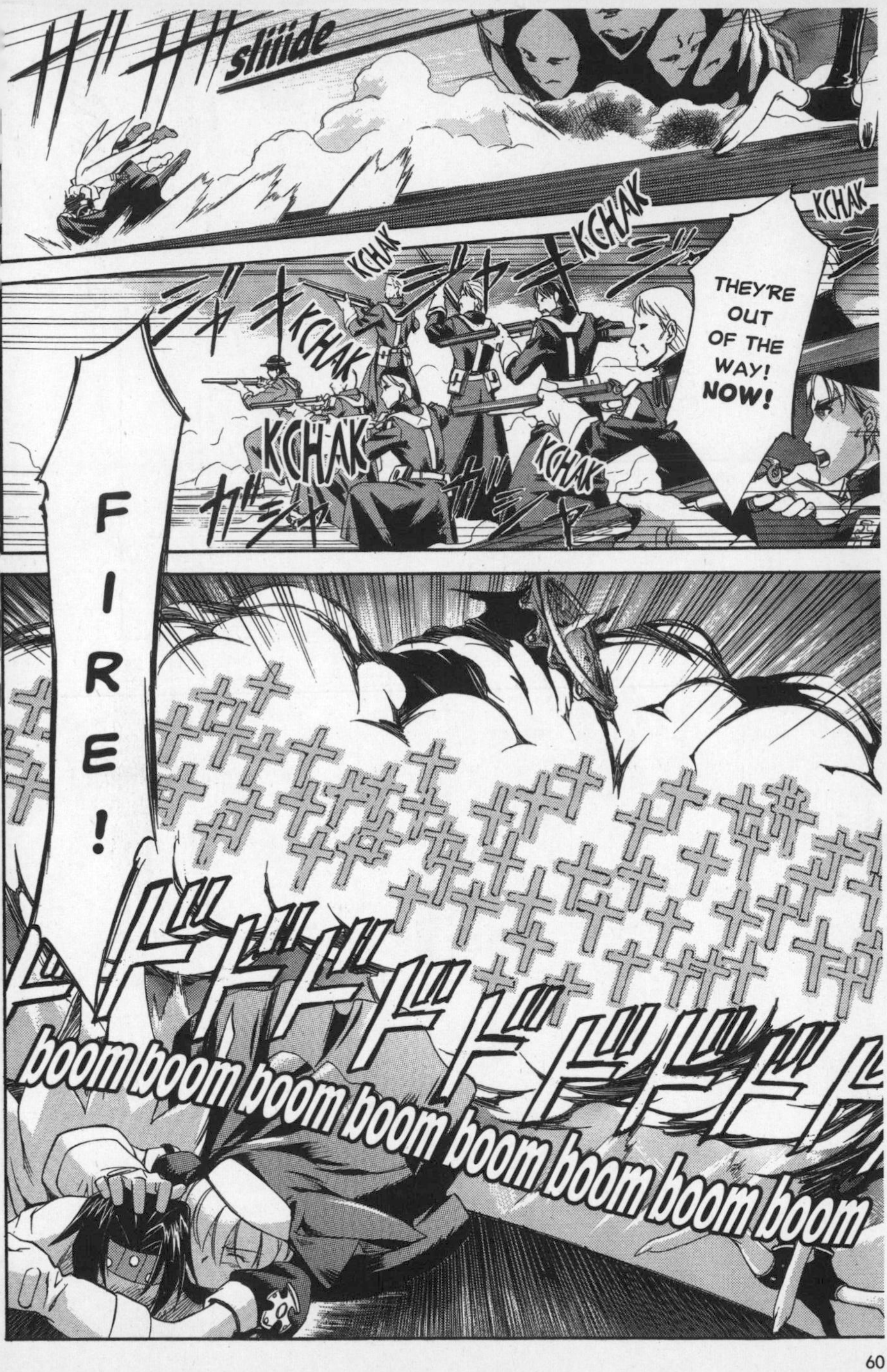
sliiide
KCHAK
THEY'RE OUT OF THE WAY! NOW!
KCHAK
KCHAK
KCHAK
KCHAK
KCHAK
FIRE!
boom boom boom boom boom boom boom boom boom

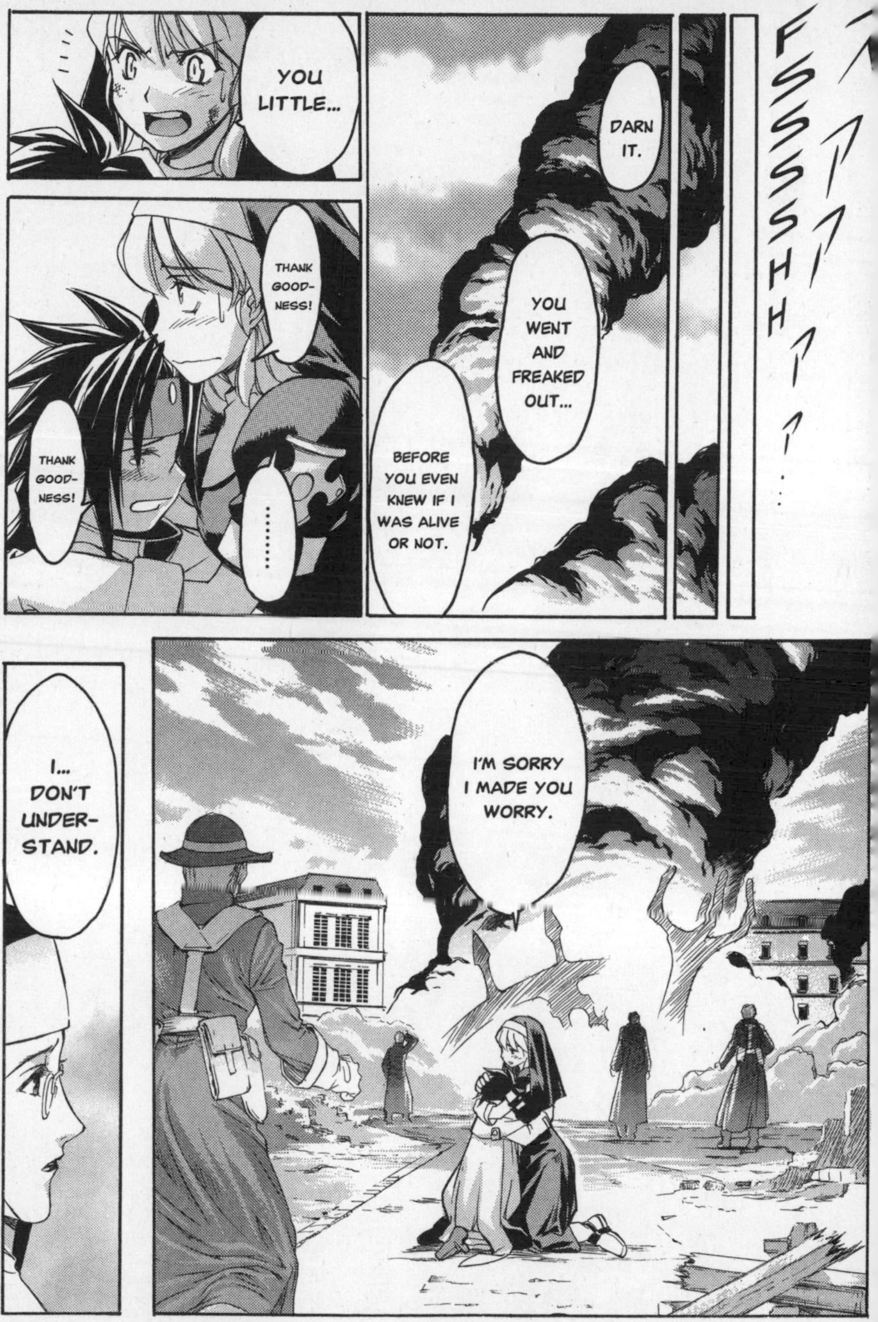
FSSSHH
DARN IT.
YOU WENT AND FREAKED OUT...
BEFORE YOU EVEN KNEW IF I WAS ALIVE OR NOT.
YOU LITTLE...
THANK GOOD-NESS!
....
THANK GOOD-NESS!
I'M SORRY I MADE YOU WORRY.
I... DON'T UNDER-STAND.

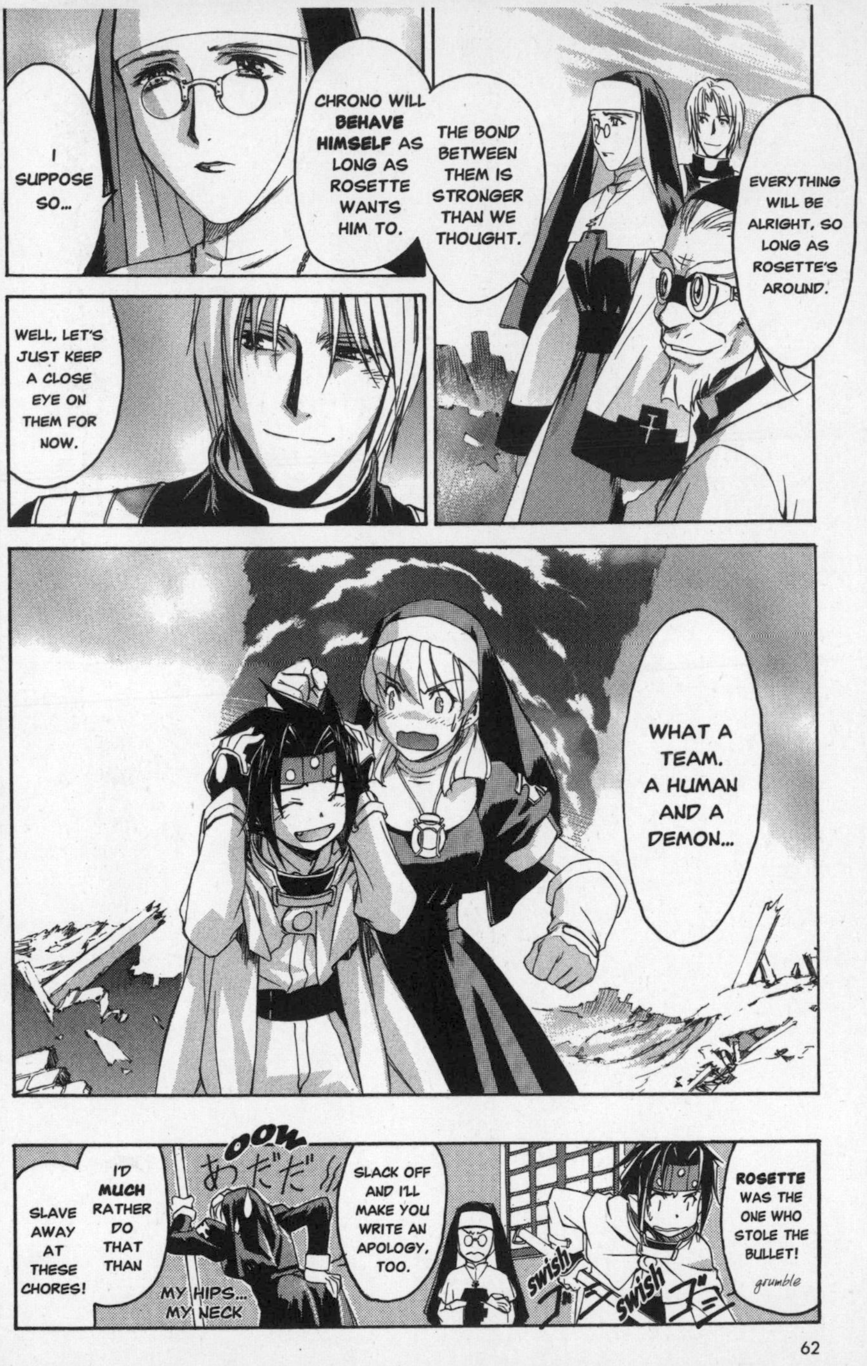

EVERYTHING WILL BE ALRIGHT, SO LONG AS ROSETTE'S AROUND.
THE BOND BETWEEN THEM IS STRONGER THAN WE THOUGHT.
CHRONO WILL BEHAVE HIMSELF AS LONG AS ROSETTE WANTS HIM TO.
I SUPPOSE SO...
WELL, LET'S JUST KEEP A CLOSE EYE ON THEM FOR NOW.
WHAT A TEAM. A HUMAN AND A DEMON...
ROSETTE WAS THE ONE WHO STOLE THE BULLET!
grumble
SWISH
SWISH
SLACK OFF AND I'LL MAKE YOU WRITE AN APOLOGY, TOO.
OOW
おだだ
MY HIPS... MY NECK
I'D MUCH RATHER DO THAT THAN
SLAVE AWAY AT THESE CHORES!

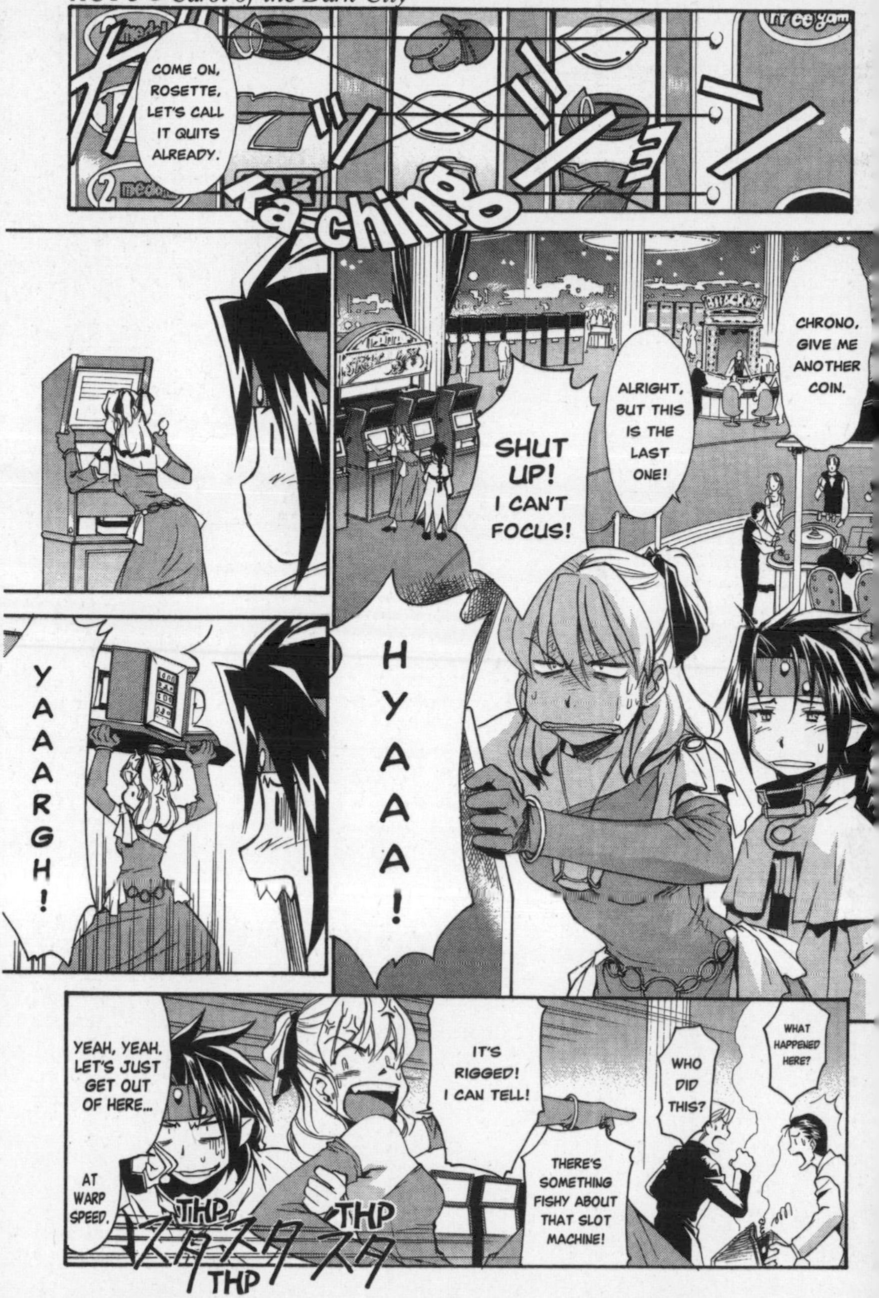
COME ON, ROSETTE, LET'S CALL IT QUITS ALREADY.
ka-chingg
CHRONO, GIVE ME ANOTHER COIN.
ALRIGHT, BUT THIS IS THE LAST ONE!
SHUT UP! I CAN'T FOCUS!
HYAAA!
YAAAARGH!
WHAT HAPPENED HERE?
WHO DID THIS?
THERE'S SOMETHING FISHY ABOUT THAT SLOT MACHINE!
IT'S RIGGED! I CAN TELL!
YEAH, YEAH. LET'S JUST GET OUT OF HERE...
AT WARP SPEED.
THP THP THP
スタスタ スタ

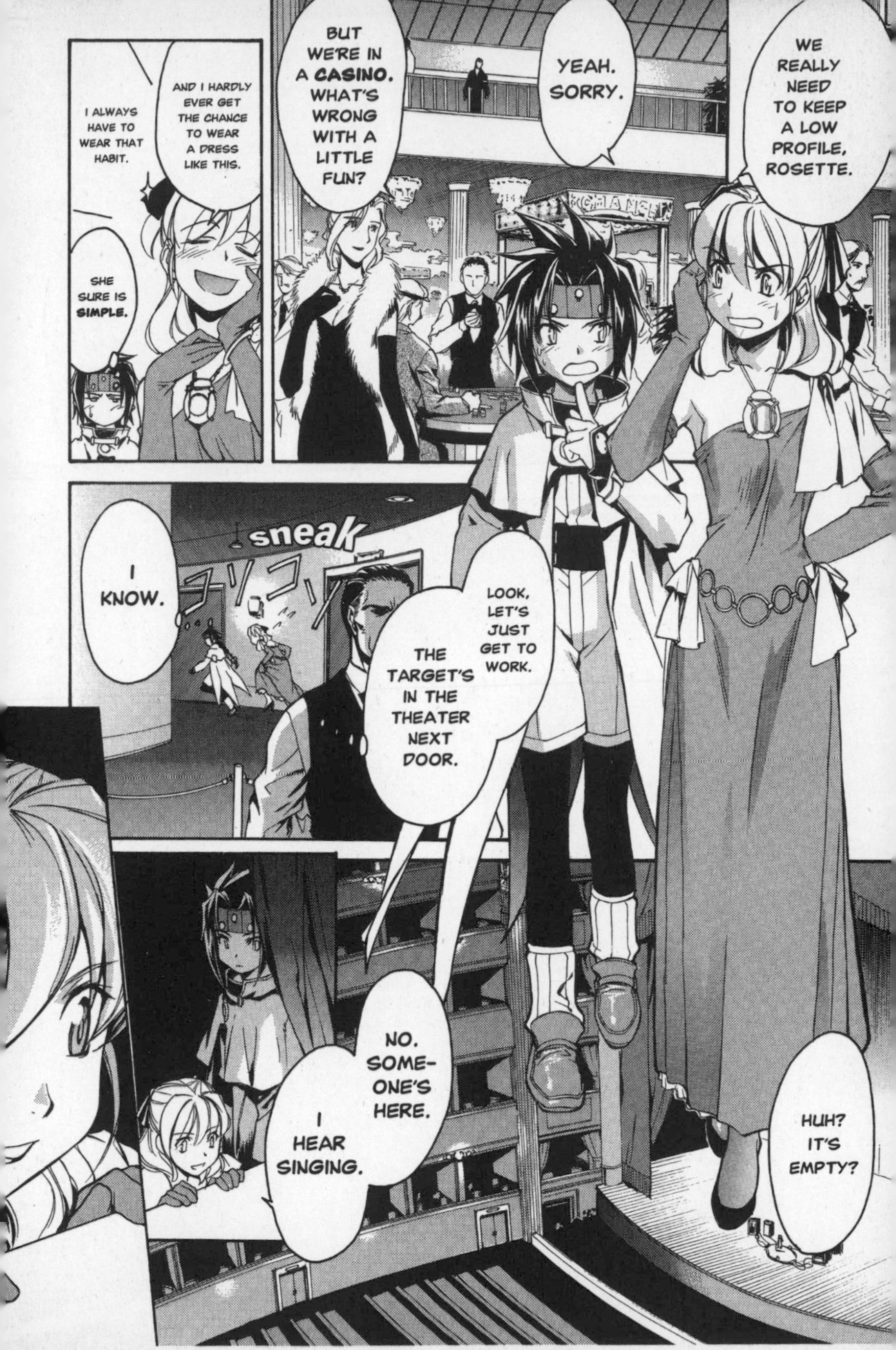
WE REALLY NEED TO KEEP A LOW PROFILE, ROSETTE.
YEAH. SORRY.
BUT WE'RE IN A **CASINO**. WHAT'S WRONG WITH A LITTLE FUN?
AND I HARDLY EVER GET THE CHANCE TO WEAR A DRESS LIKE THIS.
I ALWAYS HAVE TO WEAR THAT HABIT.
SHE SURE IS **SIMPLE**.
LOOK, LET'S JUST GET TO WORK.
THE TARGET'S IN THE THEATER NEXT DOOR.
I KNOW.
sneak
HUH? IT'S EMPTY?
NO. SOME-ONE'S HERE.
I HEAR SINGING.

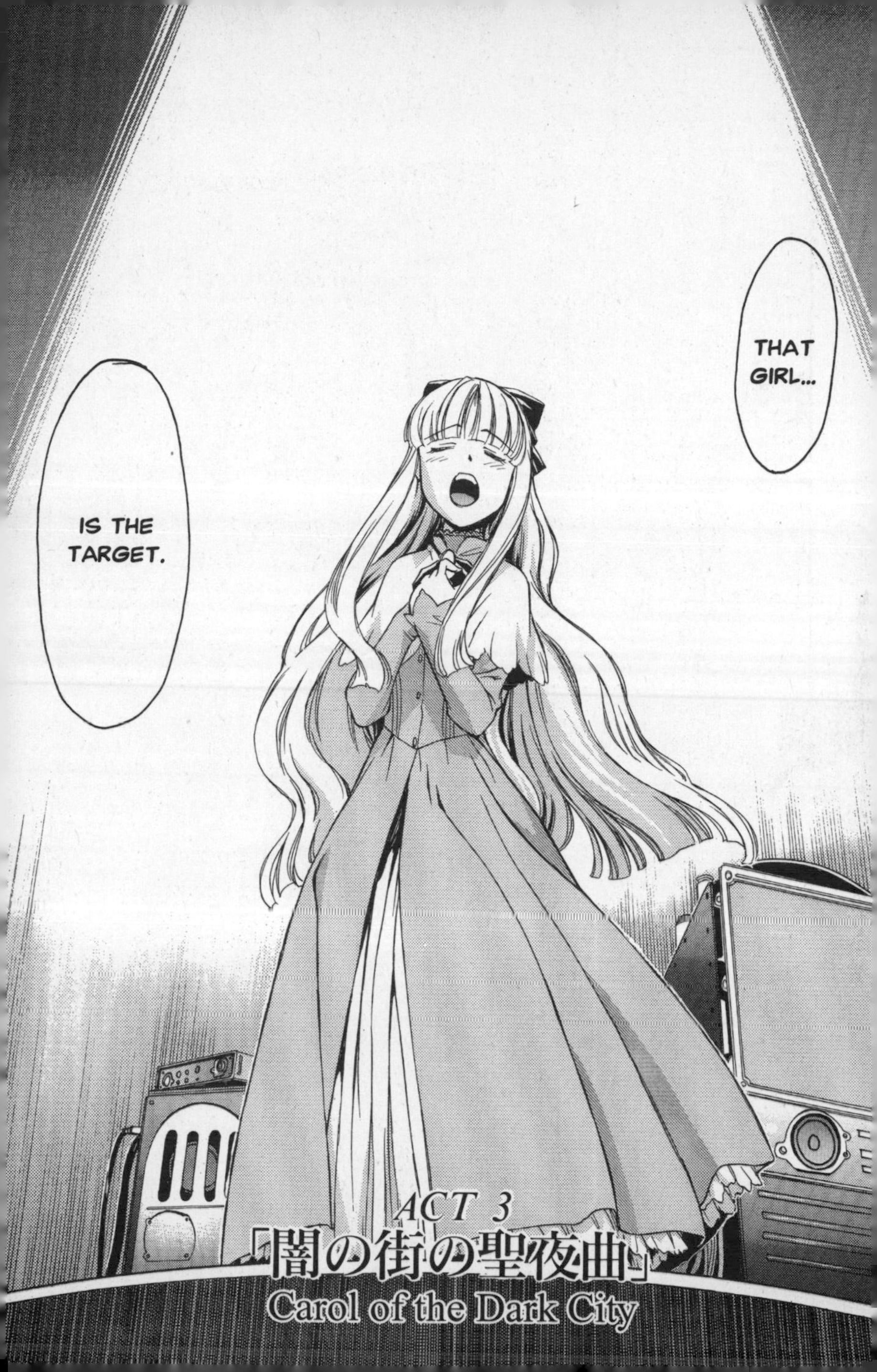
THAT GIRL...
IS THE TARGET.
ACT 3
「闇の街の聖夜曲」
Carol of the Dark City

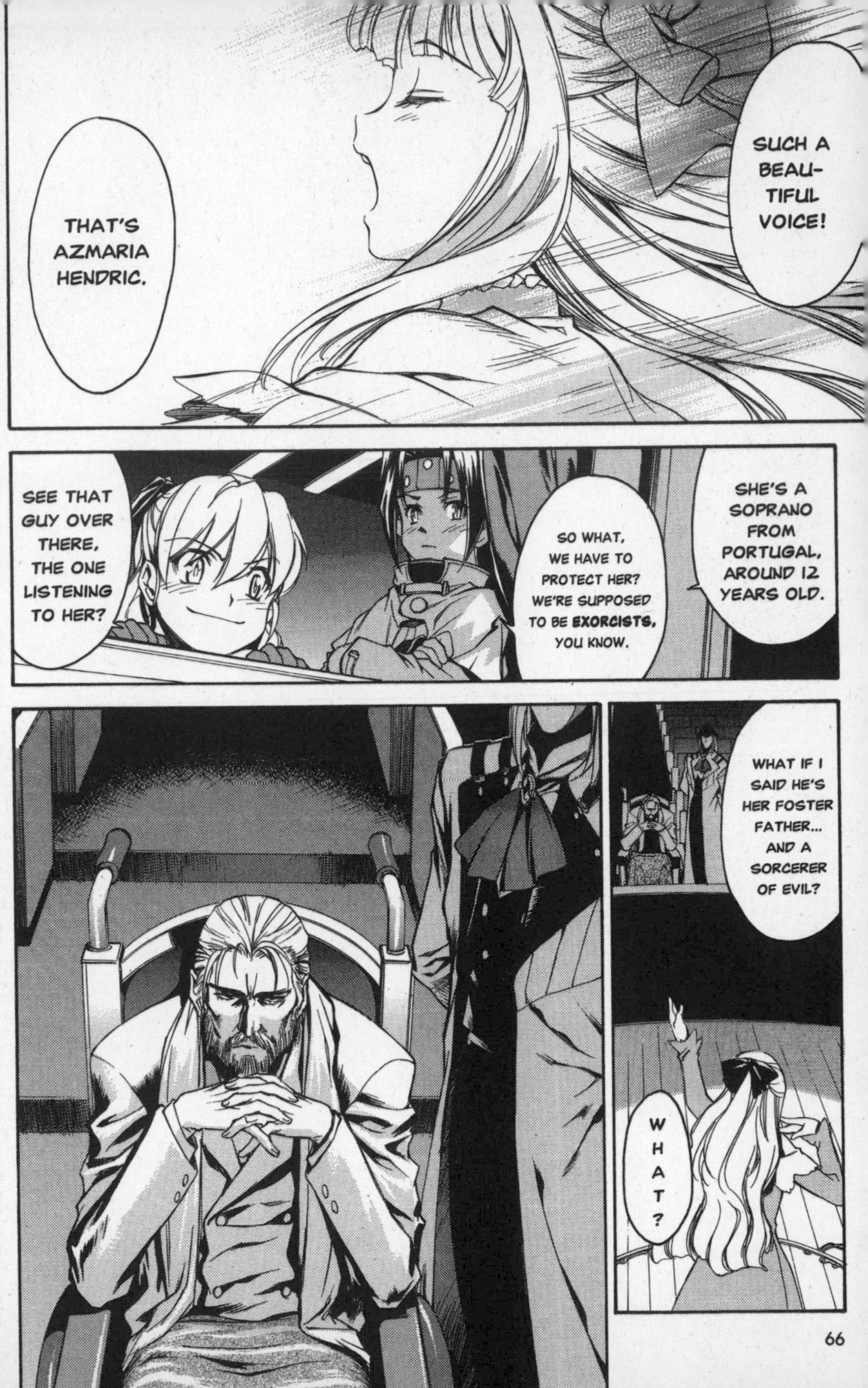
SUCH A BEAU-TIFUL VOICE!
THAT'S AZMARIA HENDRIC.
SHE'S A SOPRANO FROM PORTUGAL, AROUND 12 YEARS OLD.
SO WHAT, WE HAVE TO PROTECT HER? WE'RE SUPPOSED TO BE **EXORCISTS,** YOU KNOW.
SEE THAT GUY OVER THERE, THE ONE LISTENING TO HER?
WHAT IF I SAID HE'S HER FOSTER FATHER... AND A SORCERER OF EVIL?
WHAT?

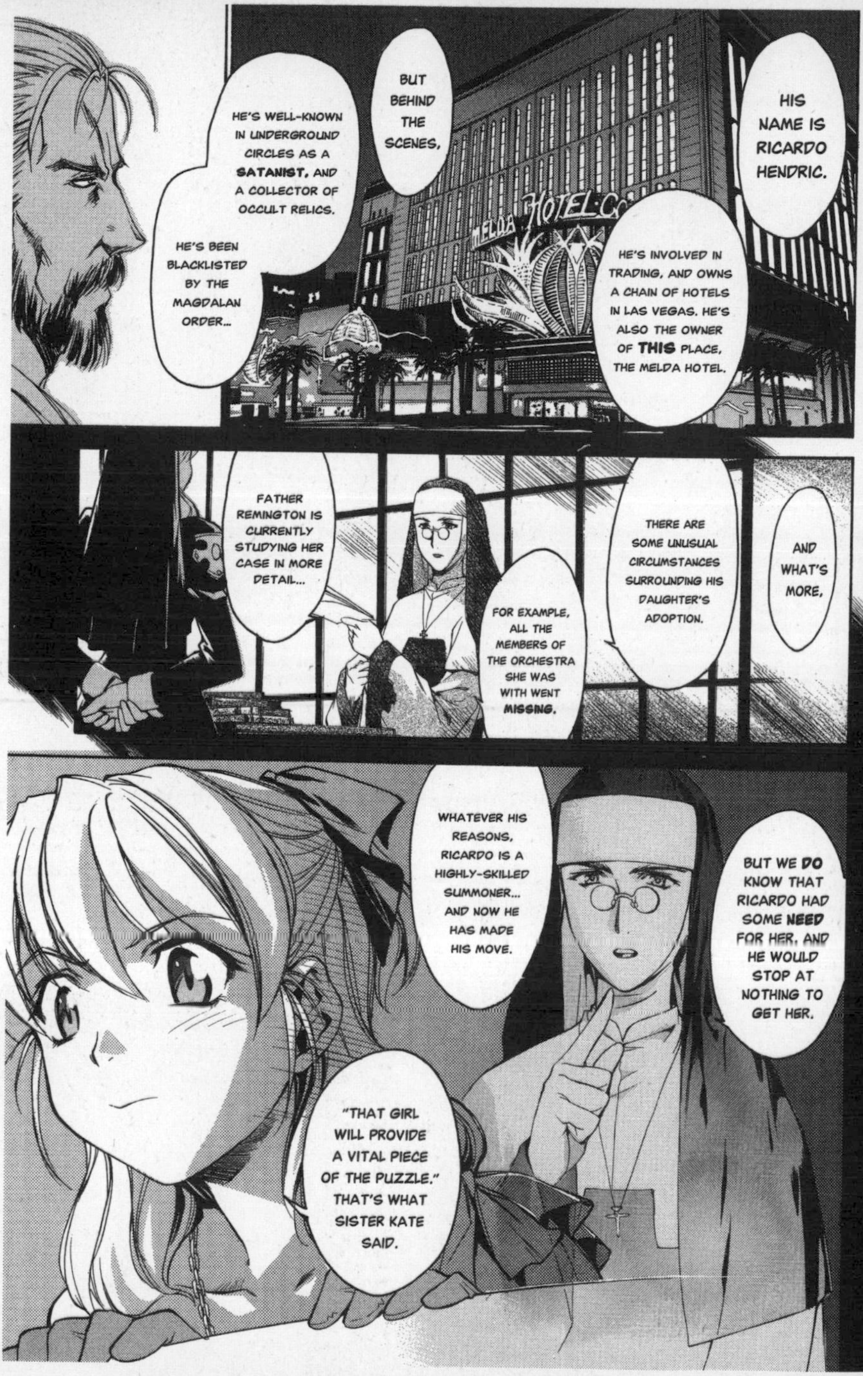
HIS NAME IS RICARDO HENDRIC.
HE'S INVOLVED IN TRADING, AND OWNS A CHAIN OF HOTELS IN LAS VEGAS. HE'S ALSO THE OWNER OF **THIS** PLACE, THE MELDA HOTEL.
MELDA
BUT BEHIND THE SCENES,
HE'S WELL-KNOWN IN UNDERGROUND CIRCLES AS A **SATANIST,** AND A COLLECTOR OF OCCULT RELICS.
HE'S BEEN BLACKLISTED BY THE MAGDALAN ORDER...
AND WHAT'S MORE,
THERE ARE SOME UNUSUAL CIRCUMSTANCES SURROUNDING HIS DAUGHTER'S ADOPTION.
FOR EXAMPLE, ALL THE MEMBERS OF THE ORCHESTRA SHE WAS WITH WENT **MISSING.**
FATHER REMINGTON IS CURRENTLY STUDYING HER CASE IN MORE DETAIL...
BUT WE **DO** KNOW THAT RICARDO HAD SOME **NEED** FOR HER, AND HE WOULD STOP AT NOTHING TO GET HER.
WHATEVER HIS REASONS, RICARDO IS A HIGHLY-SKILLED SUMMONER... AND NOW HE HAS MADE HIS MOVE.
"THAT GIRL WILL PROVIDE A VITAL PIECE OF THE PUZZLE." THAT'S WHAT SISTER KATE SAID.

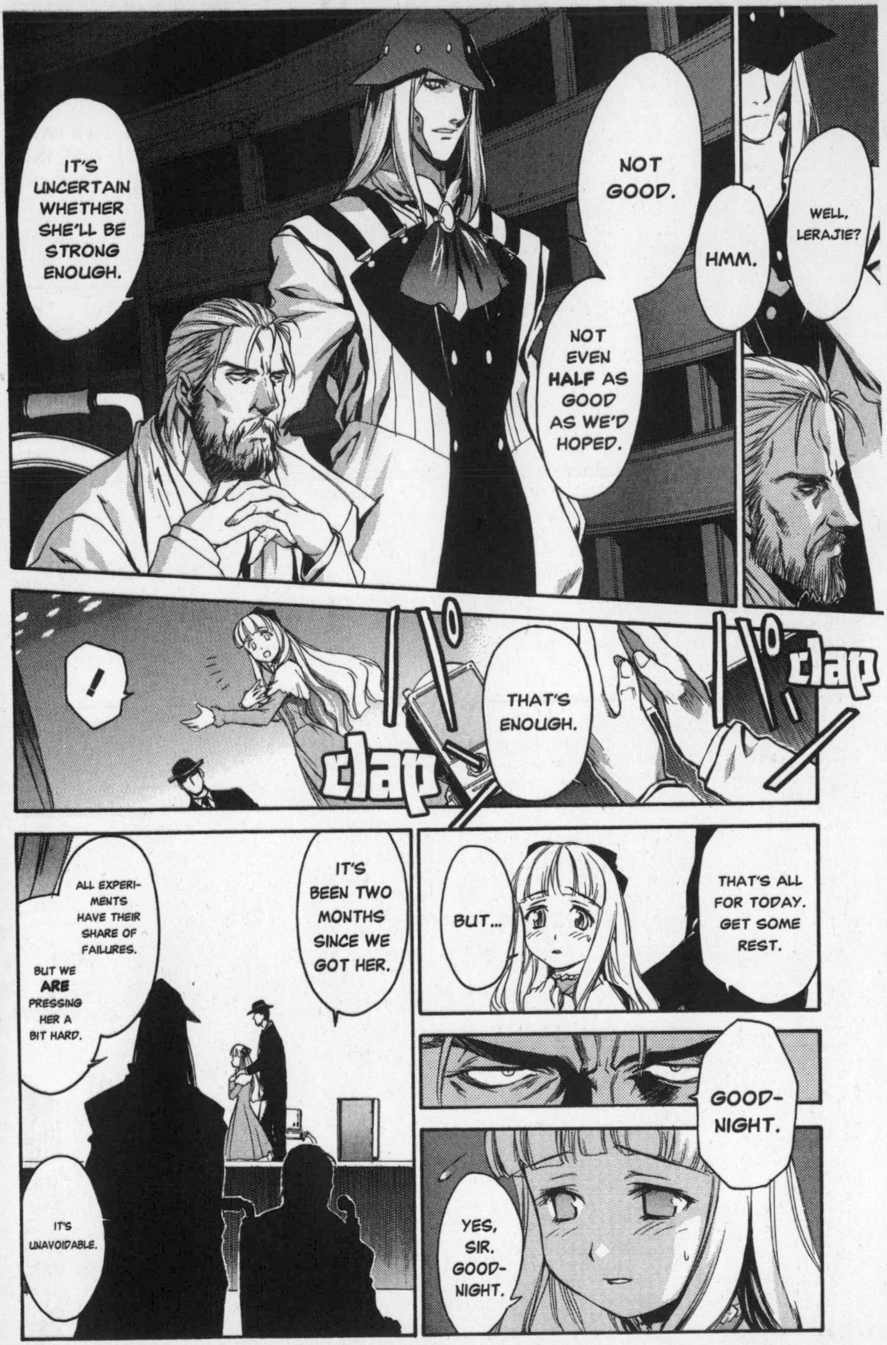
WELL, LERAJIE?
HMM.
NOT GOOD.
NOT EVEN **HALF** AS GOOD AS WE'D HOPED.
IT'S UNCERTAIN WHETHER SHE'LL BE STRONG ENOUGH.
clap
THAT'S ENOUGH.
clap
!
THAT'S ALL FOR TODAY. GET SOME REST.
BUT...
GOOD-NIGHT.
YES, SIR. GOOD-NIGHT.
IT'S BEEN TWO MONTHS SINCE WE GOT HER.
ALL EXPERI-MENTS HAVE THEIR SHARE OF FAILURES.
BUT WE **ARE** PRESSING HER A BIT HARD.
IT'S UNAVOIDABLE.

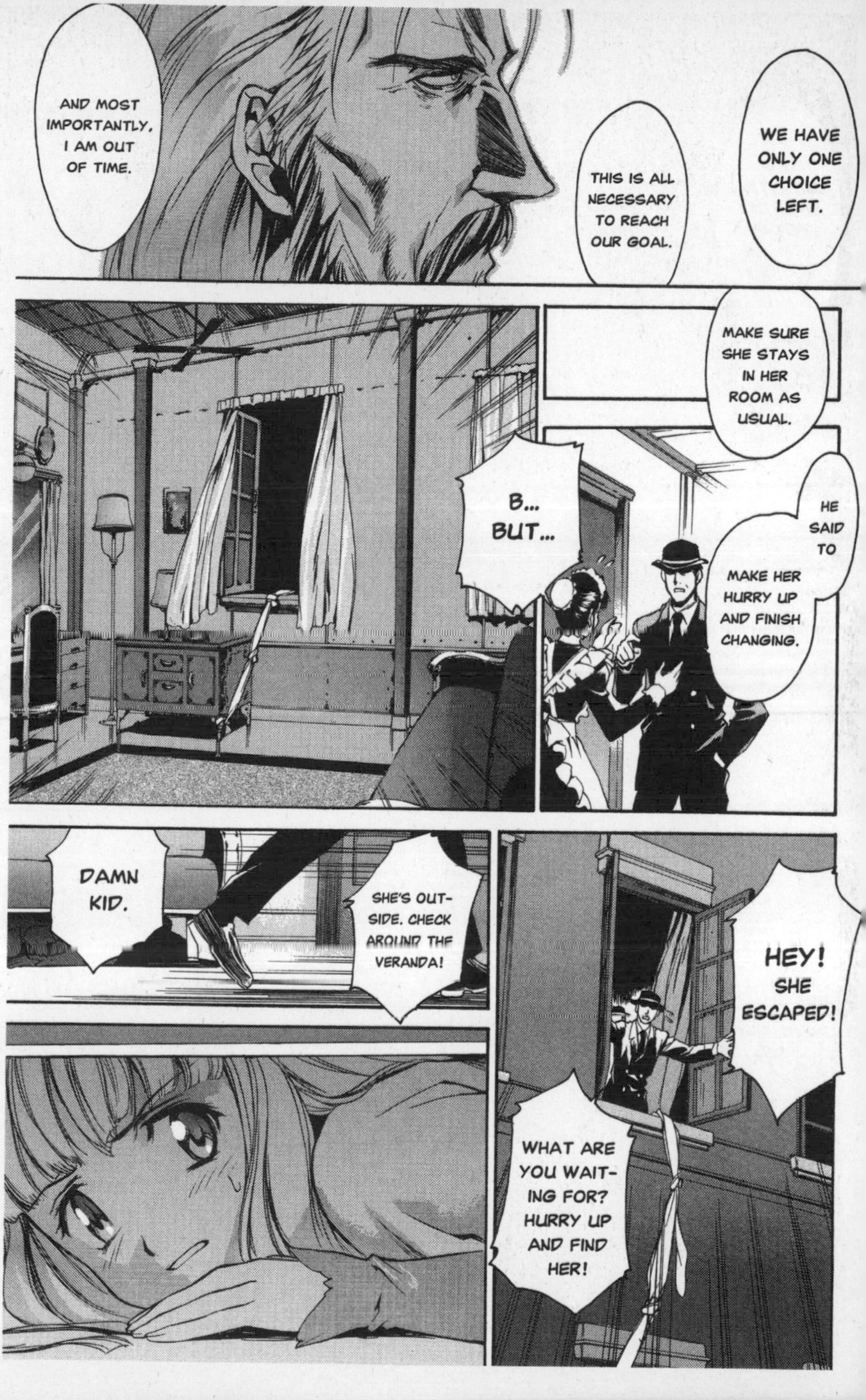
WE HAVE ONLY ONE CHOICE LEFT.
THIS IS ALL NECESSARY TO REACH OUR GOAL.
AND MOST IMPORTANTLY, I AM OUT OF TIME.
MAKE SURE SHE STAYS IN HER ROOM AS USUAL.
HE SAID TO MAKE HER HURRY UP AND FINISH CHANGING.
B... BUT...
HEY! SHE ESCAPED!
WHAT ARE YOU WAIT-ING FOR? HURRY UP AND FIND HER!
SHE'S OUT-SIDE. CHECK AROUND THE VERANDA!
DAMN KID.

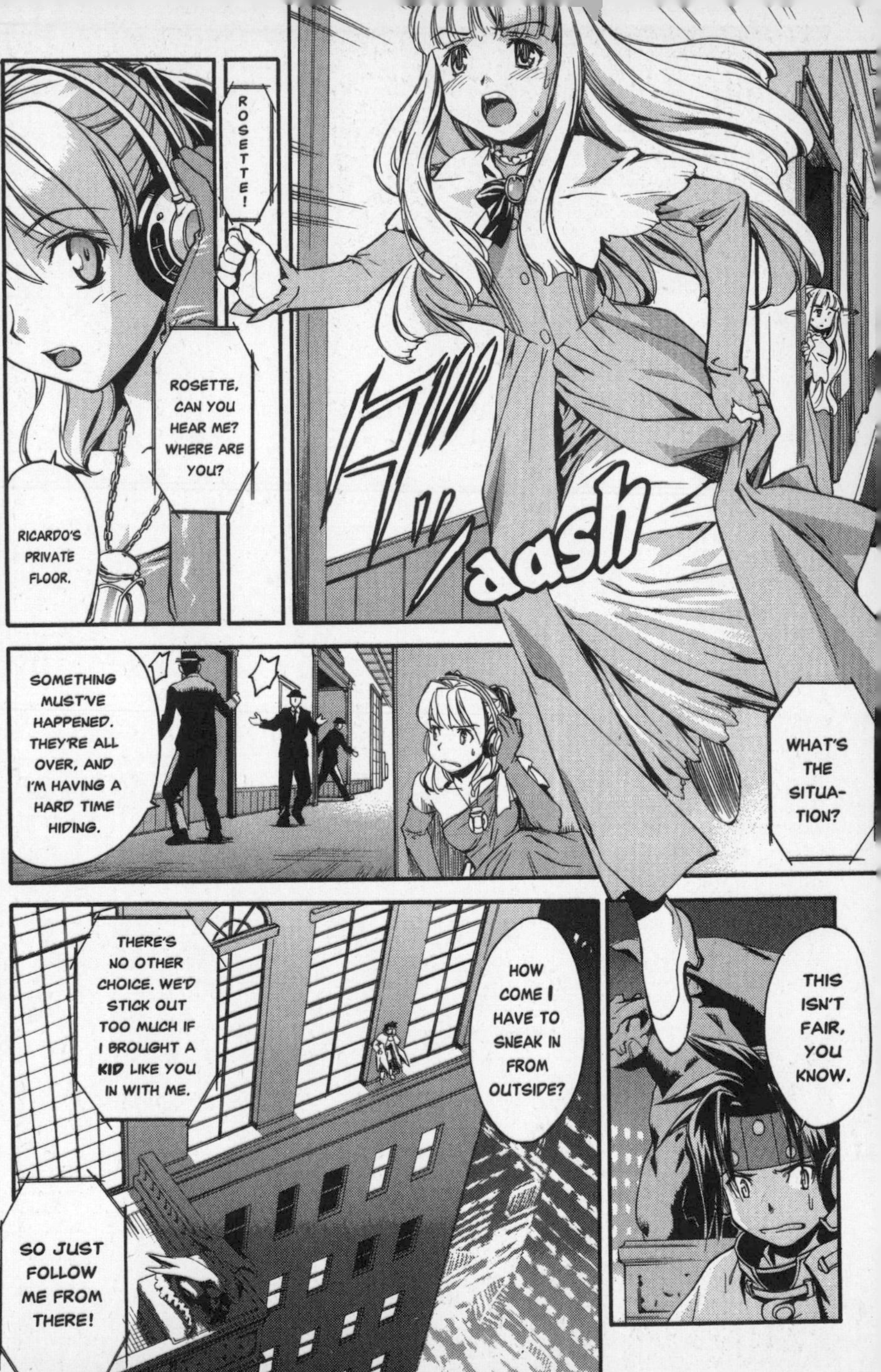
aash
ROSETTE!
ROSETTE, CAN YOU HEAR ME? WHERE ARE YOU?
RICARDO'S PRIVATE FLOOR.
WHAT'S THE SITUATION?
SOMETHING MUST'VE HAPPENED. THEY'RE ALL OVER, AND I'M HAVING A HARD TIME HIDING.
THIS ISN'T FAIR, YOU KNOW.
HOW COME I HAVE TO SNEAK IN FROM OUTSIDE?
THERE'S NO OTHER CHOICE. WE'D STICK OUT TOO MUCH IF I BROUGHT A KID LIKE YOU IN WITH ME.
SO JUST FOLLOW ME FROM THERE!

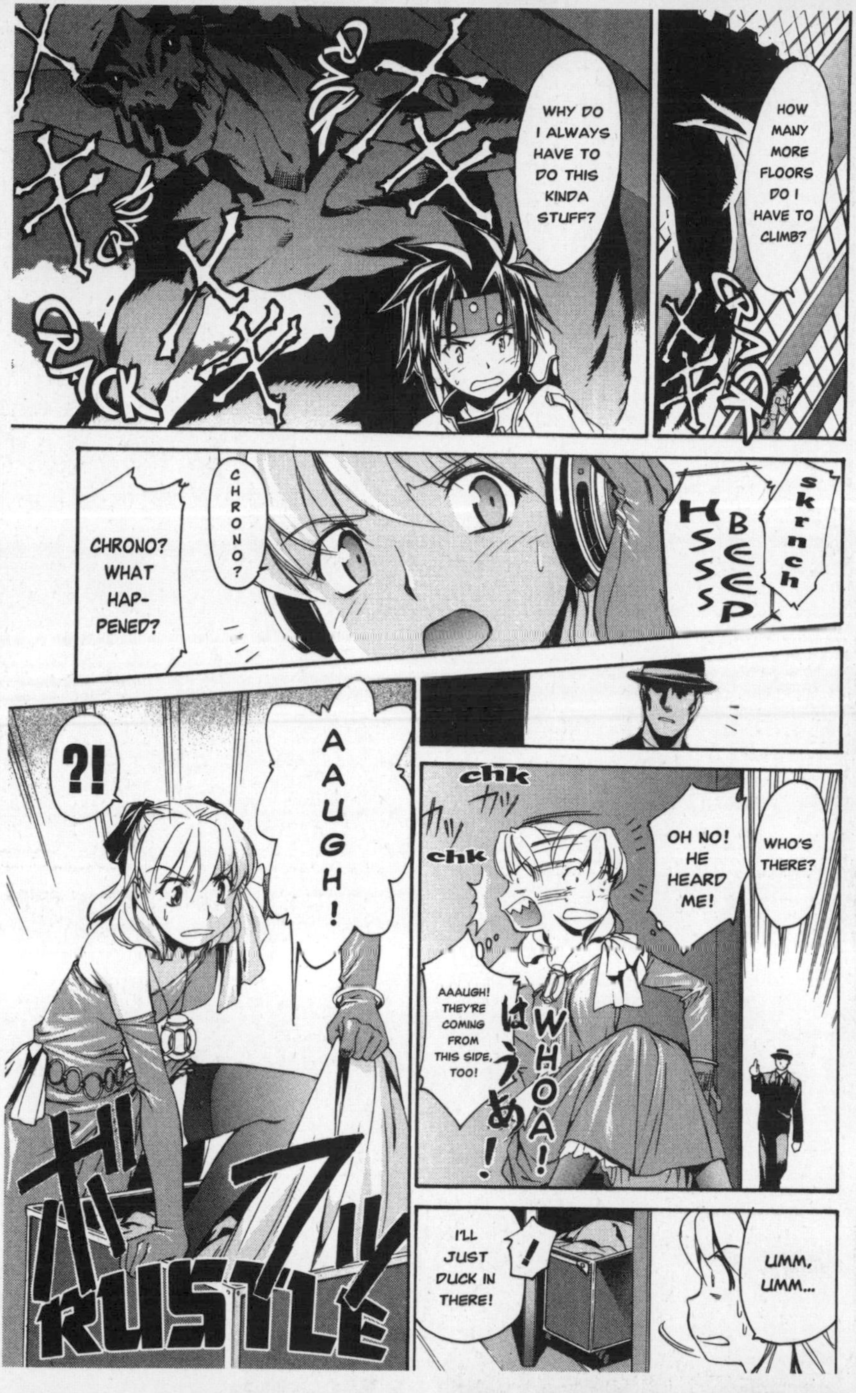
HOW MANY MORE FLOORS DO I HAVE TO CLIMB?
CRACK
WHY DO I ALWAYS HAVE TO DO THIS KINDA STUFF?
CRACK
CRACK
CRACK
skrnch
BEEP
HSSS
CHRONO?
CHRONO? WHAT HAP-PENED?
WHO'S THERE?
OH NO! HE HEARD ME!
chk
chk
AAAUGH! THEY'RE COMING FROM THIS SIDE, TOO!
WHOA!
はうあ!
UMM, UMM...
!
I'LL JUST DUCK IN THERE!
AAUGH!
?!
RUSTLE

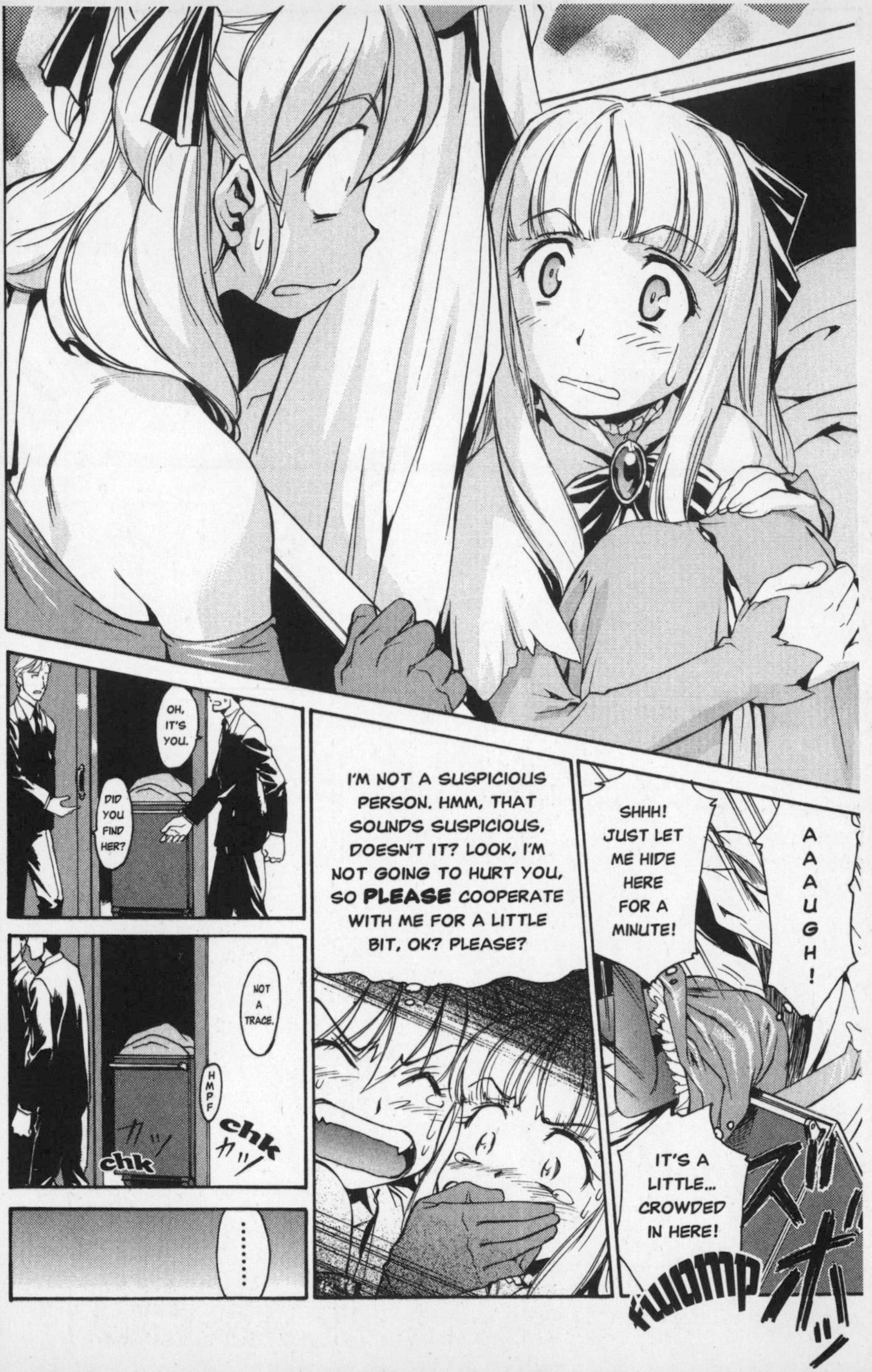
AAAUGH!
SHHH! JUST LET ME HIDE HERE FOR A MINUTE!
IT'S A LITTLE... CROWDED IN HERE!
fwoomp
I'M NOT A SUSPICIOUS PERSON. HMM, THAT SOUNDS SUSPICIOUS, DOESN'T IT? LOOK, I'M NOT GOING TO HURT YOU, SO **PLEASE** COOPERATE WITH ME FOR A LITTLE BIT, OK? PLEASE?
OH, IT'S YOU.
DID YOU FIND HER?
NOT A TRACE.
HMPF
chk
chk
......

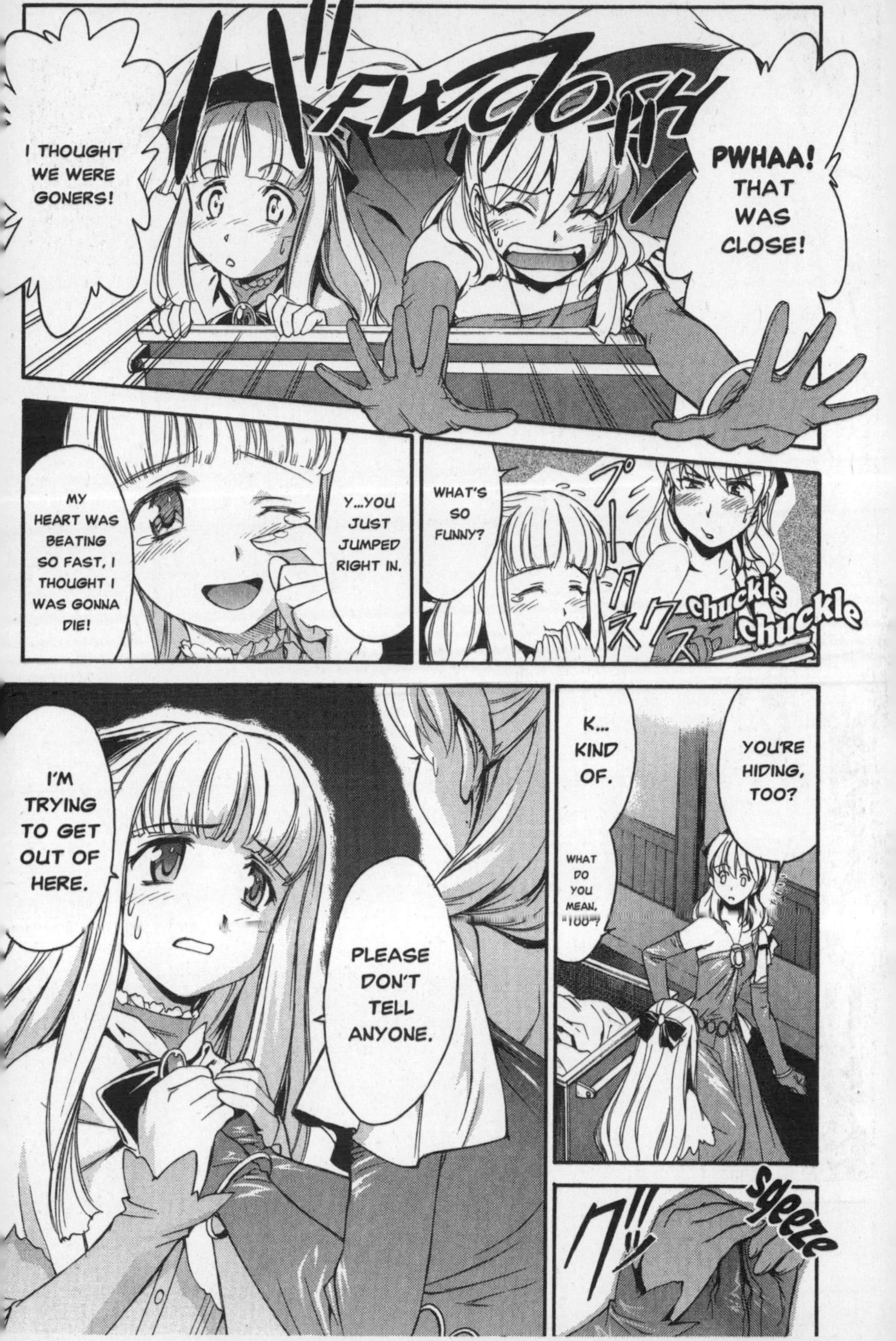
PWHAA! THAT WAS CLOSE!
FWOOSH
I THOUGHT WE WERE GONERS!
WHAT'S SO FUNNY?
Chuckle Chuckle
Y...YOU JUST JUMPED RIGHT IN.
MY HEART WAS BEATING SO FAST, I THOUGHT I WAS GONNA DIE!
YOU'RE HIDING, TOO?
K... KIND OF.
WHAT DO YOU MEAN, "TOO"?
sqeeze
PLEASE DON'T TELL ANYONE.
I'M TRYING TO GET OUT OF HERE.

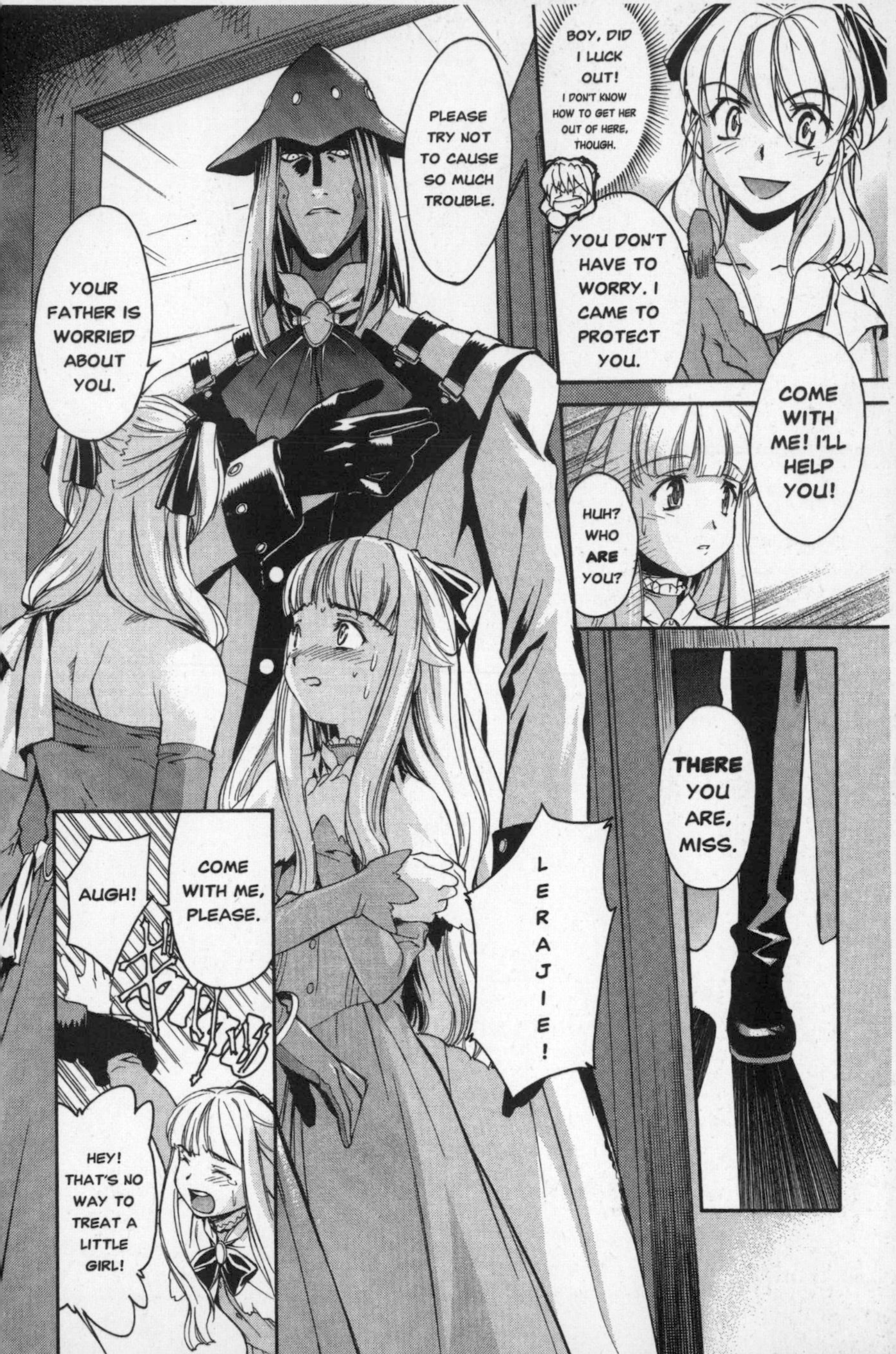
BOY, DID I LUCK OUT!
I DON'T KNOW HOW TO GET HER OUT OF HERE, THOUGH.
YOU DON'T HAVE TO WORRY. I CAME TO PROTECT YOU.
COME WITH ME! I'LL HELP YOU!
HUH? WHO ARE YOU?
THERE YOU ARE, MISS.
PLEASE TRY NOT TO CAUSE SO MUCH TROUBLE.
YOUR FATHER IS WORRIED ABOUT YOU.
LERAJIE!
COME WITH ME, PLEASE.
AUGH!
HEY! THAT'S NO WAY TO TREAT A LITTLE GIRL!

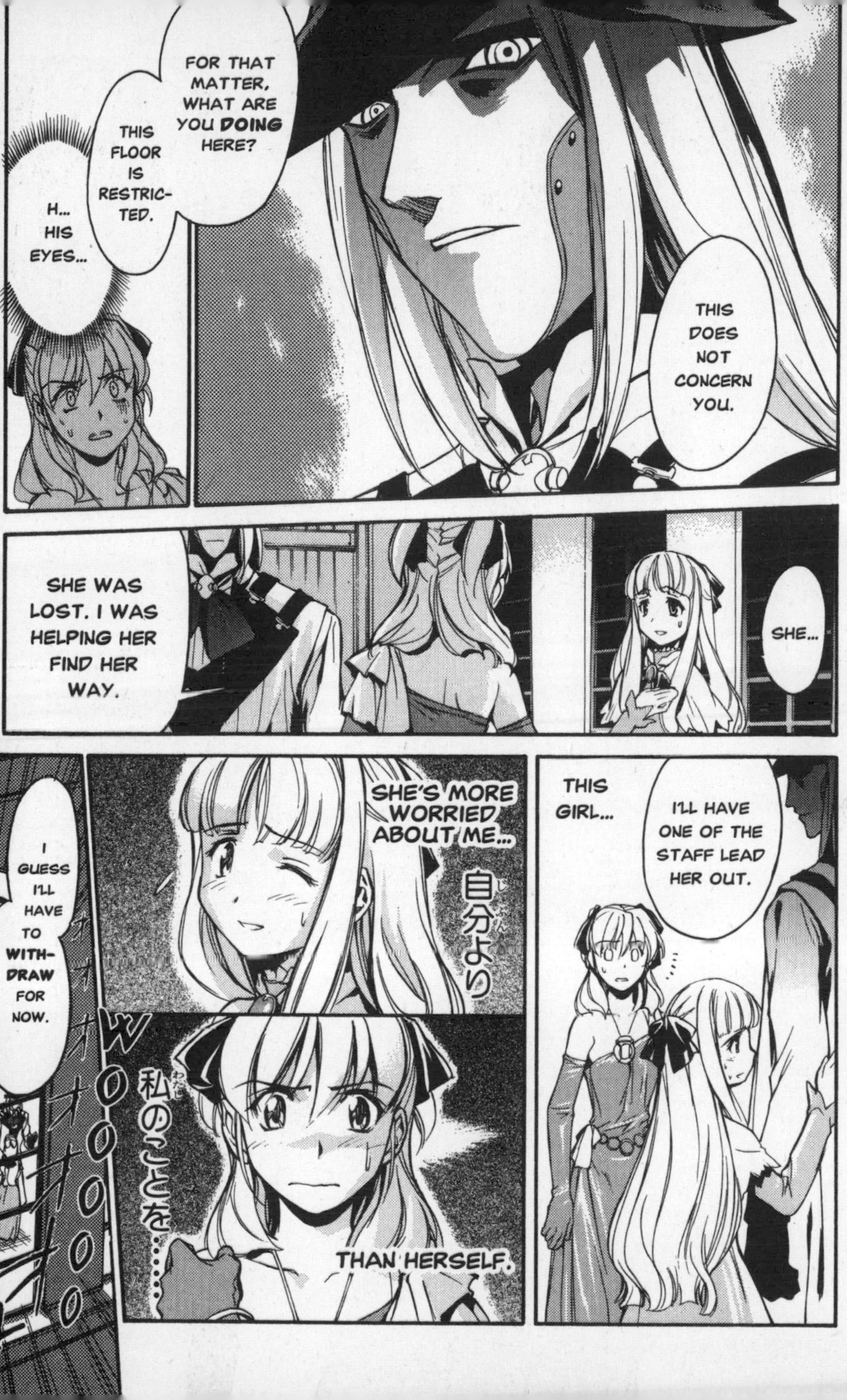
THIS DOES NOT CONCERN YOU.
THIS FLOOR IS RESTRICTED.
FOR THAT MATTER, WHAT ARE YOU DOING HERE?
H... HIS EYES...
SHE...
SHE WAS LOST. I WAS HELPING HER FIND HER WAY.
I'LL HAVE ONE OF THE STAFF LEAD HER OUT.
THIS GIRL...
SHE'S MORE WORRIED ABOUT ME...
自分より
私のことを…
THAN HERSELF.
I GUESS I'LL HAVE TO WITHDRAW FOR NOW.
WOOOOOO

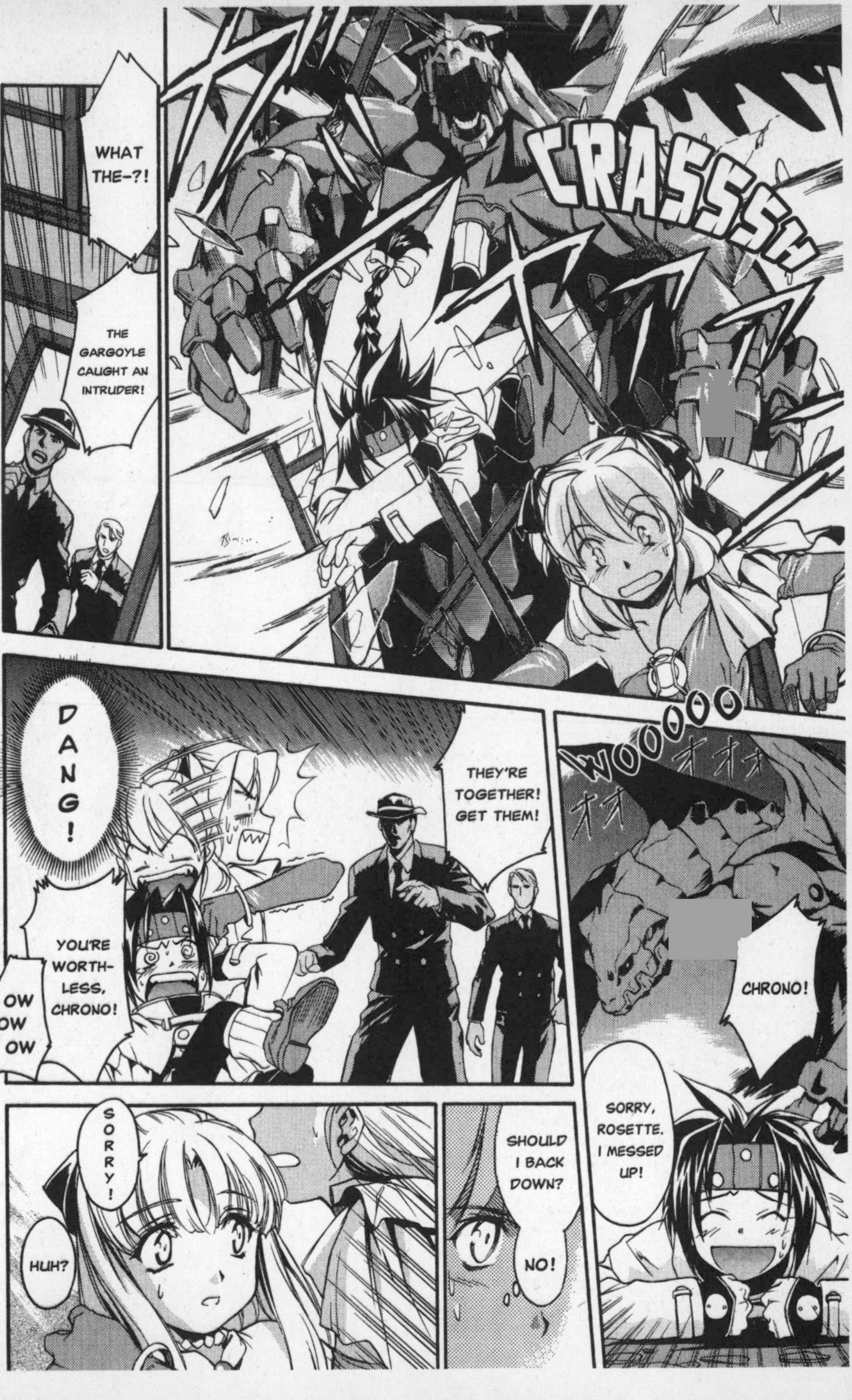
CRASSSSH
WHAT THE-?!
THE GARGOYLE CAUGHT AN INTRUDER!
WOOOOOO
CHRONO!
SORRY, ROSETTE. I MESSED UP!
DANG!
THEY'RE TOGETHER! GET THEM!
YOU'RE WORTH-LESS, CHRONO!
OW OW OW
SHOULD I BACK DOWN?
NO!
SORRY!
HUH?

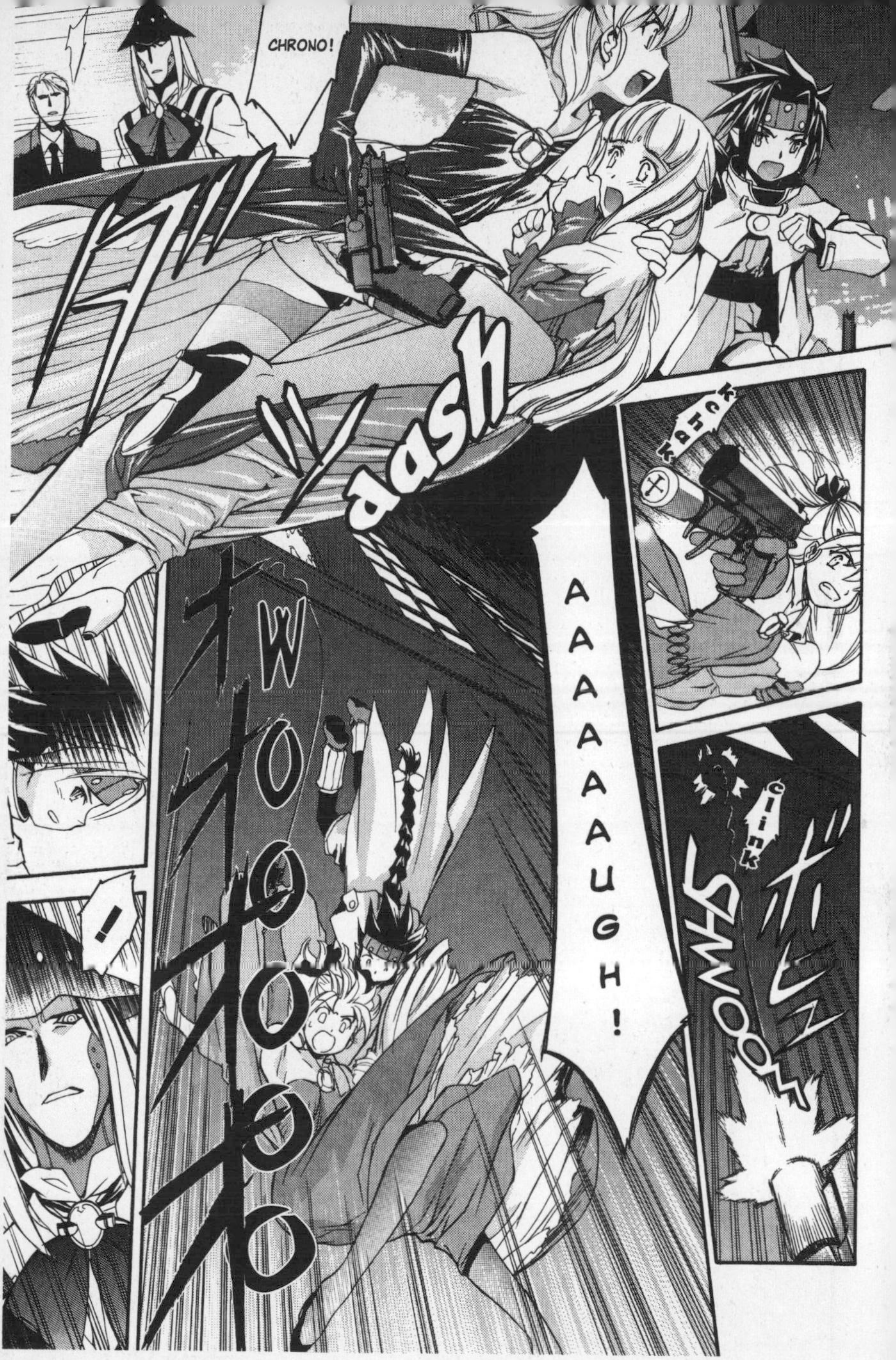
CHRONO!
aash
kachck
AAAAAAAAUGH!
cliink
SHWOOM
WOOOO
!

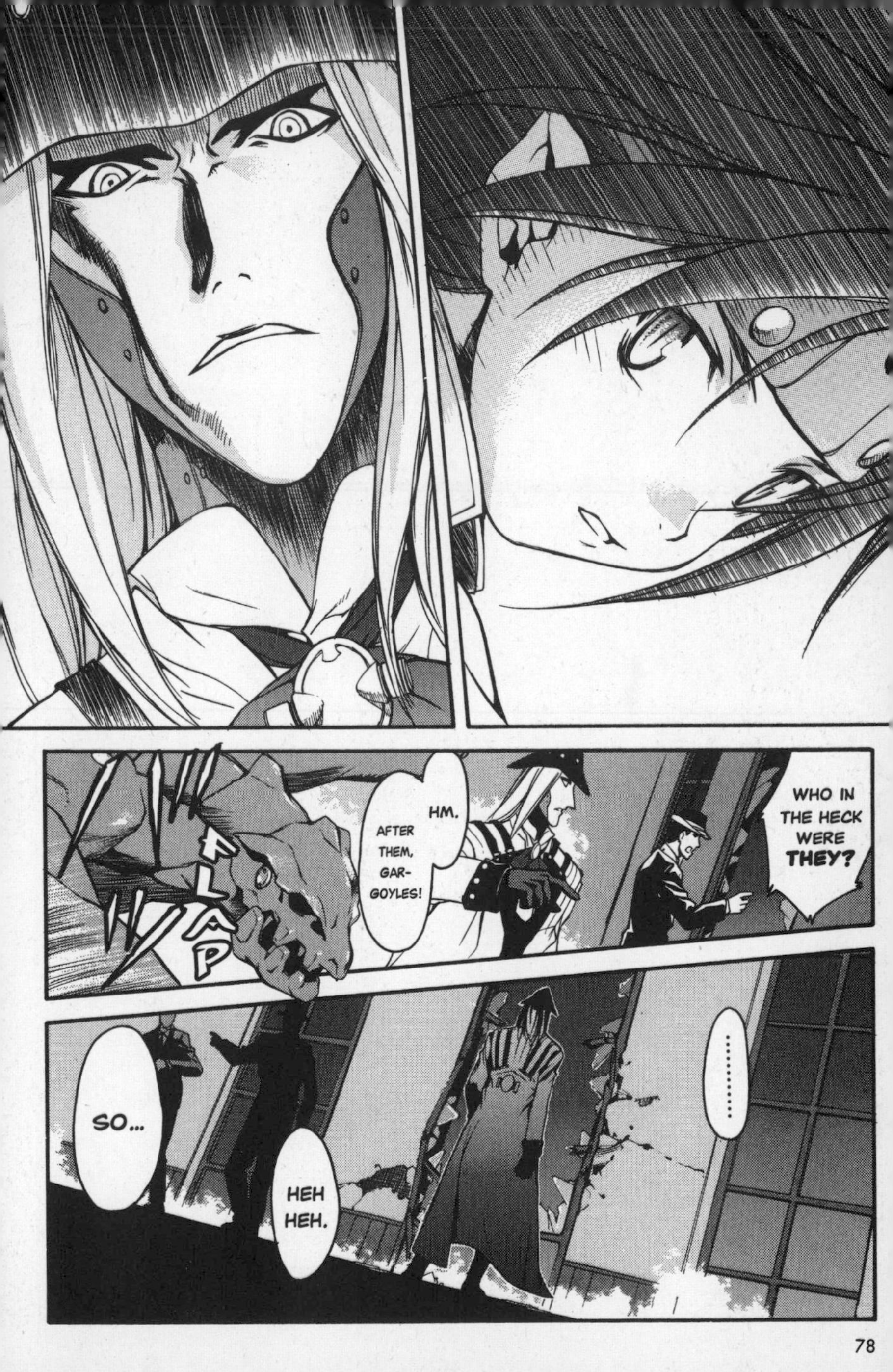
WHO IN THE HECK WERE THEY?
HM.
AFTER THEM, GAR-GOYLES!
FLAP
FLAP
....
SO...
HEH HEH.

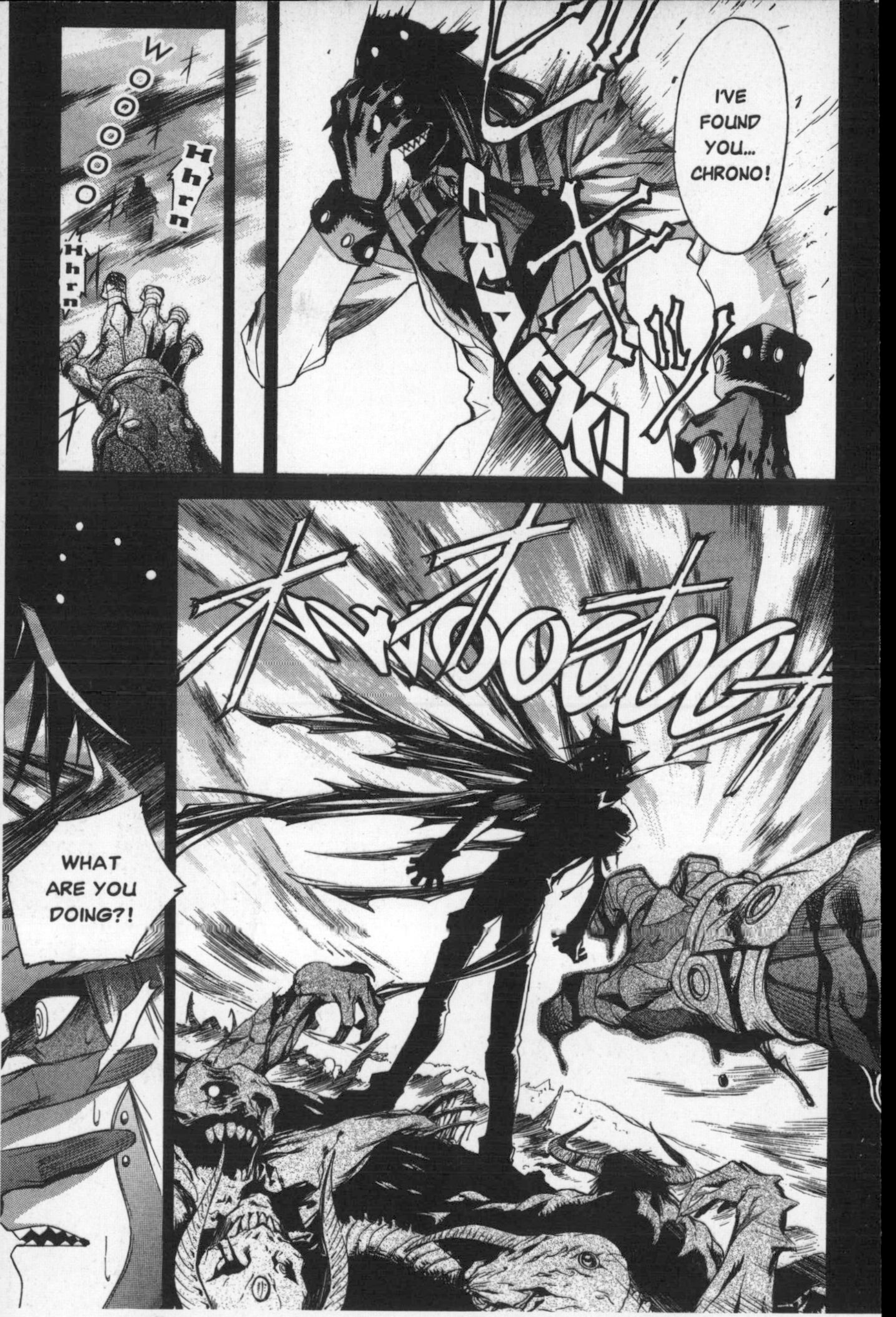
I'VE FOUND YOU... CHRONO!
CRACK!
WOOOOOOO
Hhrn
Hhrn
WHAT ARE YOU DOING?!

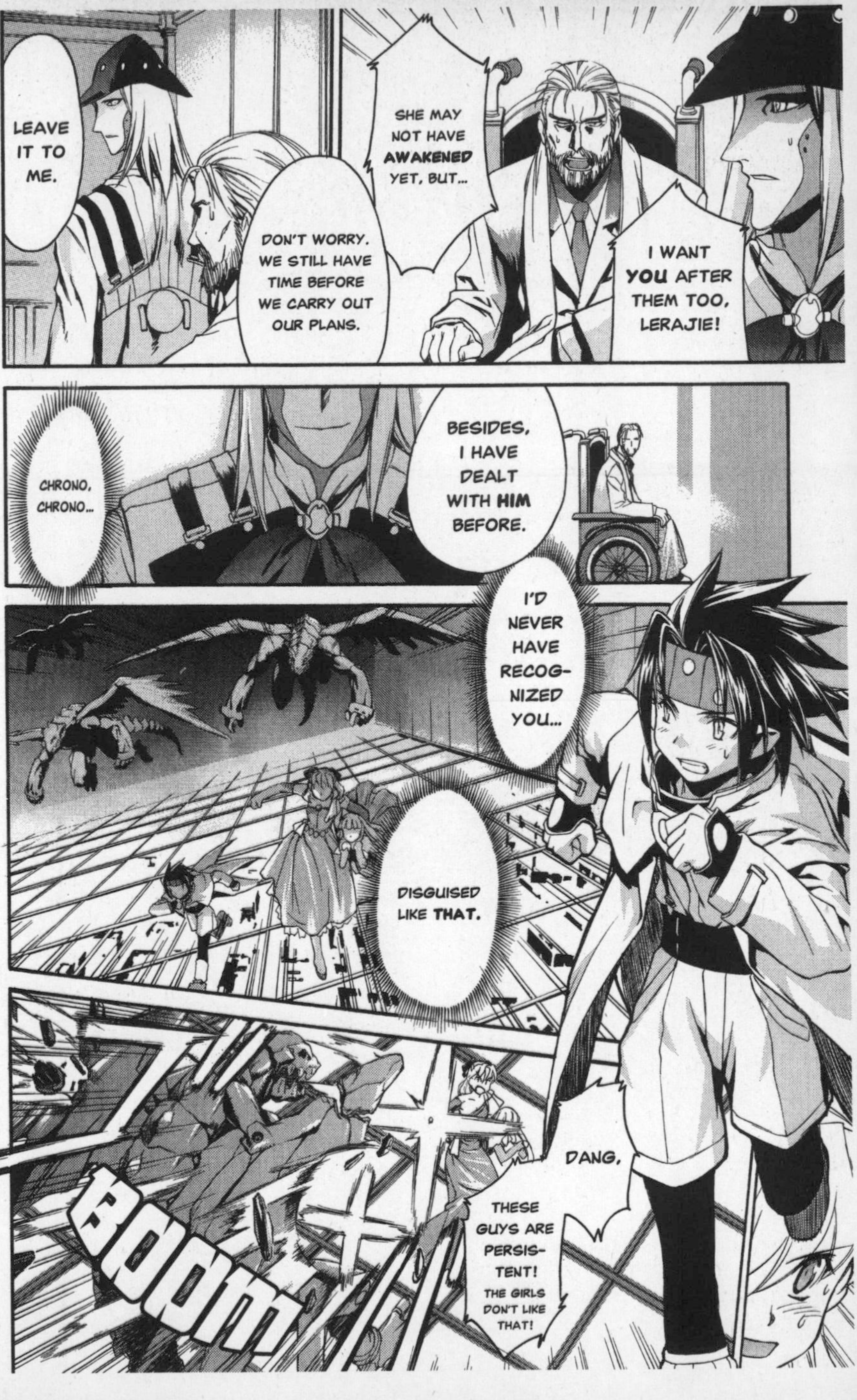
SHE MAY NOT HAVE AWAKENED YET, BUT...
I WANT YOU AFTER THEM TOO, LERAJIE!
DON'T WORRY. WE STILL HAVE TIME BEFORE WE CARRY OUT OUR PLANS.
LEAVE IT TO ME.
BESIDES, I HAVE DEALT WITH HIM BEFORE.
CHRONO, CHRONO...
I'D NEVER HAVE RECOG-NIZED YOU...
DISGUISED LIKE THAT.
DANG,
THESE GUYS ARE PERSIS-TENT!
THE GIRLS DON'T LIKE THAT!
BOOM

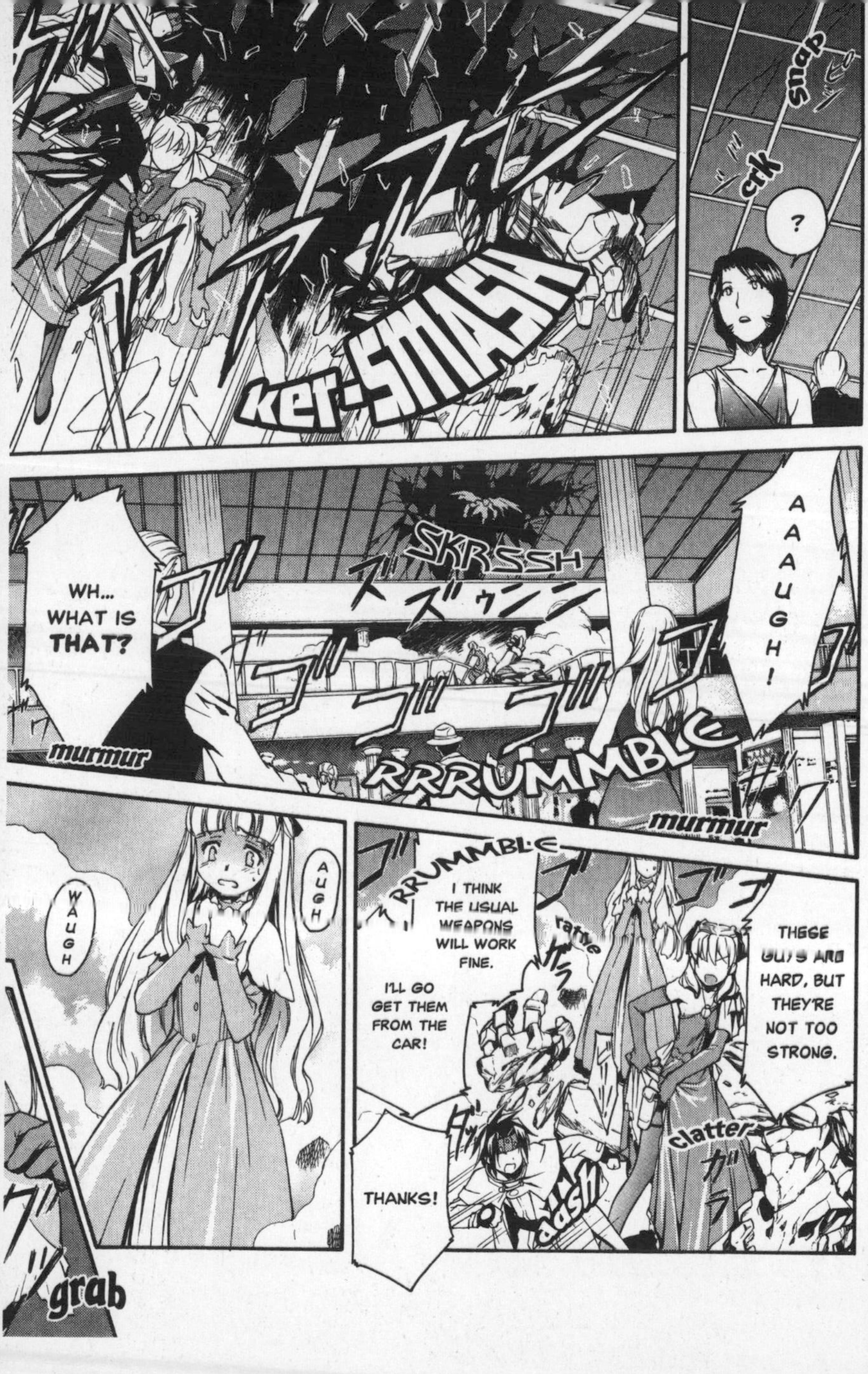

snap
crk
?
ker-SMASH
AAAAUGH!
SKRSSH
WH... WHAT IS THAT?
RRRUMMBLE
murmur
murmur
THESE GUYS ARE HARD, BUT THEY'RE NOT TOO STRONG.
RRUMMBLE
I THINK THE USUAL WEAPONS WILL WORK FINE.
rattle
I'LL GO GET THEM FROM THE CAR!
clatter
dash
THANKS!
AUGH
WAUGH
grab

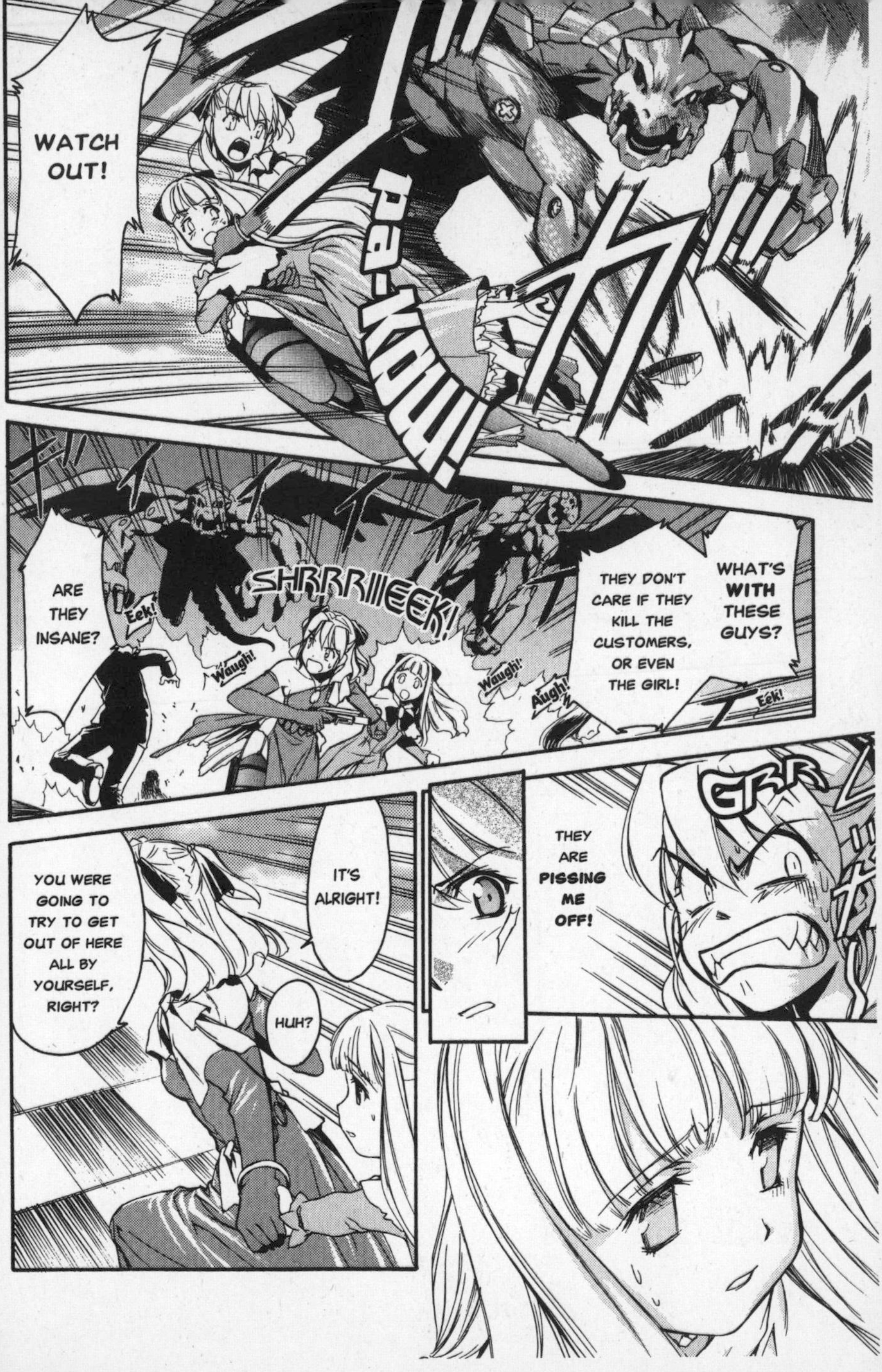
Pa-Kouu!
WATCH OUT!
WHAT'S WITH THESE GUYS?
THEY DON'T CARE IF THEY KILL THE CUSTOMERS, OR EVEN THE GIRL!
Eek!
Augh!
Waugh!
SHRRRIIIEEK!
Waugh!
Eek!
ARE THEY INSANE?
GRR
THEY ARE PISSING ME OFF!
IT'S ALRIGHT!
YOU WERE GOING TO TRY TO GET OUT OF HERE ALL BY YOURSELF, RIGHT?
HUH?

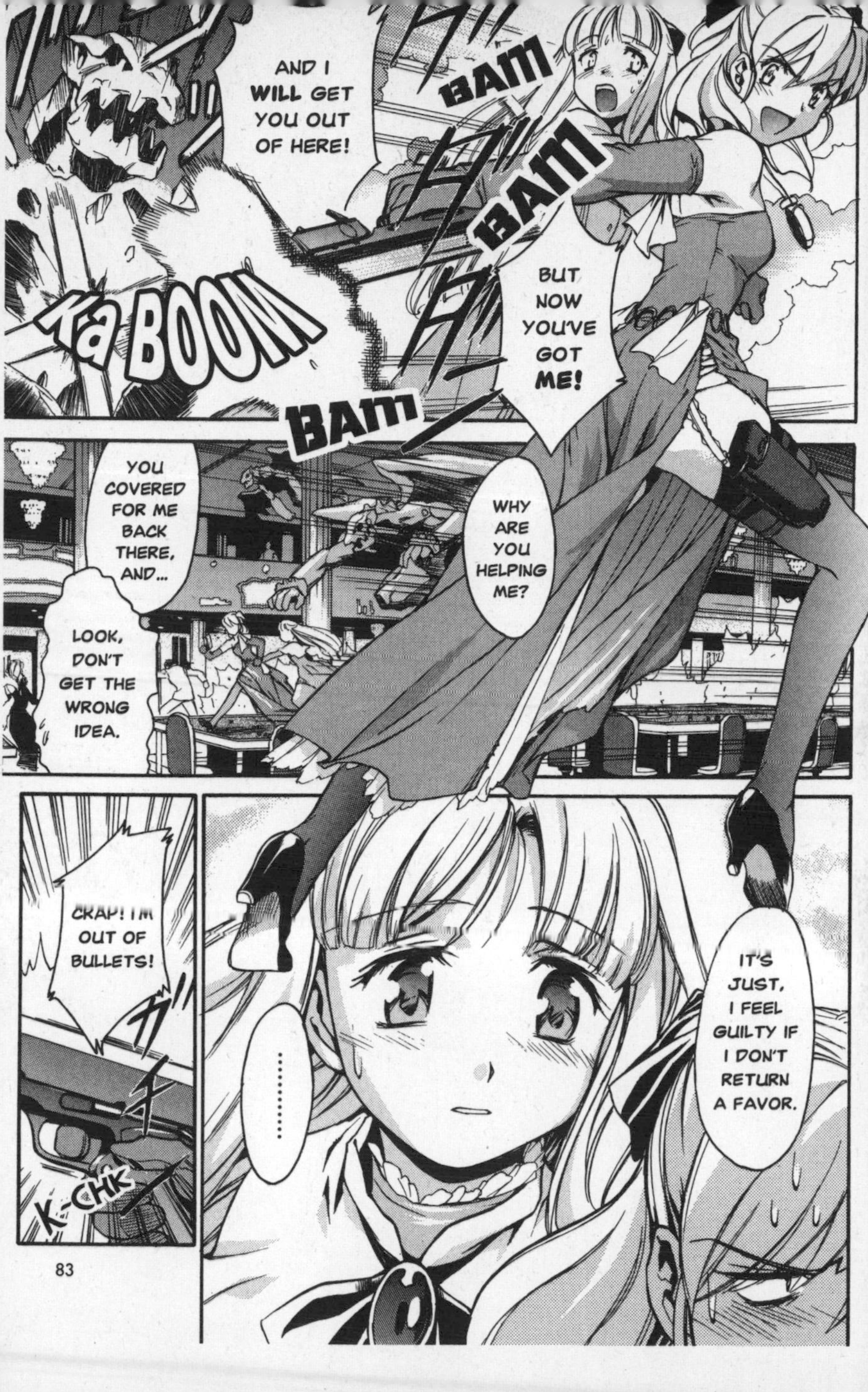
BAM
BAM
BAM
BUT NOW YOU'VE GOT ME!
AND I WILL GET YOU OUT OF HERE!
Ka BOOM
BAM
WHY ARE YOU HELPING ME?
YOU COVERED FOR ME BACK THERE, AND...
LOOK, DON'T GET THE WRONG IDEA.
IT'S JUST, I FEEL GUILTY IF I DON'T RETURN A FAVOR.
....
CRAP! I'M OUT OF BULLETS!
K-CHK

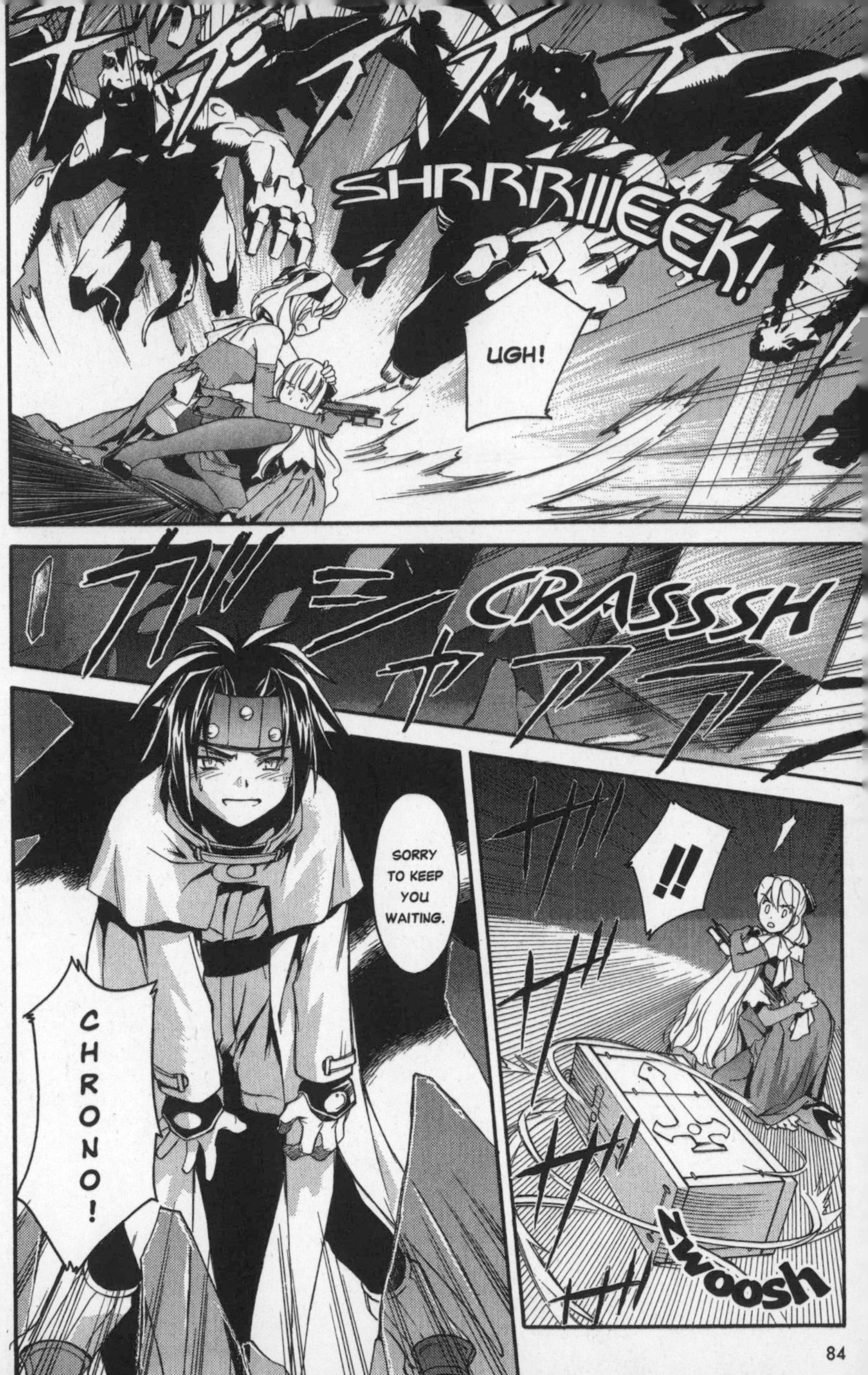
SHRRRIIIEEK!
UGH!
CRASSSH
!!
Zwoosh
SORRY TO KEEP YOU WAITING.
CHRONO!

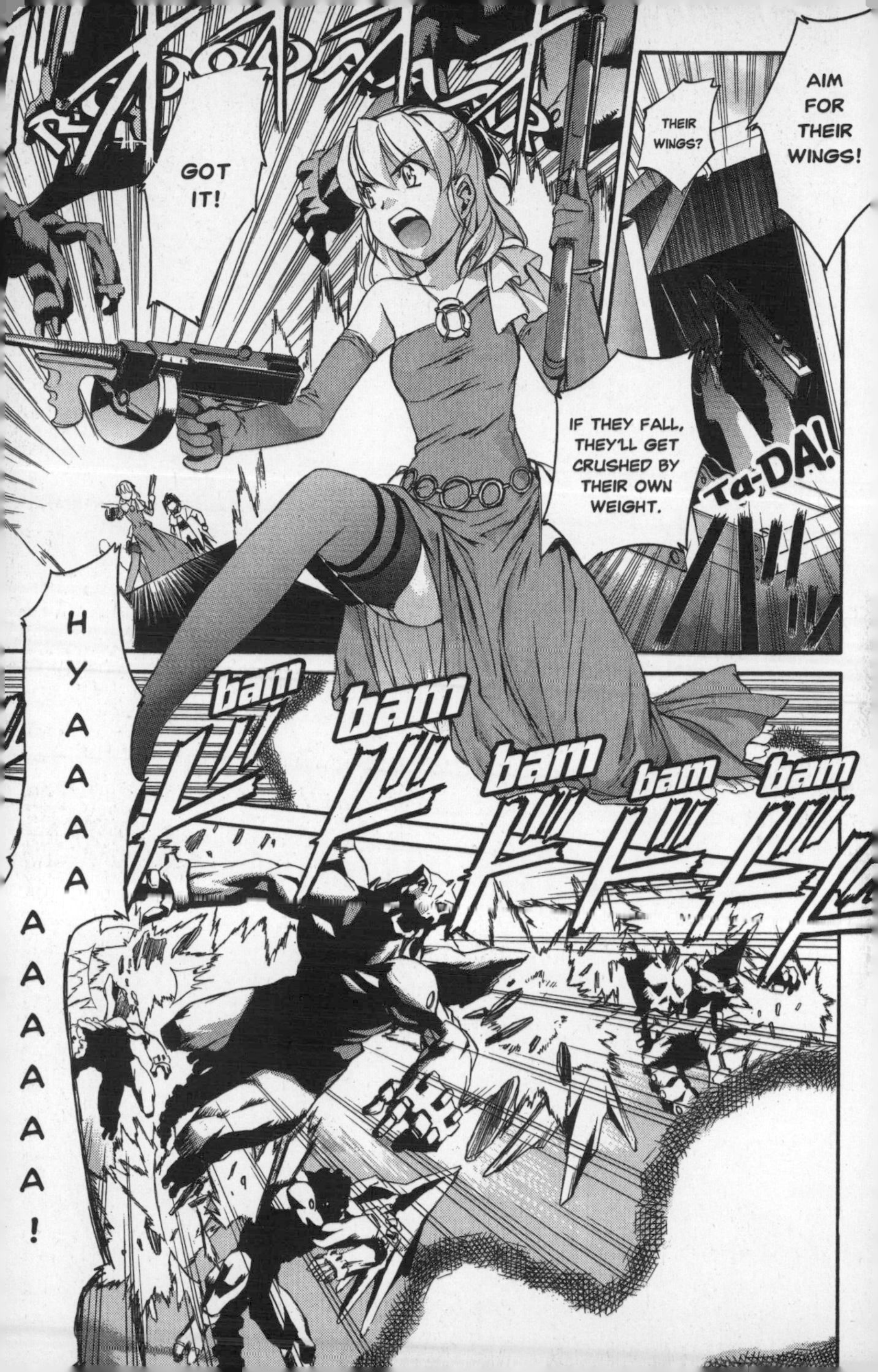
AIM FOR THEIR WINGS!
THEIR WINGS?
GOT IT!
IF THEY FALL, THEY'LL GET CRUSHED BY THEIR OWN WEIGHT.
Ta-DA!
bam
bam
bam
bam
bam
HYAAAAAAAAAA!

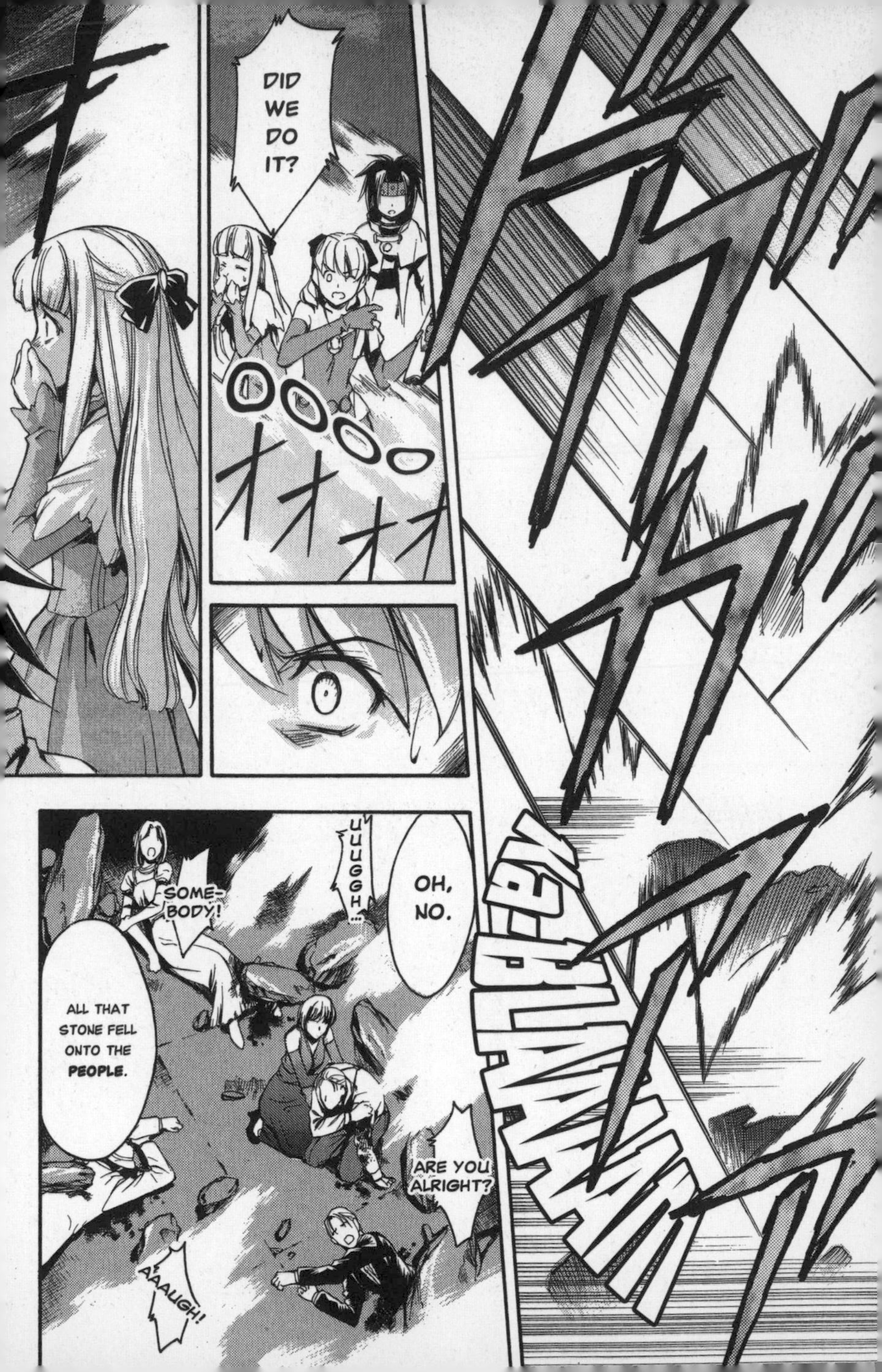
KA-BLAAAM!
DID WE DO IT?
OOOO
オオオオ
OH, NO.
UUUGGH...
SOME-BODY!
ARE YOU ALRIGHT?
ALL THAT STONE FELL ONTO THE **PEOPLE**.
AAAUGH!

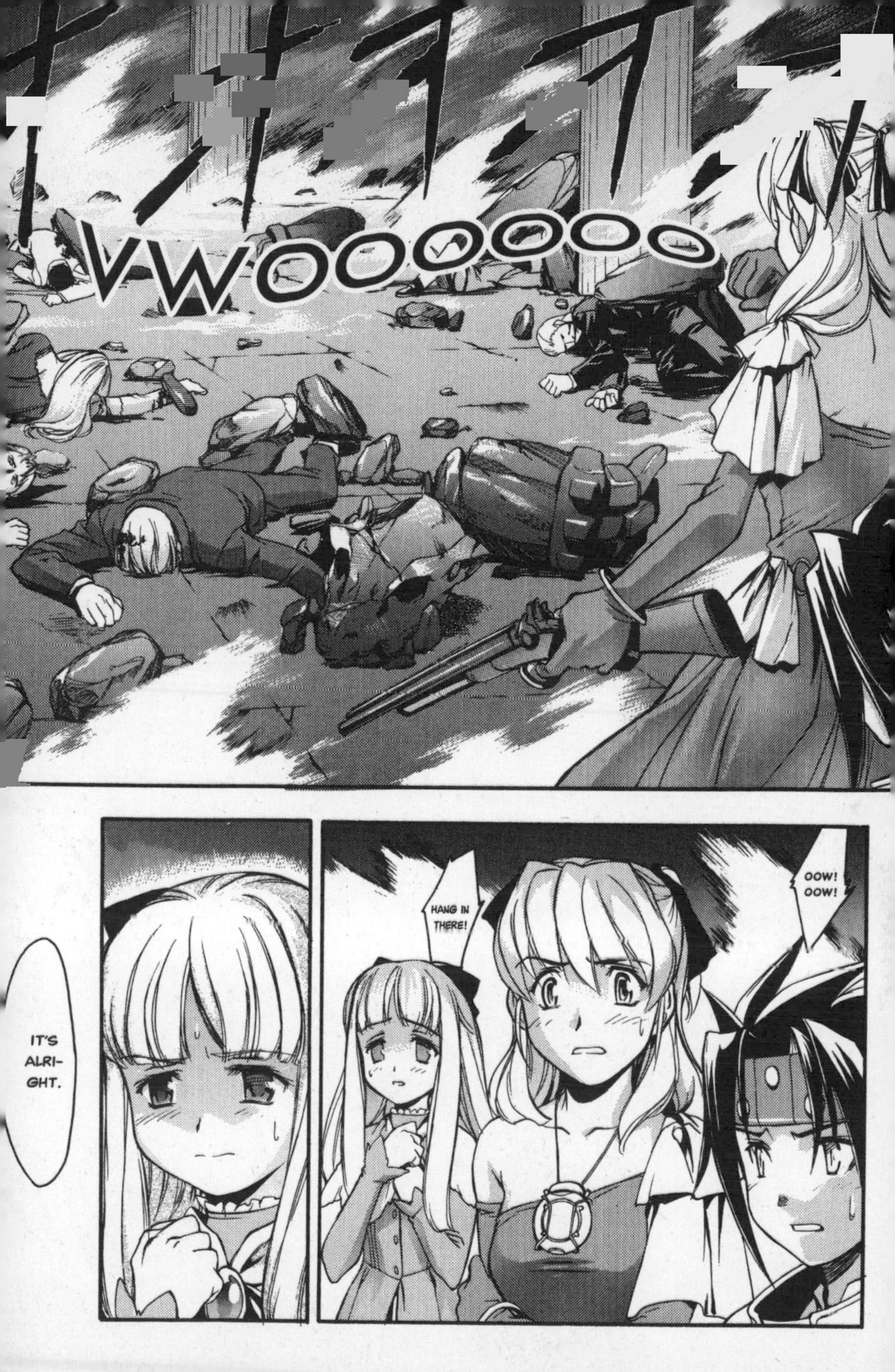
VWOOOOOOO
OOW! OOW!
HANG IN THERE!
IT'S ALRIGHT.

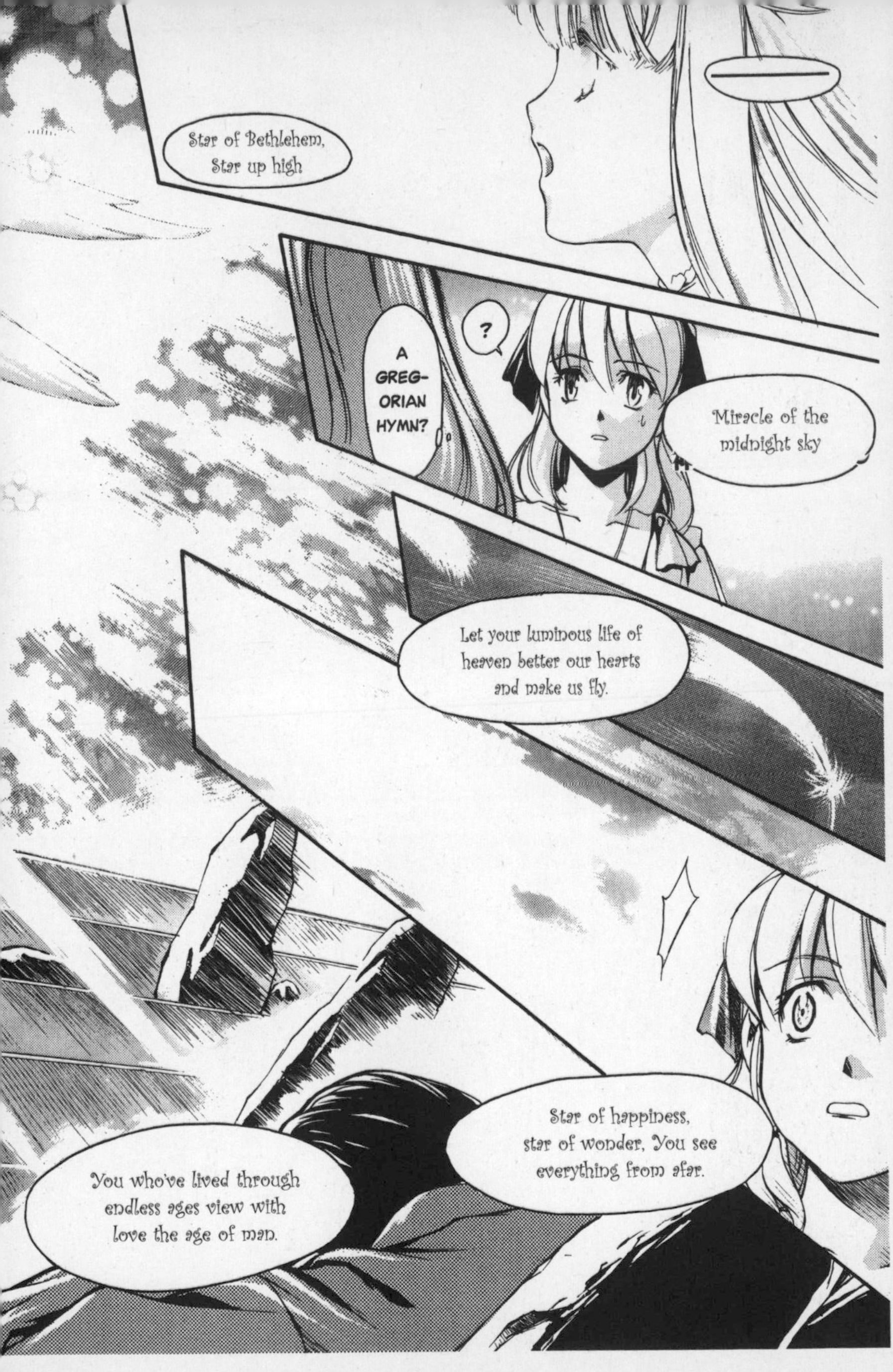
Star of Bethlehem, Star up high
?
A GREG-ORIAN HYMN?
Miracle of the midnight sky
Let your luminous life of heaven better our hearts and make us fly.
Star of happiness, star of wonder, You see everything from afar.
You who've lived through endless ages view with love the age of man.

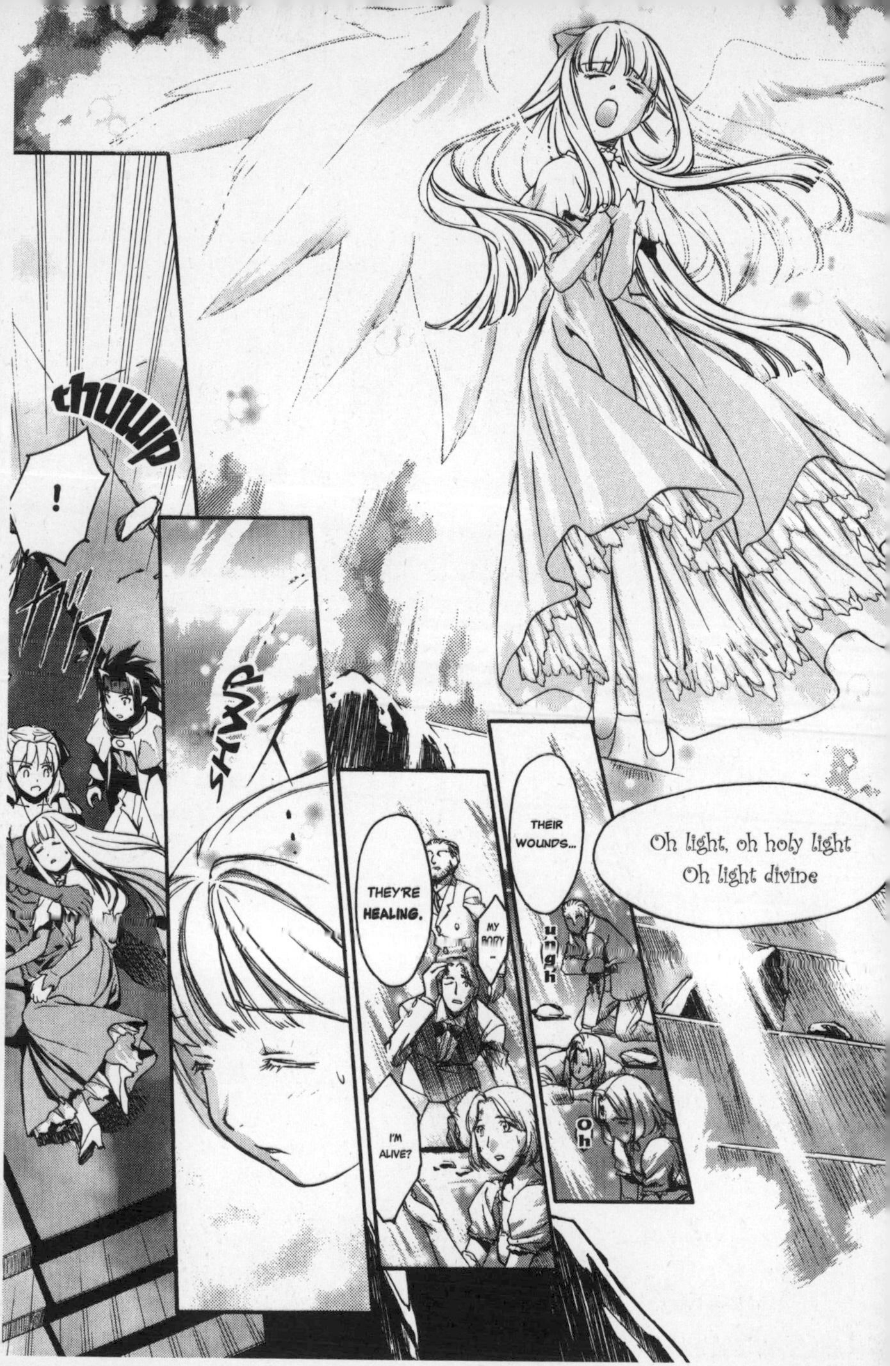
Oh light, oh holy light
Oh light divine
THEIR WOUNDS...
ungh
Oh
THEY'RE HEALING.
MY BODY...
I'M ALIVE?
SHWUP
thuwp
!

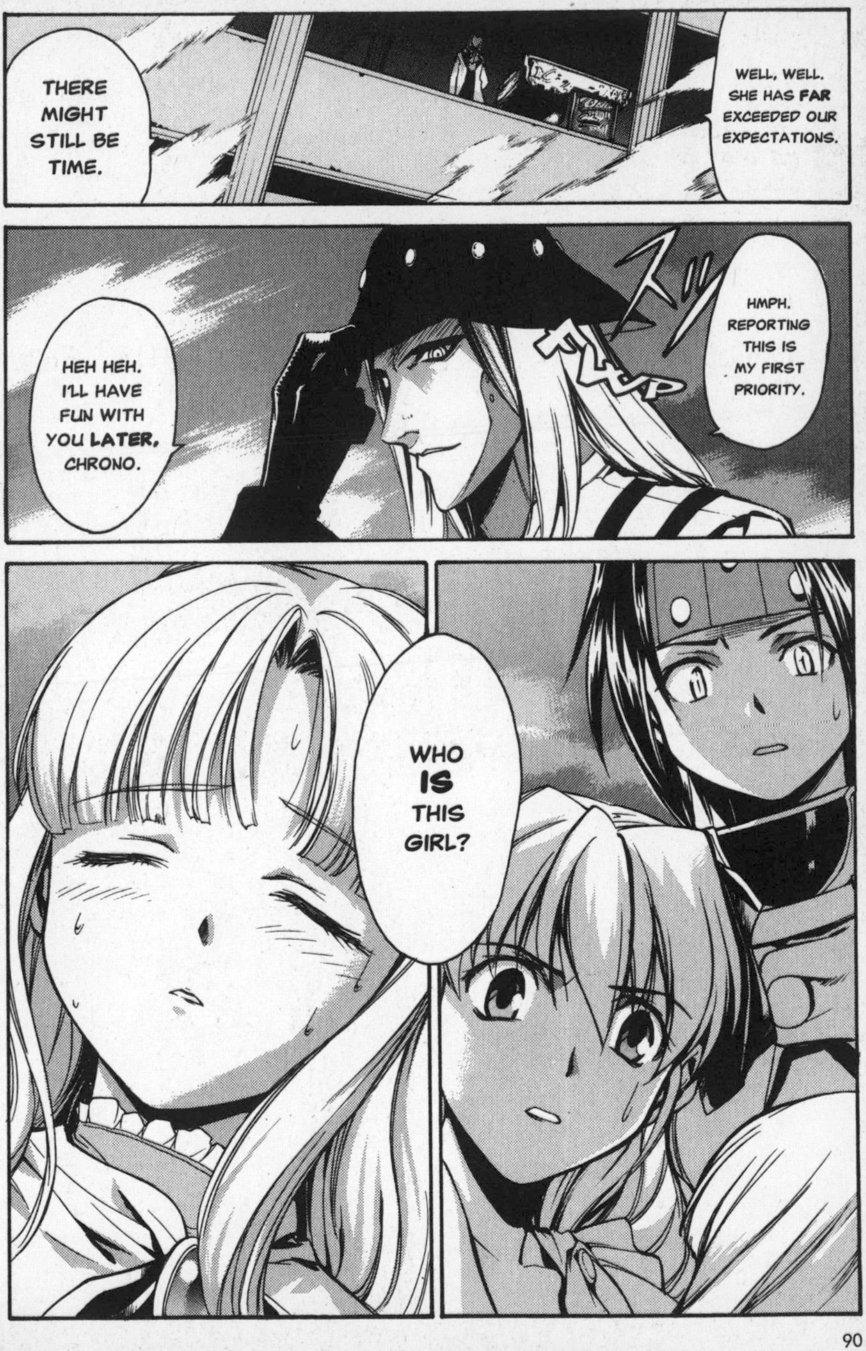
WELL, WELL. SHE HAS FAR EXCEEDED OUR EXPECTATIONS.
THERE MIGHT STILL BE TIME.
HMPH. REPORTING THIS IS MY FIRST PRIORITY.
FWAP
HEH HEH. I'LL HAVE FUN WITH YOU LATER, CHRONO.
WHO IS THIS GIRL?

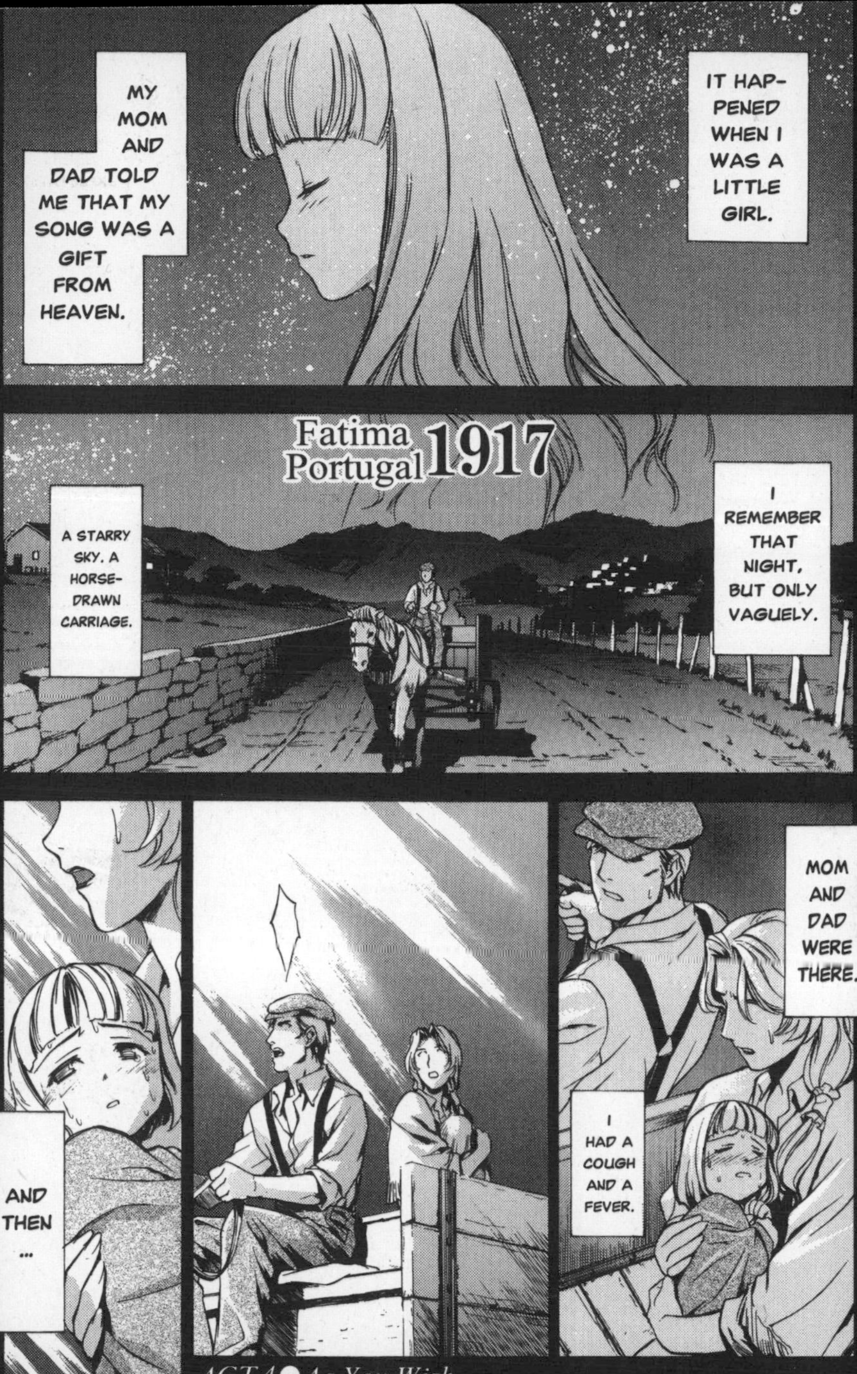
IT HAPPENED WHEN I WAS A LITTLE GIRL.
MY MOM AND DAD TOLD ME THAT MY SONG WAS A GIFT FROM HEAVEN.
Fatima Portugal 1917
I REMEMBER THAT NIGHT, BUT ONLY VAGUELY.
A STARRY SKY. A HORSE-DRAWN CARRIAGE.
MOM AND DAD WERE THERE.
I HAD A COUGH AND A FEVER.
AND THEN ...

ACT 4 ● As You Wish

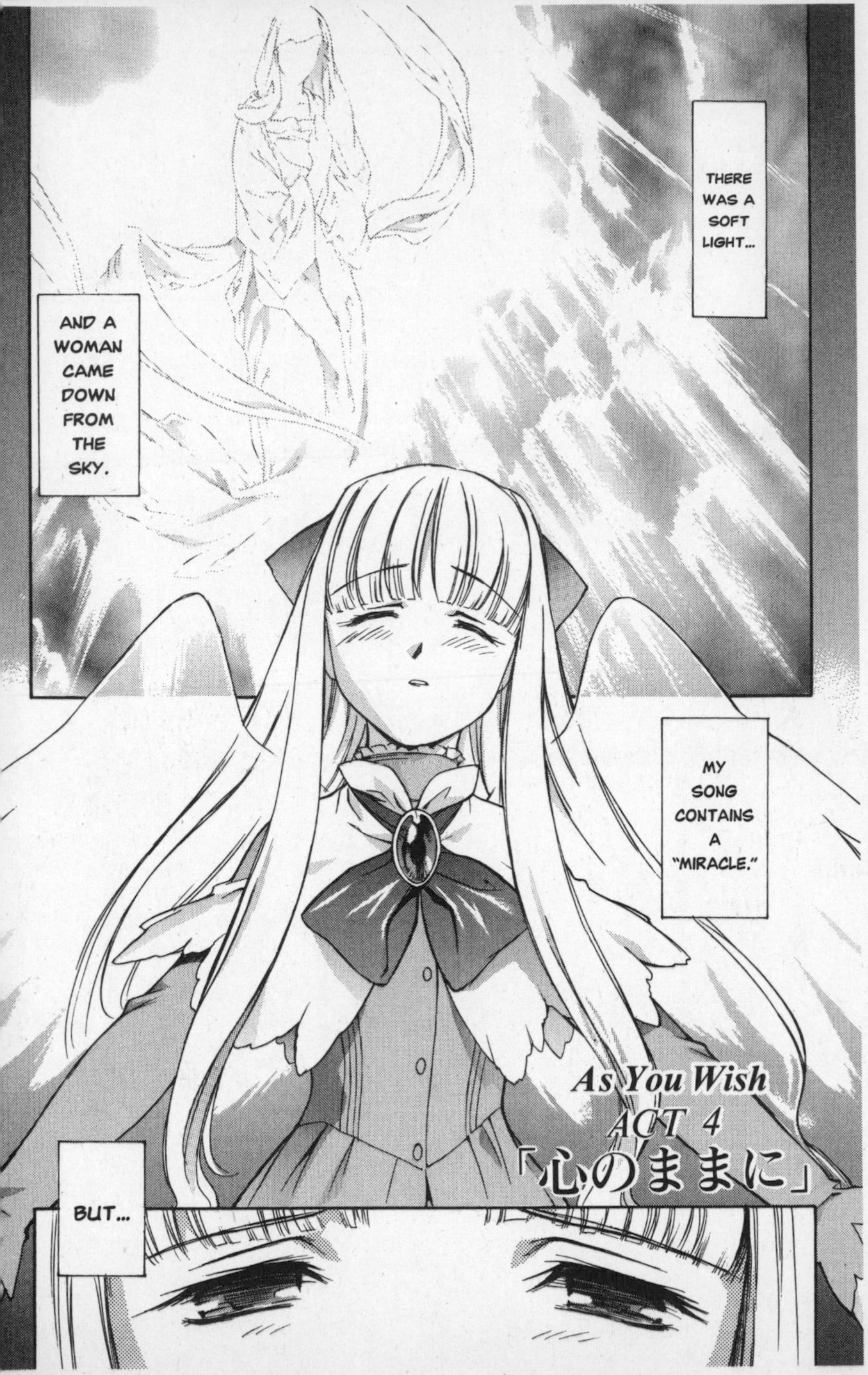
THERE WAS A SOFT LIGHT...
AND A WOMAN CAME DOWN FROM THE SKY.
MY SONG CONTAINS A "MIRACLE."
As You Wish
ACT 4
「心のままに」
BUT...

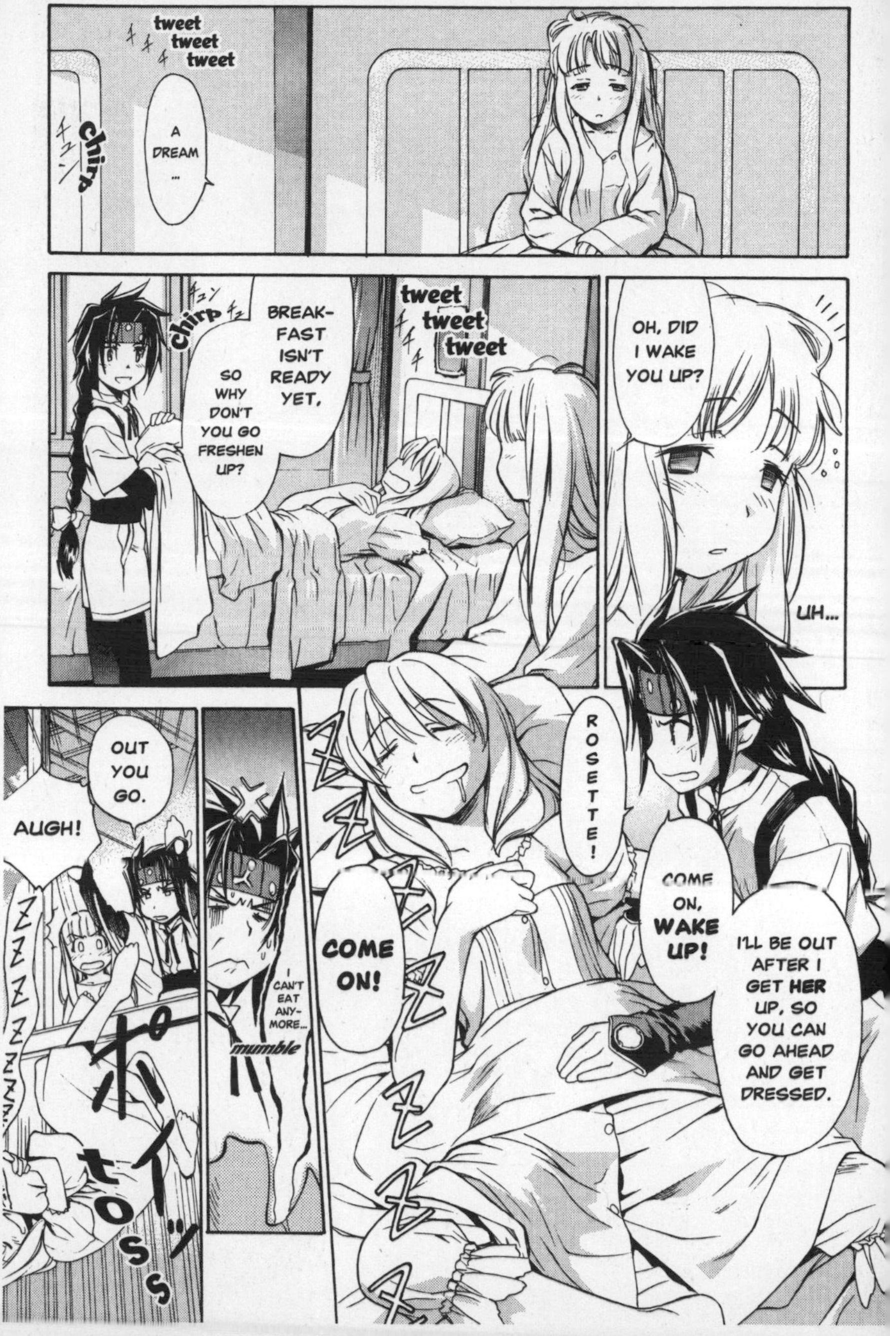
tweet tweet tweet
chirp
A DREAM ...
OH, DID I WAKE YOU UP?
UH...
tweet tweet tweet
BREAK-FAST ISN'T READY YET,
SO WHY DON'T YOU GO FRESHEN UP?
chirp
ROSETTE!
COME ON, WAKE UP!
I'LL BE OUT AFTER I GET HER UP, SO YOU CAN GO AHEAD AND GET DRESSED.
COME ON!
I CAN'T EAT ANYMORE...
mumble
OUT YOU GO.
AUGH!
toss

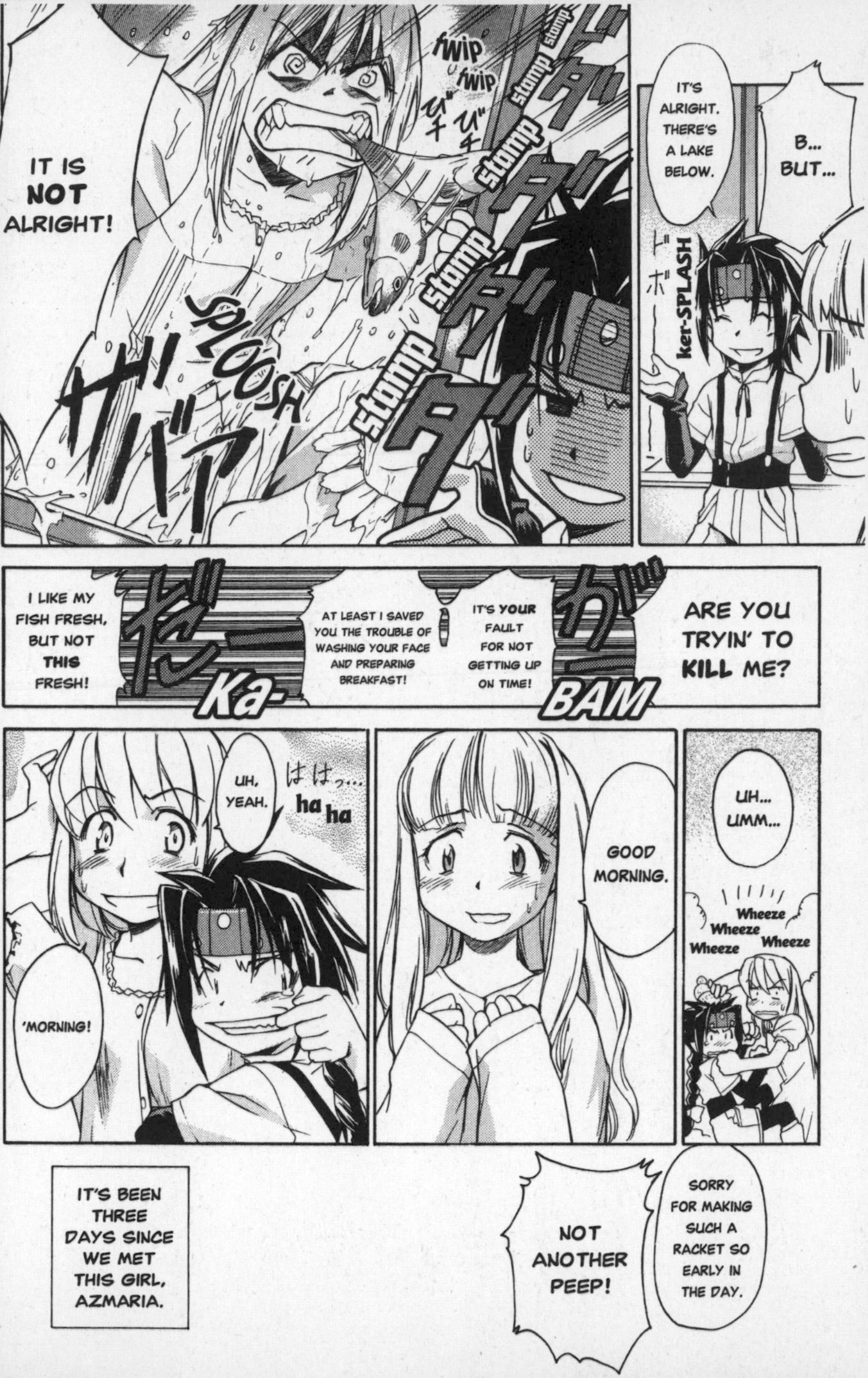
IT'S ALRIGHT. THERE'S A LAKE BELOW.
B... BUT...
ker-SPLASH
IT IS NOT ALRIGHT!
fwip fwip
stamp stamp stamp stamp stamp stamp stamp
SPLOOSH
ARE YOU TRYIN' TO KILL ME?
BAM
IT'S YOUR FAULT FOR NOT GETTING UP ON TIME!
AT LEAST I SAVED YOU THE TROUBLE OF WASHING YOUR FACE AND PREPARING BREAKFAST!
Ka-
I LIKE MY FISH FRESH, BUT NOT THIS FRESH!
UH... UMM...
Wheeze Wheeze Wheeze Wheeze
GOOD MORNING.
UH, YEAH.
ha ha
'MORNING!
SORRY FOR MAKING SUCH A RACKET SO EARLY IN THE DAY.
NOT ANOTHER PEEP!
IT'S BEEN THREE DAYS SINCE WE MET THIS GIRL, AZMARIA.

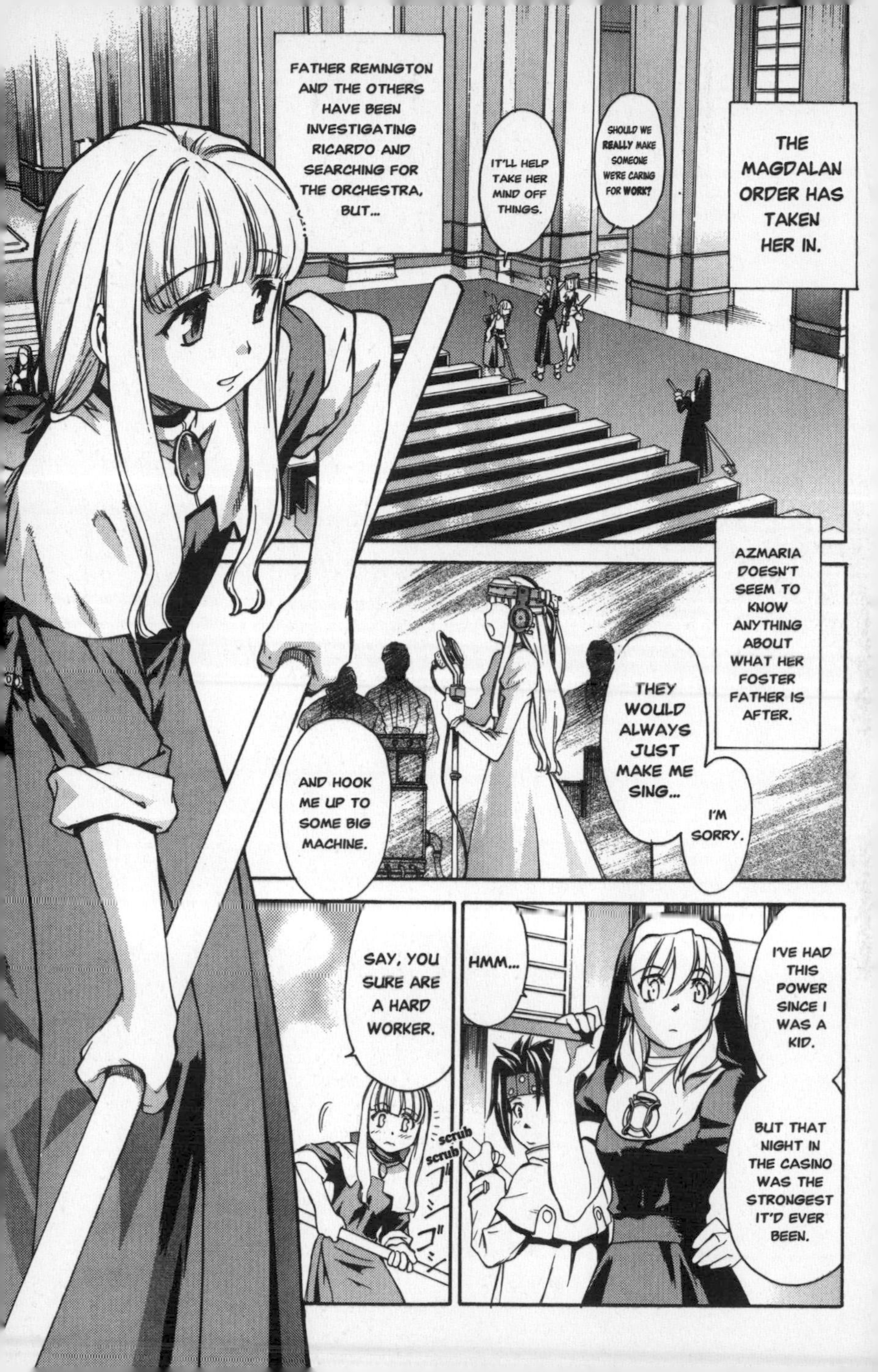
THE MAGDALAN ORDER HAS TAKEN HER IN.
SHOULD WE REALLY MAKE SOMEONE WE'RE CARING FOR WORK?
IT'LL HELP TAKE HER MIND OFF THINGS.
FATHER REMINGTON AND THE OTHERS HAVE BEEN INVESTIGATING RICARDO AND SEARCHING FOR THE ORCHESTRA, BUT...
AZMARIA DOESN'T SEEM TO KNOW ANYTHING ABOUT WHAT HER FOSTER FATHER IS AFTER.
I'M SORRY.
THEY WOULD ALWAYS JUST MAKE ME SING...
AND HOOK ME UP TO SOME BIG MACHINE.
I'VE HAD THIS POWER SINCE I WAS A KID.
BUT THAT NIGHT IN THE CASINO WAS THE STRONGEST IT'D EVER BEEN.
HMM...
scrub scrub
SAY, YOU SURE ARE A HARD WORKER.

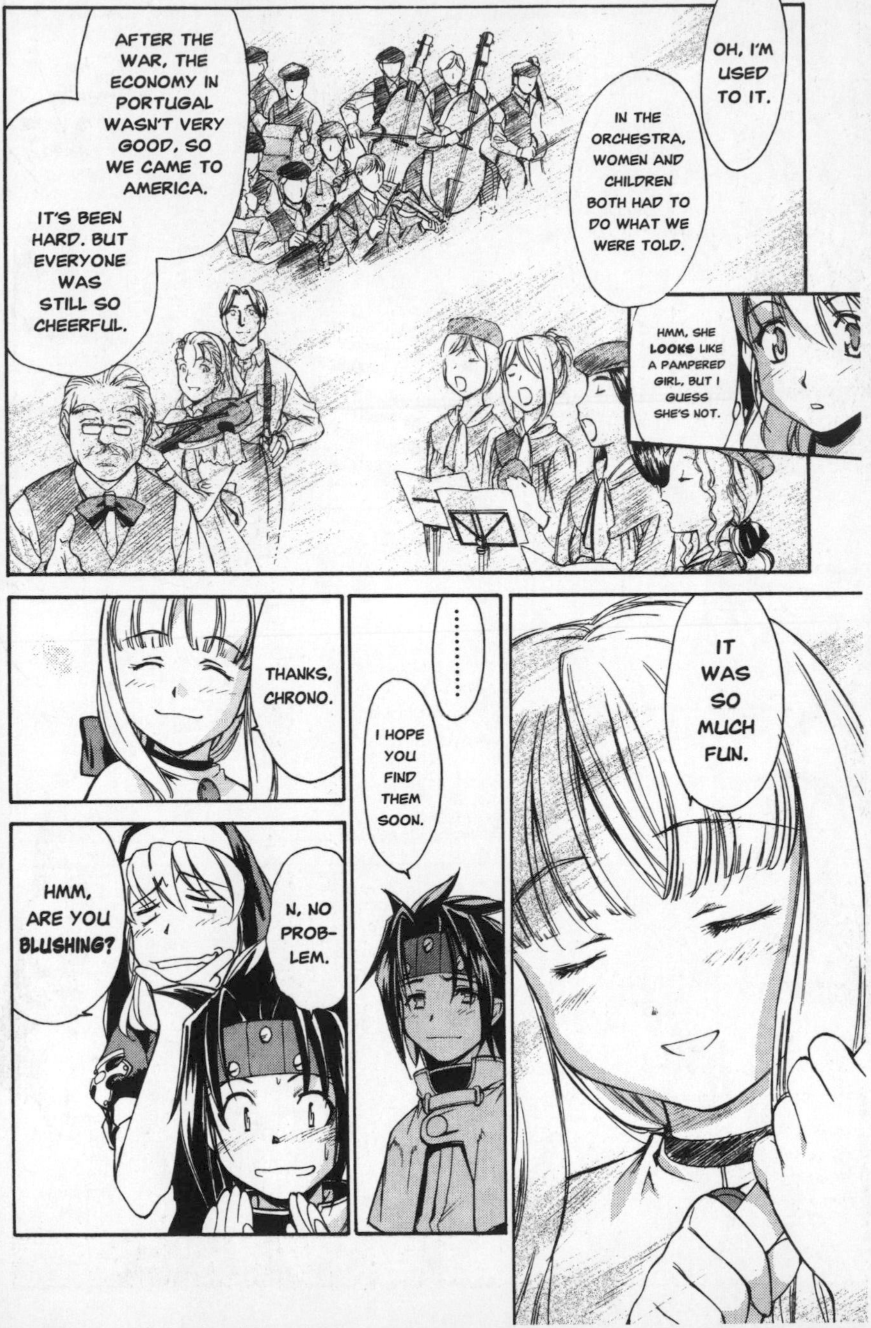
OH, I'M USED TO IT.
IN THE ORCHESTRA, WOMEN AND CHILDREN BOTH HAD TO DO WHAT WE WERE TOLD.
AFTER THE WAR, THE ECONOMY IN PORTUGAL WASN'T VERY GOOD, SO WE CAME TO AMERICA.
IT'S BEEN HARD. BUT EVERYONE WAS STILL SO CHEERFUL.
HMM, SHE LOOKS LIKE A PAMPERED GIRL, BUT I GUESS SHE'S NOT.
IT WAS SO MUCH FUN.
......
I HOPE YOU FIND THEM SOON.
THANKS, CHRONO.
N, NO PROB-LEM.
HMM, ARE YOU BLUSHING?

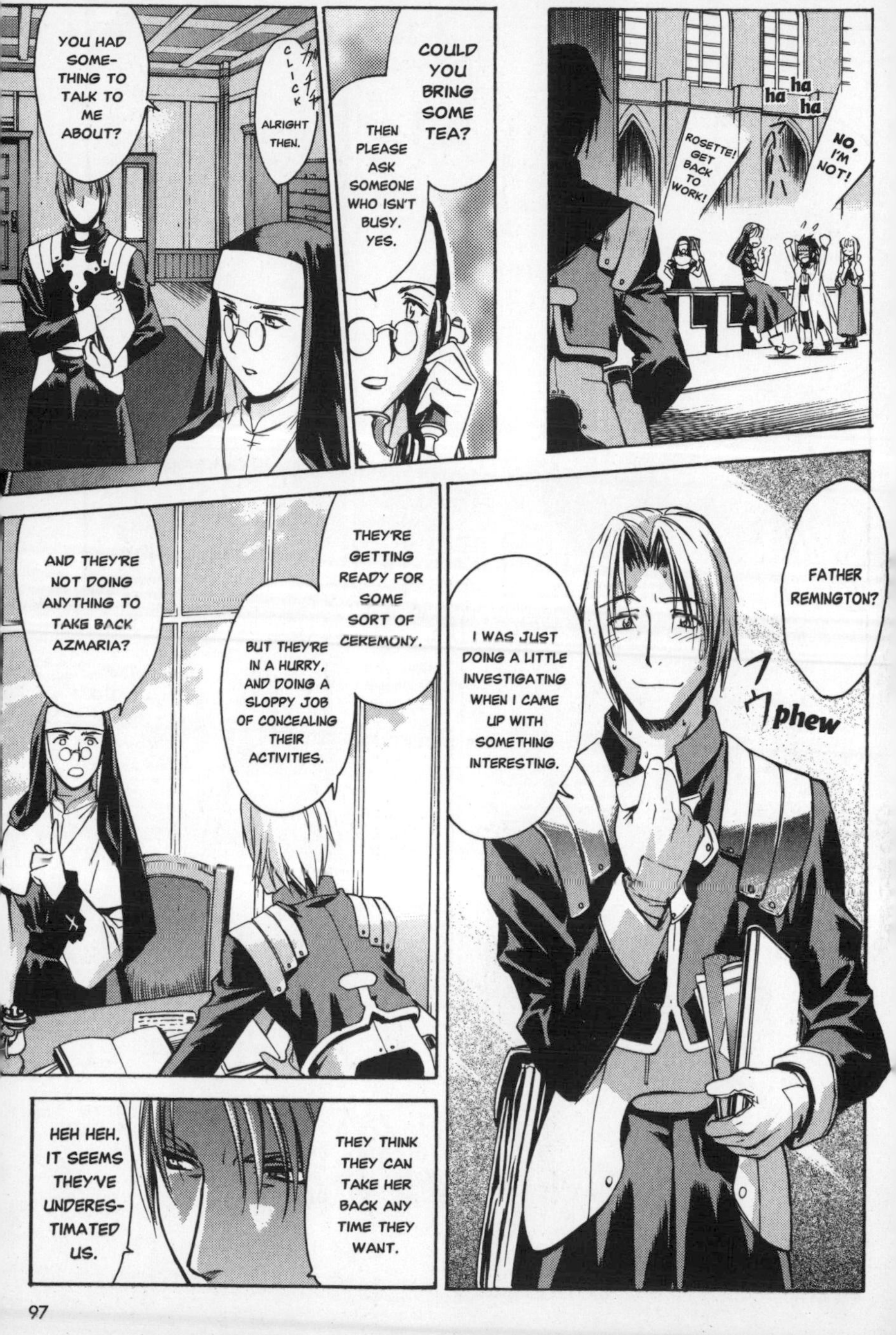
ha ha ha
NO, I'M NOT!
ROSETTE! GET BACK TO WORK!
COULD YOU BRING SOME TEA?
THEN PLEASE ASK SOMEONE WHO ISN'T BUSY. YES.
CLICK
ALRIGHT THEN.
YOU HAD SOME-THING TO TALK TO ME ABOUT?
FATHER REMINGTON?
phew
I WAS JUST DOING A LITTLE INVESTIGATING WHEN I CAME UP WITH SOMETHING INTERESTING.
THEY'RE GETTING READY FOR SOME SORT OF CEREMONY.
BUT THEY'RE IN A HURRY, AND DOING A SLOPPY JOB OF CONCEALING THEIR ACTIVITIES.
AND THEY'RE NOT DOING ANYTHING TO TAKE BACK AZMARIA?
THEY THINK THEY CAN TAKE HER BACK ANY TIME THEY WANT.
HEH HEH. IT SEEMS THEY'VE UNDERES-TIMATED US.

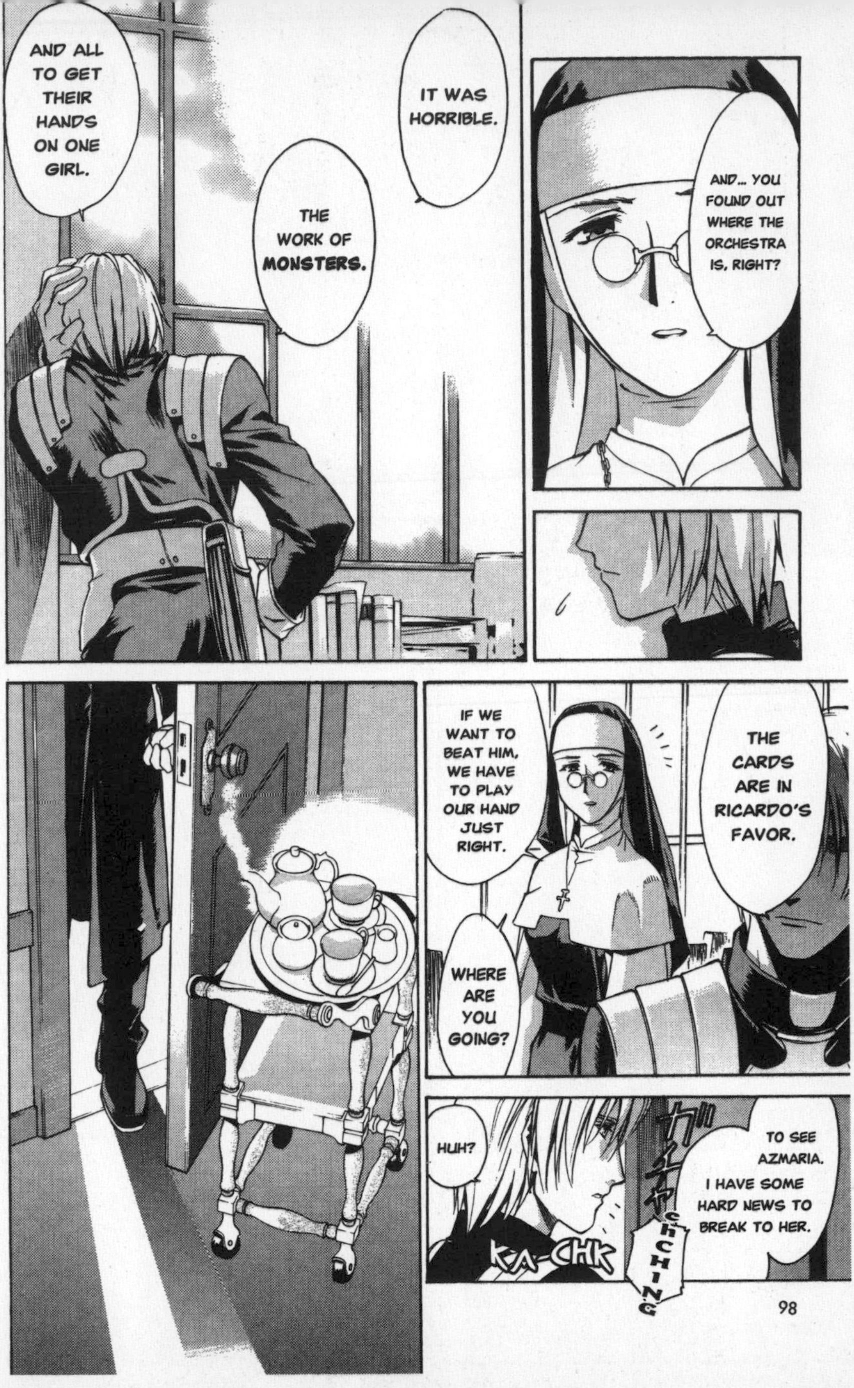
AND... YOU FOUND OUT WHERE THE ORCHESTRA IS, RIGHT?
IT WAS HORRIBLE.
THE WORK OF MONSTERS.
AND ALL TO GET THEIR HANDS ON ONE GIRL.
THE CARDS ARE IN RICARDO'S FAVOR.
IF WE WANT TO BEAT HIM, WE HAVE TO PLAY OUR HAND JUST RIGHT.
WHERE ARE YOU GOING?
TO SEE AZMARIA. I HAVE SOME HARD NEWS TO BREAK TO HER.
ガチャ
CHCHING
HUH?
KA-CHK

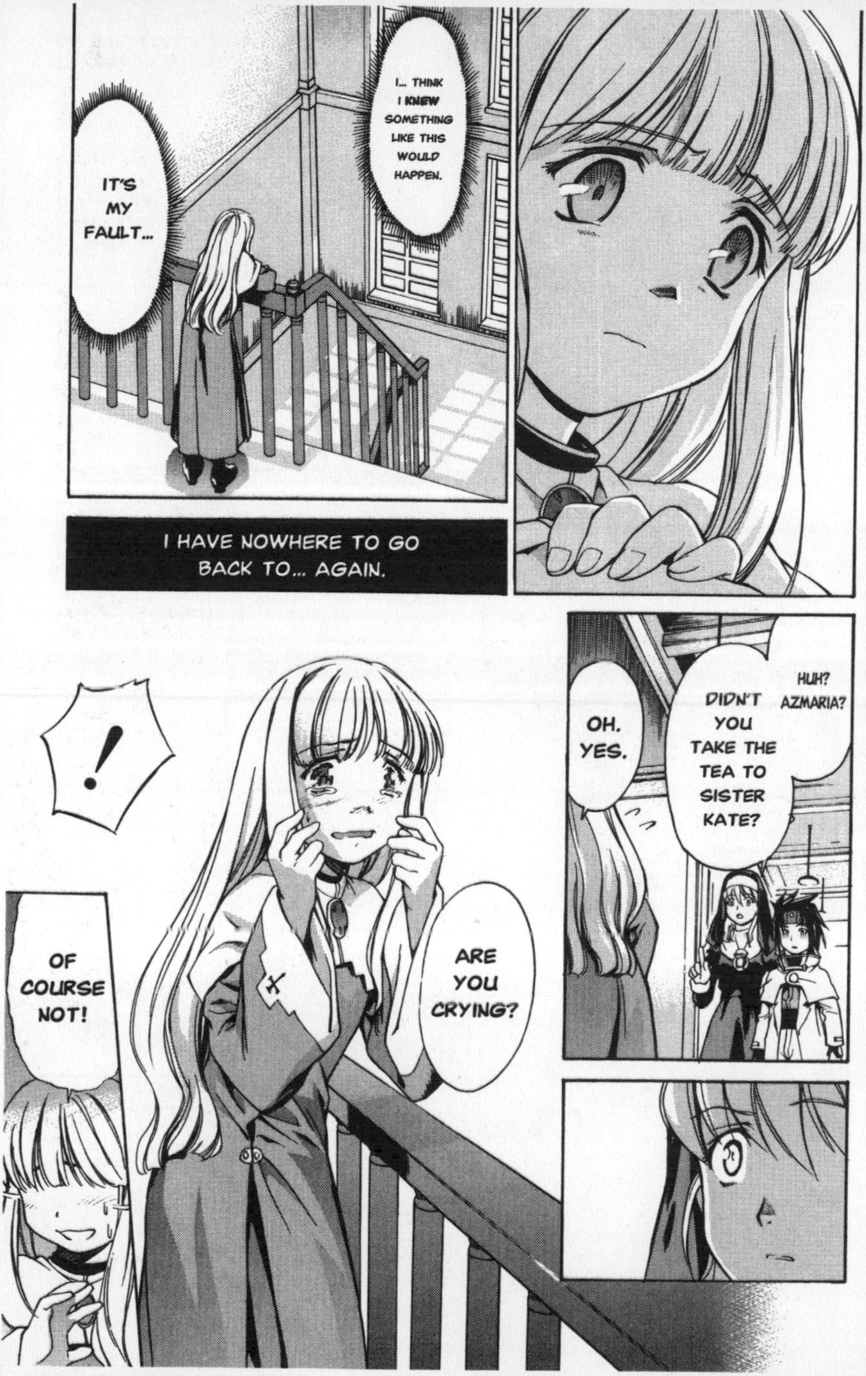
I... THINK I KNEW SOMETHING LIKE THIS WOULD HAPPEN.
IT'S MY FAULT...
I HAVE NOWHERE TO GO BACK TO... AGAIN.
HUH? AZMARIA?
DIDN'T YOU TAKE THE TEA TO SISTER KATE?
OH. YES.
!
ARE YOU CRYING?
OF COURSE NOT!

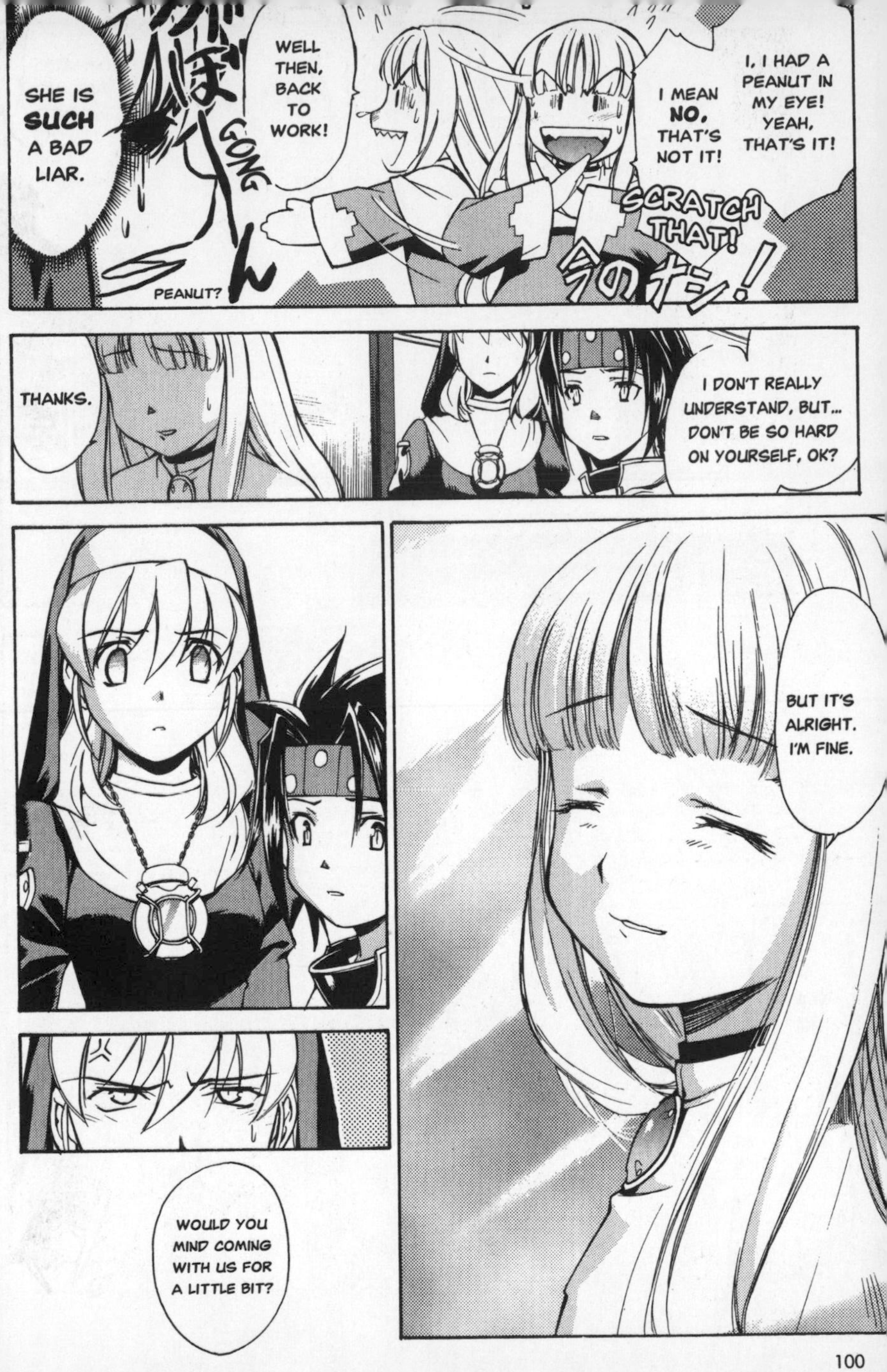
I, I HAD A PEANUT IN MY EYE! YEAH, THAT'S IT!
I MEAN NO, THAT'S NOT IT!
SCRATCH THAT!
今のナシ!
WELL THEN, BACK TO WORK!
GONG
PEANUT?
SHE IS SUCH A BAD LIAR.
I DON'T REALLY UNDERSTAND, BUT... DON'T BE SO HARD ON YOURSELF, OK?
THANKS.
BUT IT'S ALRIGHT. I'M FINE.
WOULD YOU MIND COMING WITH US FOR A LITTLE BIT?

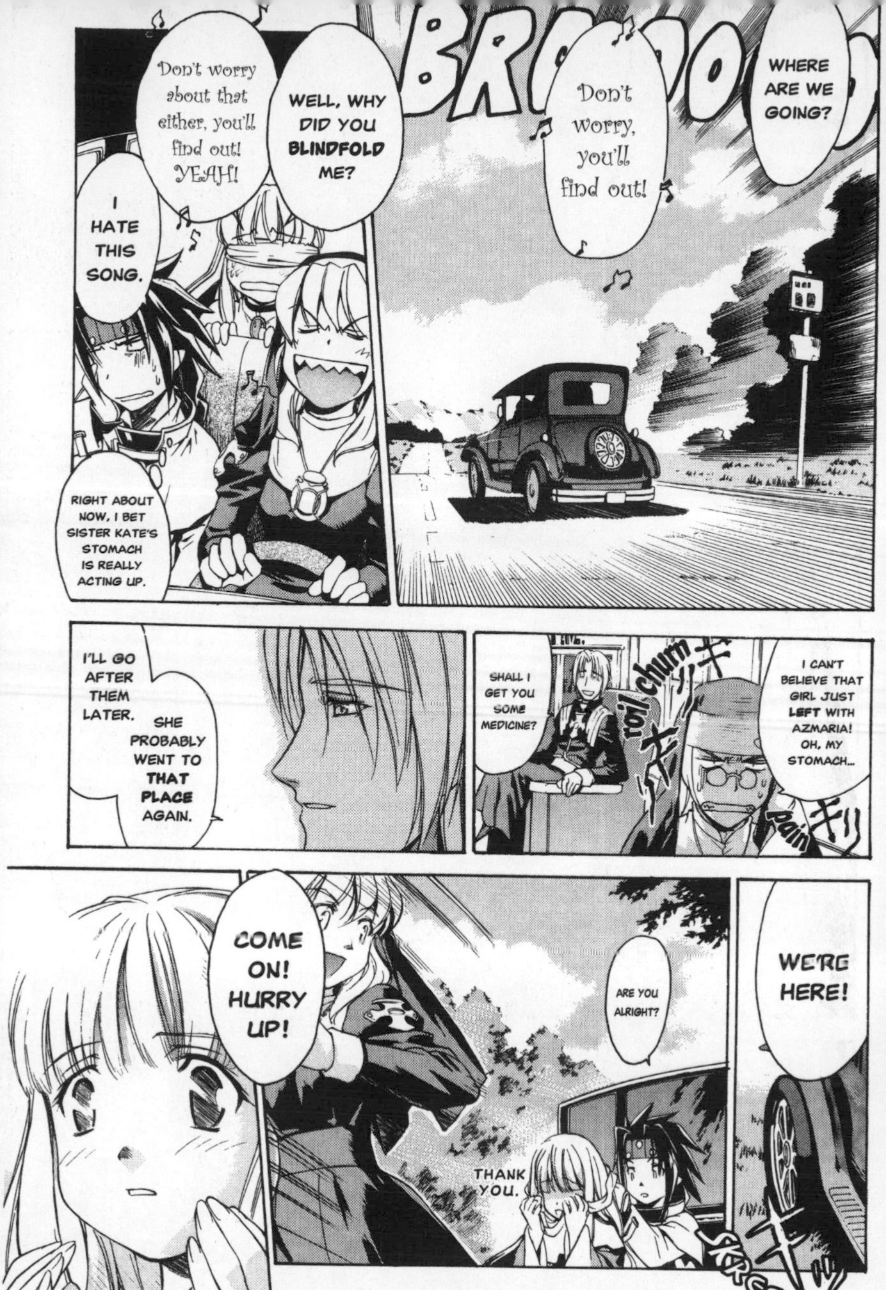
WHERE ARE WE GOING?
Don't worry, you'll find out!
WELL, WHY DID YOU BLINDFOLD ME?
Don't worry about that either, you'll find out! YEAH!
I HATE THIS SONG.
RIGHT ABOUT NOW, I BET SISTER KATE'S STOMACH IS REALLY ACTING UP.
I CAN'T BELIEVE THAT GIRL JUST LEFT WITH AZMARIA! OH, MY STOMACH...
roil churn
pain
SHALL I GET YOU SOME MEDICINE?
I'LL GO AFTER THEM LATER.
SHE PROBABLY WENT TO THAT PLACE AGAIN.
WE'RE HERE!
SKREE
ARE YOU ALRIGHT?
THANK YOU.
COME ON! HURRY UP!

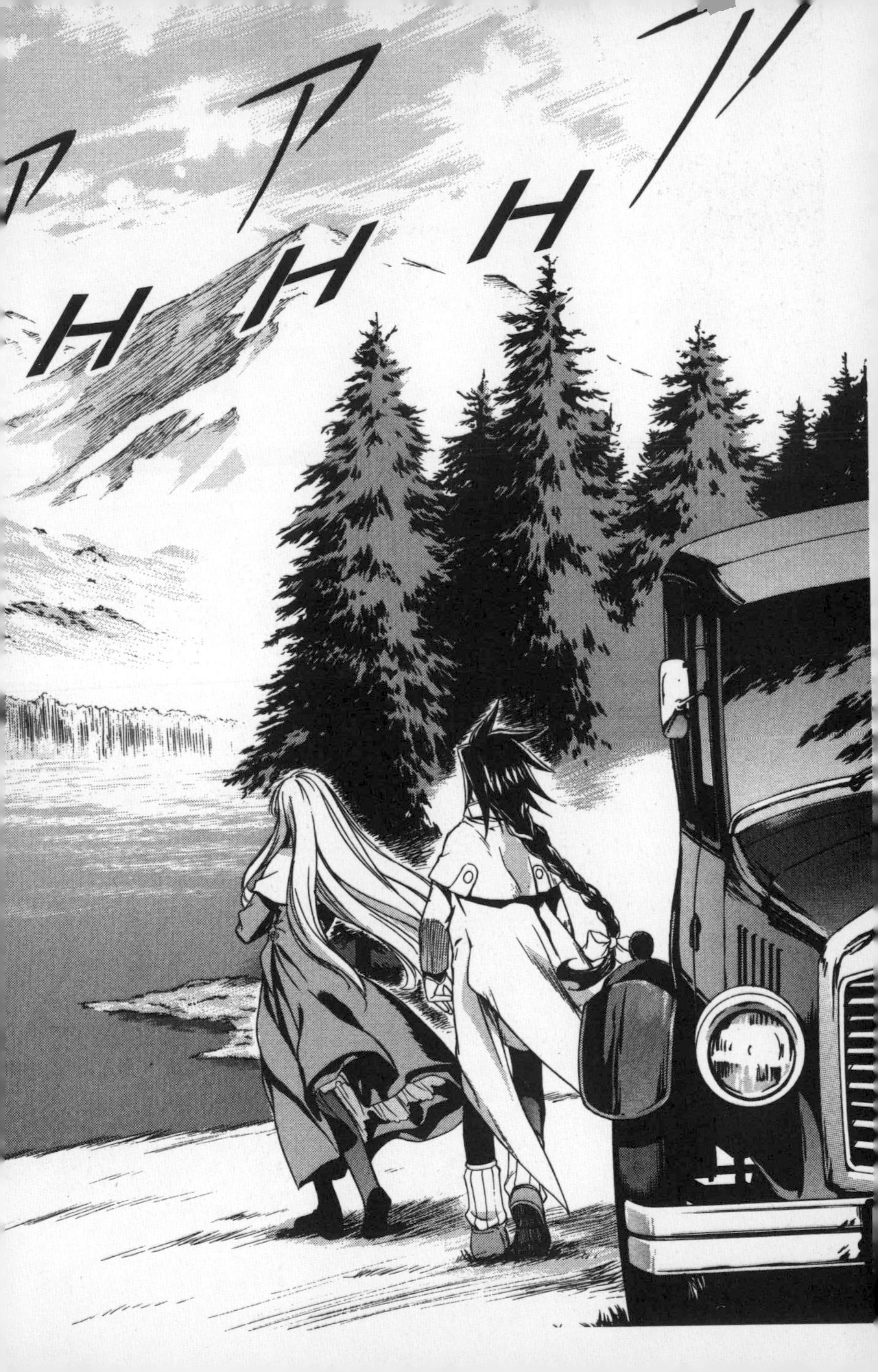

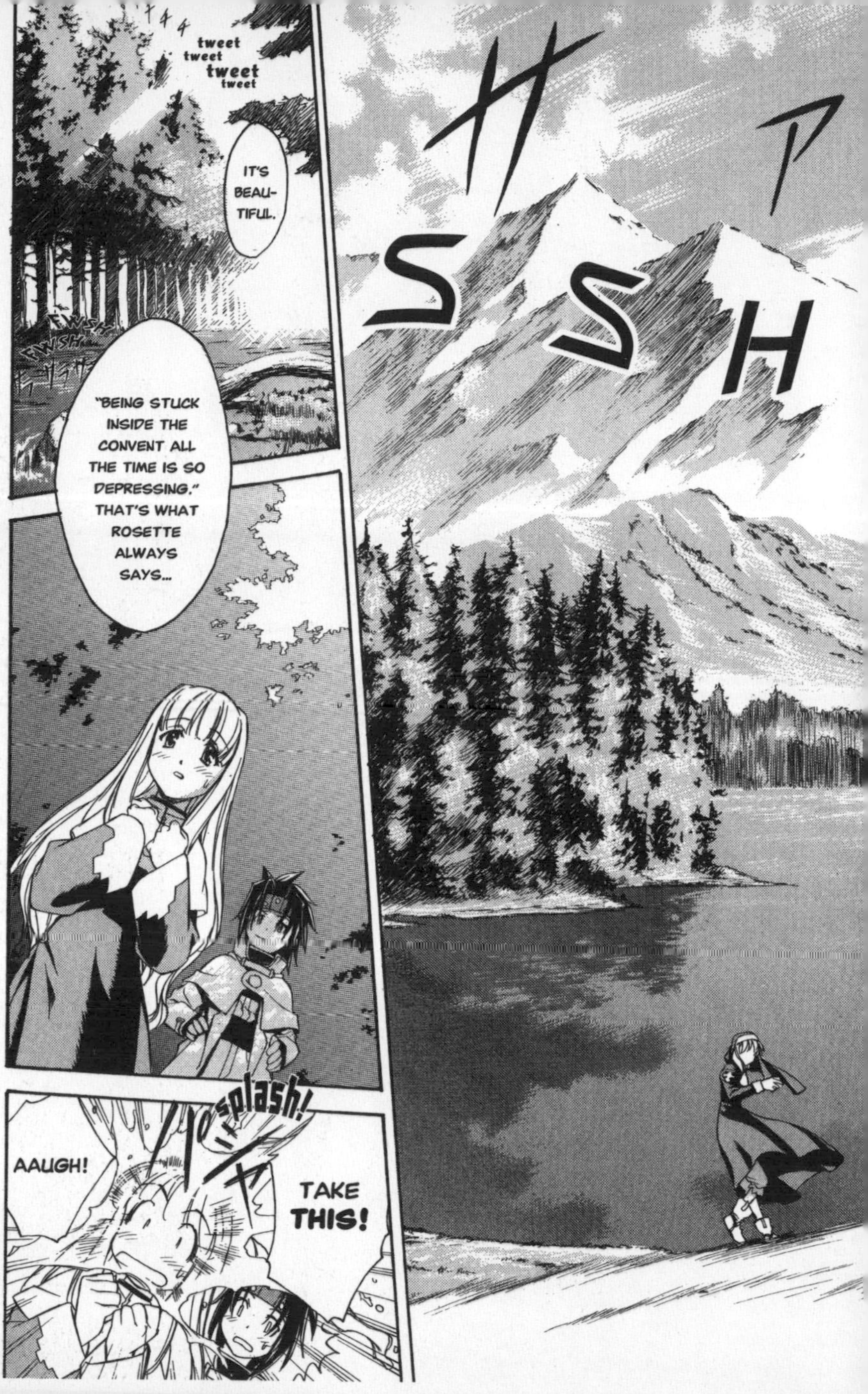
SSH
tweet
tweet
tweet
tweet
IT'S BEAUTIFUL.
FWSH
FWSH
"BEING STUCK INSIDE THE CONVENT ALL THE TIME IS SO DEPRESSING." THAT'S WHAT ROSETTE ALWAYS SAYS...
splash!
TAKE THIS!
AAUGH!

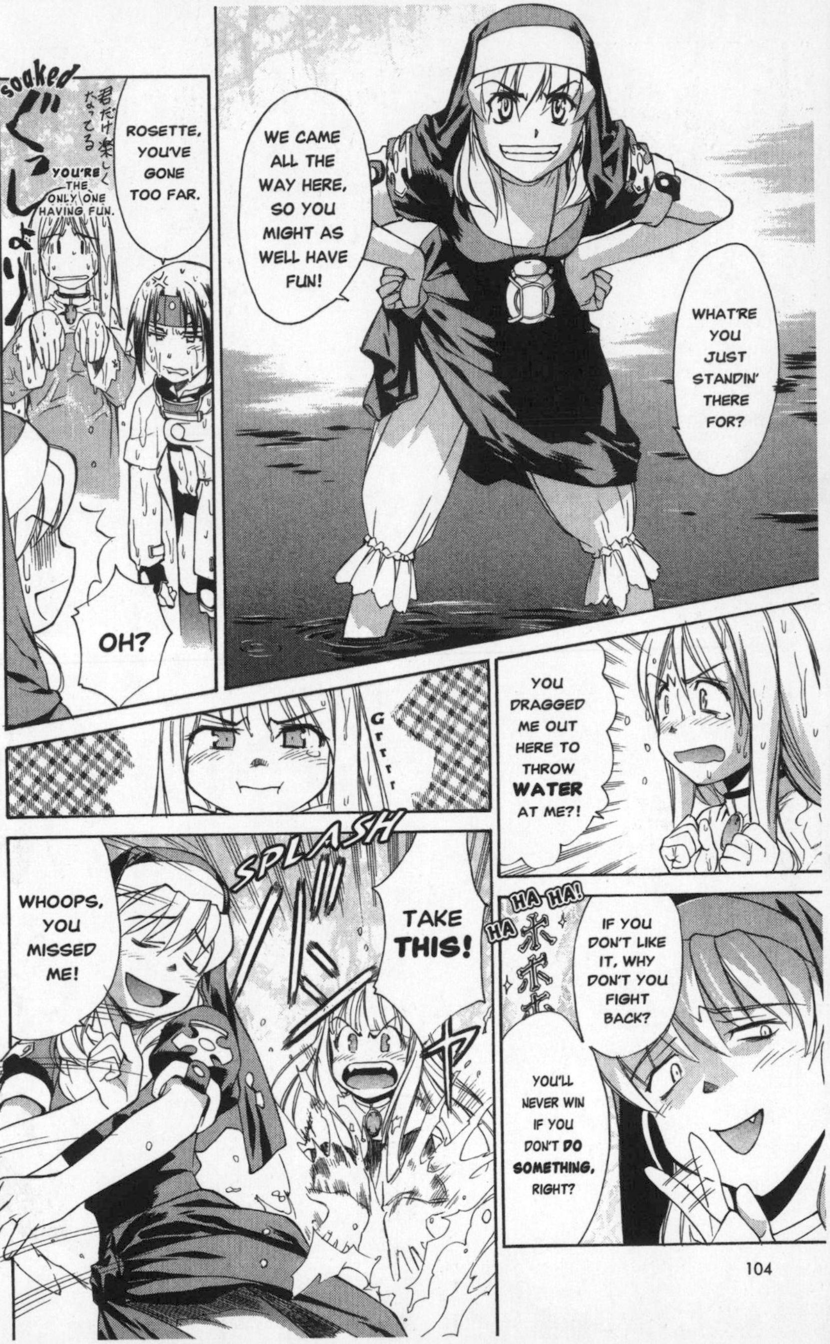
WHAT'RE YOU JUST STANDIN' THERE FOR?
WE CAME ALL THE WAY HERE, SO YOU MIGHT AS WELL HAVE FUN!
ROSETTE, YOU'VE GONE TOO FAR.
soaked
君だけ楽しくなってる
YOU'RE THE ONLY ONE HAVING FUN.
OH?
YOU DRAGGED ME OUT HERE TO THROW WATER AT ME?!
Grrrr
HA HA! HA
ホホホ
IF YOU DON'T LIKE IT, WHY DON'T YOU FIGHT BACK?
YOU'LL NEVER WIN IF YOU DON'T DO SOMETHING, RIGHT?
TAKE THIS!
SPLASH
WHOOPS, YOU MISSED ME!

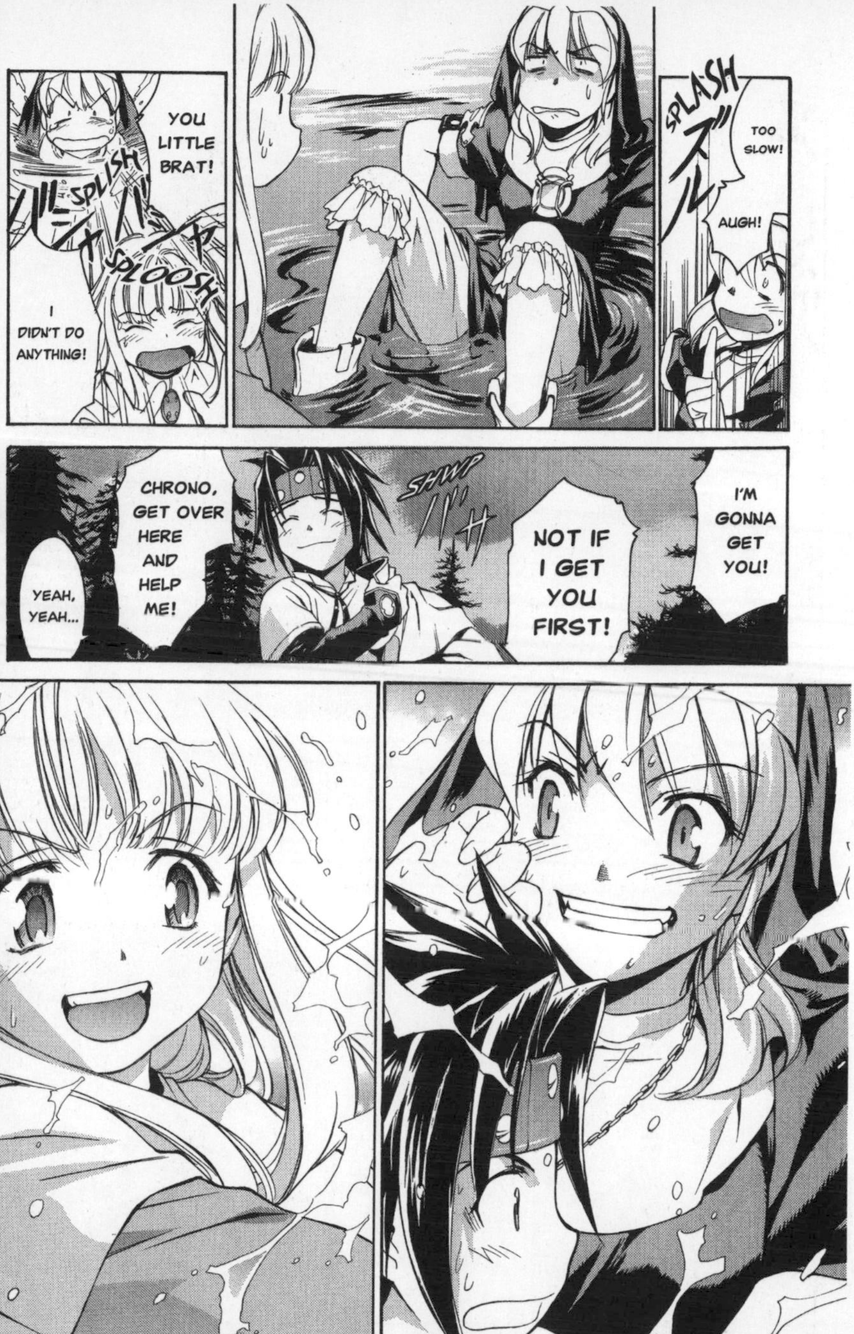
SPLASH
TOO SLOW!
AUGH!
YOU LITTLE BRAT!
SPLISH
SPLOOSH
I DIDN'T DO ANYTHING!
I'M GONNA GET YOU!
NOT IF I GET YOU FIRST!
SHWP
CHRONO, GET OVER HERE AND HELP ME!
YEAH, YEAH...

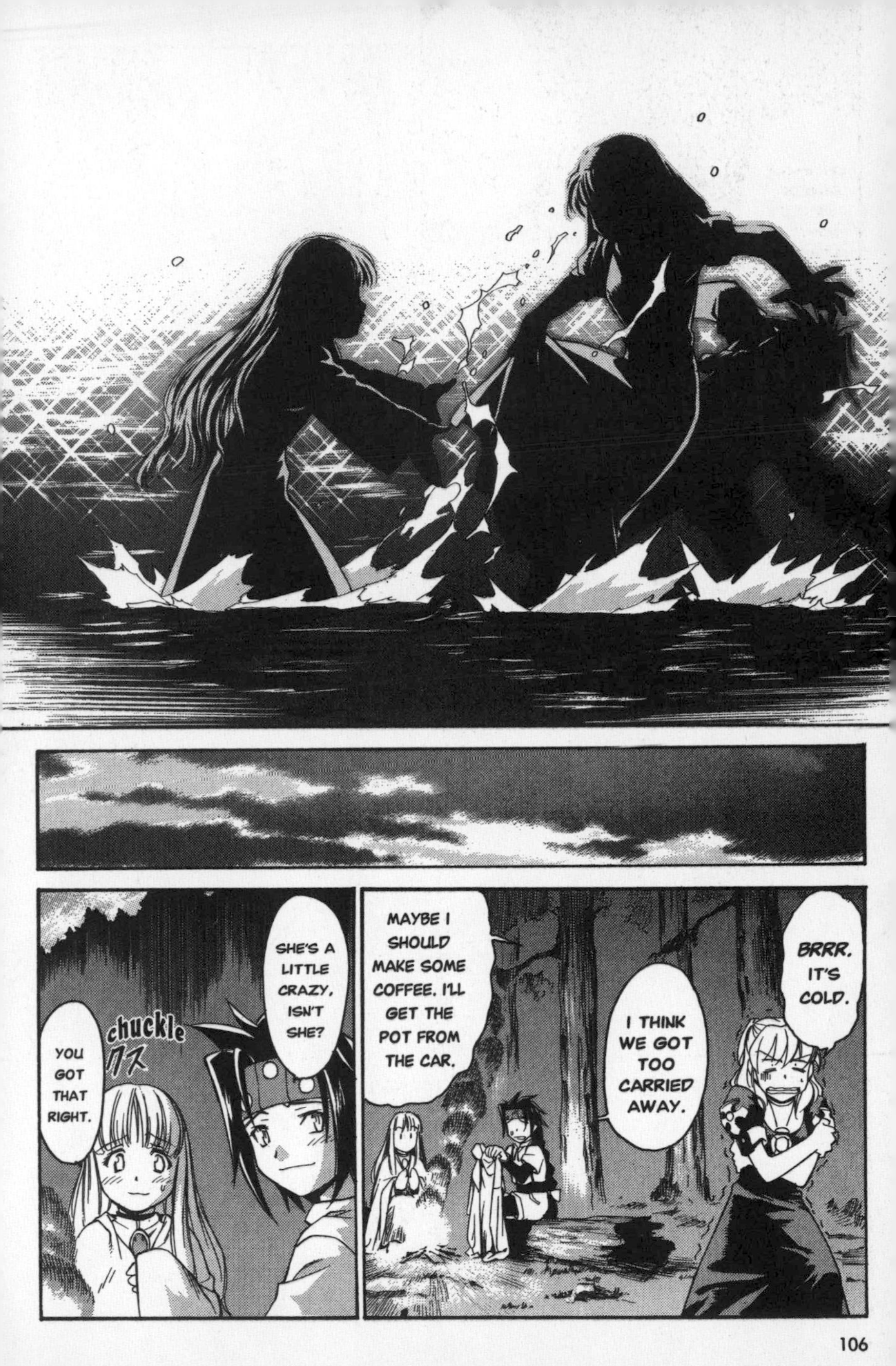
BRRR. IT'S COLD.
I THINK WE GOT TOO CARRIED AWAY.
MAYBE I SHOULD MAKE SOME COFFEE. I'LL GET THE POT FROM THE CAR.
SHE'S A LITTLE CRAZY, ISN'T SHE?
chuckle クス
YOU GOT THAT RIGHT.

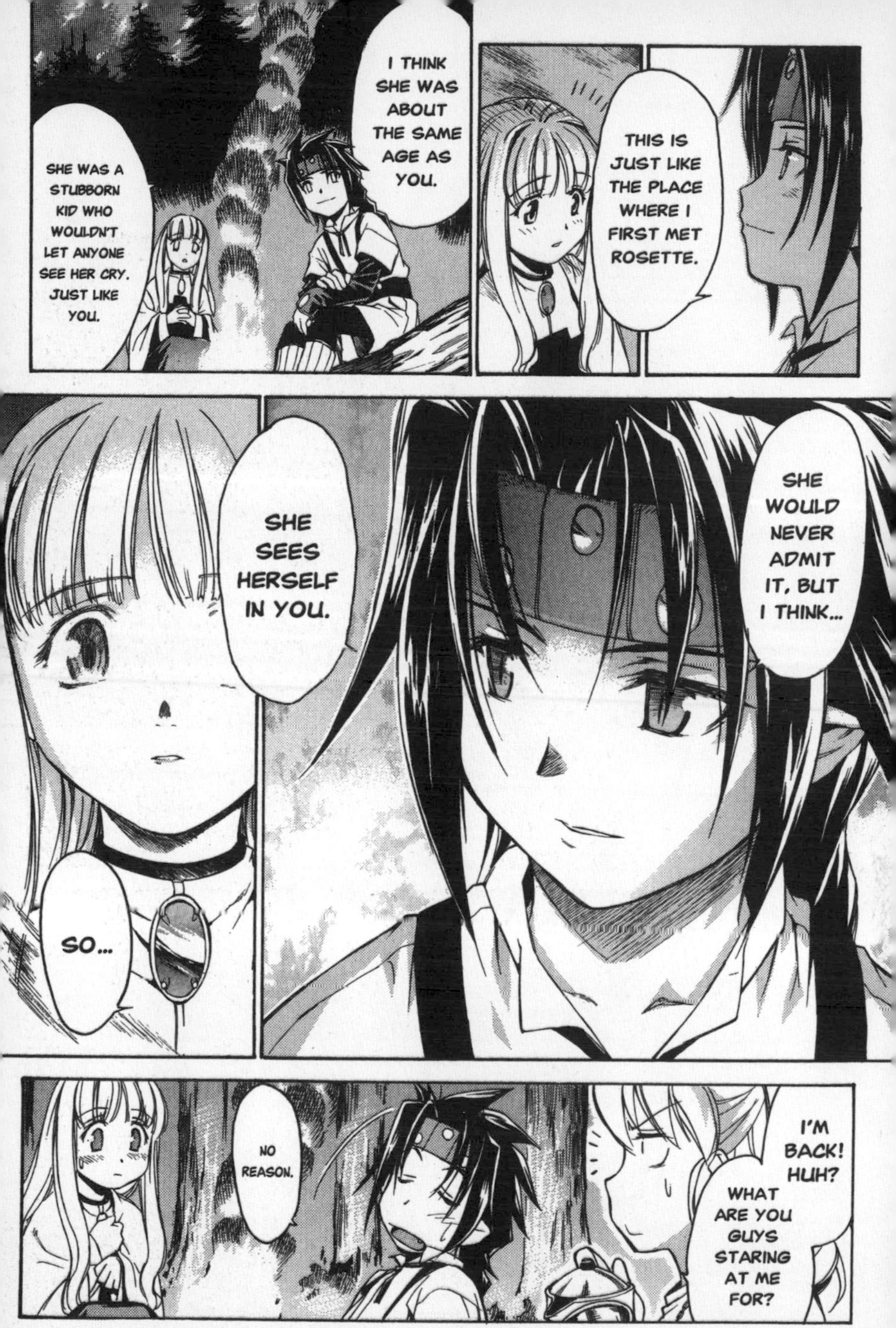
THIS IS JUST LIKE THE PLACE WHERE I FIRST MET ROSETTE.
I THINK SHE WAS ABOUT THE SAME AGE AS YOU.
SHE WAS A STUBBORN KID WHO WOULDN'T LET ANYONE SEE HER CRY. JUST LIKE YOU.
SHE WOULD NEVER ADMIT IT, BUT I THINK...
SHE SEES HERSELF IN YOU.
SO...
I'M BACK! HUH?
WHAT ARE YOU GUYS STARING AT ME FOR?
NO REASON.

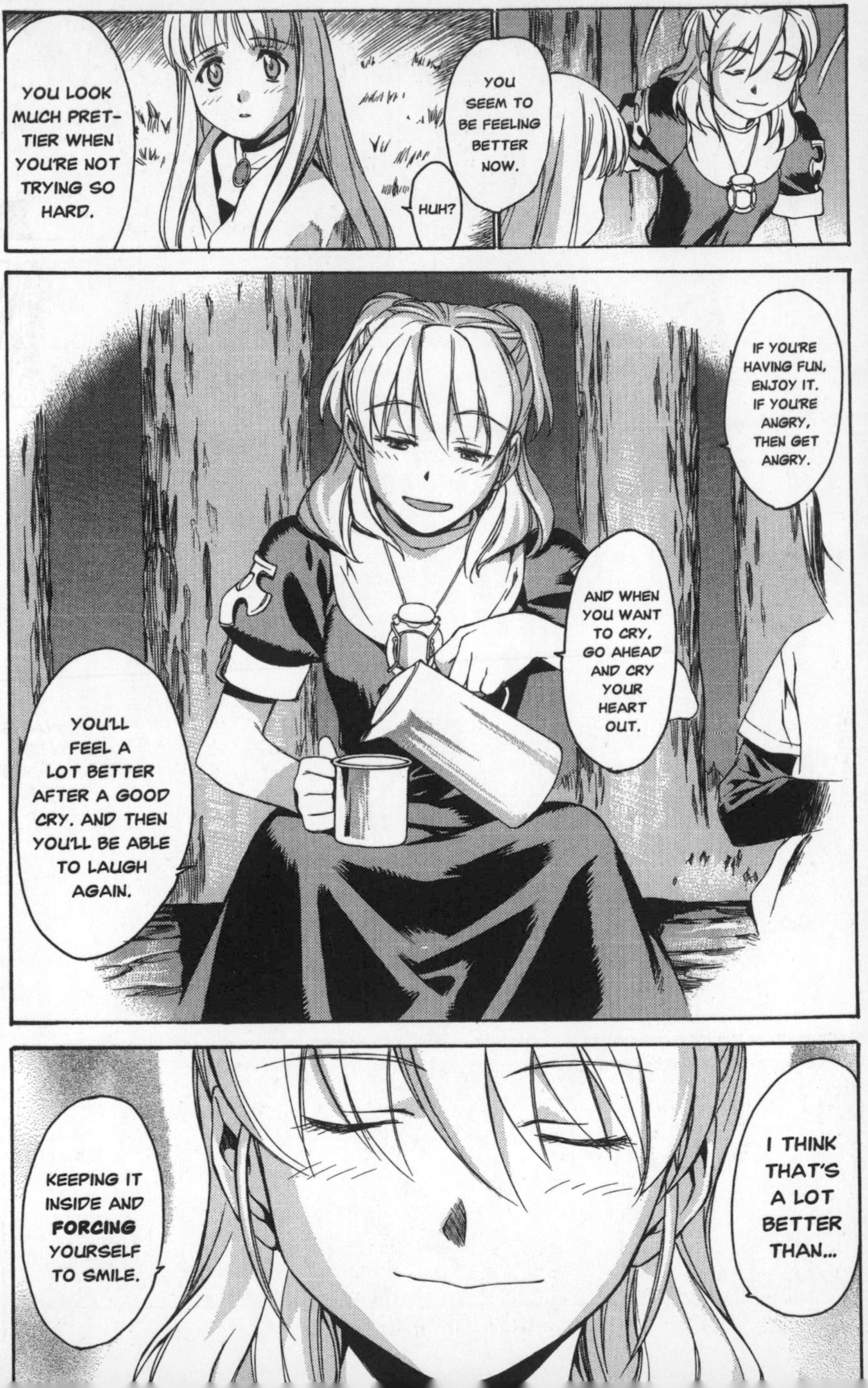
YOU SEEM TO BE FEELING BETTER NOW.
HUH?
YOU LOOK MUCH PRET-TIER WHEN YOU'RE NOT TRYING SO HARD.
IF YOU'RE HAVING FUN, ENJOY IT. IF YOU'RE ANGRY, THEN GET ANGRY.
AND WHEN YOU WANT TO CRY, GO AHEAD AND CRY YOUR HEART OUT.
YOU'LL FEEL A LOT BETTER AFTER A GOOD CRY. AND THEN YOU'LL BE ABLE TO LAUGH AGAIN.
I THINK THAT'S A LOT BETTER THAN...
KEEPING IT INSIDE AND **FORCING** YOURSELF TO SMILE.

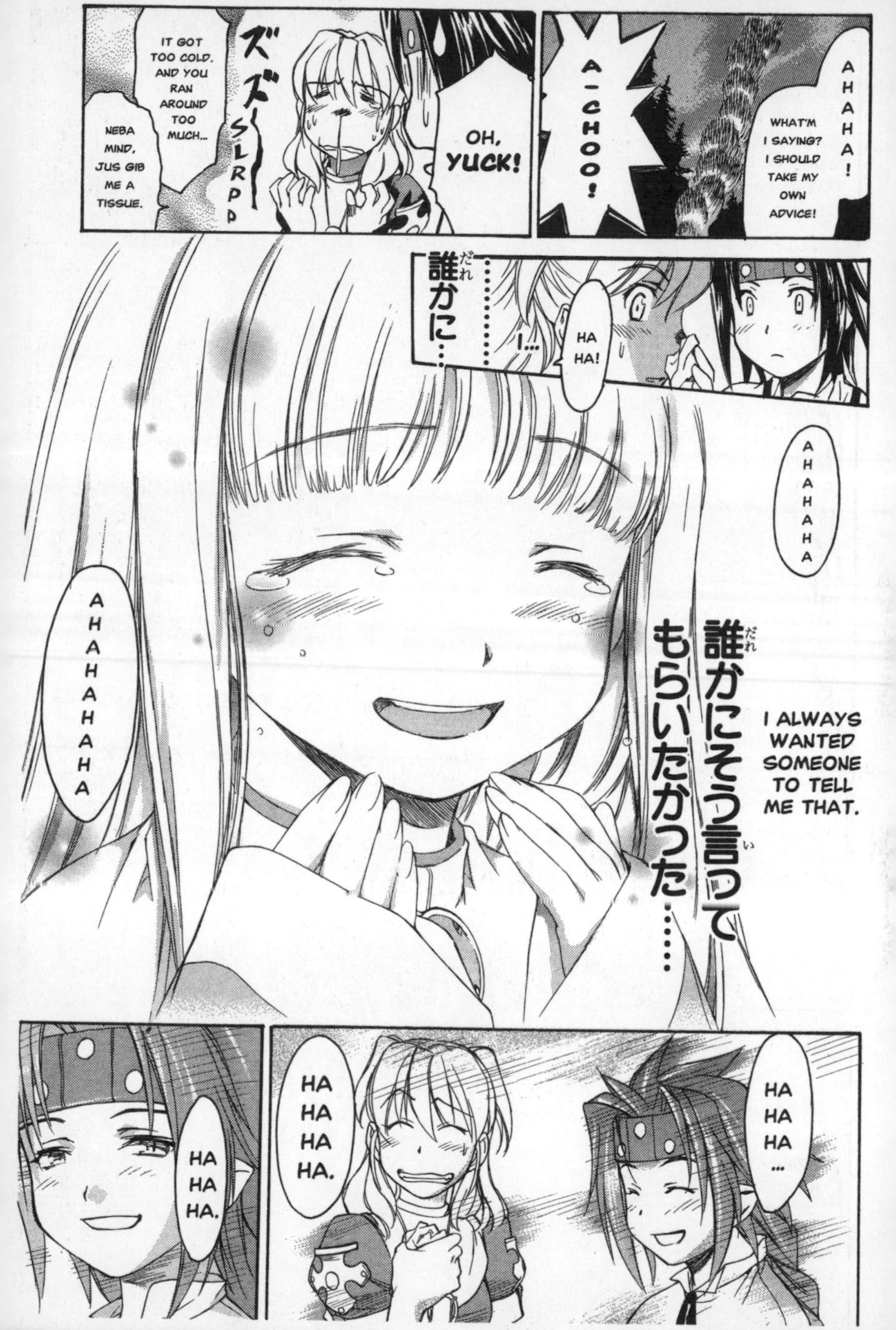
AHAHAHA!
WHAT'M I SAYING? I SHOULD TAKE MY OWN ADVICE!
A-CHOO!
OH, YUCK!
ズズー
SLRPP
IT GOT TOO COLD. AND YOU RAN AROUND TOO MUCH...
NEBA MIND, JUS GIB ME A TISSUE.
HA HA!
I...
誰かに……
AHAHAHAHA
誰かにそう言ってもらいたかった……
I ALWAYS WANTED SOMEONE TO TELL ME THAT.
AHAHAHAHAHA
HA HA HA ...
HA HA HA HA.
HA HA HA.

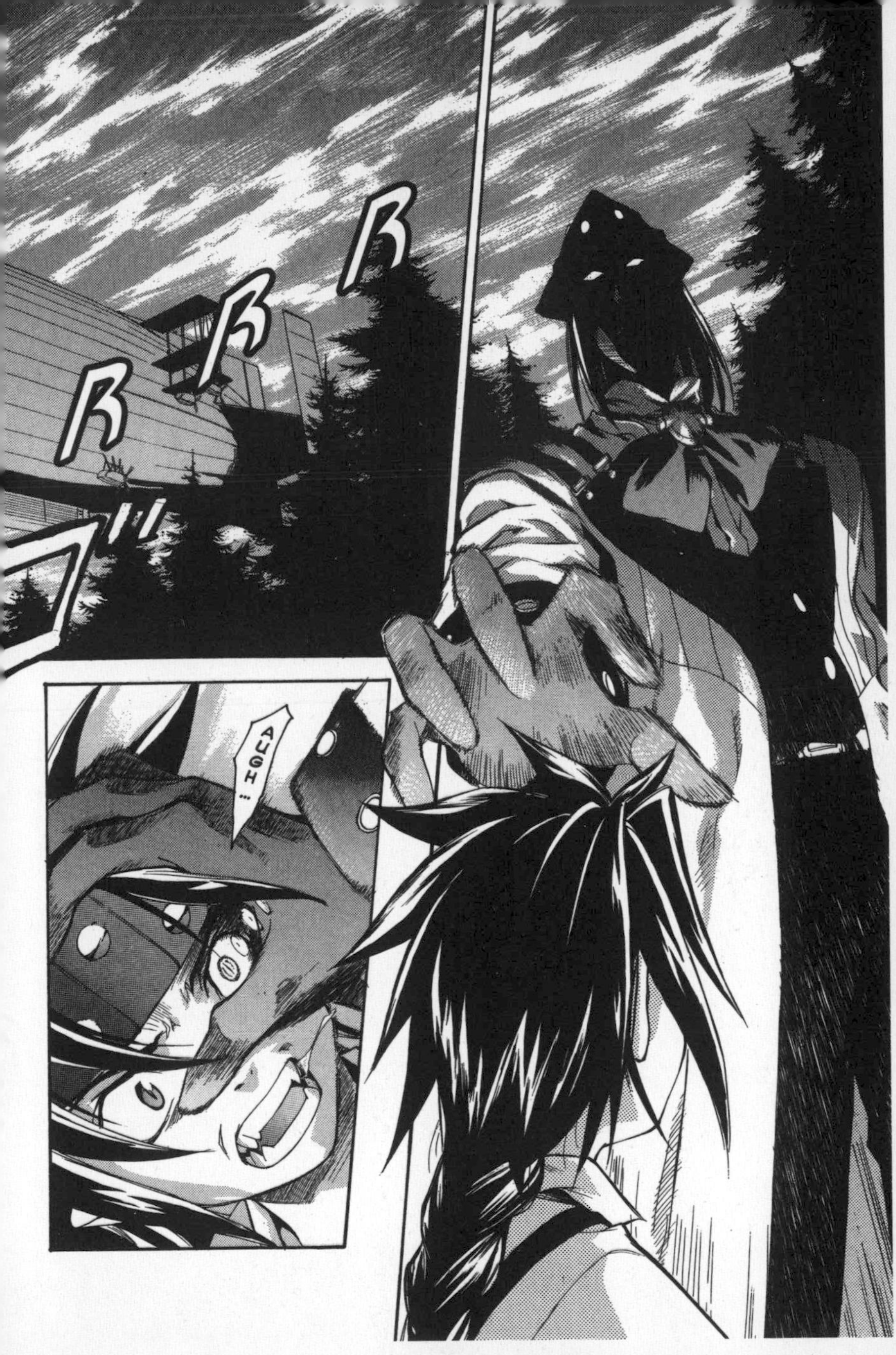
RRR
AUGH...

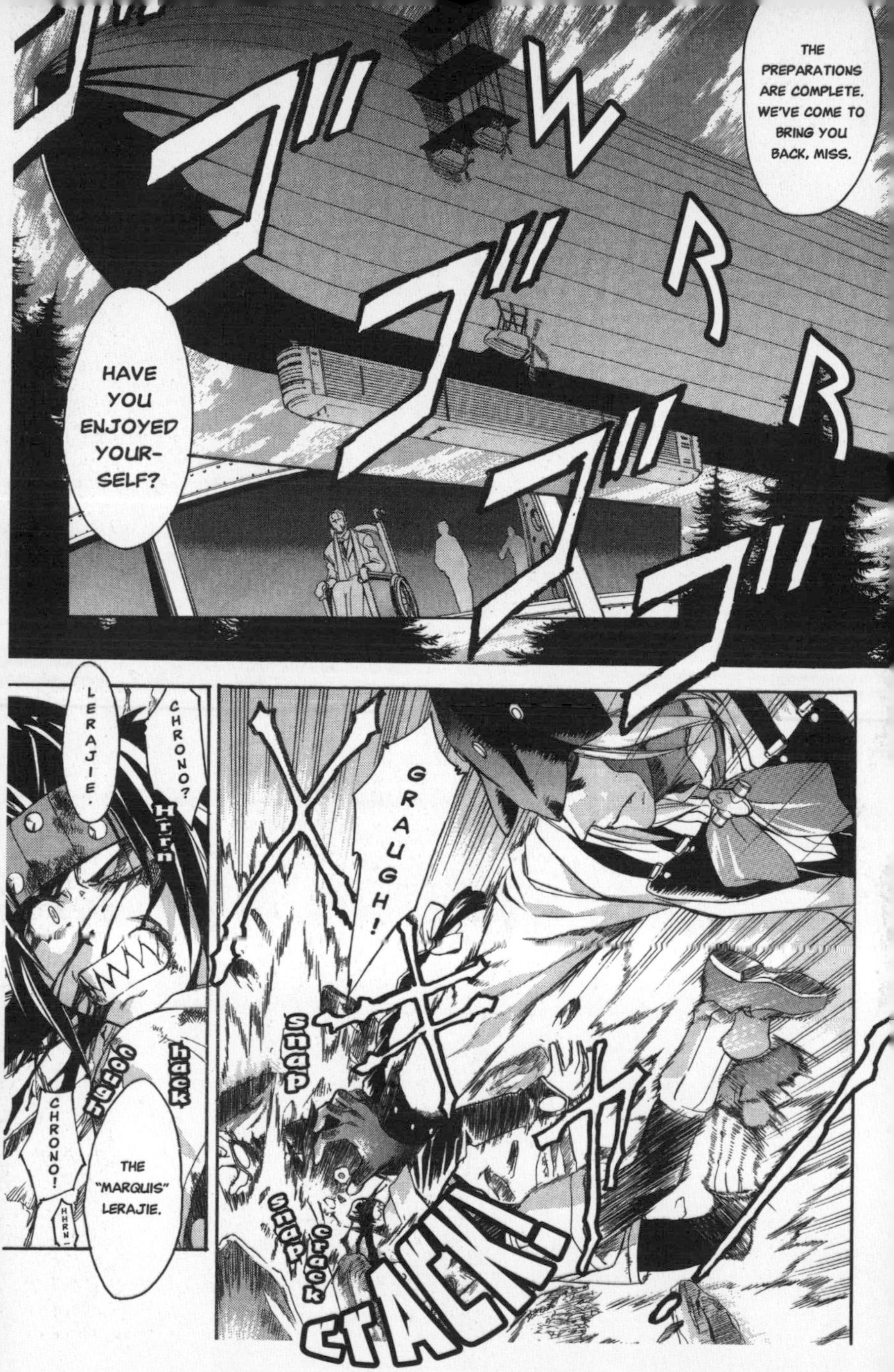
THE PREPARATIONS ARE COMPLETE. WE'VE COME TO BRING YOU BACK, MISS.
WRRR
HAVE YOU ENJOYED YOUR-SELF?
GRAUGH!
snap
crack
snap
CTACK!
CHRONO?
LERAJIE.
Hrrn
hack
cough
THE "MARQUIS" LERAJIE.
CHRONO!
HHRN-

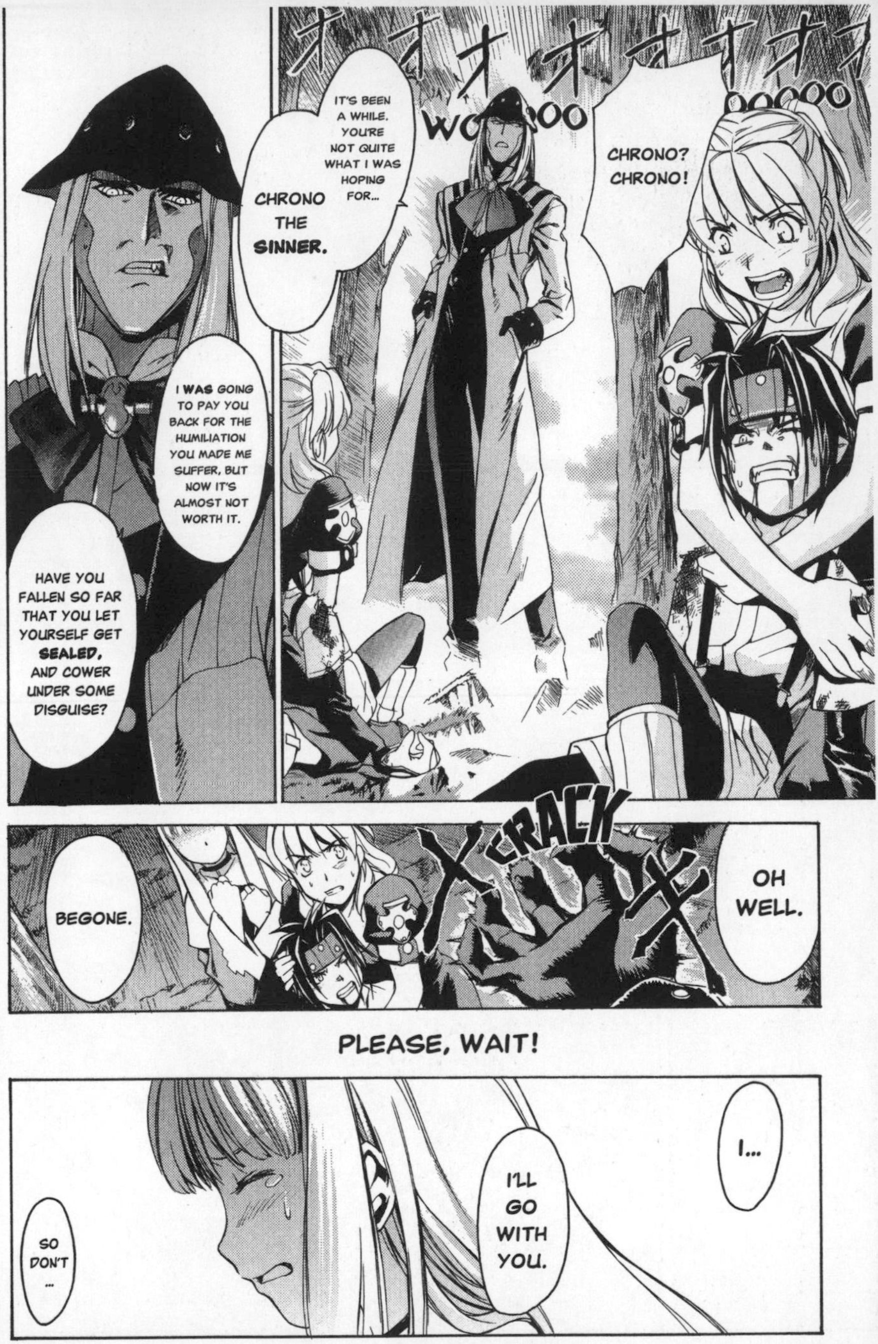
オオオオオオオオ
OOOOO
WO
OO
CHRONO? CHRONO!
IT'S BEEN A WHILE. YOU'RE NOT QUITE WHAT I WAS HOPING FOR...
CHRONO THE SINNER.
I WAS GOING TO PAY YOU BACK FOR THE HUMILIATION YOU MADE ME SUFFER, BUT NOW IT'S ALMOST NOT WORTH IT.
HAVE YOU FALLEN SO FAR THAT YOU LET YOURSELF GET SEALED, AND COWER UNDER SOME DISGUISE?
OH WELL.
CRACK
BEGONE.
PLEASE, WAIT!
I...
I'LL GO WITH YOU.
SO DON'T ...

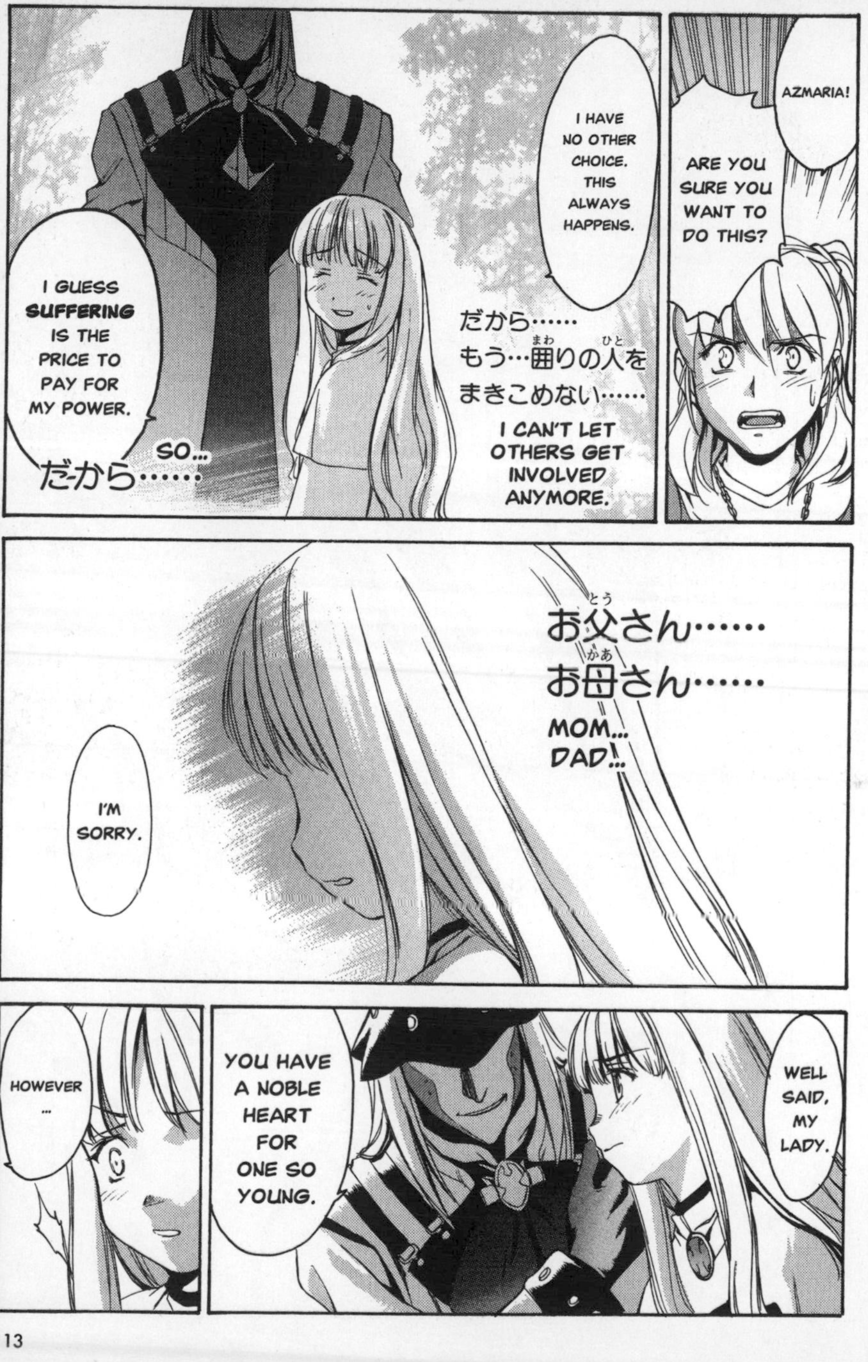
AZMARIA!
ARE YOU SURE YOU WANT TO DO THIS?
I HAVE NO OTHER CHOICE. THIS ALWAYS HAPPENS.
I GUESS **SUFFERING** IS THE PRICE TO PAY FOR MY POWER.
SO...
だ-から……
だから……
もう…囲りの人をまきこめない……
I CAN'T LET OTHERS GET INVOLVED ANYMORE.
お父さん……
お母さん……
MOM... DAD!...
I'M SORRY.
WELL SAID, MY LADY.
YOU HAVE A NOBLE HEART FOR ONE SO YOUNG.
HOWEVER...

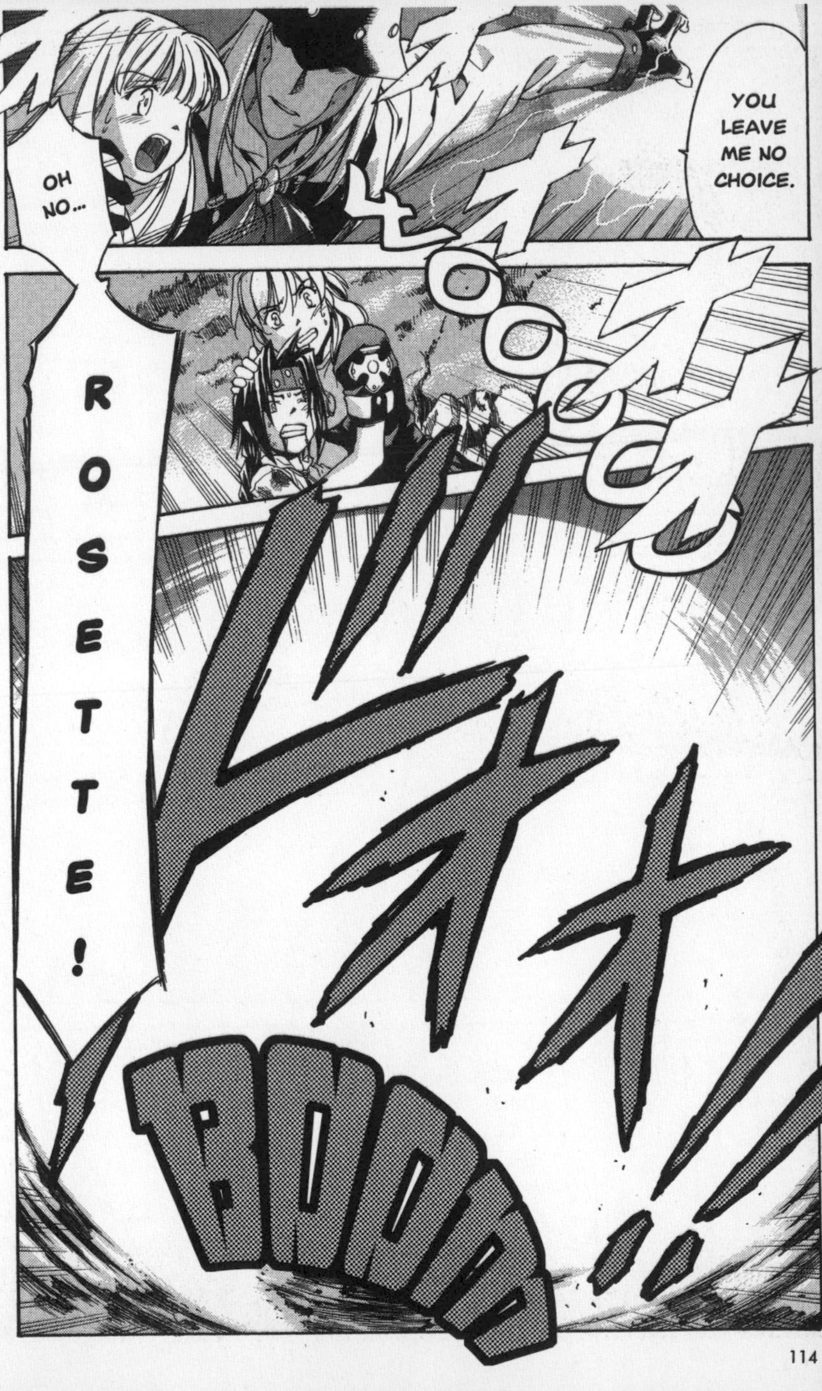
YOU LEAVE ME NO CHOICE.
OH NO...
ROSETTE!
BOOM!!

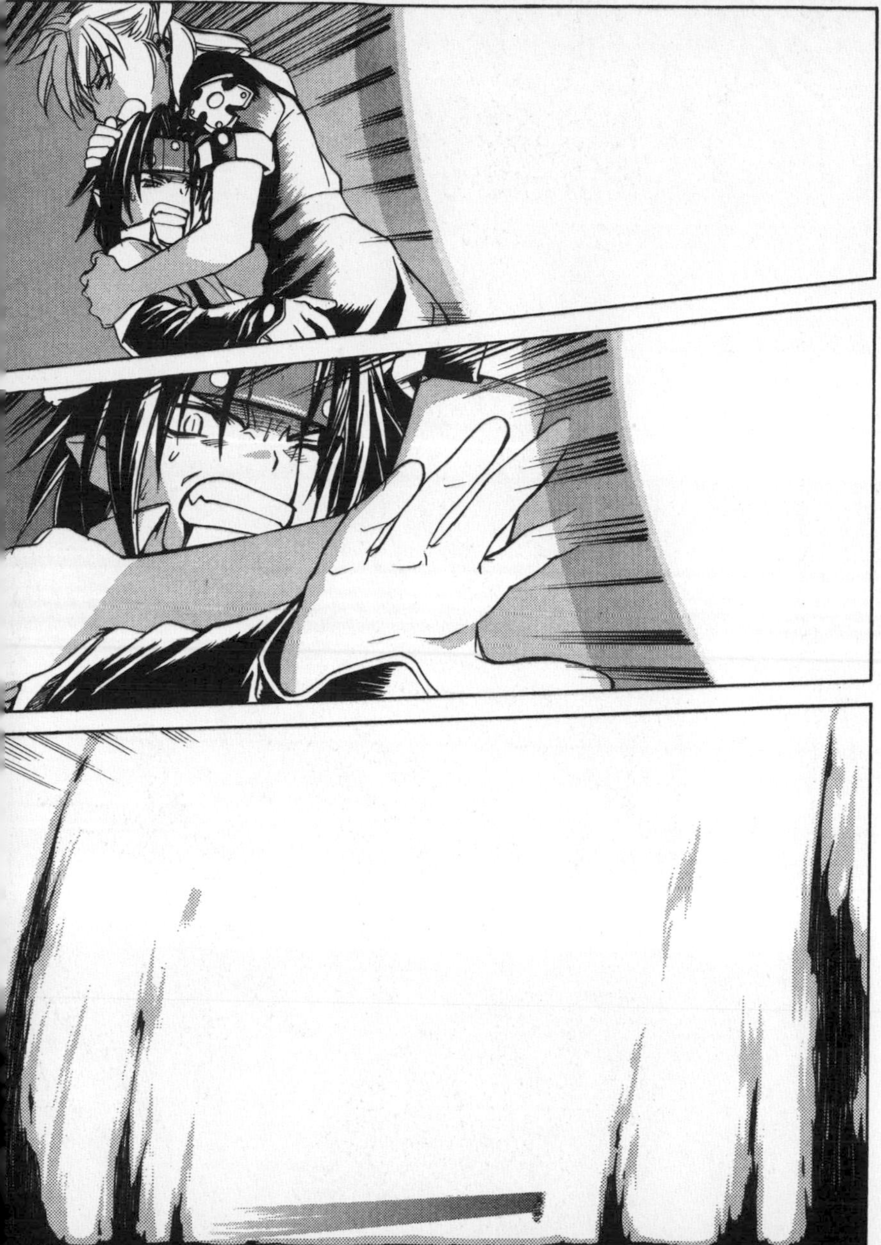

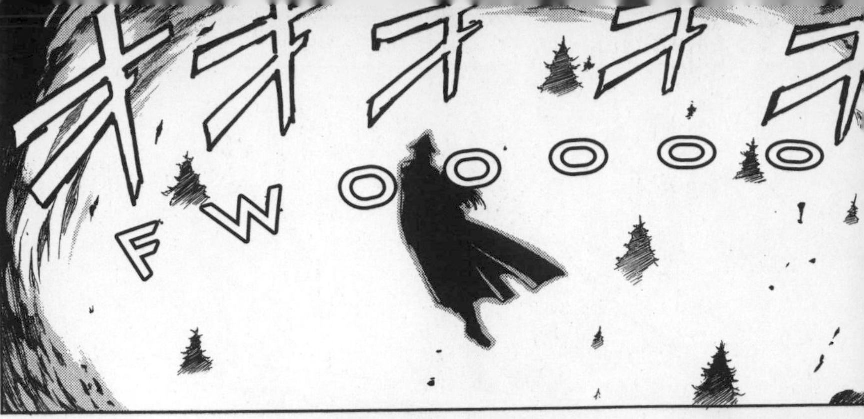
FWOOOOOO

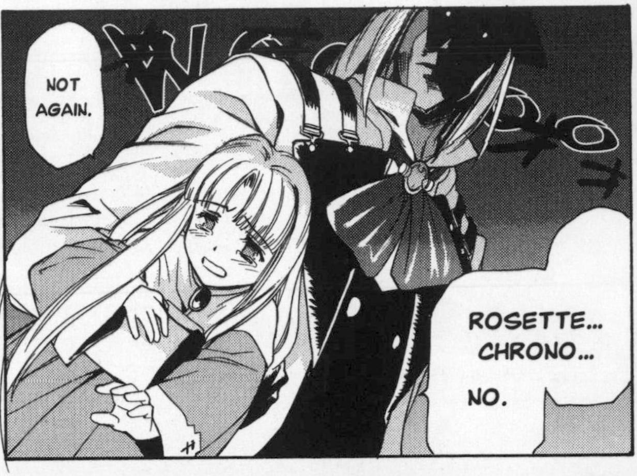
NOT AGAIN.
ROSETTE... CHRONO...
NO.

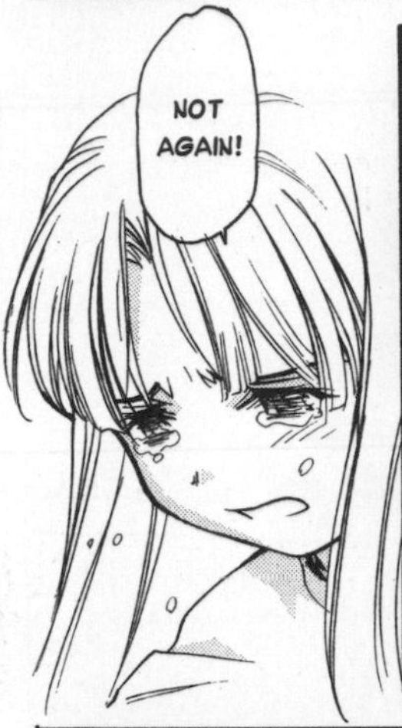
NOT AGAIN!

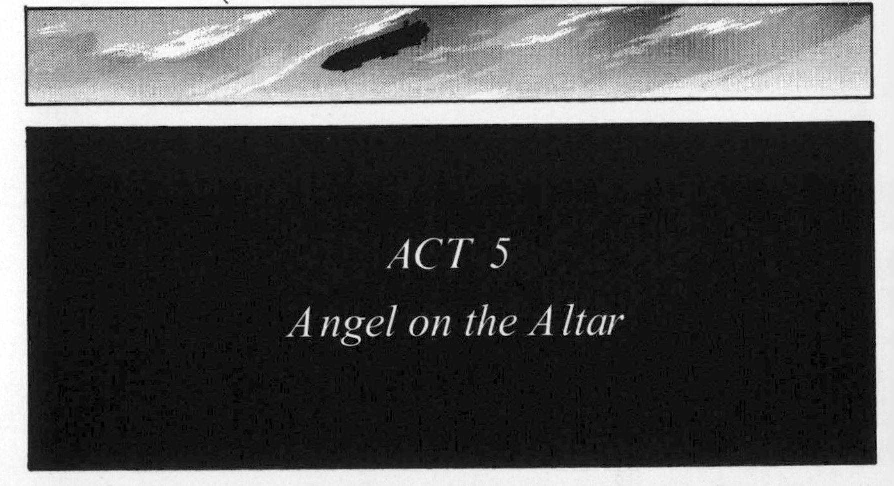

ACT 5

Angel on the Altar

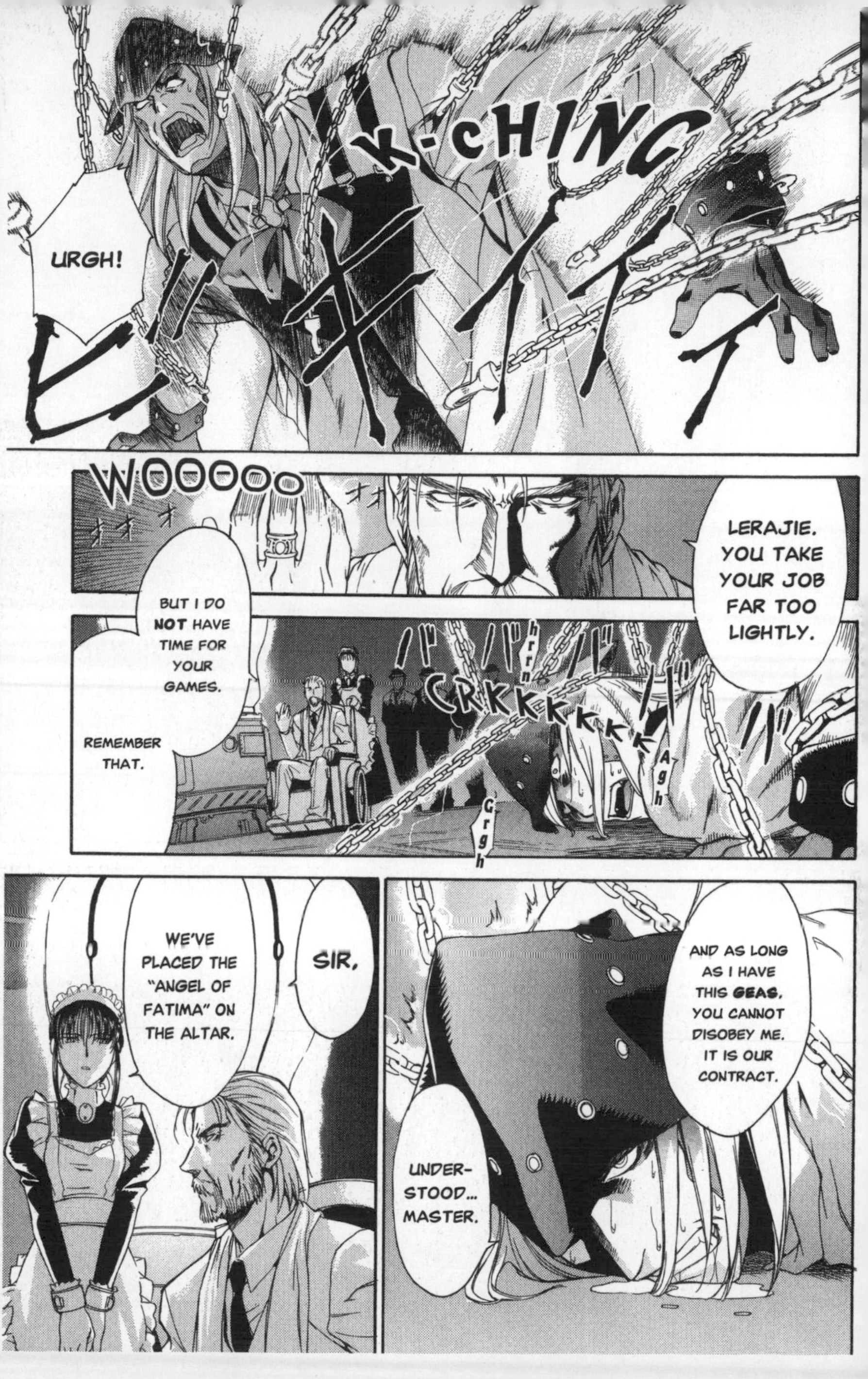
K-CHING
URGH!
WOOOOO
LERAJIE. YOU TAKE YOUR JOB FAR TOO LIGHTLY.
BUT I DO NOT HAVE TIME FOR YOUR GAMES.
hrrn
CRKKKKKKK
Agh
Grgh
REMEMBER THAT.
AND AS LONG AS I HAVE THIS GEAS, YOU CANNOT DISOBEY ME. IT IS OUR CONTRACT.
UNDER-STOOD... MASTER.
SIR,
WE'VE PLACED THE "ANGEL OF FATIMA" ON THE ALTAR.

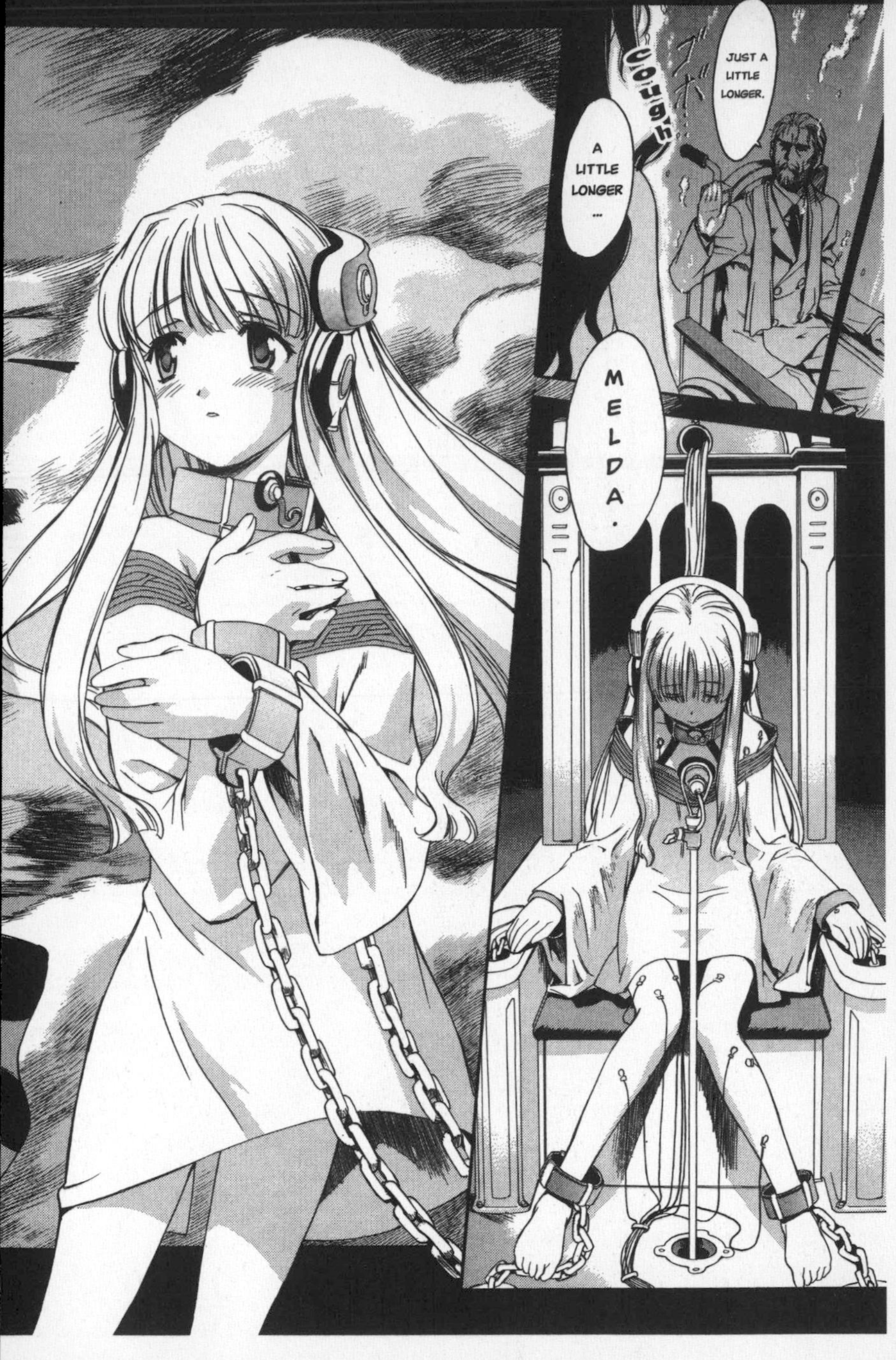
JUST A LITTLE LONGER.
Cough
A LITTLE LONGER ...
MELDA.

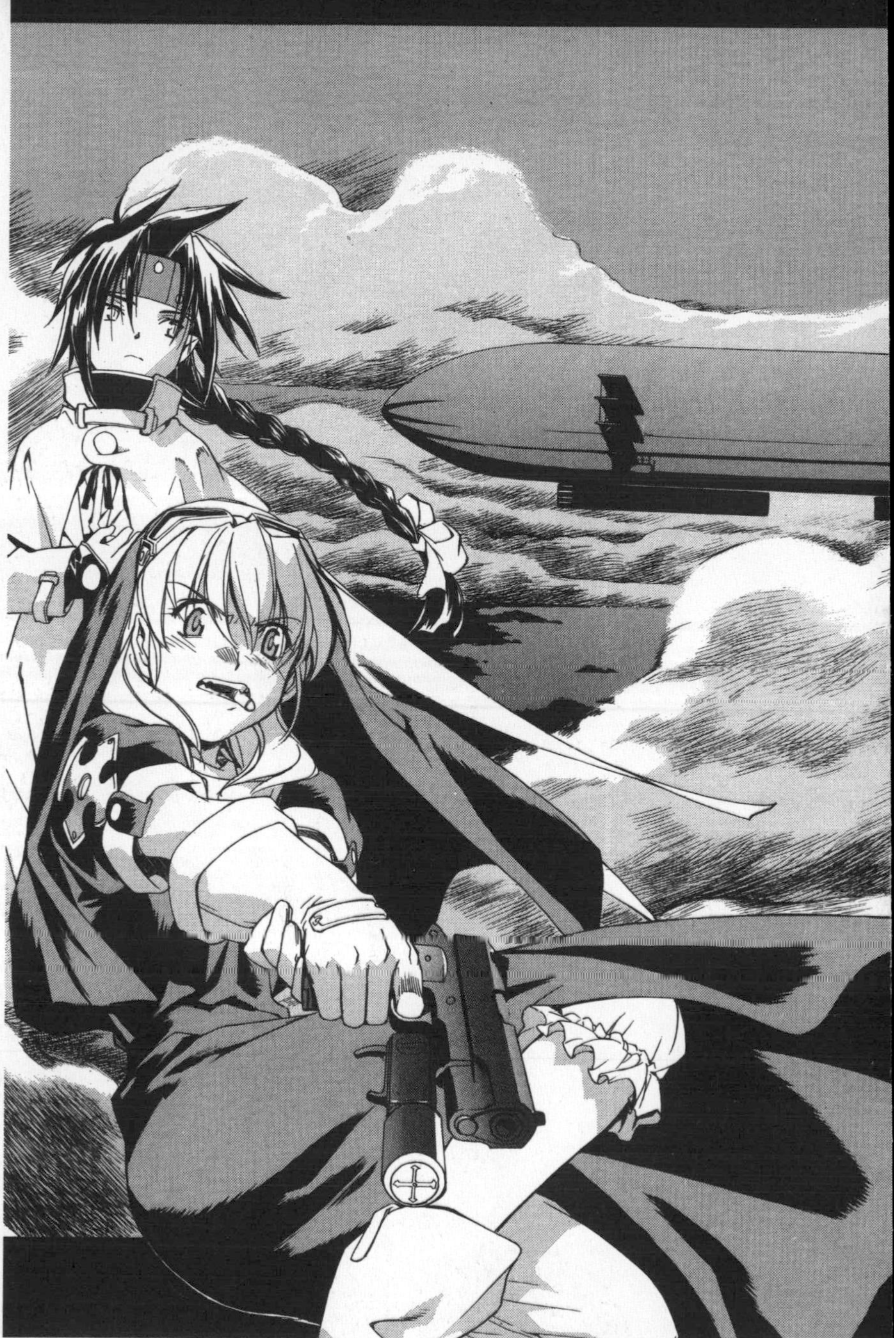

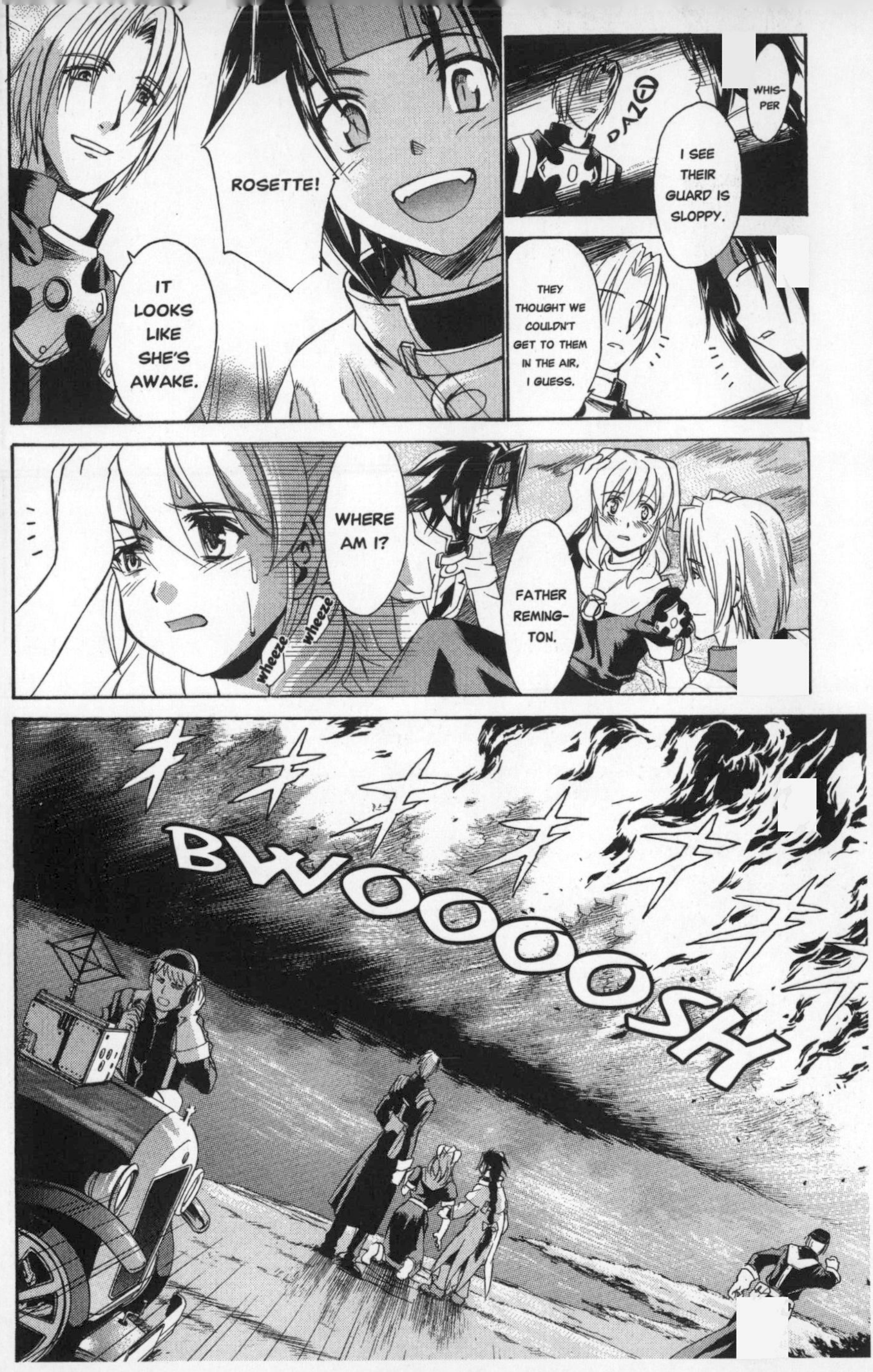
WHISPER
DAZE
I SEE THEIR GUARD IS SLOPPY.
THEY THOUGHT WE COULDN'T GET TO THEM IN THE AIR, I GUESS.
ROSETTE!
IT LOOKS LIKE SHE'S AWAKE.
FATHER REMINGTON.
WHERE AM I?
wheeze wheeze
BWOOOOOSH

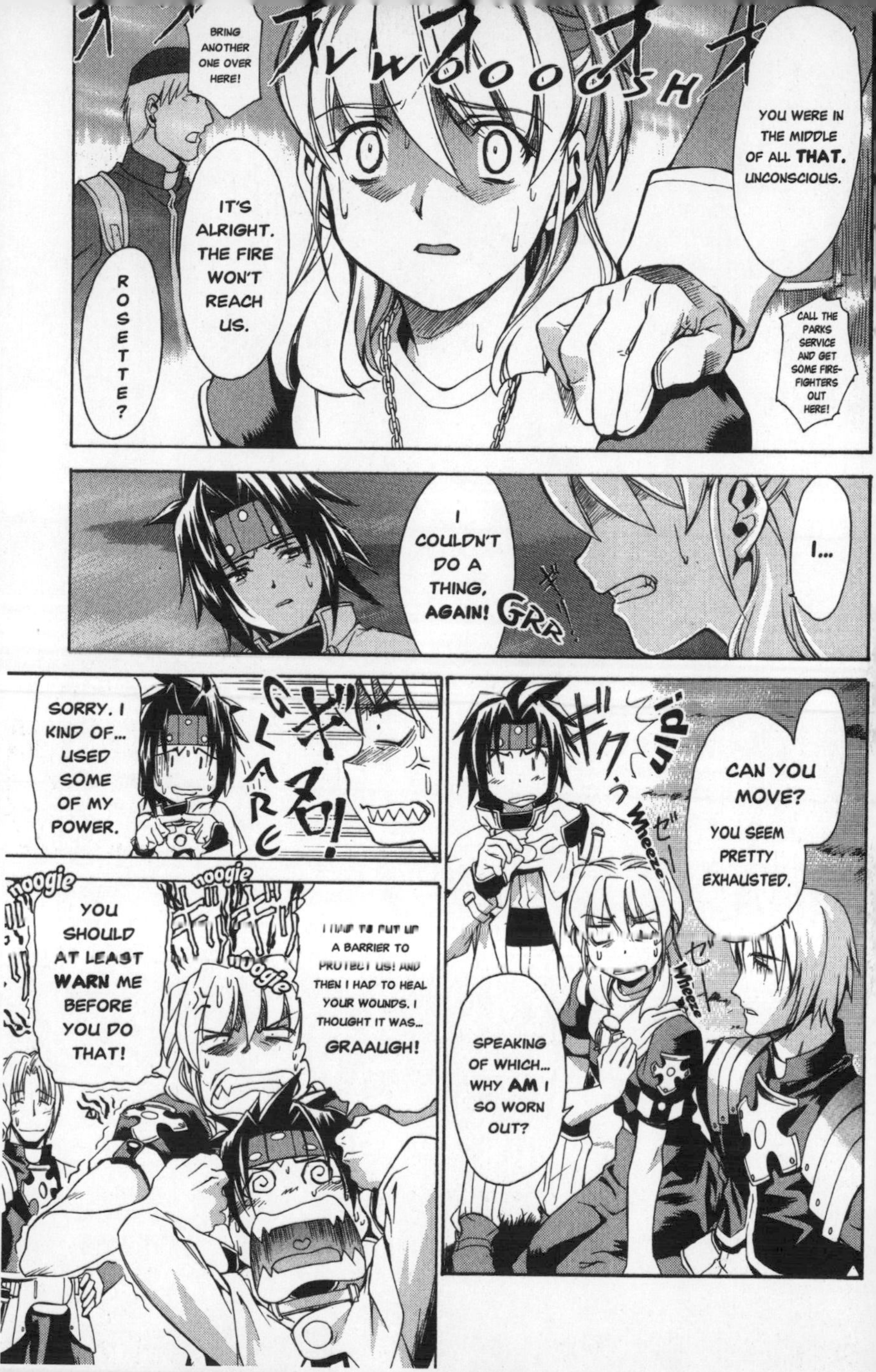

YOU WERE IN THE MIDDLE OF ALL THAT. UNCONSCIOUS.
CALL THE PARKS SERVICE AND GET SOME FIRE-FIGHTERS OUT HERE!
VWOOOOSH
BRING ANOTHER ONE OVER HERE!
IT'S ALRIGHT. THE FIRE WON'T REACH US.
ROSETTE?
I...
I COULDN'T DO A THING, AGAIN!
GRR
CAN YOU MOVE? YOU SEEM PRETTY EXHAUSTED.
gulp
Wheeze
Wheeze
SPEAKING OF WHICH... WHY AM I SO WORN OUT?
SORRY. I KIND OF... USED SOME OF MY POWER.
GLARE
noogie
noogie
noogie
YOU SHOULD AT LEAST WARN ME BEFORE YOU DO THAT!
I HAD TO PUT UP A BARRIER TO PROTECT US! AND THEN I HAD TO HEAL YOUR WOUNDS. I THOUGHT IT WAS... GRAAUGH!

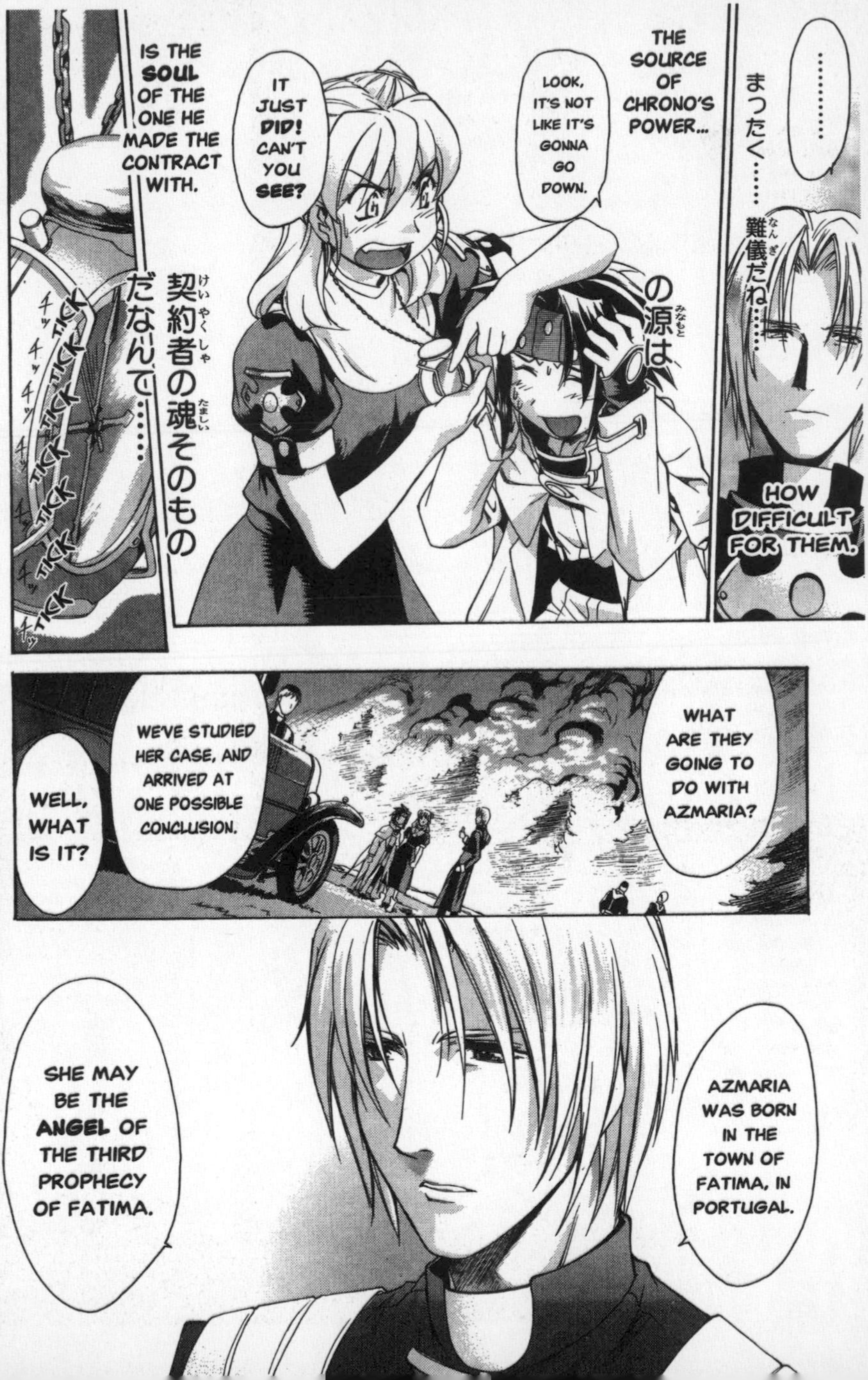
……
まったく……難儀だね……
HOW DIFFICULT FOR THEM.
THE SOURCE OF CHRONO'S POWER...
の源は、
LOOK, IT'S NOT LIKE IT'S GONNA GO DOWN.
IT JUST DID! CAN'T YOU SEE?
IS THE SOUL OF THE ONE HE MADE THE CONTRACT WITH.
契約者の魂そのものだなんて……
TICK TICK TICK TICK TICK TICK
チッ チッ チッ チッ チッ
WHAT ARE THEY GOING TO DO WITH AZMARIA?
WE'VE STUDIED HER CASE, AND ARRIVED AT ONE POSSIBLE CONCLUSION.
WELL, WHAT IS IT?
AZMARIA WAS BORN IN THE TOWN OF FATIMA, IN PORTUGAL.
SHE MAY BE THE ANGEL OF THE THIRD PROPHECY OF FATIMA.

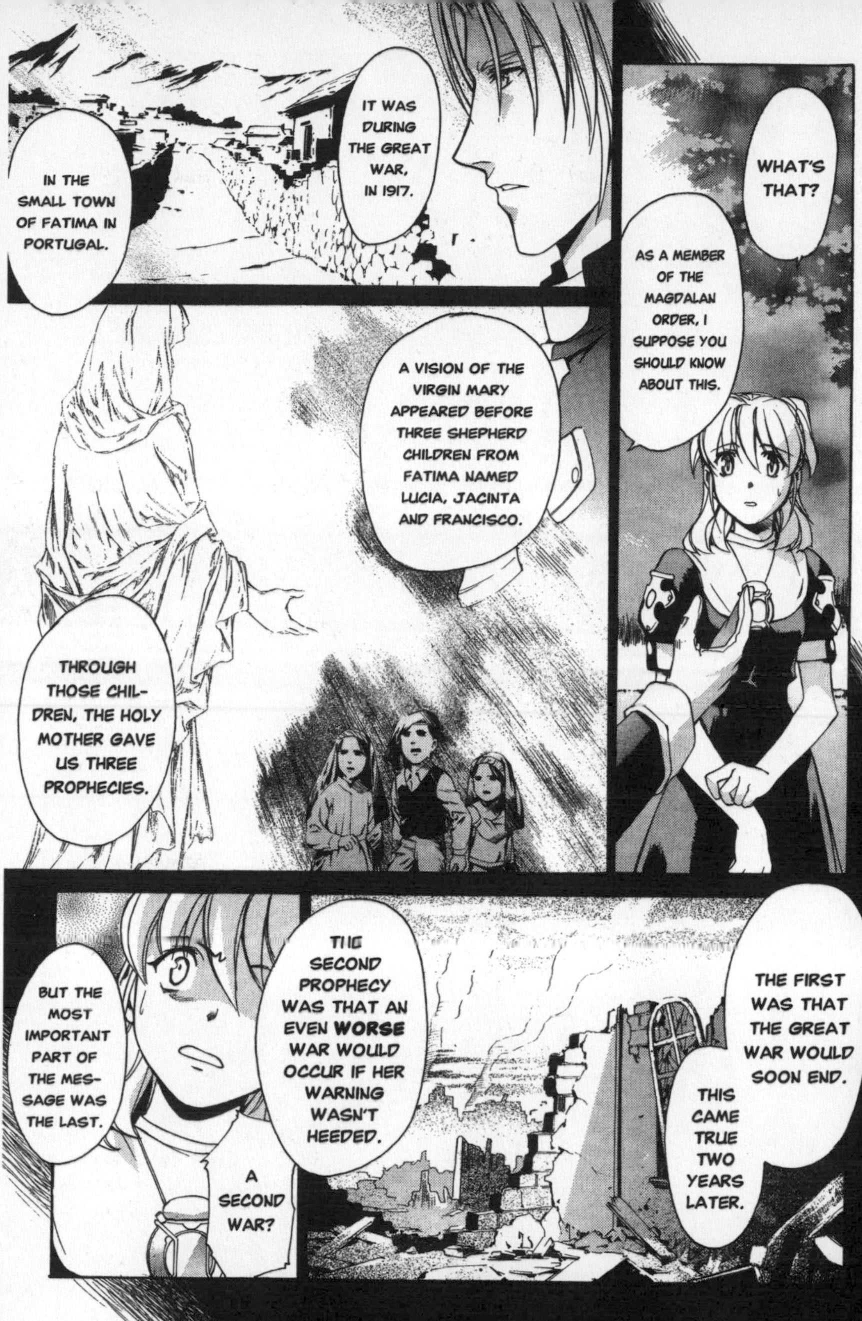
WHAT'S THAT?
AS A MEMBER OF THE MAGDALAN ORDER, I SUPPOSE YOU SHOULD KNOW ABOUT THIS.
IT WAS DURING THE GREAT WAR, IN 1917.
IN THE SMALL TOWN OF FATIMA IN PORTUGAL.
A VISION OF THE VIRGIN MARY APPEARED BEFORE THREE SHEPHERD CHILDREN FROM FATIMA NAMED LUCIA, JACINTA AND FRANCISCO.
THROUGH THOSE CHIL-DREN, THE HOLY MOTHER GAVE US THREE PROPHECIES.
THE FIRST WAS THAT THE GREAT WAR WOULD SOON END.
THIS CAME TRUE TWO YEARS LATER.
THE SECOND PROPHECY WAS THAT AN EVEN WORSE WAR WOULD OCCUR IF HER WARNING WASN'T HEEDED.
A SECOND WAR?
BUT THE MOST IMPORTANT PART OF THE MES-SAGE WAS THE LAST.

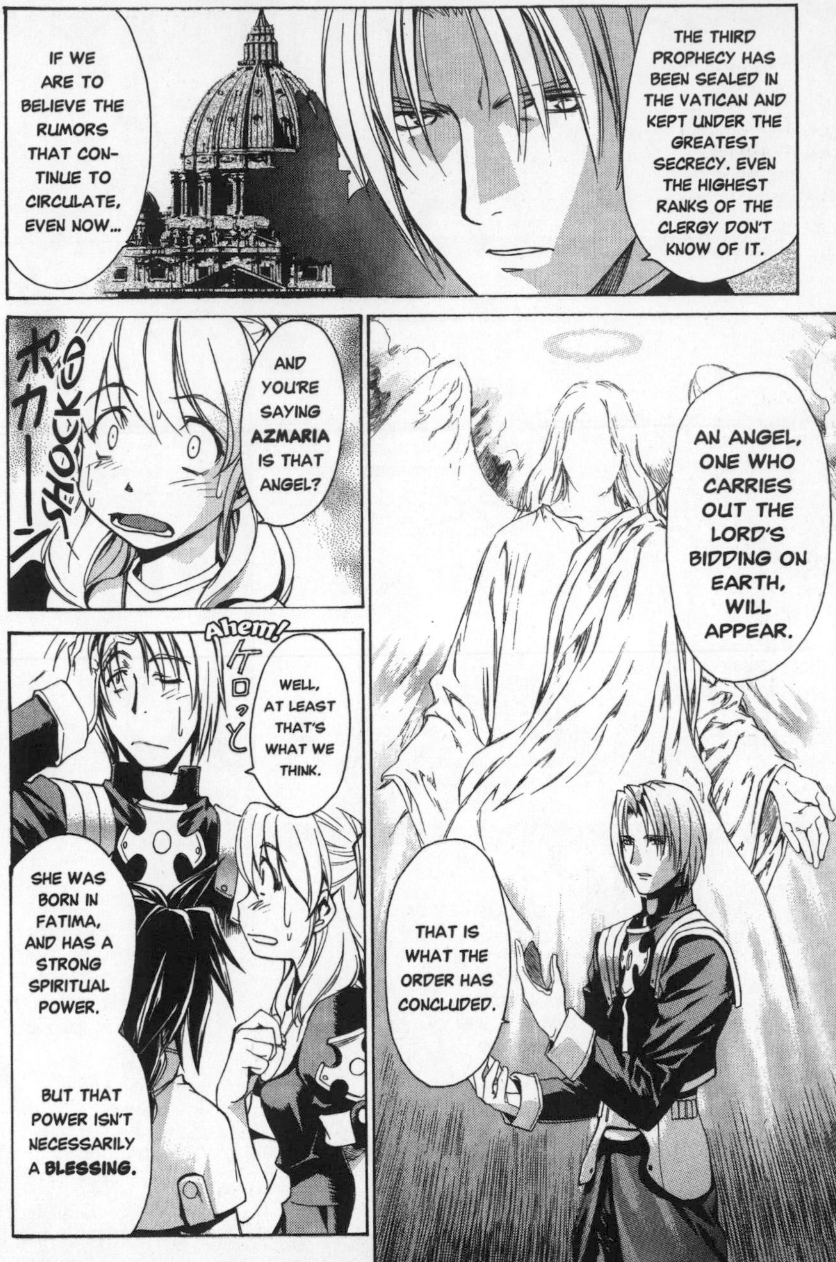
THE THIRD PROPHECY HAS BEEN SEALED IN THE VATICAN AND KEPT UNDER THE GREATEST SECRECY. EVEN THE HIGHEST RANKS OF THE CLERGY DON'T KNOW OF IT.
IF WE ARE TO BELIEVE THE RUMORS THAT CON-TINUE TO CIRCULATE, EVEN NOW...
AN ANGEL, ONE WHO CARRIES OUT THE LORD'S BIDDING ON EARTH, WILL APPEAR.
THAT IS WHAT THE ORDER HAS CONCLUDED.
AND YOU'RE SAYING **AZMARIA** IS THAT ANGEL?
SHOCKED
Ahem!
WELL, AT LEAST THAT'S WHAT WE THINK.
SHE WAS BORN IN FATIMA, AND HAS A STRONG SPIRITUAL POWER.
BUT THAT POWER ISN'T NECESSARILY A **BLESSING.**

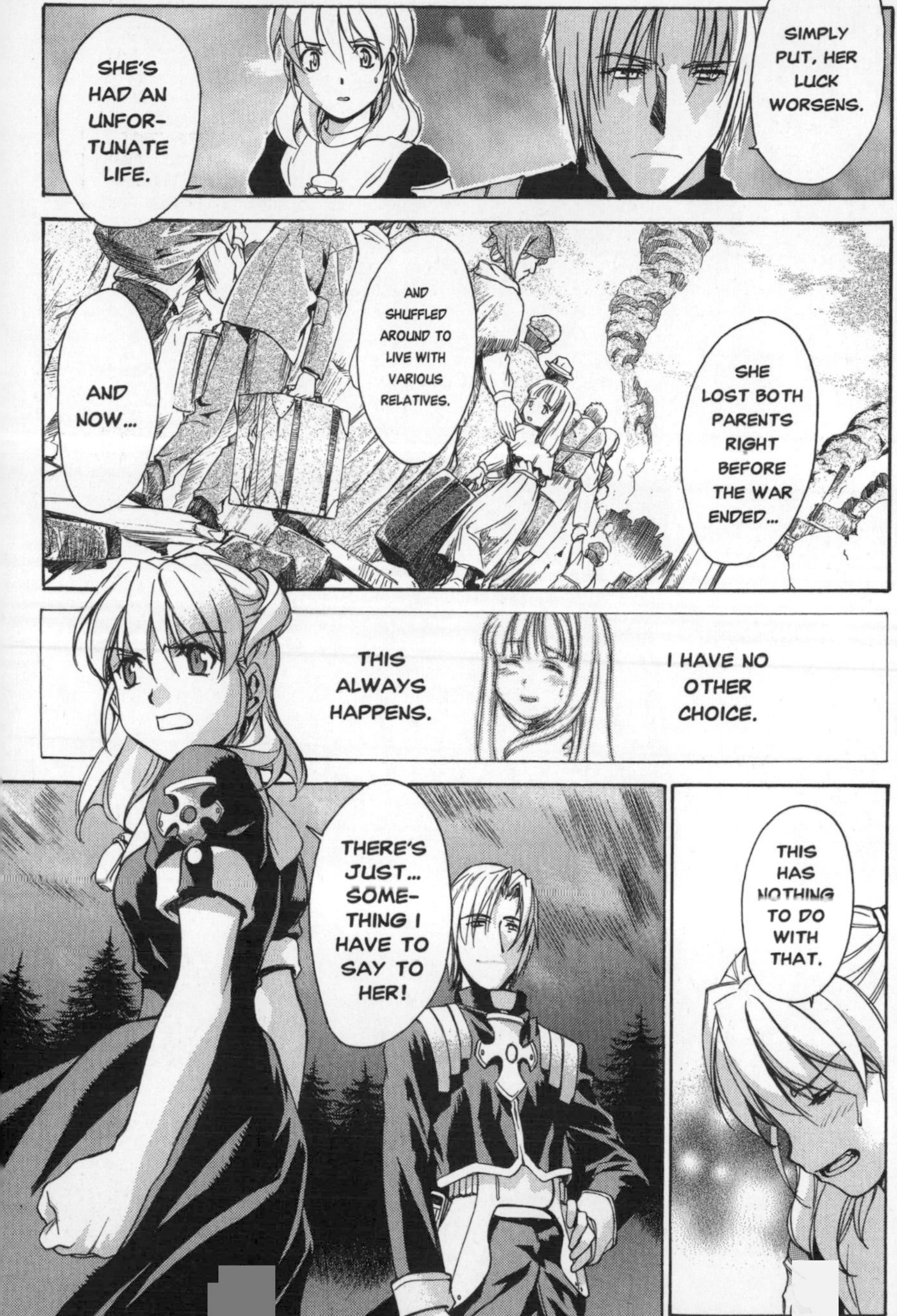
SIMPLY PUT, HER LUCK WORSENS.
SHE'S HAD AN UNFOR-TUNATE LIFE.
SHE LOST BOTH PARENTS RIGHT BEFORE THE WAR ENDED...
AND SHUFFLED AROUND TO LIVE WITH VARIOUS RELATIVES.
AND NOW...
I HAVE NO OTHER CHOICE.
THIS ALWAYS HAPPENS.
THIS HAS NOTHING TO DO WITH THAT.
THERE'S JUST... SOME-THING I HAVE TO SAY TO HER!

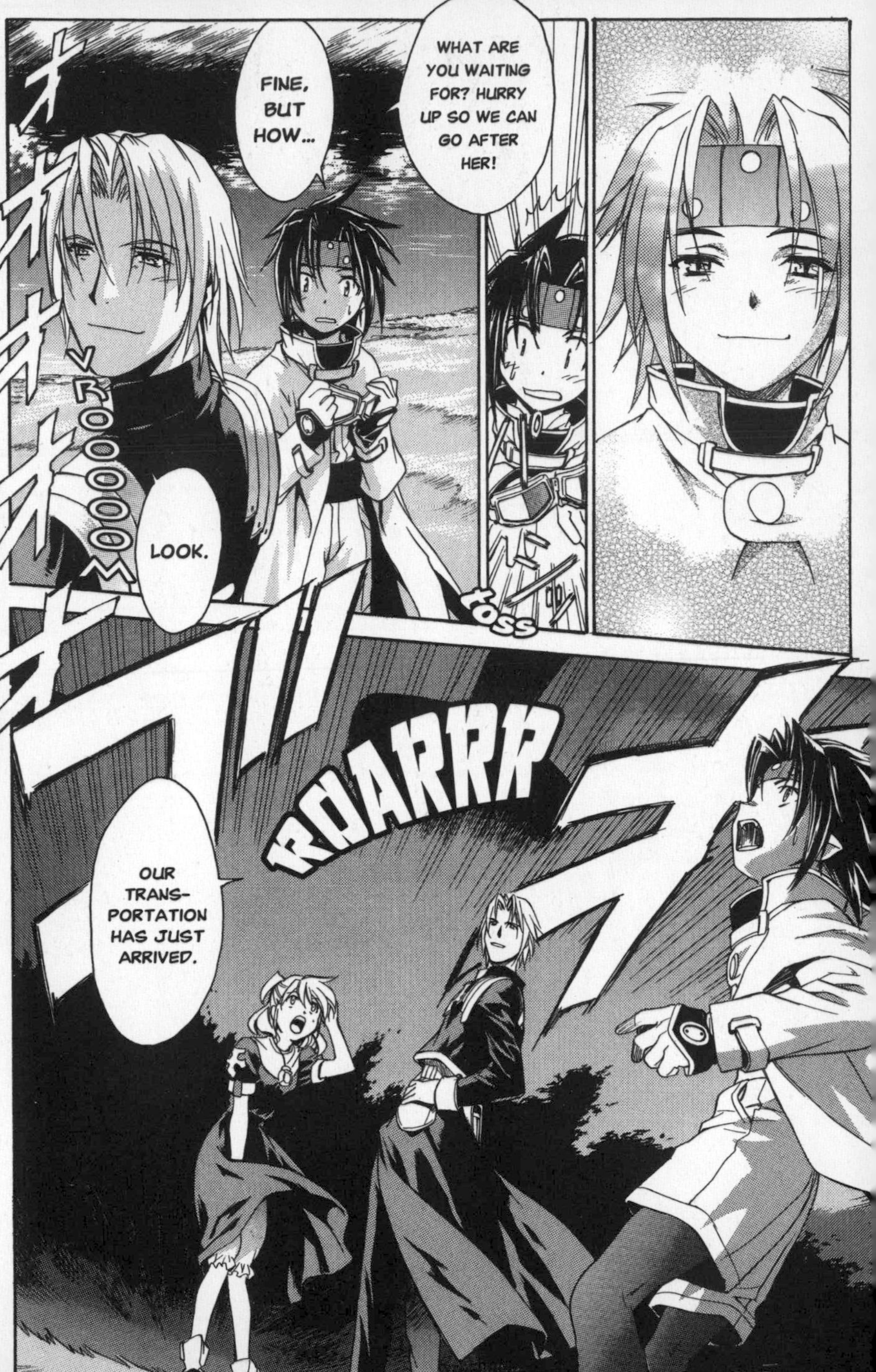
WHAT ARE YOU WAITING FOR? HURRY UP SO WE CAN GO AFTER HER!
toss
FINE, BUT HOW...
VROOOOOM
オオオオオオ
LOOK.
ROARRR
OUR TRANS-PORTATION HAS JUST ARRIVED.

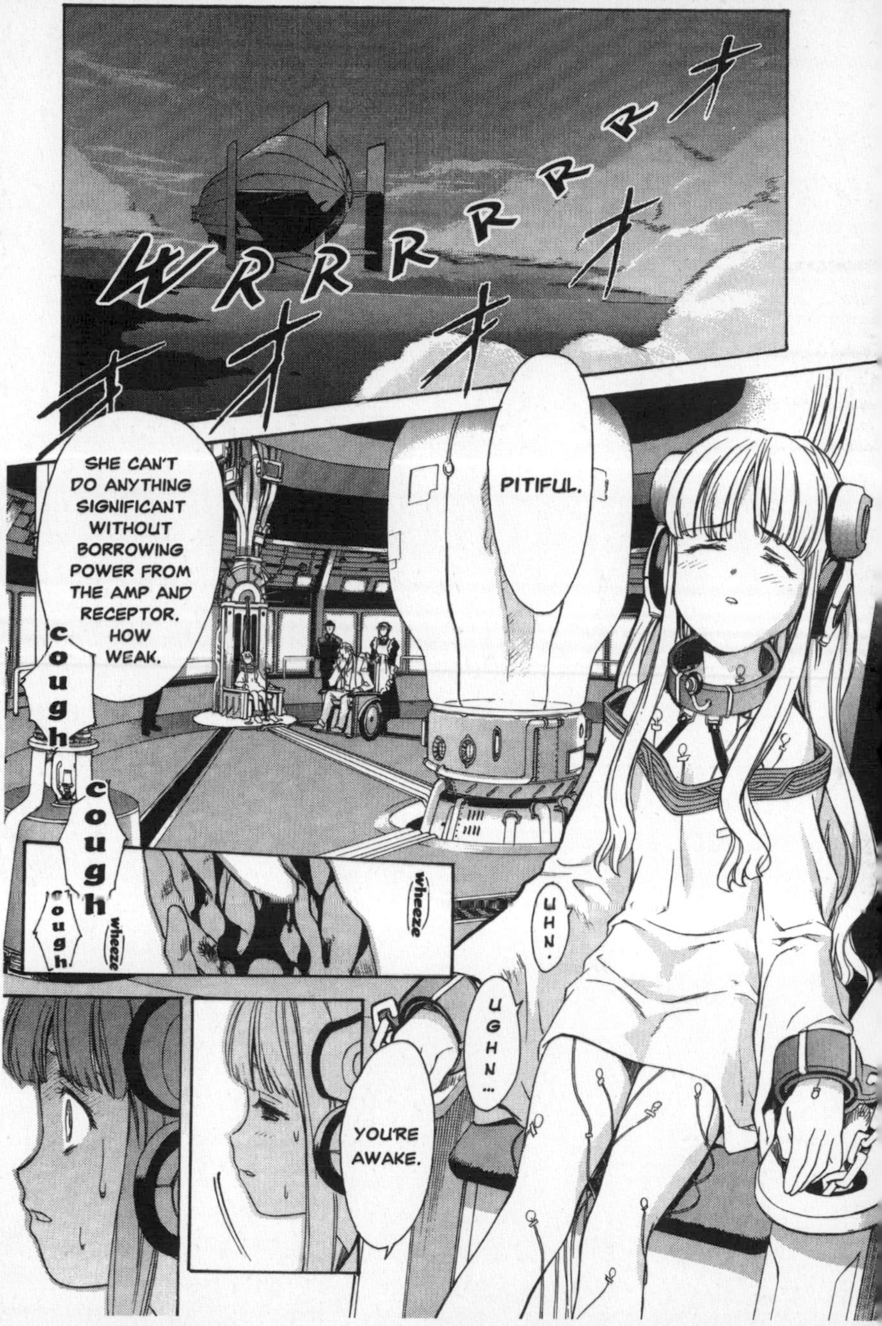

WRRRRRRR
PITIFUL.
SHE CAN'T DO ANYTHING SIGNIFICANT WITHOUT BORROWING POWER FROM THE AMP AND RECEPTOR. HOW WEAK.
cough
cough
cough
wheeze
wheeze
UHN.
UGHN...
YOU'RE AWAKE.

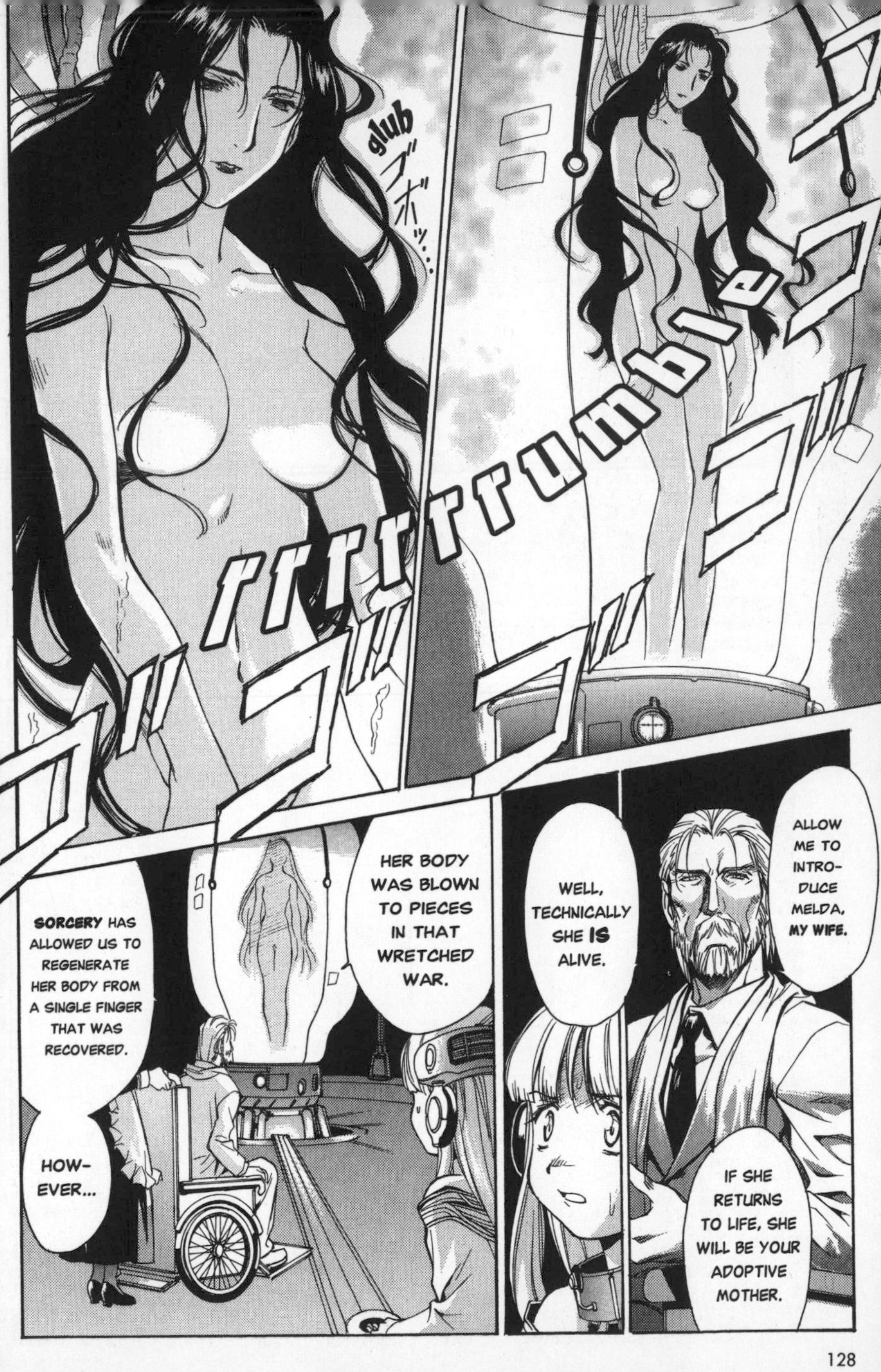

rrrrrrrumble
glub
ゴボッ…
ALLOW ME TO INTRO-DUCE MELDA, MY WIFE.
WELL, TECHNICALLY SHE IS ALIVE.
IF SHE RETURNS TO LIFE, SHE WILL BE YOUR ADOPTIVE MOTHER.
HER BODY WAS BLOWN TO PIECES IN THAT WRETCHED WAR.
SORCERY HAS ALLOWED US TO REGENERATE HER BODY FROM A SINGLE FINGER THAT WAS RECOVERED.
HOW-EVER...

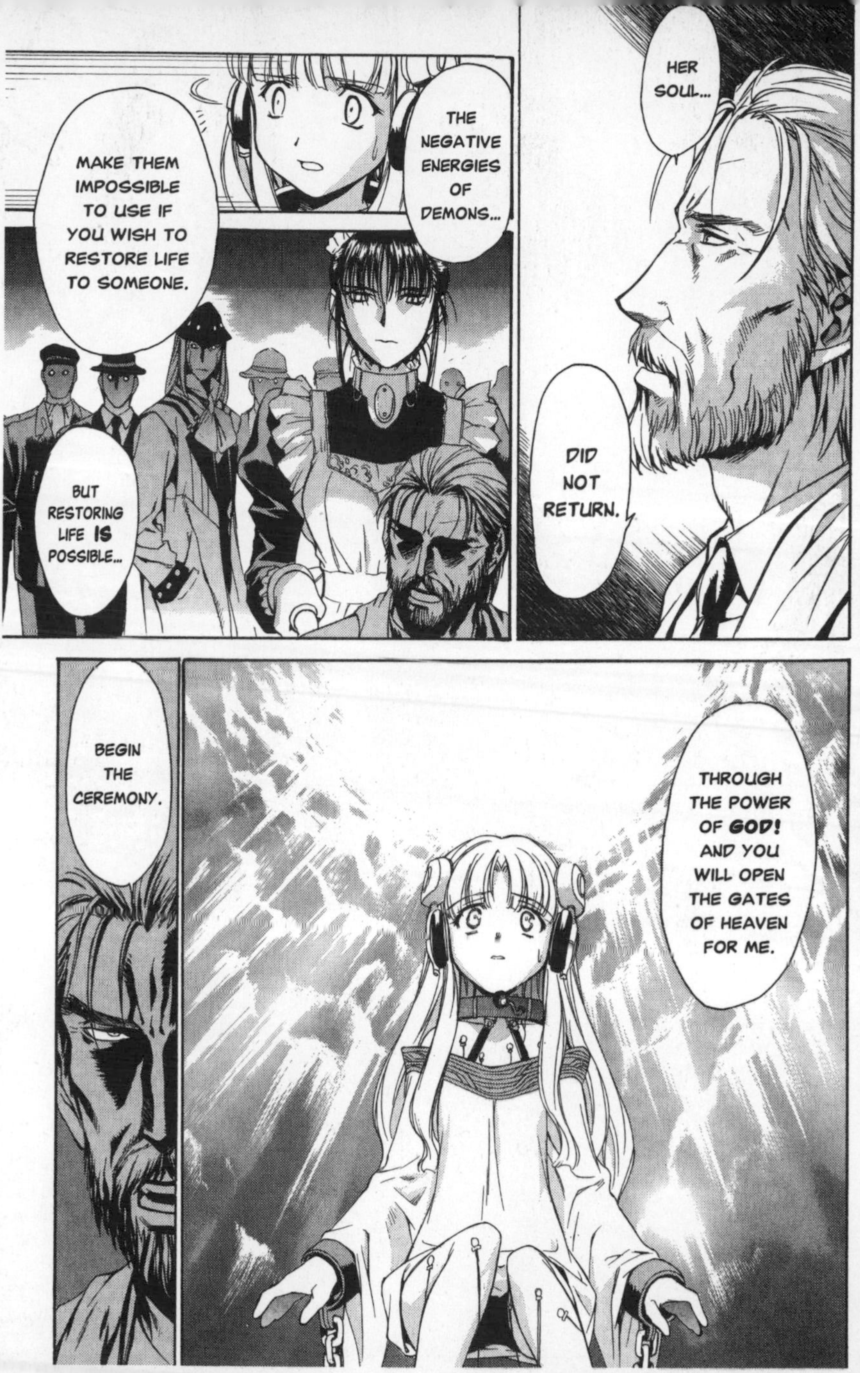
HER SOUL...
DID NOT RETURN.
THE NEGATIVE ENERGIES OF DEMONS...
MAKE THEM IMPOSSIBLE TO USE IF YOU WISH TO RESTORE LIFE TO SOMEONE.
BUT RESTORING LIFE **IS** POSSIBLE...
THROUGH THE POWER OF **GOD!** AND YOU WILL OPEN THE GATES OF HEAVEN FOR ME.
BEGIN THE CEREMONY.

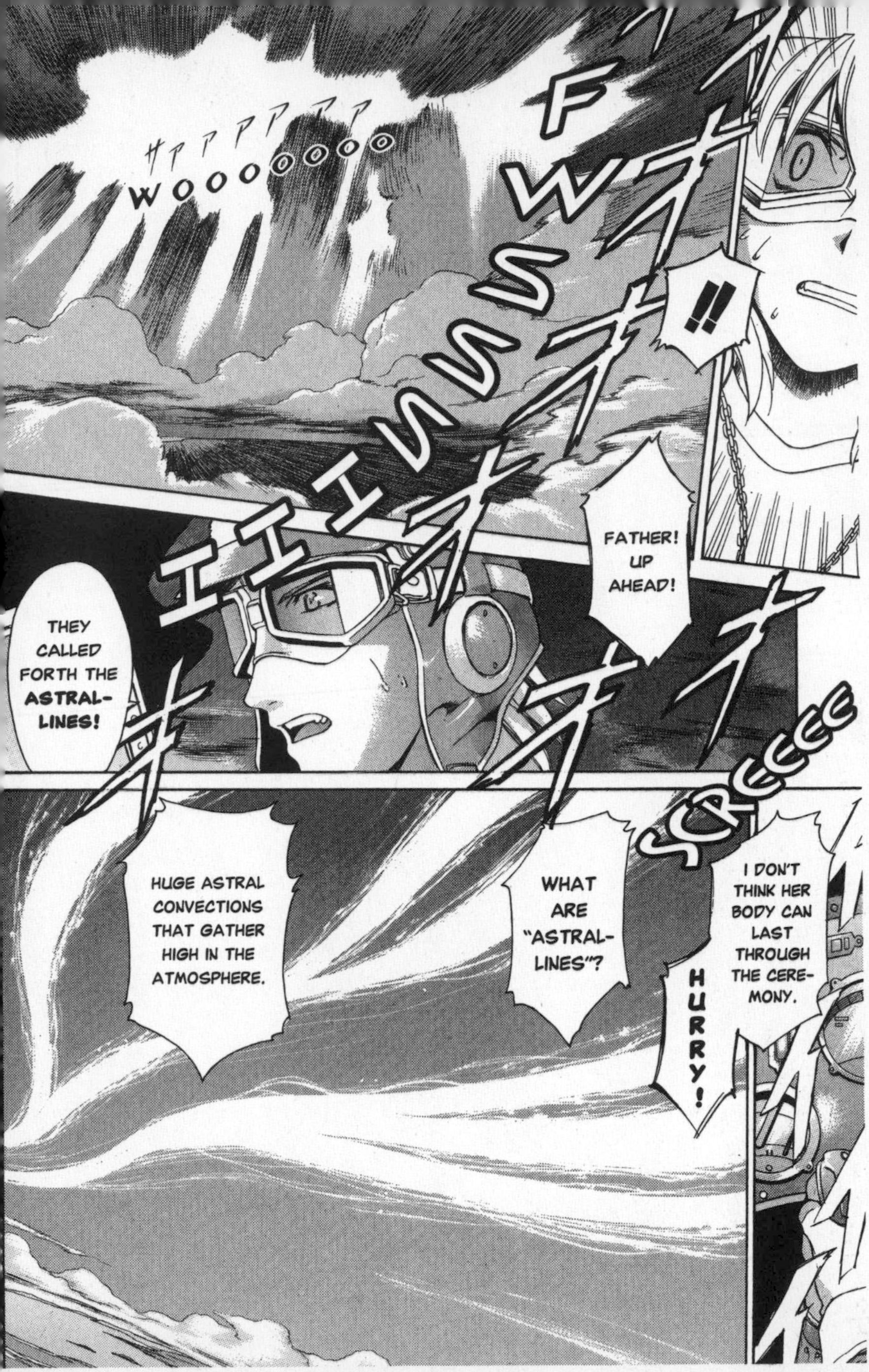
WOOOOOOO
FWSSSHHH
!!
FATHER! UP AHEAD!
THEY CALLED FORTH THE ASTRAL-LINES!
SCREEEE
I DON'T THINK HER BODY CAN LAST THROUGH THE CERE-MONY.
HURRY!
WHAT ARE "ASTRAL-LINES"?
HUGE ASTRAL CONVECTIONS THAT GATHER HIGH IN THE ATMOSPHERE.

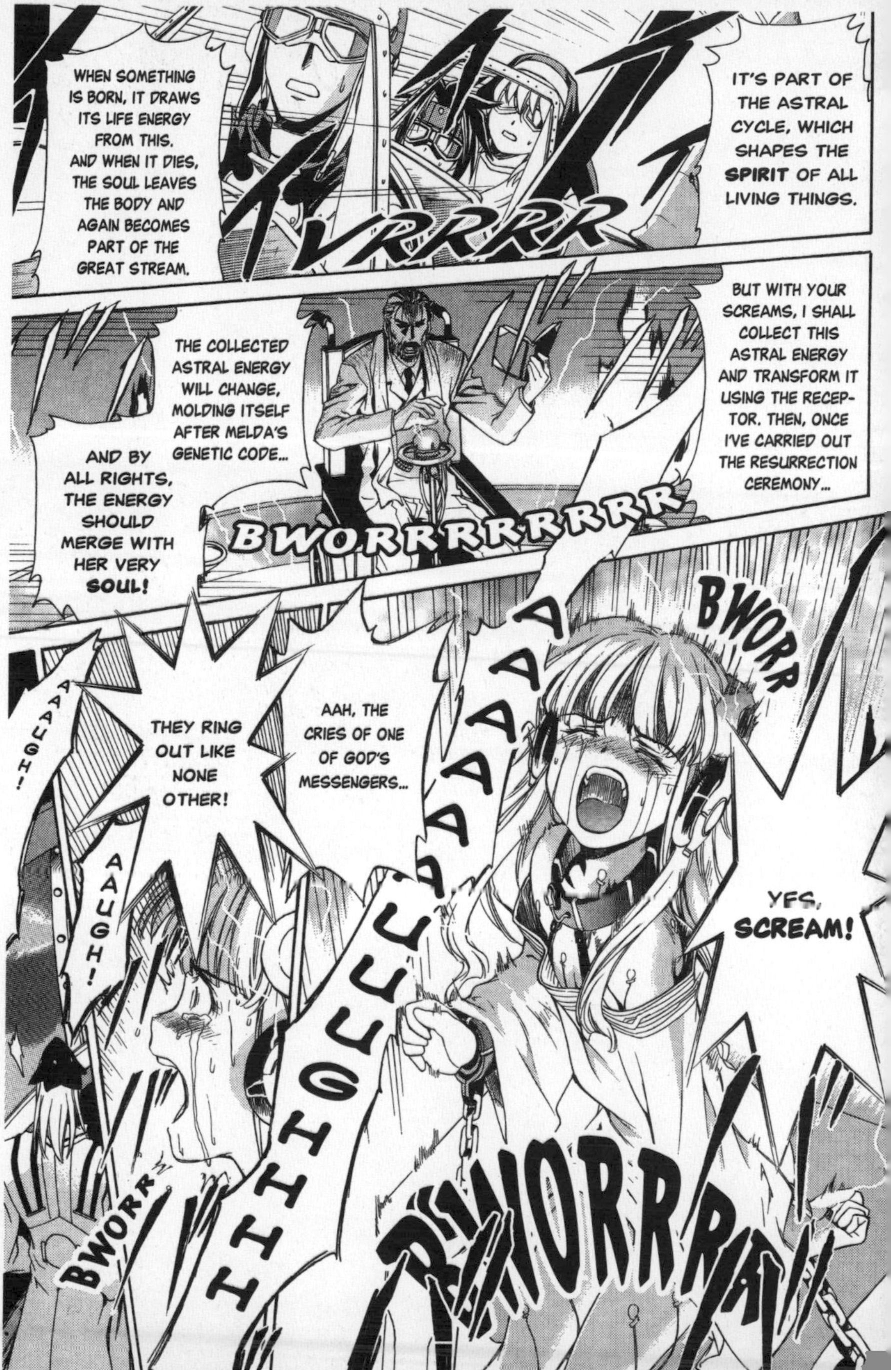

IT'S PART OF THE ASTRAL CYCLE, WHICH SHAPES THE **SPIRIT** OF ALL LIVING THINGS.
WHEN SOMETHING IS BORN, IT DRAWS ITS LIFE ENERGY FROM THIS. AND WHEN IT DIES, THE SOUL LEAVES THE BODY AND AGAIN BECOMES PART OF THE GREAT STREAM.
VRRRR
BUT WITH YOUR SCREAMS, I SHALL COLLECT THIS ASTRAL ENERGY AND TRANSFORM IT USING THE RECEPTOR. THEN, ONCE I'VE CARRIED OUT THE RESURRECTION CEREMONY...
THE COLLECTED ASTRAL ENERGY WILL CHANGE, MOLDING ITSELF AFTER MELDA'S GENETIC CODE...
AND BY ALL RIGHTS, THE ENERGY SHOULD MERGE WITH HER VERY **SOUL!**
BWORRRRRRRRR
BWORR
YES, SCREAM!
AAAAAAAUUUGHHHH
AAH, THE CRIES OF ONE OF GOD'S MESSENGERS...
THEY RING OUT LIKE NONE OTHER!
AAUGH!
AAAUGH!
BWORR

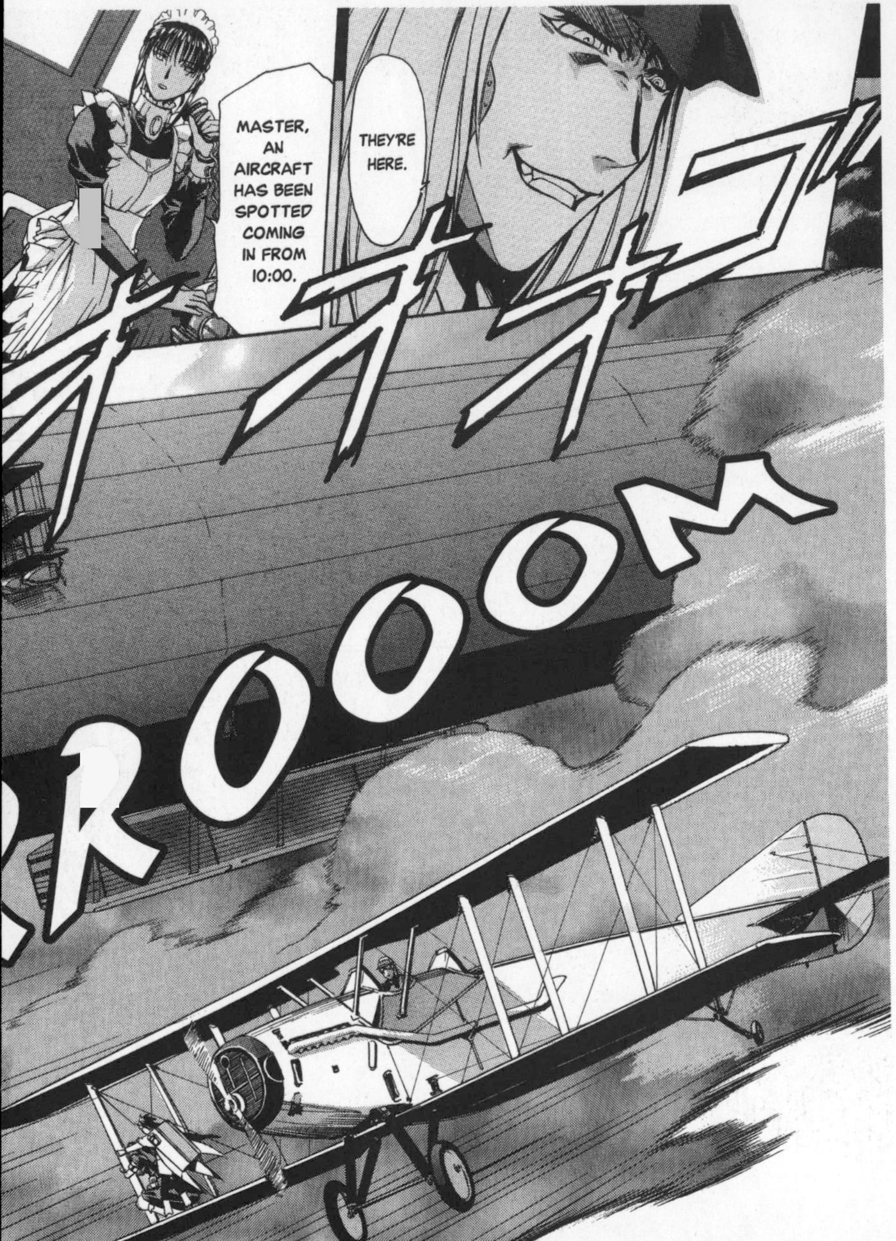

THEY'RE HERE.
MASTER, AN AIRCRAFT HAS BEEN SPOTTED COMING IN FROM 10:00.
RROOM

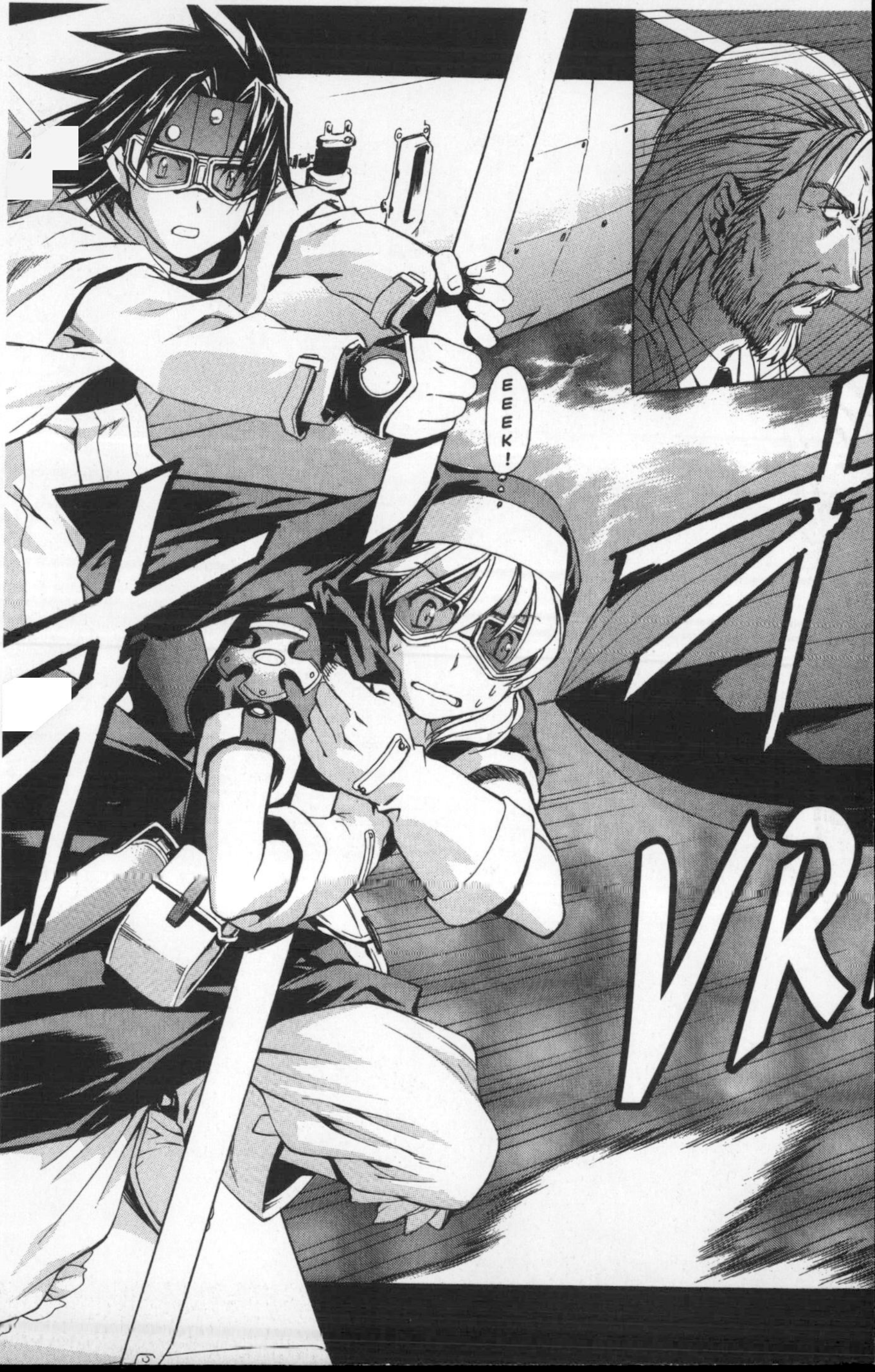
EEEK!
VR

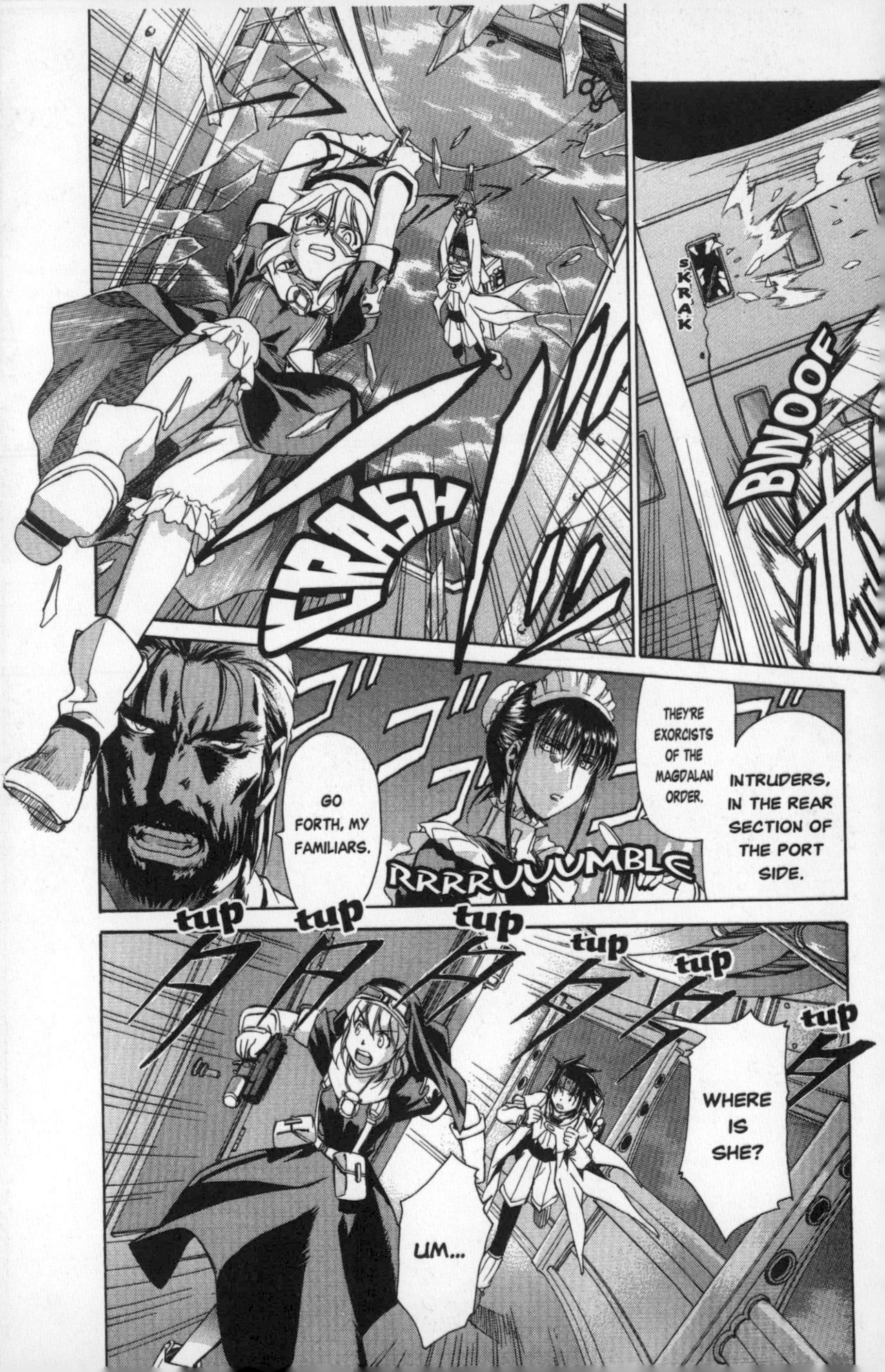
SKRAK
BWOOF
CRASH
INTRUDERS, IN THE REAR SECTION OF THE PORT SIDE.
THEY'RE EXORCISTS OF THE MAGDALAN ORDER.
RRRRUUUMBLE
GO FORTH, MY FAMILIARS.
tup
tup
tup
tup
tup
tup
WHERE IS SHE?
UM...

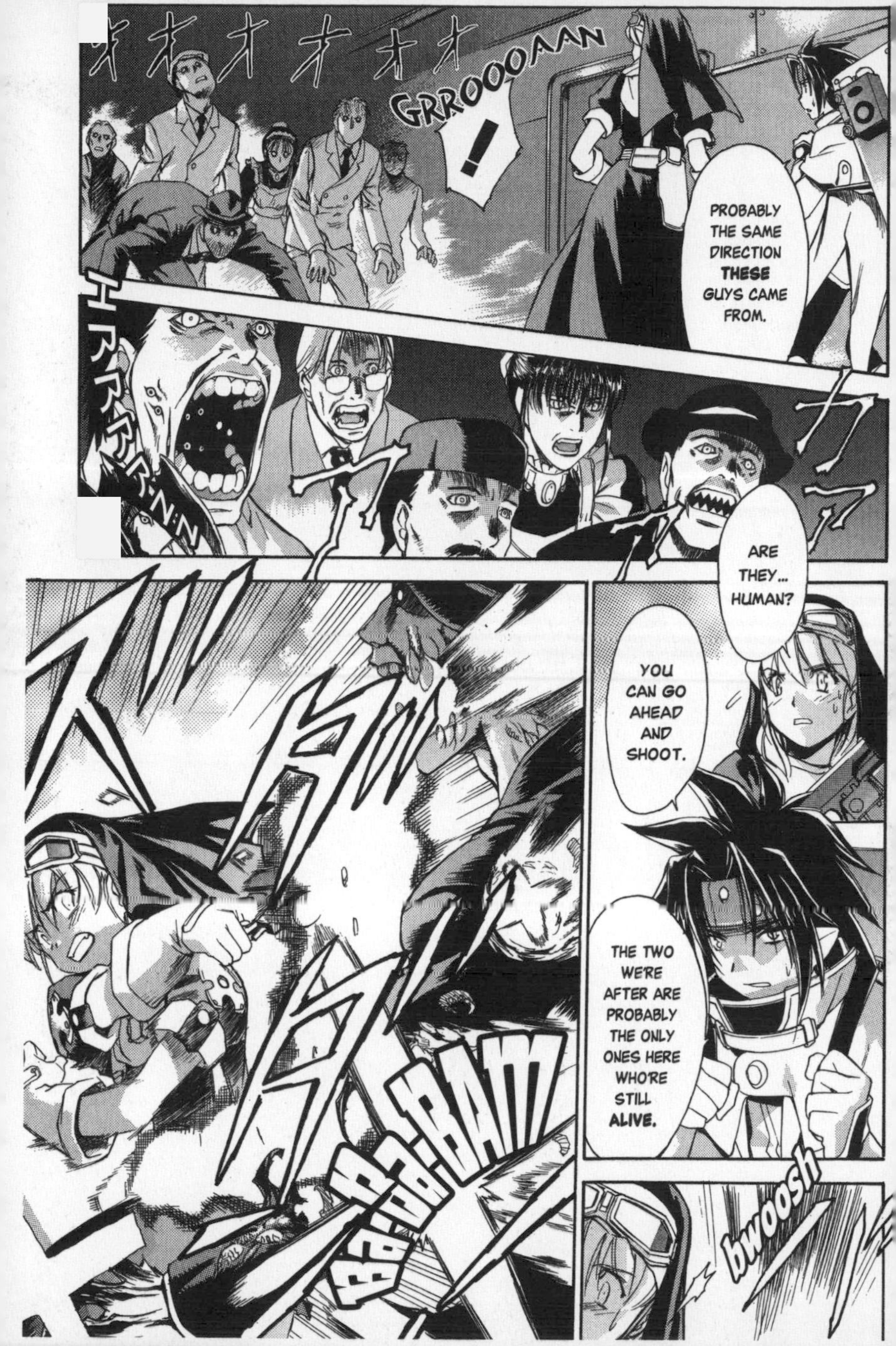
PROBABLY THE SAME DIRECTION THESE GUYS CAME FROM.
GRROOOAAN
!
オオオオオオ
ARE THEY... HUMAN?
YOU CAN GO AHEAD AND SHOOT.
THE TWO WE'RE AFTER ARE PROBABLY THE ONLY ONES HERE WHO'RE STILL ALIVE.
bwoosh
BA-BA-BAM

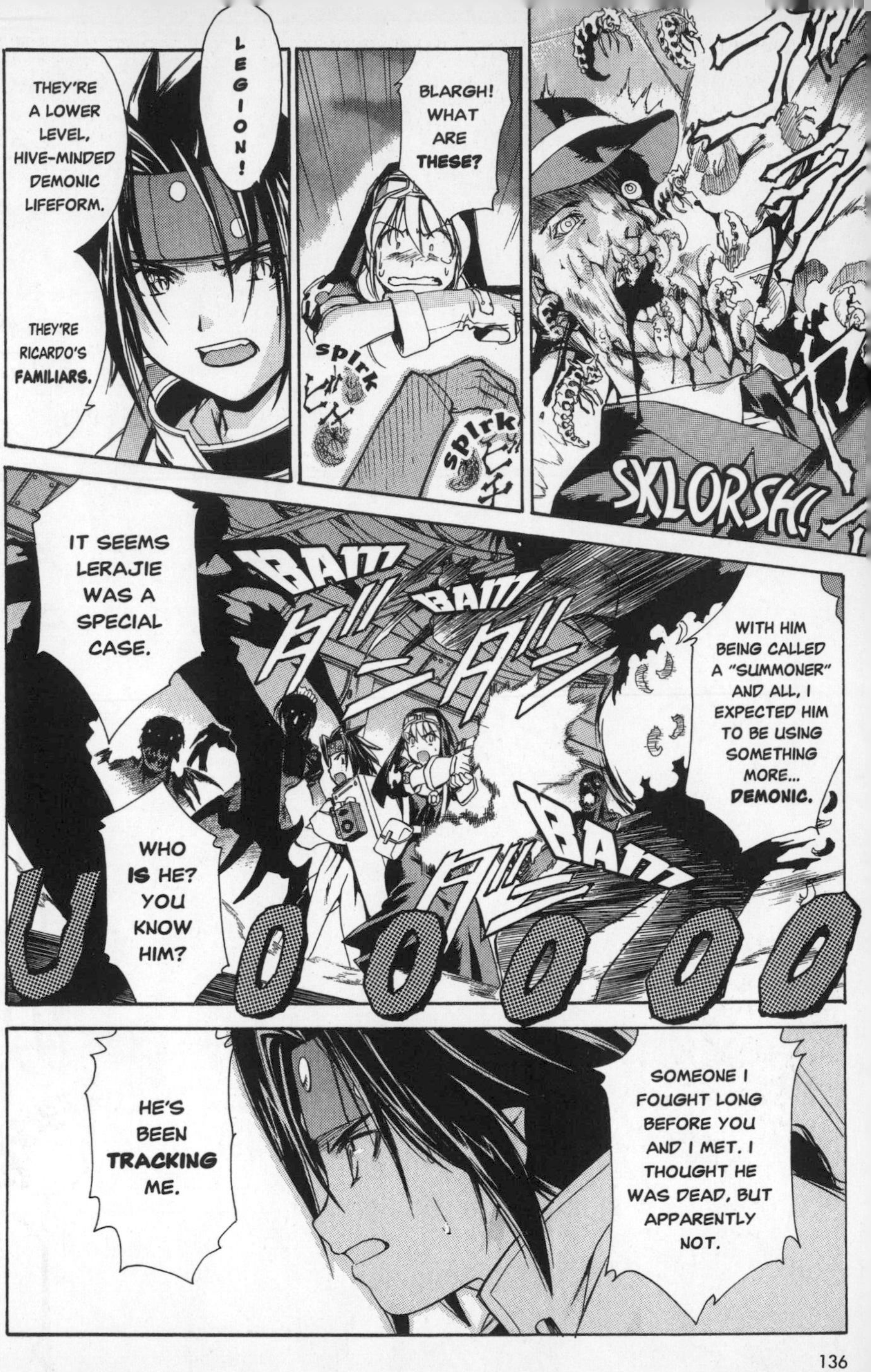
SKLORSH!
BLARGH! WHAT ARE THESE?
splrk
splrk
LEGION!
THEY'RE A LOWER LEVEL, HIVE-MINDED DEMONIC LIFEFORM.
THEY'RE RICARDO'S FAMILIARS.
BAM
BAM
WITH HIM BEING CALLED A "SUMMONER" AND ALL, I EXPECTED HIM TO BE USING SOMETHING MORE... DEMONIC.
IT SEEMS LERAJIE WAS A SPECIAL CASE.
BAM
WHO IS HE? YOU KNOW HIM?
UOOOOOO
SOMEONE I FOUGHT LONG BEFORE YOU AND I MET. I THOUGHT HE WAS DEAD, BUT APPARENTLY NOT.
HE'S BEEN TRACKING ME.

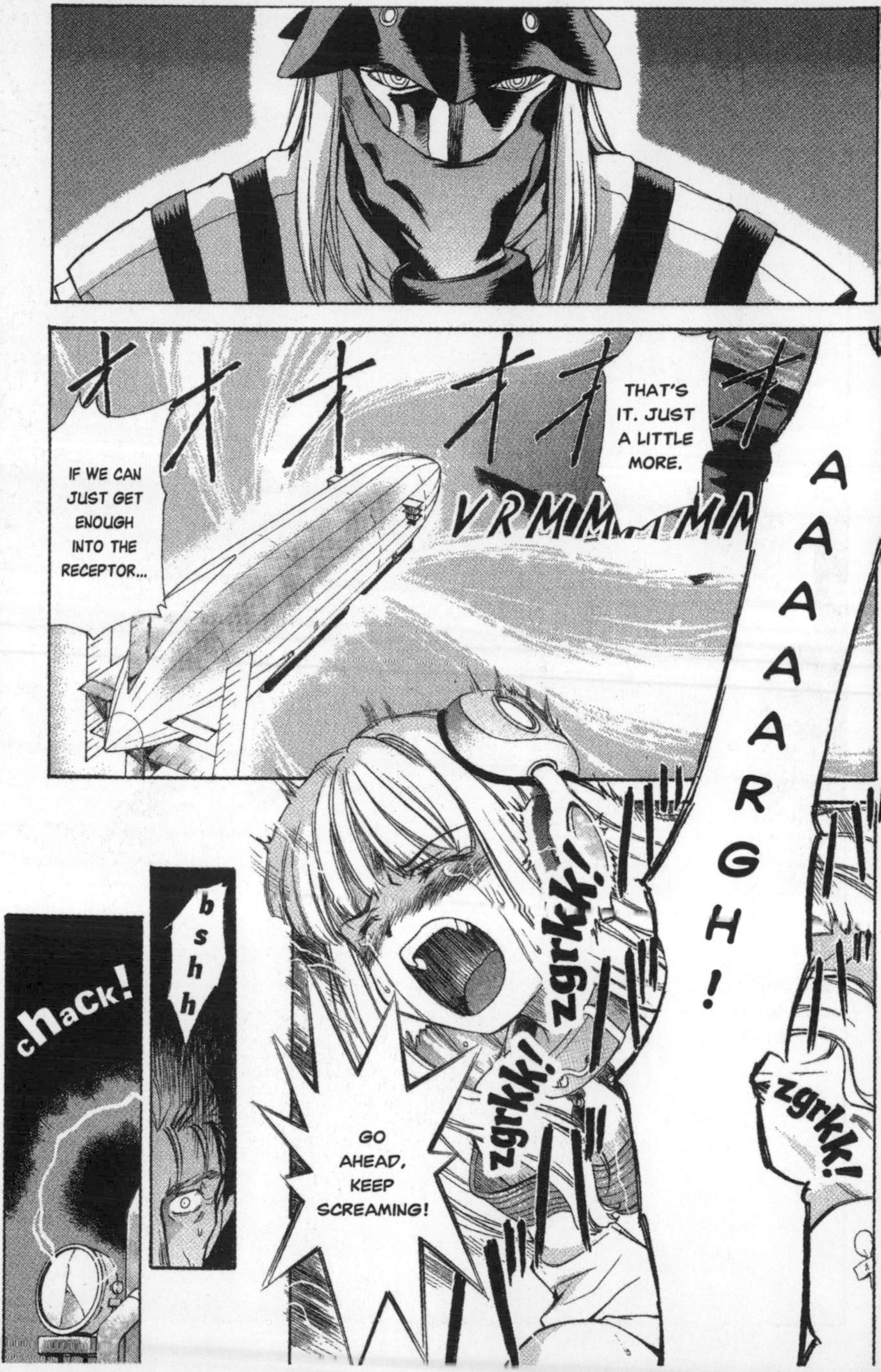

THAT'S IT. JUST A LITTLE MORE.
オオオオオオ
VRMMMMMM
IF WE CAN JUST GET ENOUGH INTO THE RECEPTOR...
AAAAAARGH!
zgrkk!
zgrkk!
zgrkk!
zgrkk!
GO AHEAD, KEEP SCREAMING!
bshh
chack!

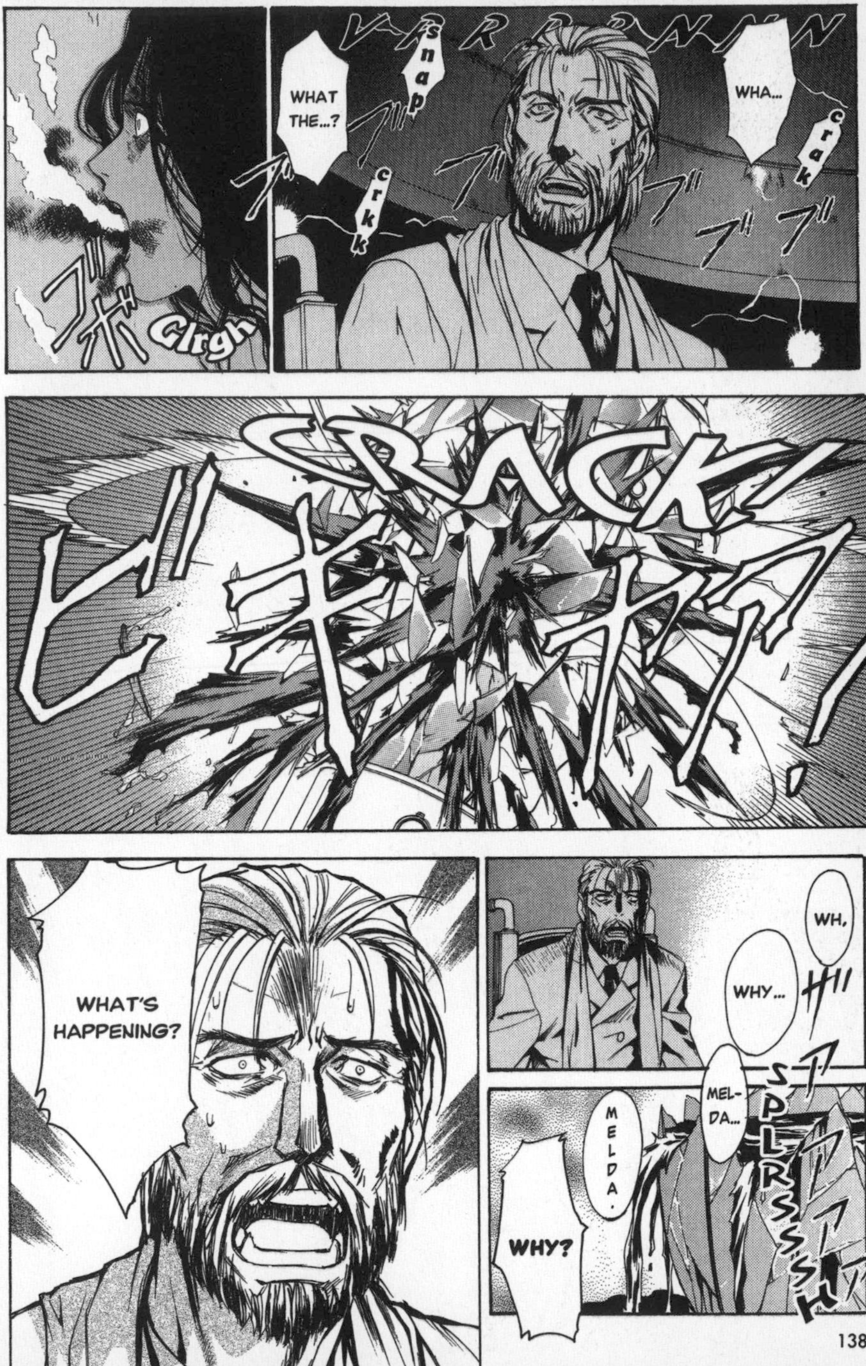
VRRRONNNN
WHA...
crak
snap
WHAT THE...?
crkk
Clrgh
CRACK!
WH,
WHY...
MEL-DA...
MELDA.
WHY?
SPLRSSSH
WHAT'S HAPPENING?

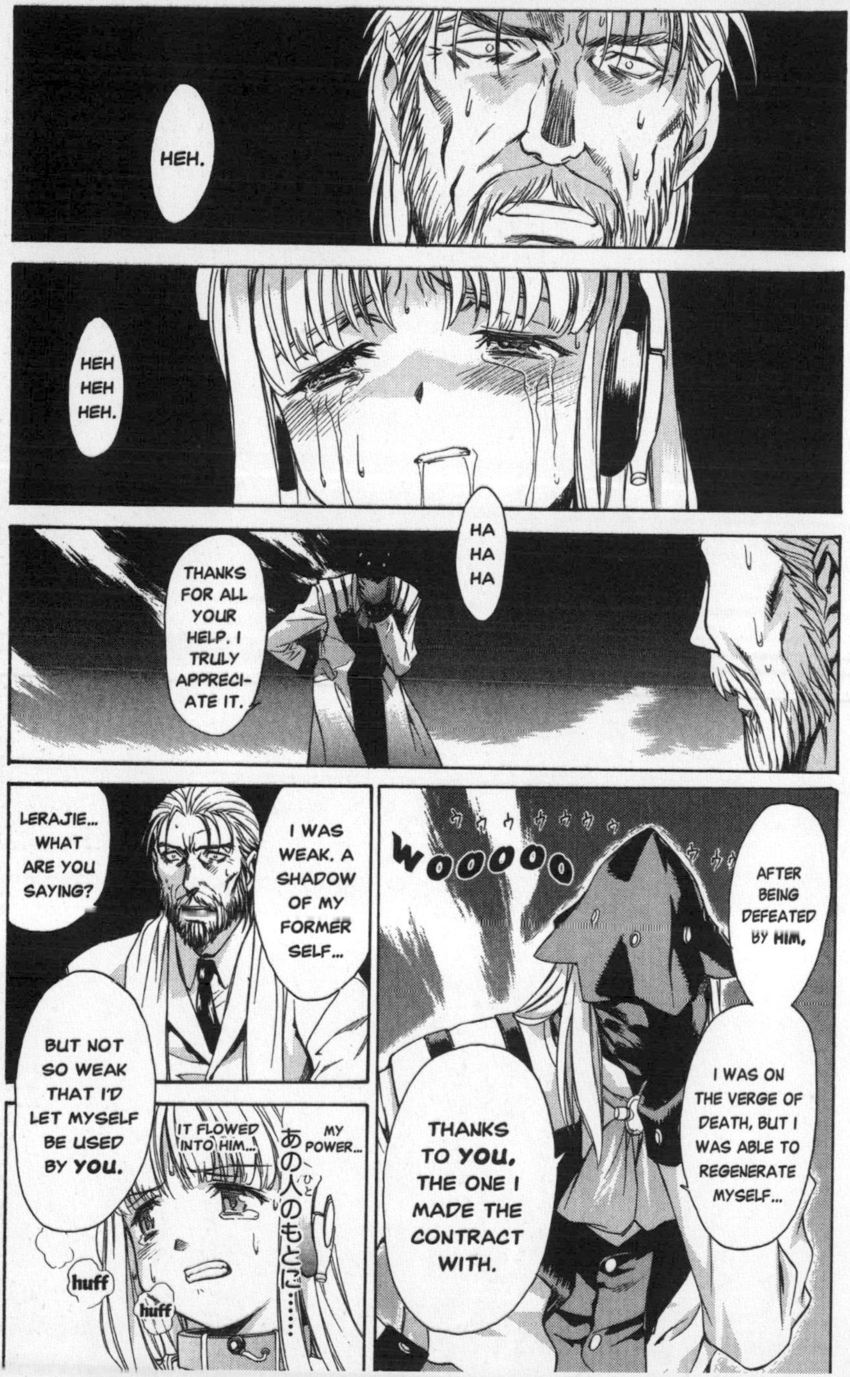
HEH.
HEH HEH HEH.
HA HA HA
THANKS FOR ALL YOUR HELP. I TRULY APPRECIATE IT.
WOOOOO
AFTER BEING DEFEATED BY HIM,
I WAS ON THE VERGE OF DEATH, BUT I WAS ABLE TO REGENERATE MYSELF...
THANKS TO YOU, THE ONE I MADE THE CONTRACT WITH.
I WAS WEAK. A SHADOW OF MY FORMER SELF...
LERAJIE... WHAT ARE YOU SAYING?
BUT NOT SO WEAK THAT I'D LET MYSELF BE USED BY YOU.
MY POWER...
あの人のもとに……
IT FLOWED INTO HIM...
huff
huff

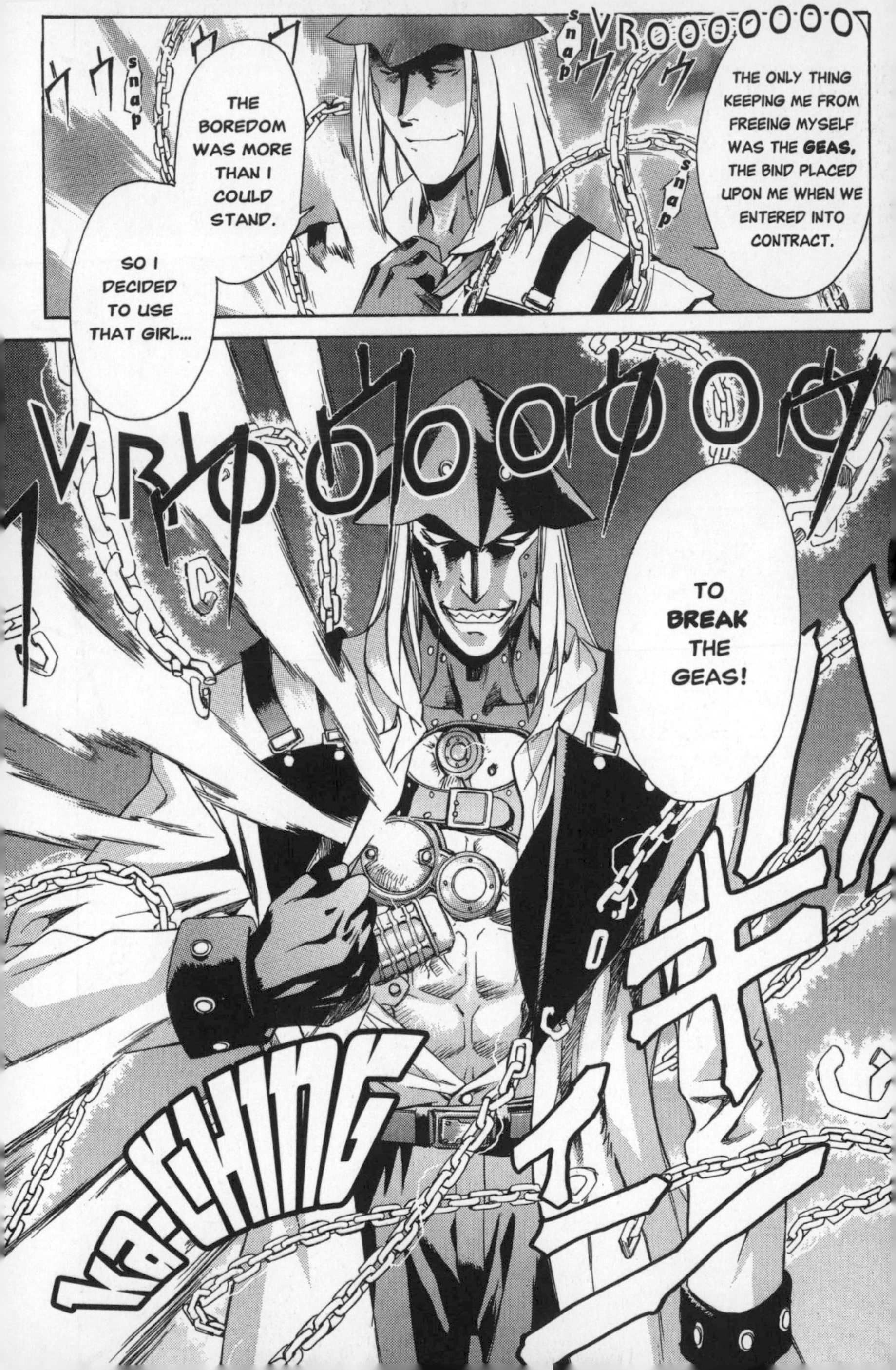
VROOOOOOOO
snap
snap
snap
THE ONLY THING KEEPING ME FROM FREEING MYSELF WAS THE **GEAS,** THE BIND PLACED UPON ME WHEN WE ENTERED INTO CONTRACT.
THE BOREDOM WAS MORE THAN I COULD STAND.
SO I DECIDED TO USE THAT GIRL...
VRYOOOOOOOO
TO **BREAK** THE GEAS!
KA-CHING

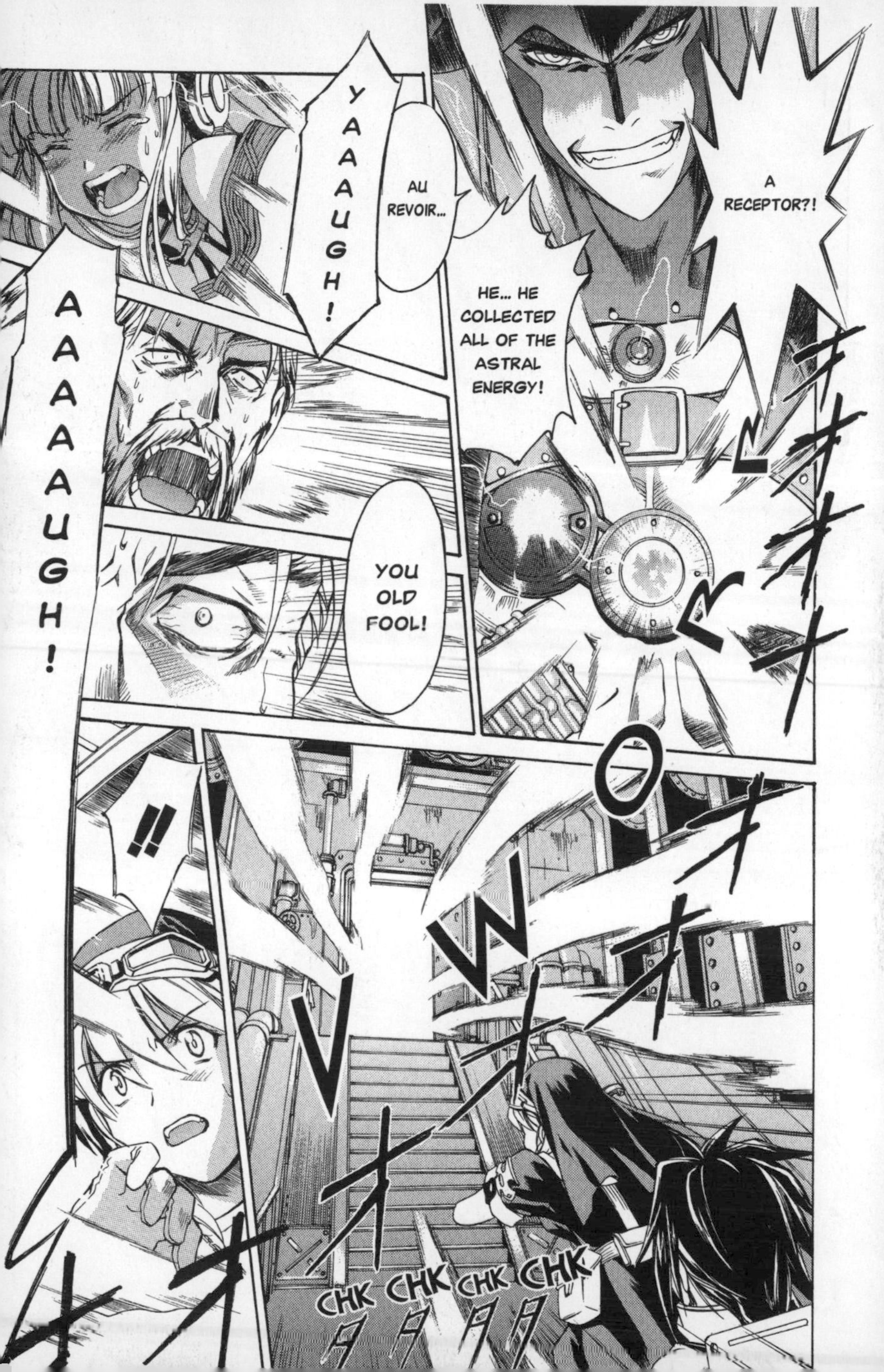
A RECEPTOR?!
HE... HE COLLECTED ALL OF THE ASTRAL ENERGY!
AU REVOIR...
YAAAAUGH!
AAAAAAAUGH!
YOU OLD FOOL!
!!
CHK CHK CHK CHK

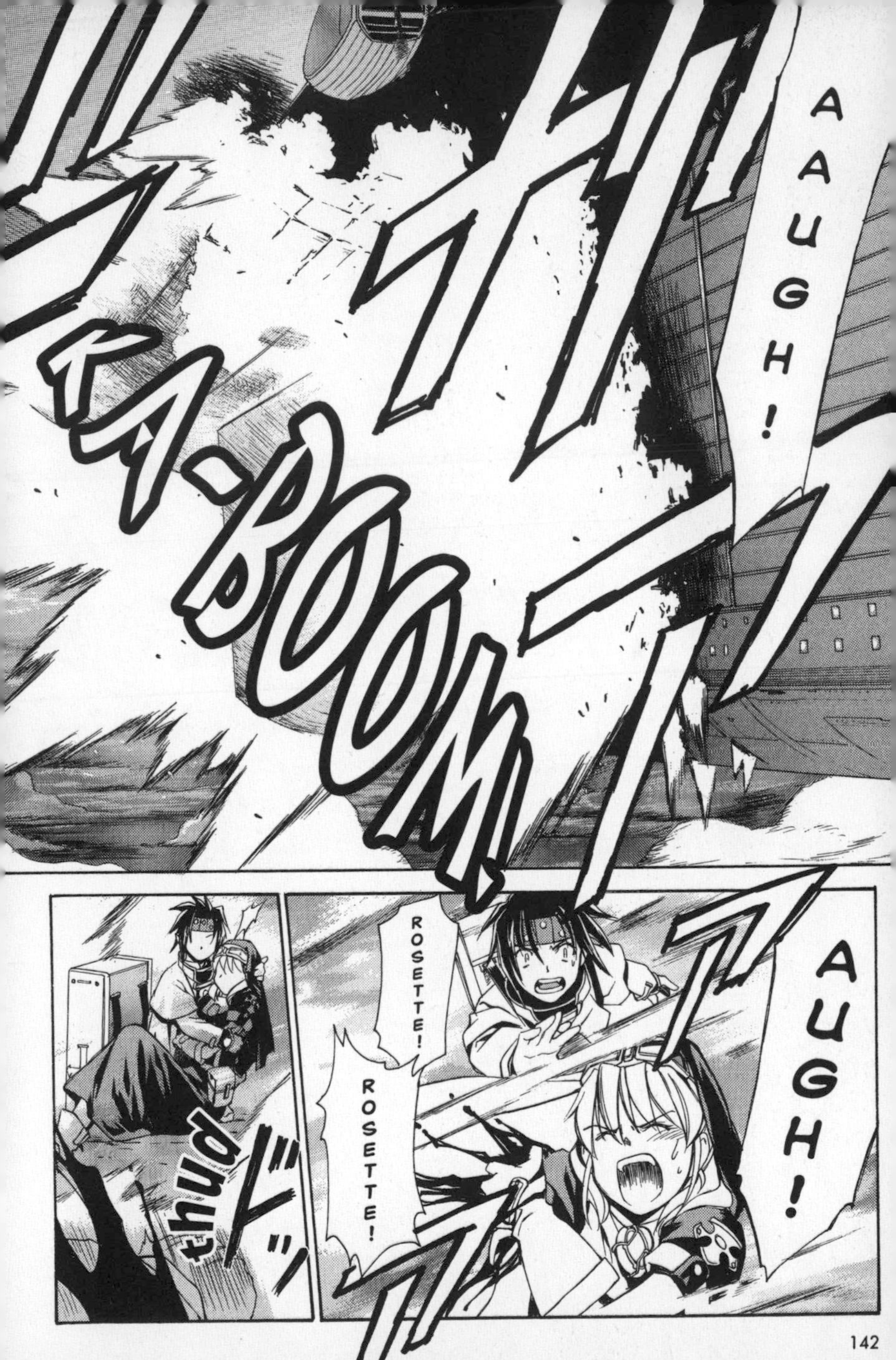
AAUGH!
KA-BOOM!
AUGH!
ROSETTE!
ROSETTE!
thud

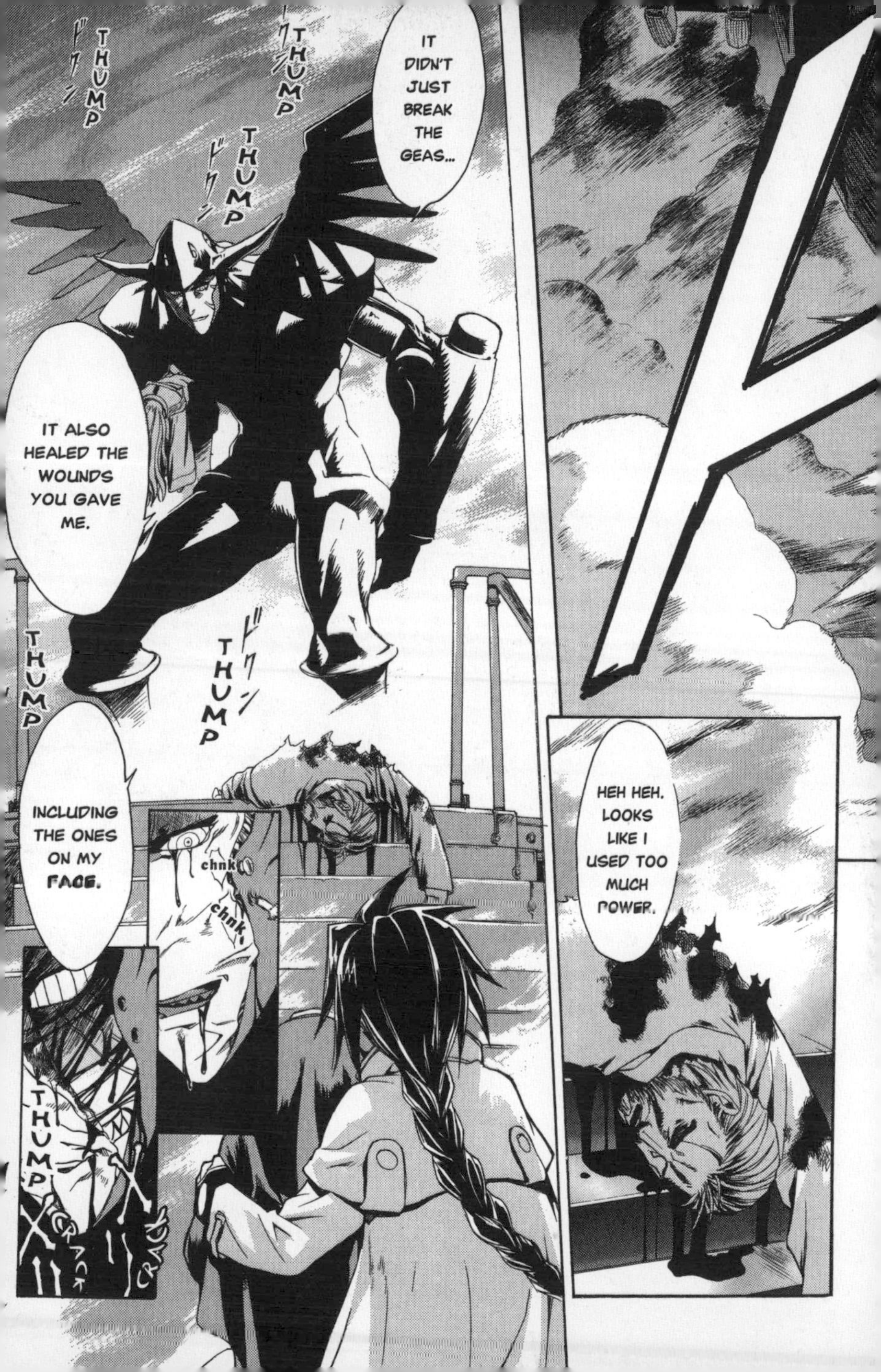
THUMP
THUMP
THUMP
IT DIDN'T JUST BREAK THE GEAS...
IT ALSO HEALED THE WOUNDS YOU GAVE ME.
THUMP
THUMP
INCLUDING THE ONES ON MY FACE.
chnk
chnk
THUMP
CRACK
CRACK
HEH HEH. LOOKS LIKE I USED TOO MUCH POWER.

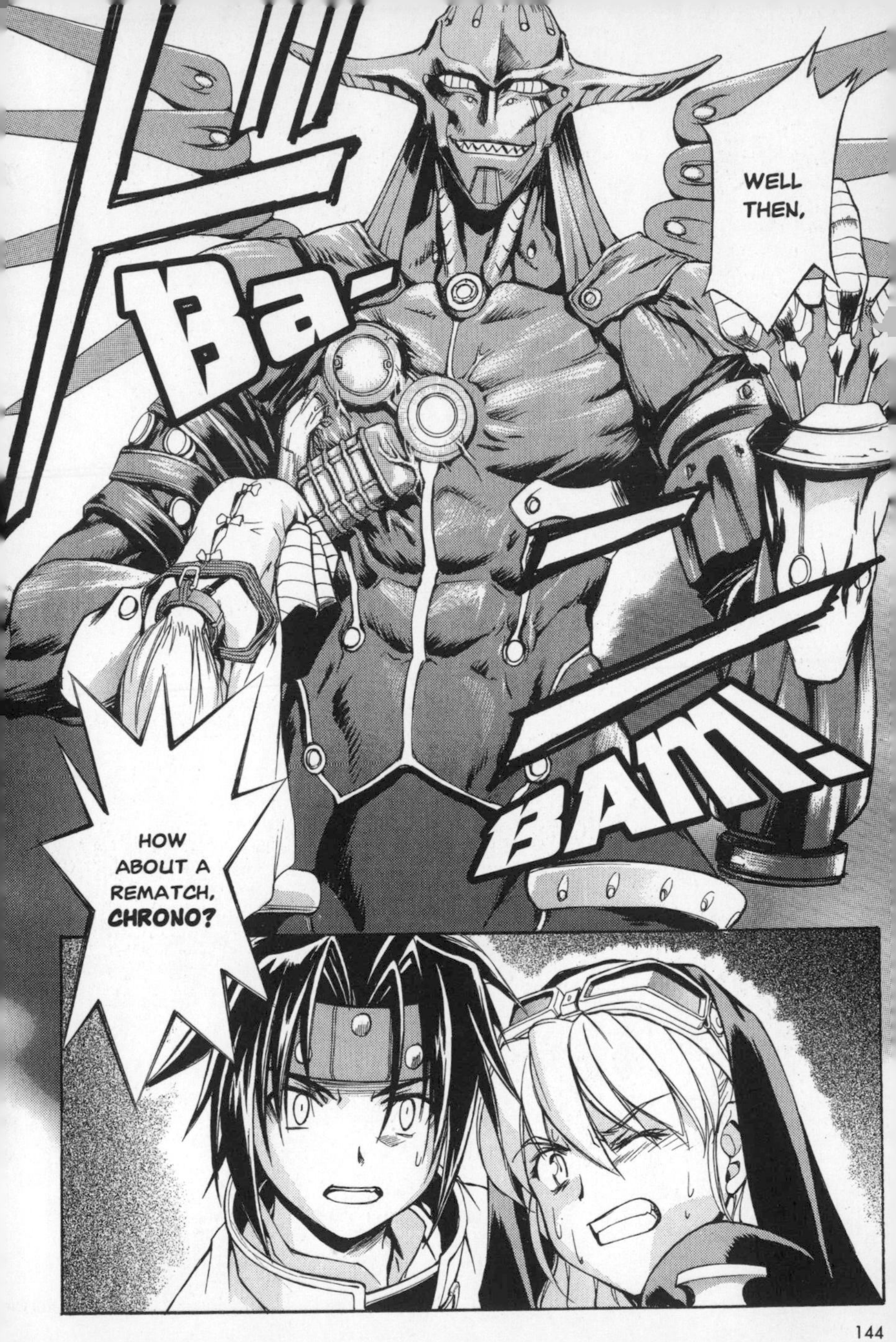
WELL THEN,
Ba-
BAM!!
HOW ABOUT A REMATCH, **CHRONO?**

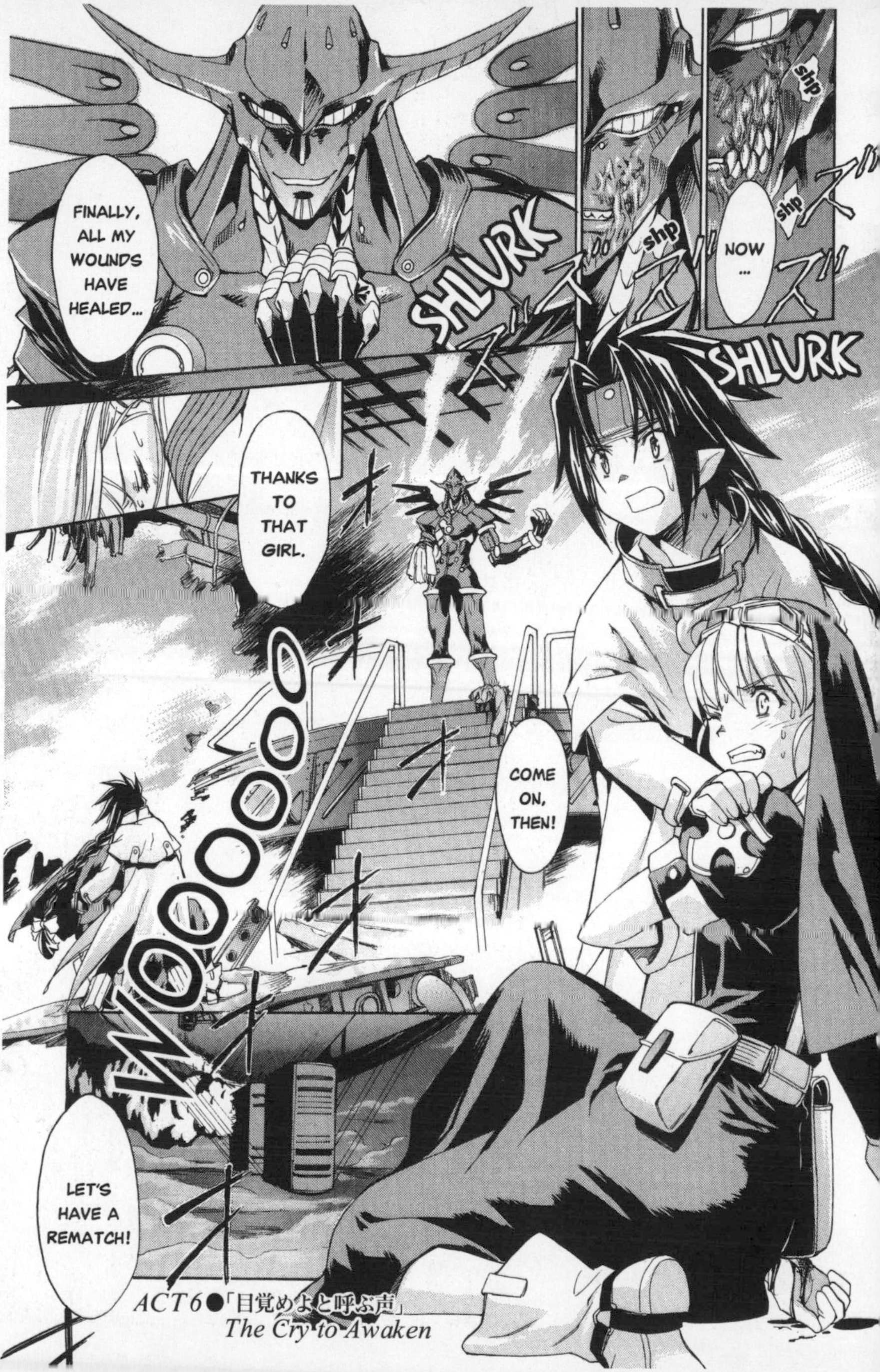
shp
NOW ...
shp
SHLURK
shp
SHLURK
FINALLY, ALL MY WOUNDS HAVE HEALED...
THANKS TO THAT GIRL.
COME ON, THEN!
WOOOOOO
LET'S HAVE A REMATCH!
ACT 6●「目覚めよと呼ぶ声」
The Cry to Awaken

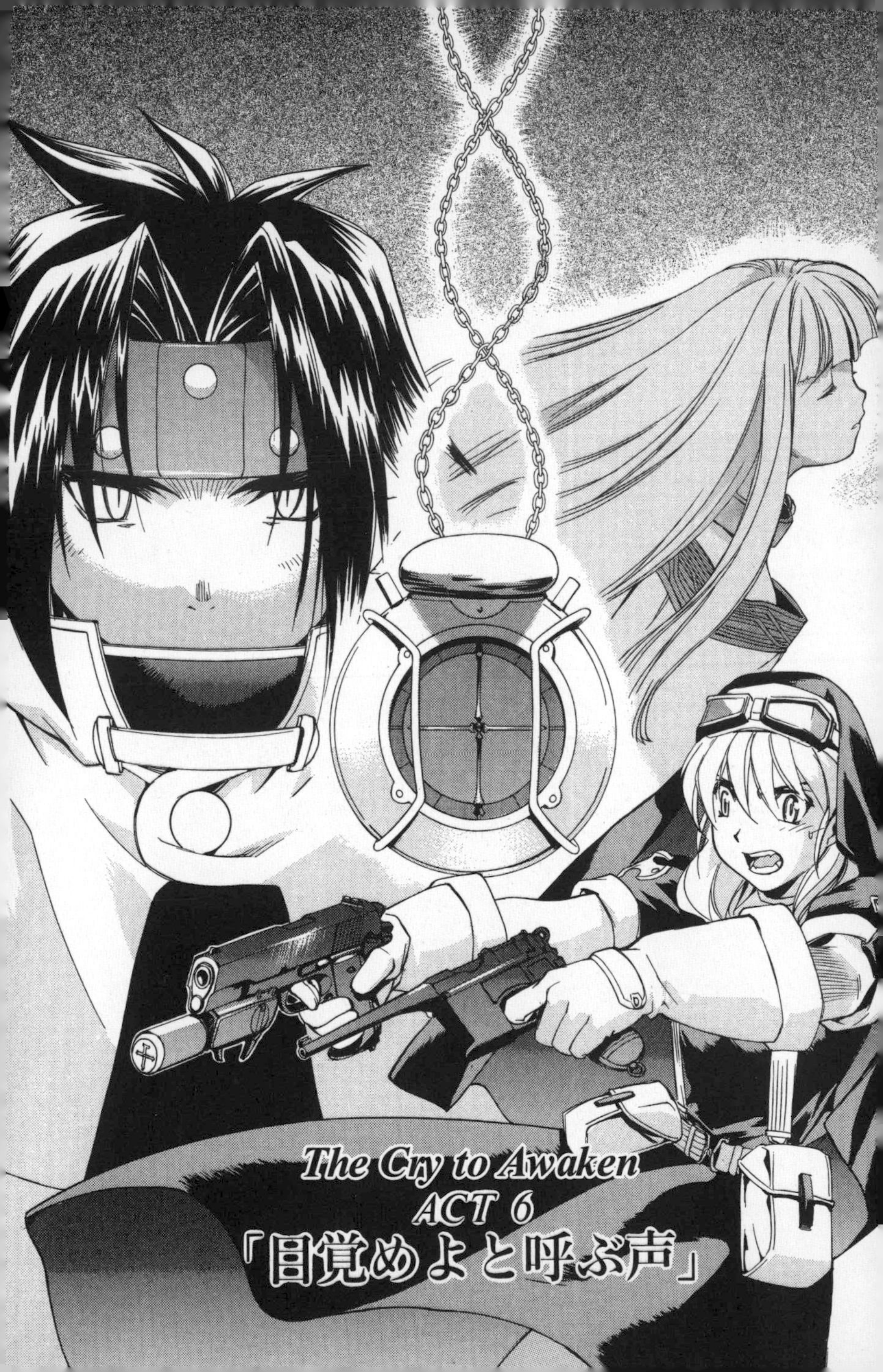
The Cry to Awaken
ACT 6
「目覚めよと呼ぶ声」

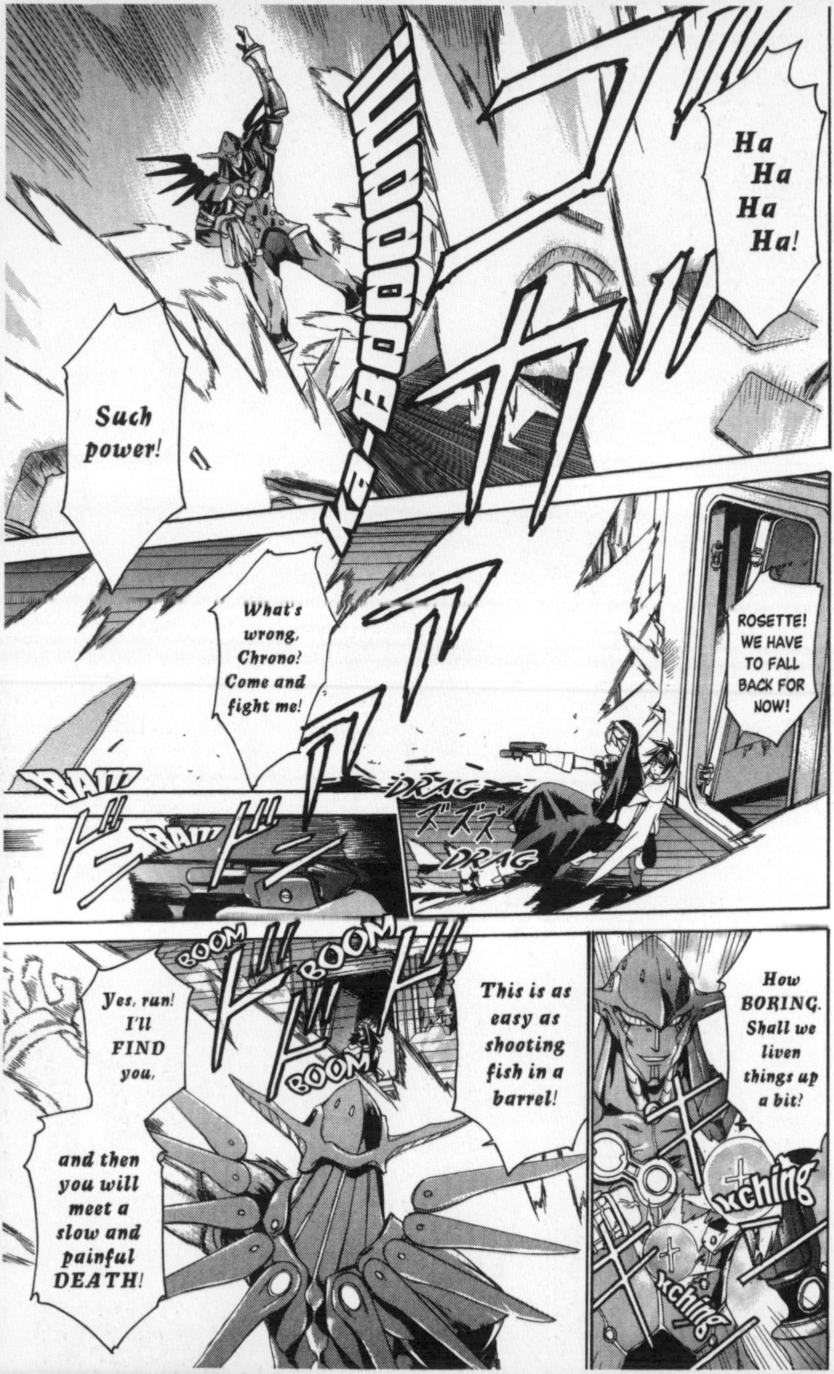
Ha Ha Ha Ha!
KA-FOOOM!
Such power!
ROSETTE! WE HAVE TO FALL BACK FOR NOW!
What's wrong, Chrono? Come and fight me!
DRAG ズズズ DRAG
BAM
BAM
How BORING. Shall we liven things up a bit?
xching
xching
This is as easy as shooting fish in a barrel!
BOOM
BOOM
BOOM
Yes, run! I'll FIND you,
and then you will meet a slow and painful DEATH!

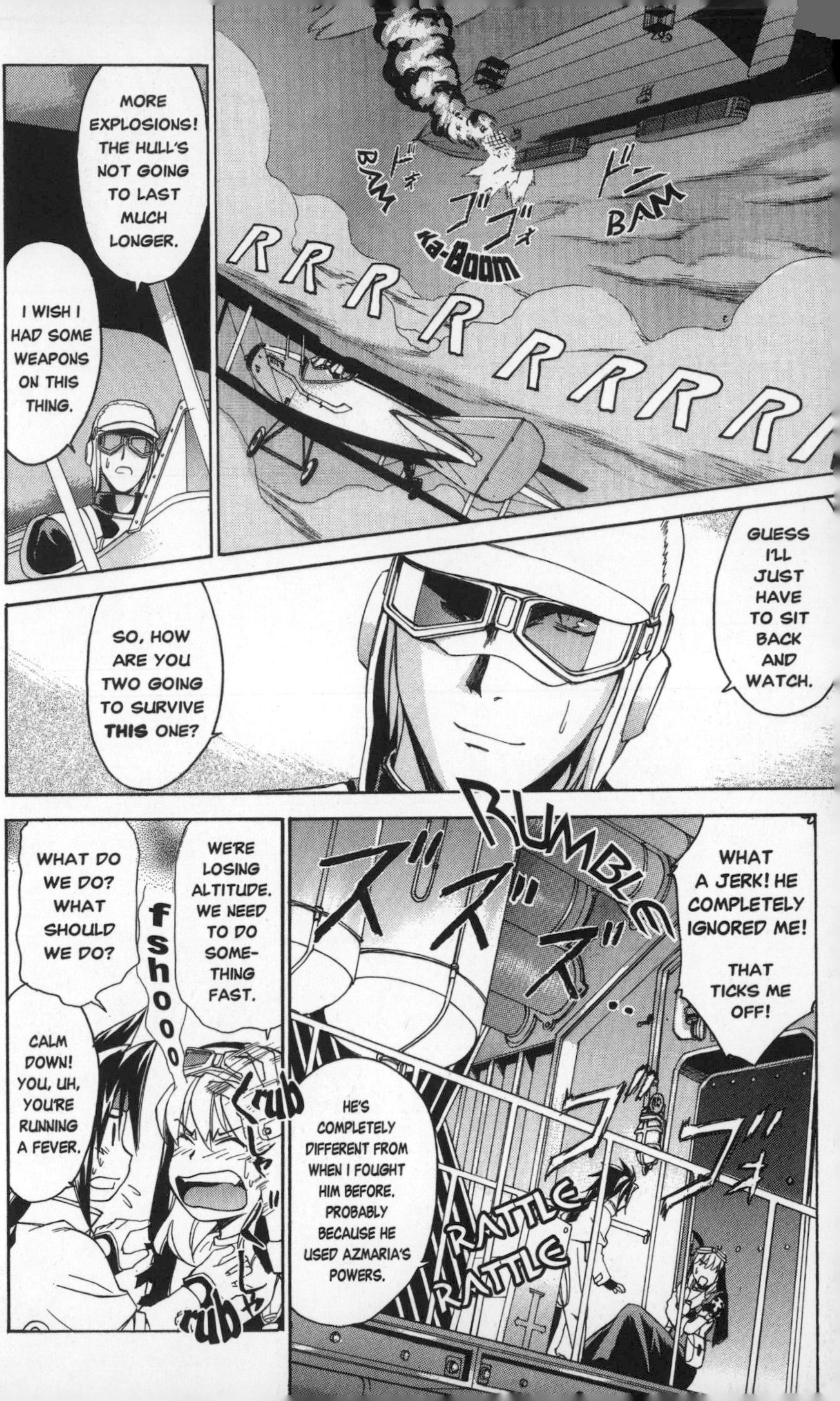
BAM
Ka-Boom
BAM
RRRRRRRRRR
MORE EXPLOSIONS! THE HULL'S NOT GOING TO LAST MUCH LONGER.
I WISH I HAD SOME WEAPONS ON THIS THING.
GUESS I'LL JUST HAVE TO SIT BACK AND WATCH.
SO, HOW ARE YOU TWO GOING TO SURVIVE **THIS** ONE?
RUMBLE
WHAT A JERK! HE COMPLETELY IGNORED ME!
THAT TICKS ME OFF!
RATTLE
RATTLE
WE'RE LOSING ALTITUDE. WE NEED TO DO SOME-THING FAST.
WHAT DO WE DO? WHAT SHOULD WE DO?
fshooo
HE'S COMPLETELY DIFFERENT FROM WHEN I FOUGHT HIM BEFORE. PROBABLY BECAUSE HE USED AZMARIA'S POWERS.
CALM DOWN! YOU, UH, YOU'RE RUNNING A FEVER.
rub
rub

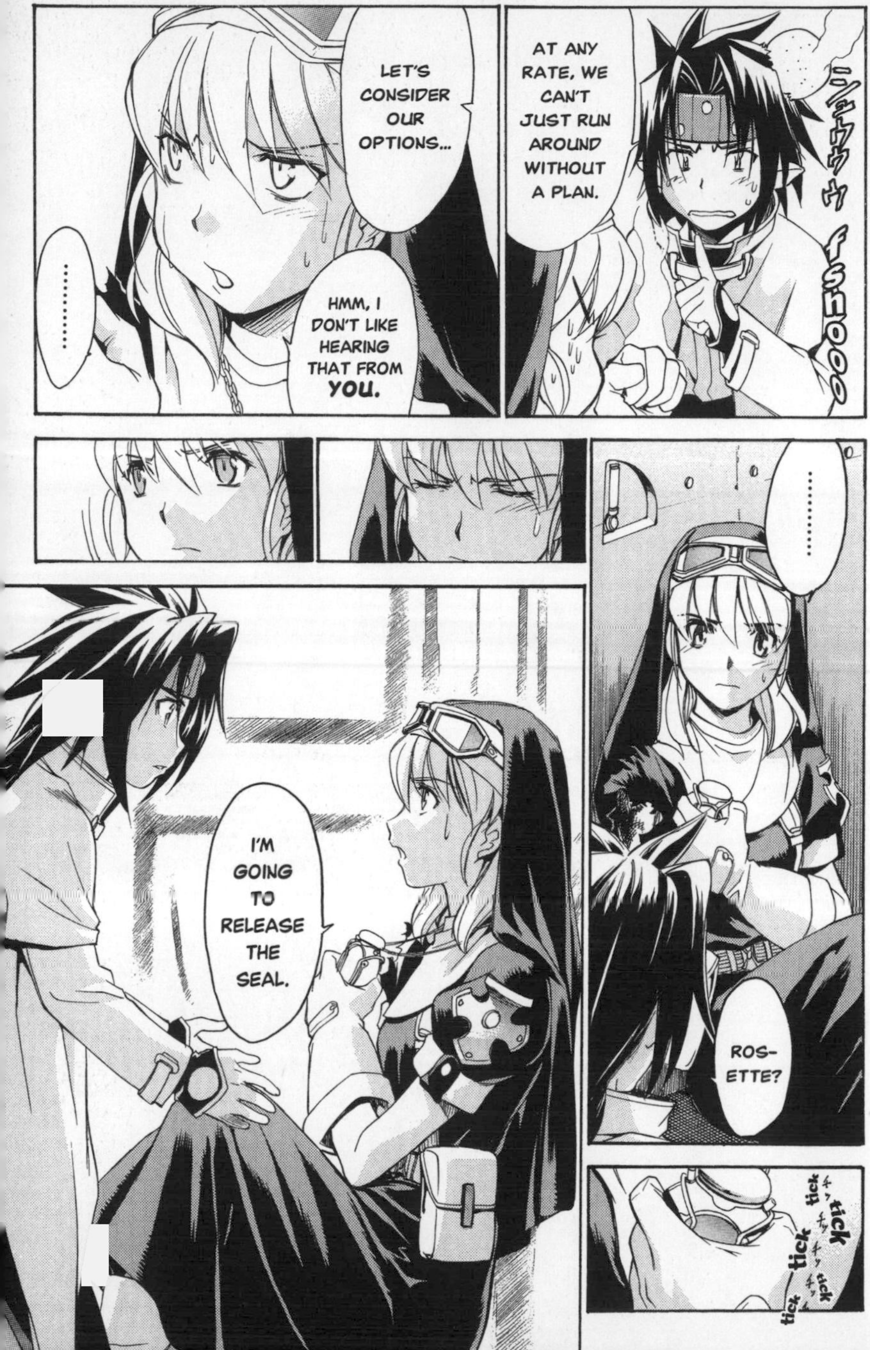
AT ANY RATE, WE CAN'T JUST RUN AROUND WITHOUT A PLAN.
fshooo
LET'S CONSIDER OUR OPTIONS...
HMM, I DON'T LIKE HEARING THAT FROM **YOU.**
......
......
ROS-ETTE?
tick tick tick tick
I'M GOING TO RELEASE THE SEAL.

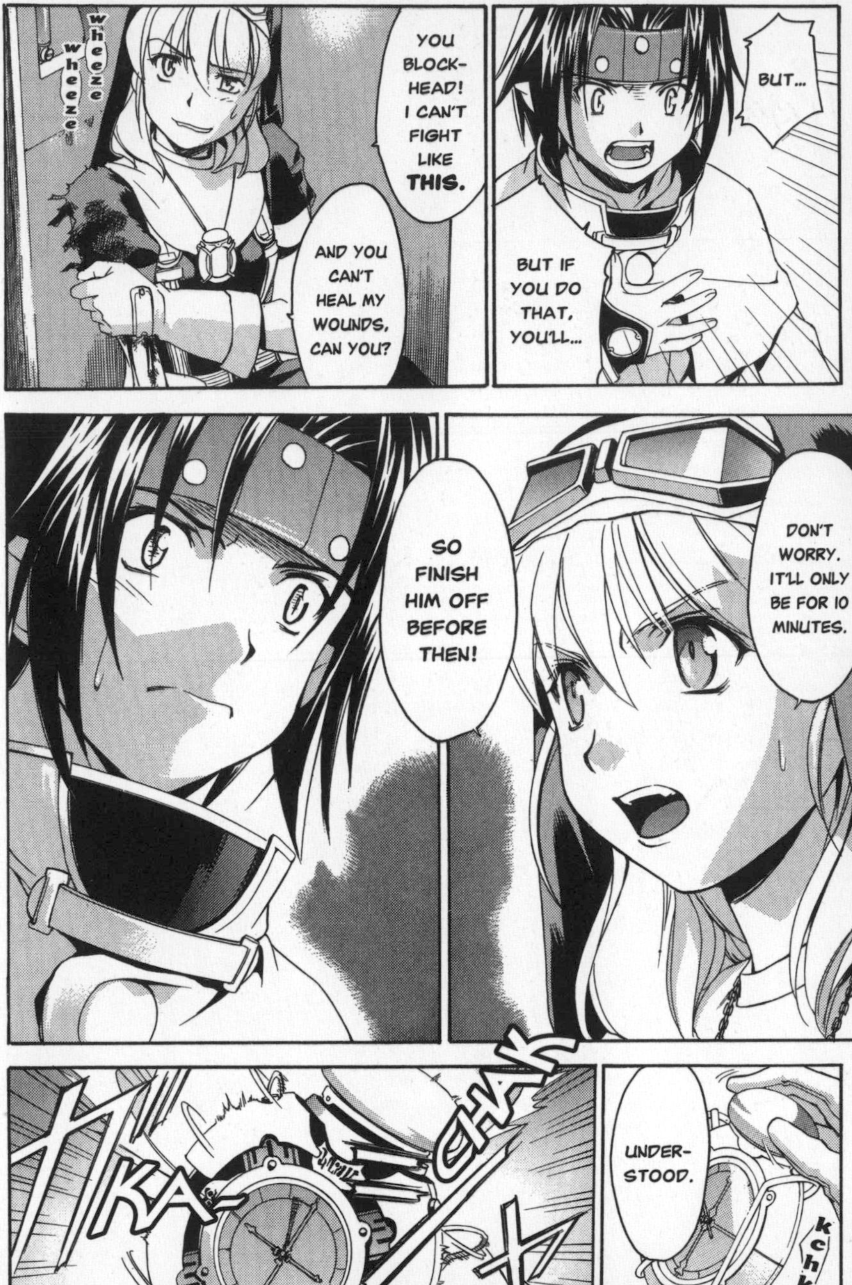
BUT...
BUT IF YOU DO THAT, YOU'LL...
wheeze wheeze
YOU BLOCK-HEAD! I CAN'T FIGHT LIKE THIS.
AND YOU CAN'T HEAL MY WOUNDS, CAN YOU?
DON'T WORRY. IT'LL ONLY BE FOR 10 MINUTES.
SO FINISH HIM OFF BEFORE THEN!
UNDER-STOOD.
kchk
KA-CHAK

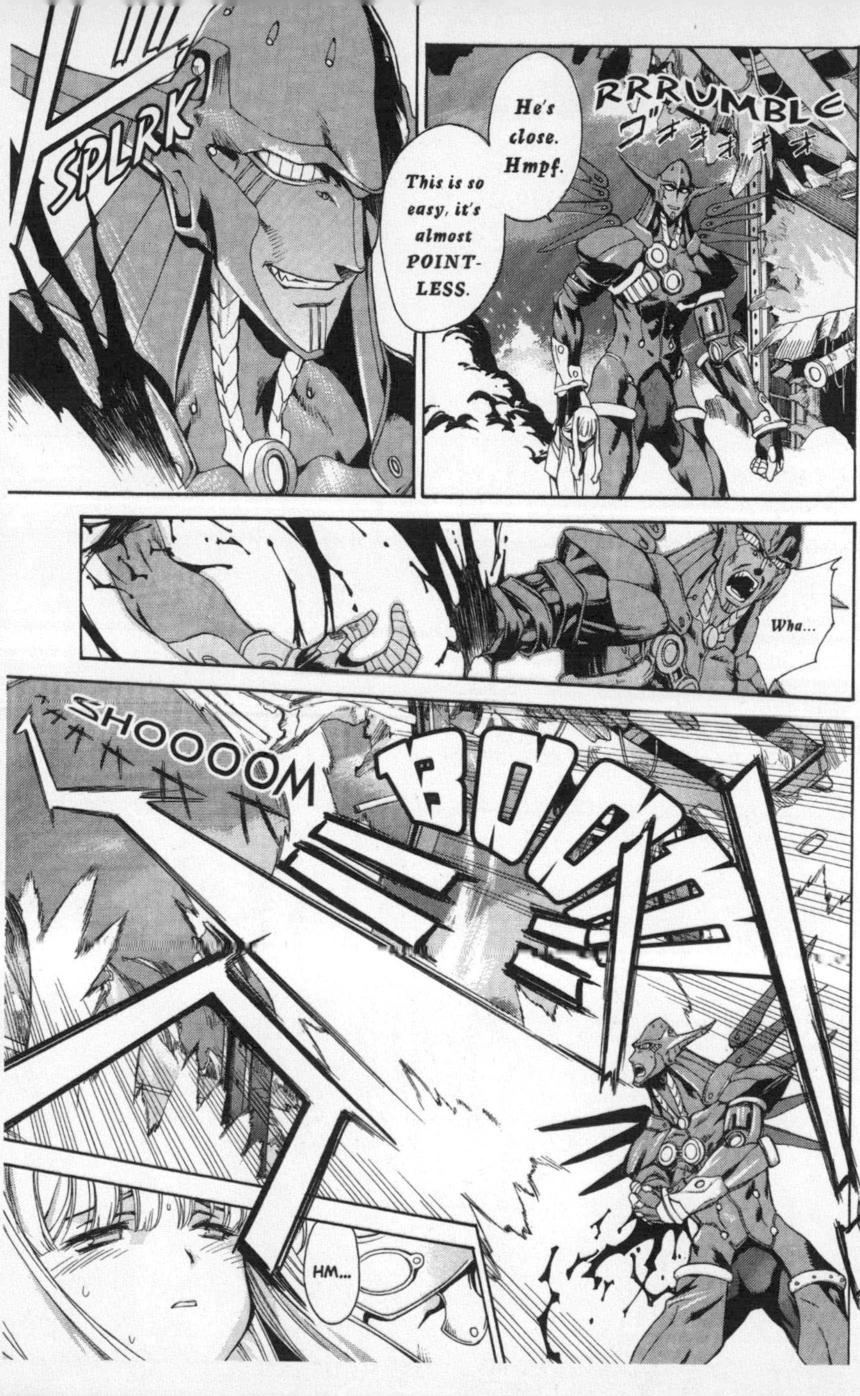
RRRUMBLE
ゴオオオオオ
He's close. Hmpf.
This is so easy, it's almost POINTLESS.
SPLRK
Wha...
SHOOOOM
BOOM
HM...

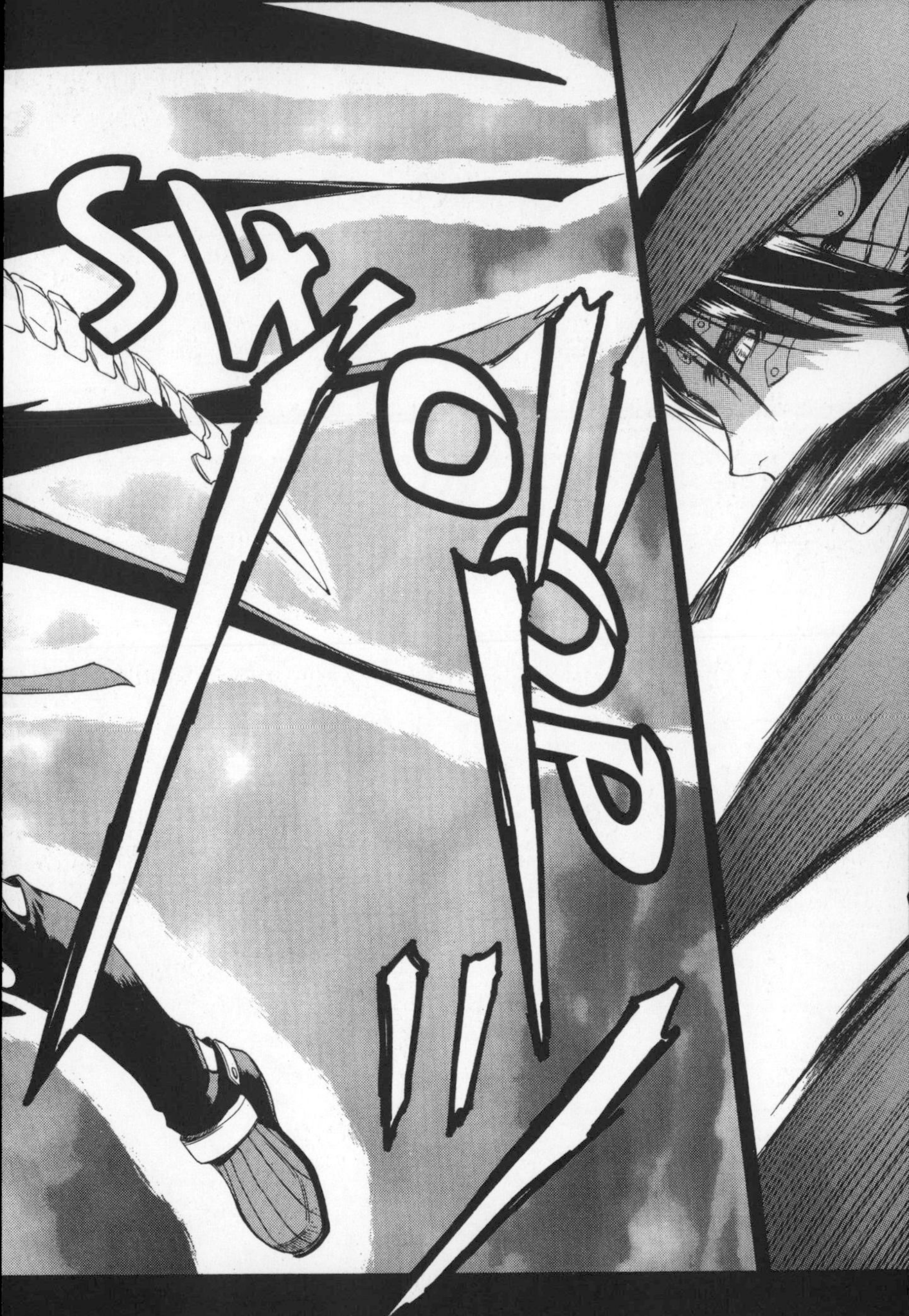

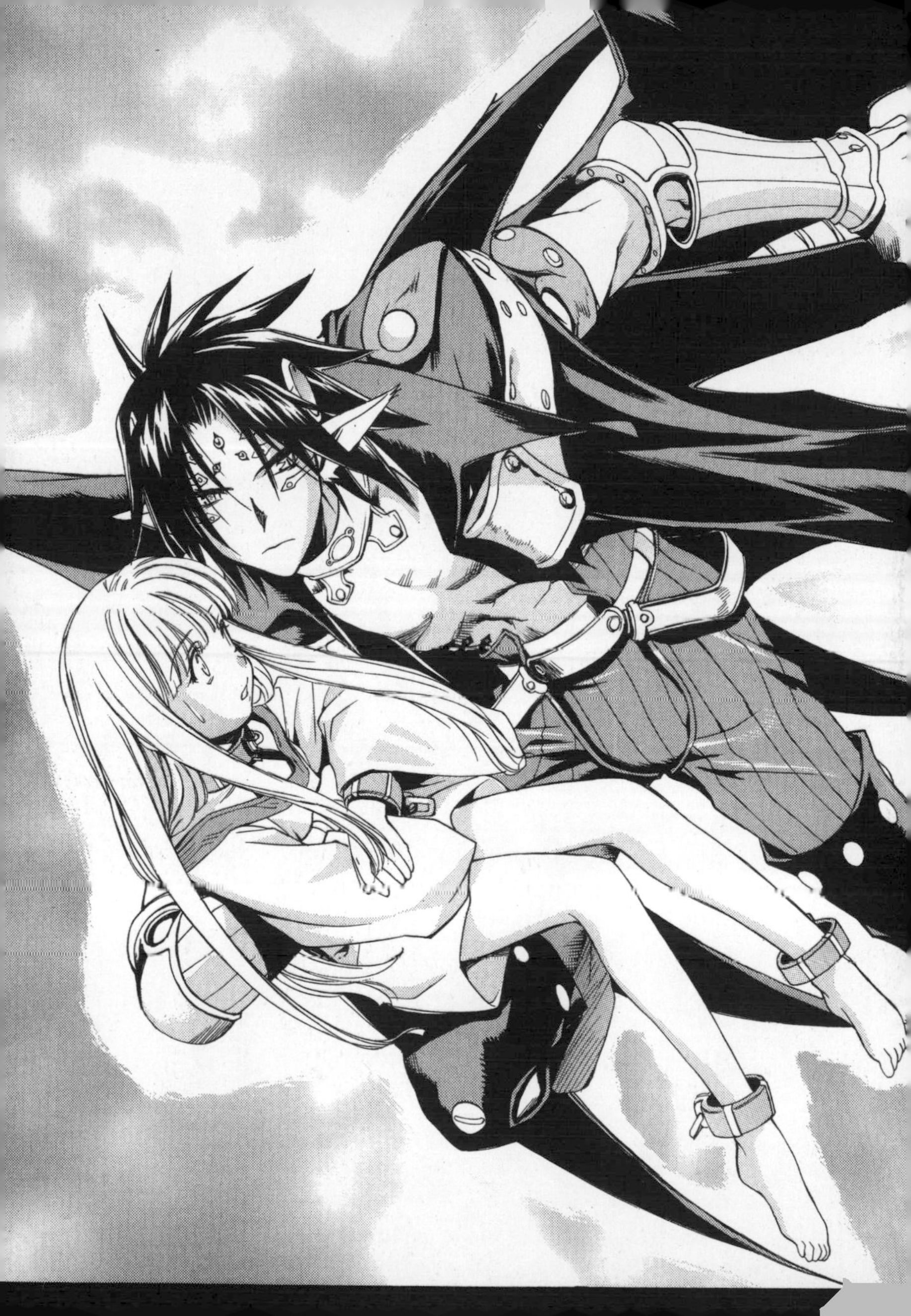

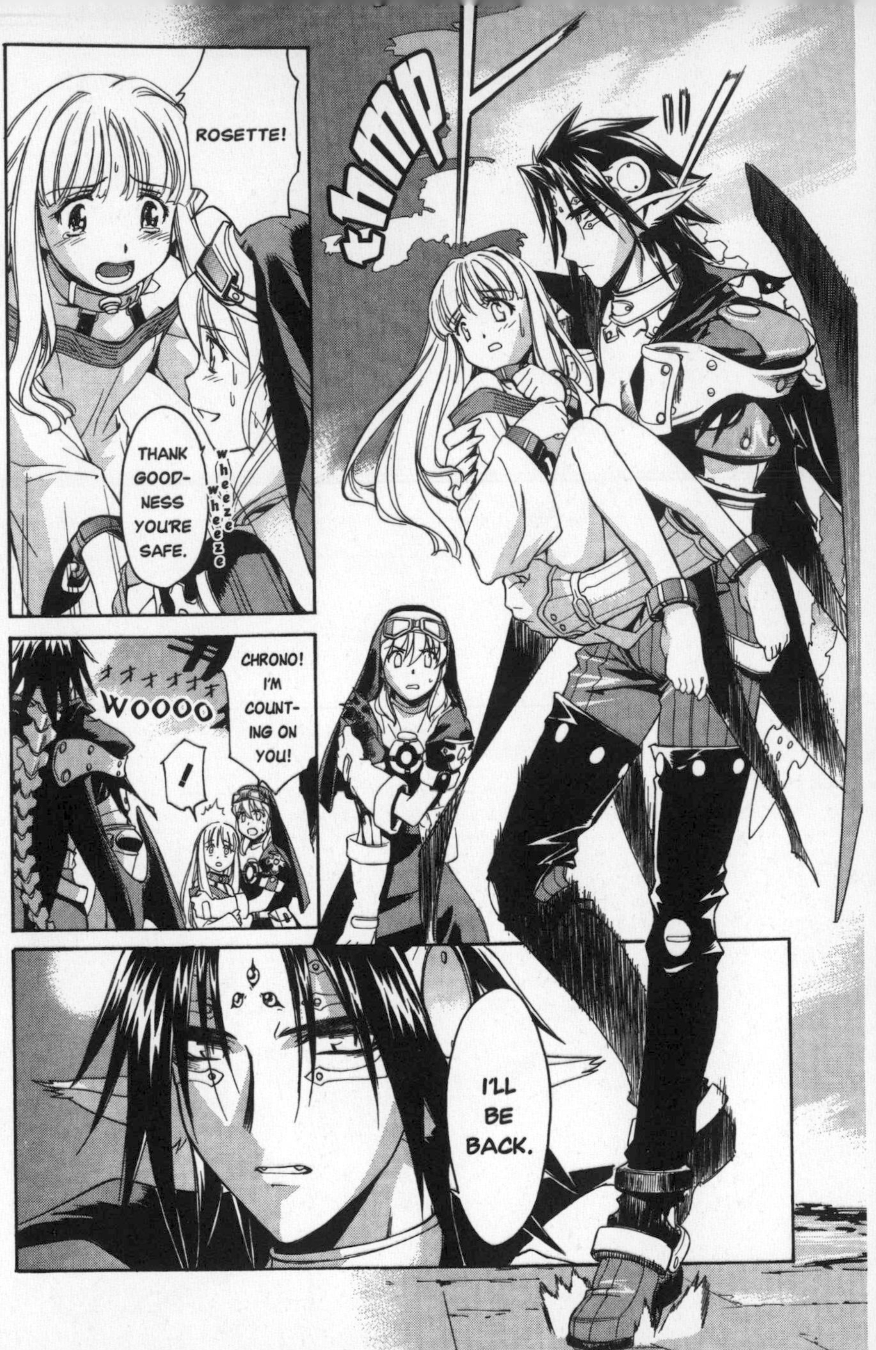
chmp
ROSETTE!
THANK GOODNESS YOU'RE SAFE.
wheeze wheeze
CHRONO! I'M COUNTING ON YOU!
オオオオオオ
WOOOO
!
I'LL BE BACK.

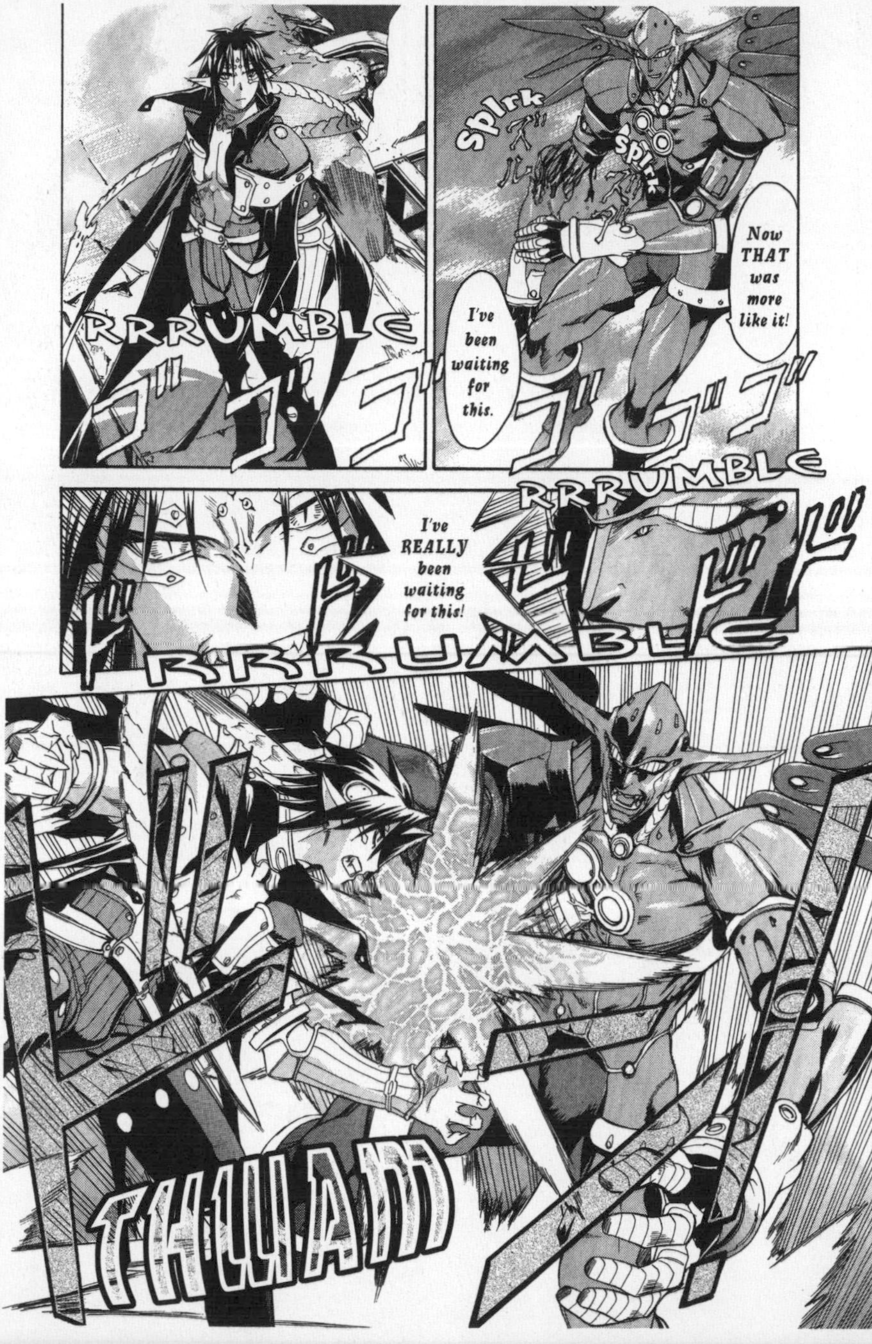
Splrk
Splrk
Now THAT was more like it!
I've been waiting for this.
RRRUMBLE
RRRUMBLE
RRRUMBLE
I've REALLY been waiting for this!
RRRUMBLE
THWAM

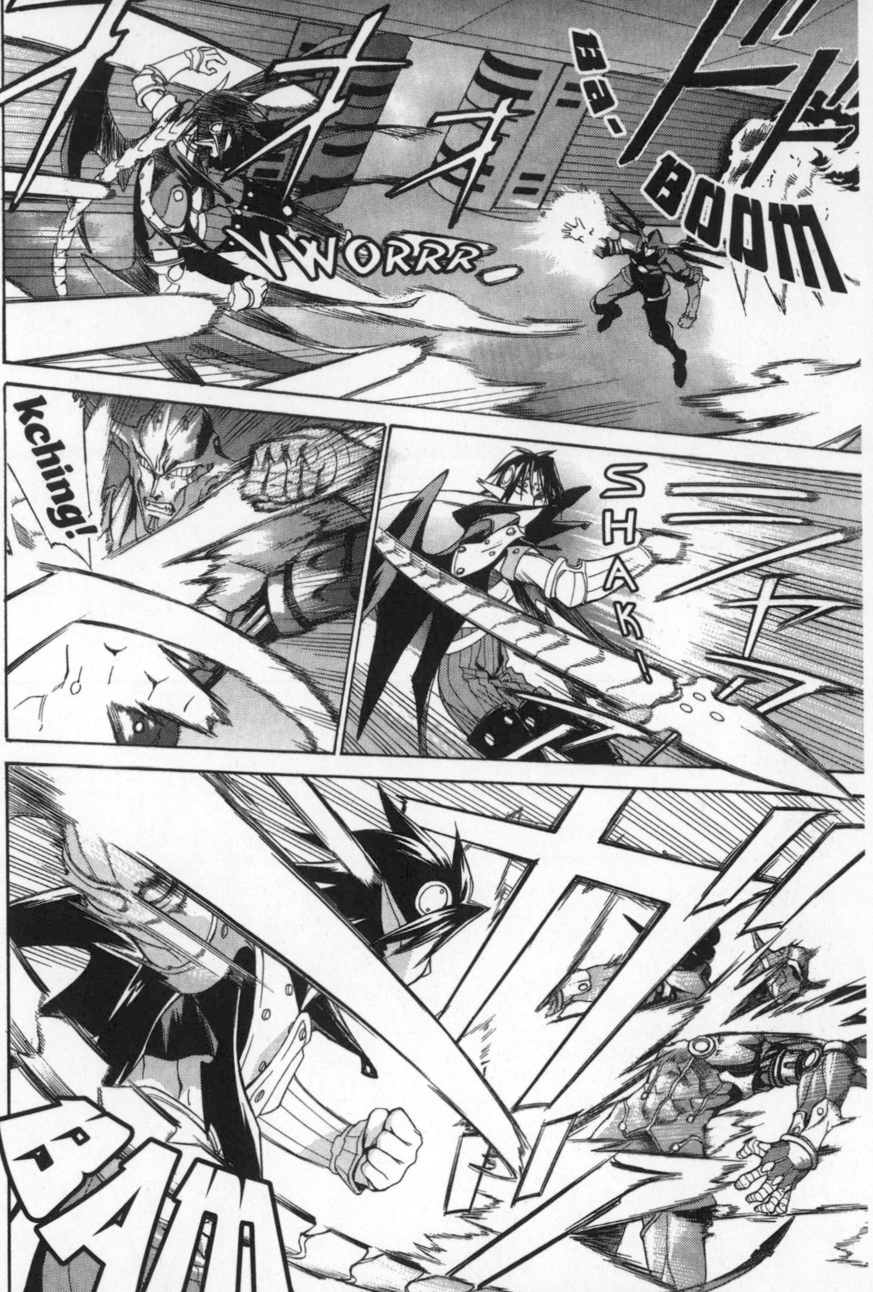
BOOM
VWORRR
SHAKI
kching!
BAM

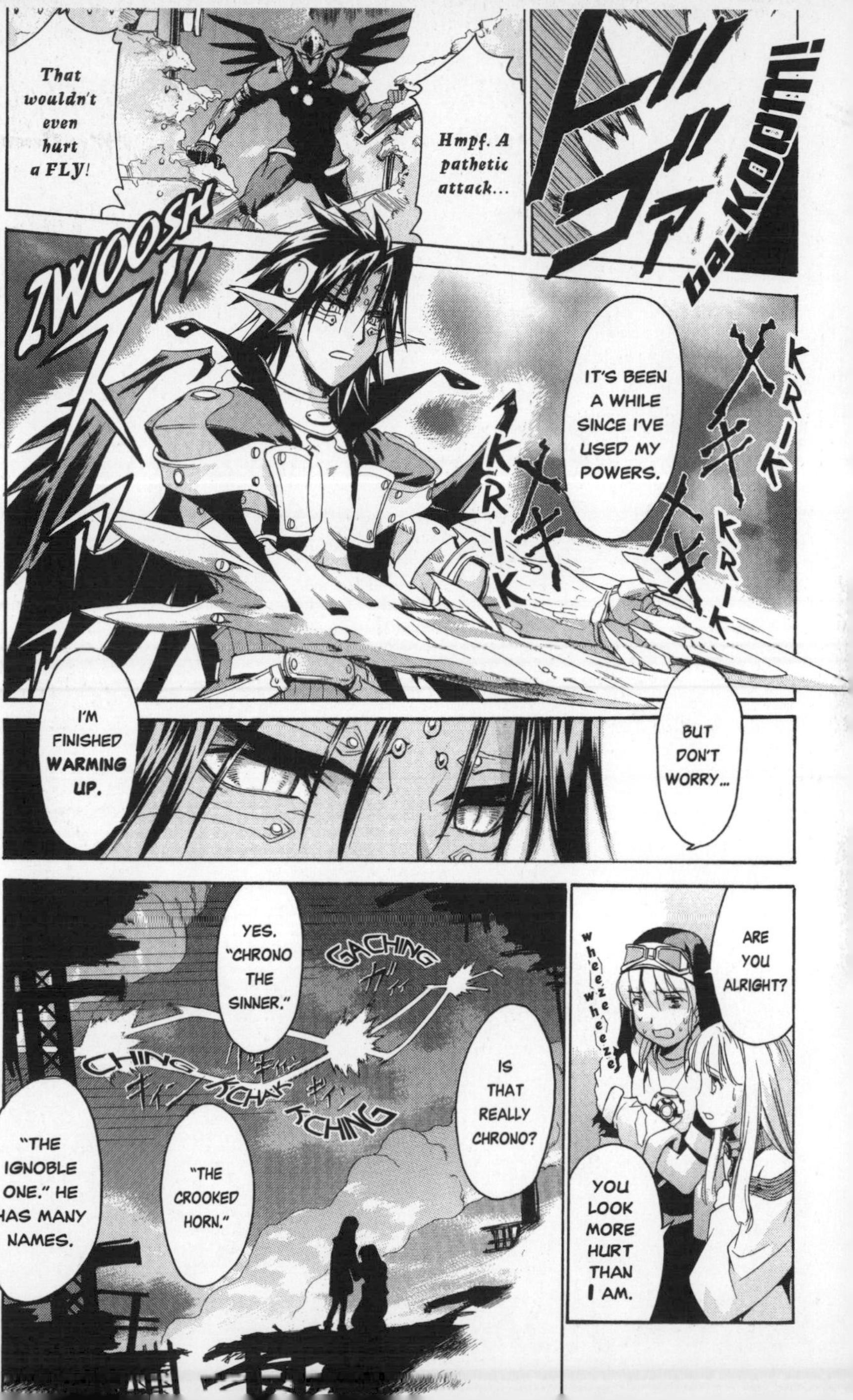
ba-KOOM!!
Hmpf. A pathetic attack...
That wouldn't even hurt a FLY!
IWOOSH
IT'S BEEN A WHILE SINCE I'VE USED MY POWERS.
KRIK
KRIK
KRIK
BUT DON'T WORRY...
I'M FINISHED WARMING UP.
ARE YOU ALRIGHT?
wheeze wheeze
YOU LOOK MORE HURT THAN I AM.
GACHING
IS THAT REALLY CHRONO?
YES. "CHRONO THE SINNER."
CHING
KCHAK
KCHING
"THE CROOKED HORN."
"THE IGNOBLE ONE." HE HAS MANY NAMES.

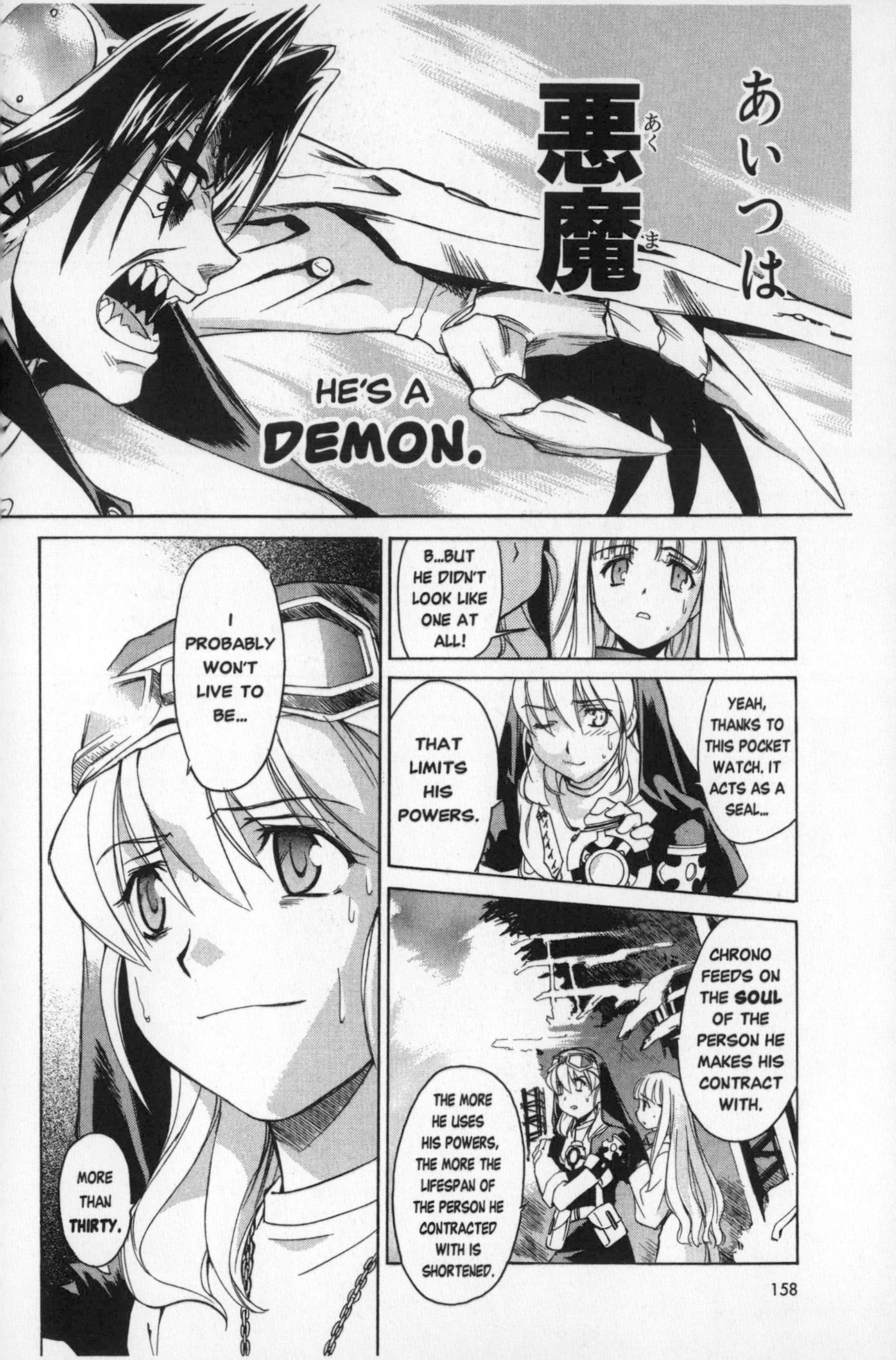
あいつは悪魔
HE'S A DEMON.
B...BUT HE DIDN'T LOOK LIKE ONE AT ALL!
YEAH, THANKS TO THIS POCKET WATCH. IT ACTS AS A SEAL...
THAT LIMITS HIS POWERS.
CHRONO FEEDS ON THE SOUL OF THE PERSON HE MAKES HIS CONTRACT WITH.
THE MORE HE USES HIS POWERS, THE MORE THE LIFESPAN OF THE PERSON HE CONTRACTED WITH IS SHORTENED.
I PROBABLY WON'T LIVE TO BE...
MORE THAN THIRTY.

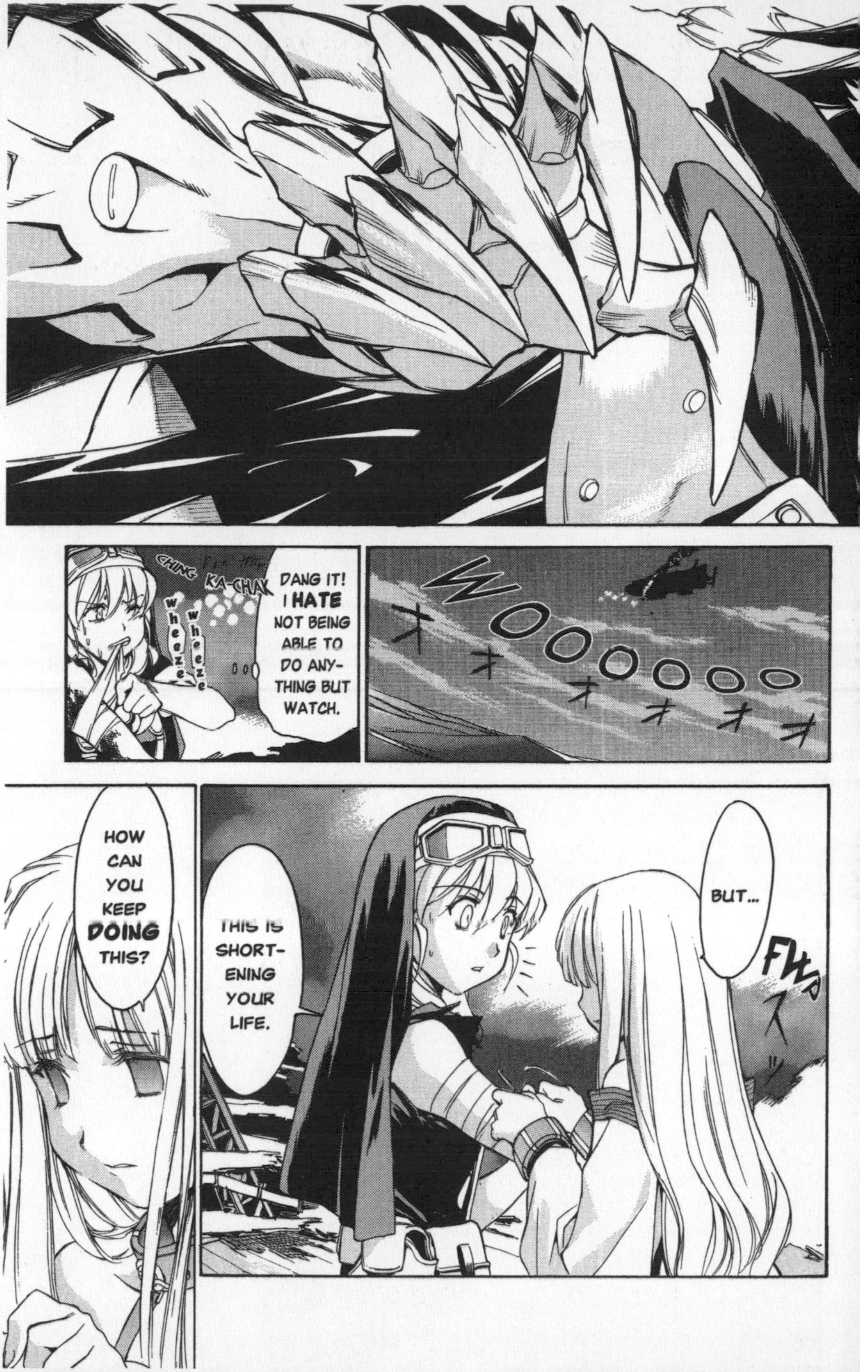
WOOOOOOO
CHING
KA-CHAK
wheeze
wheeze
DANG IT! I HATE NOT BEING ABLE TO DO ANY-THING BUT WATCH.
BUT...
FWP
THIS IS SHORT-ENING YOUR LIFE.
HOW CAN YOU KEEP DOING THIS?

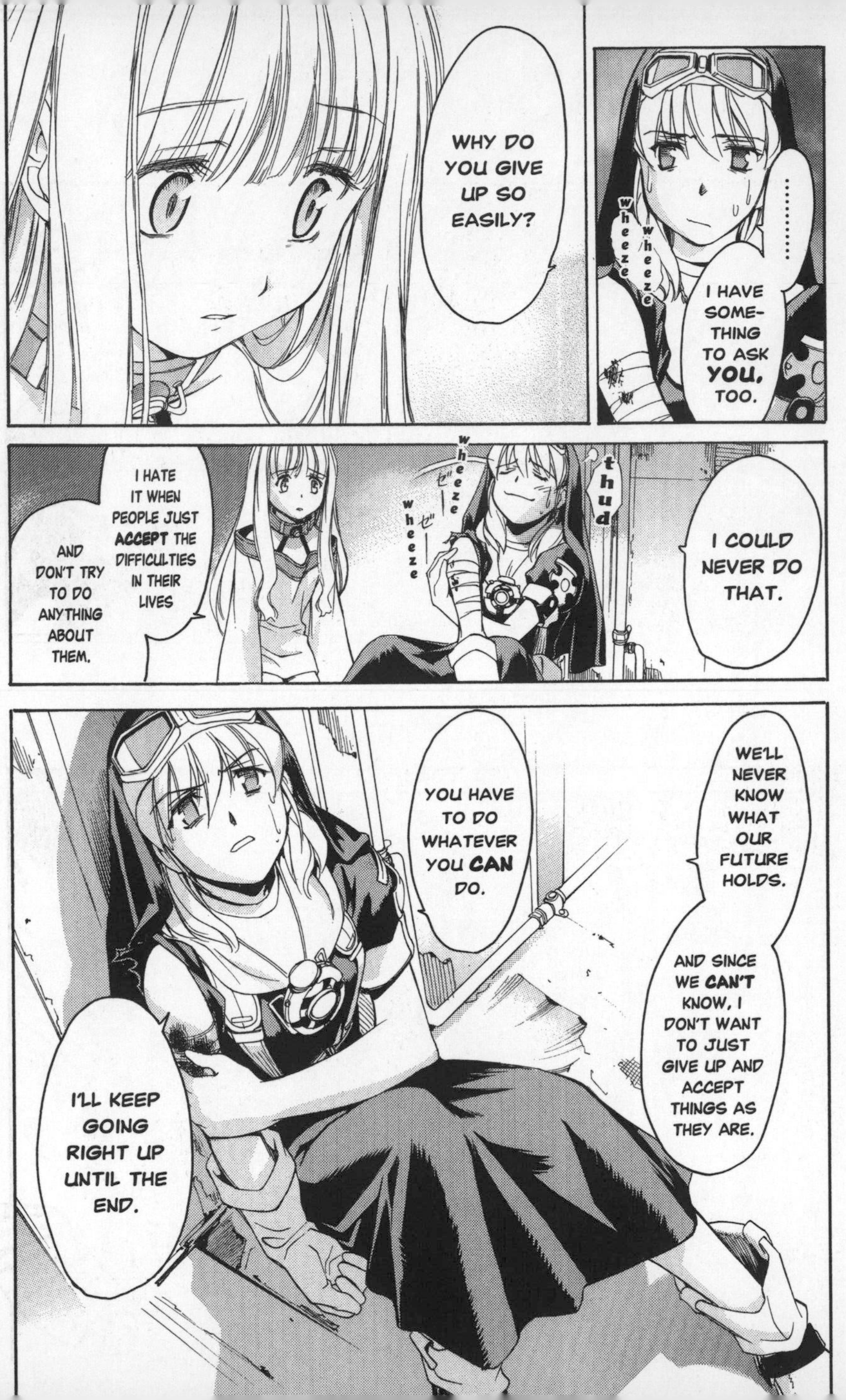
wheeze
wheeze
……
I HAVE SOMETHING TO ASK YOU, TOO.
WHY DO YOU GIVE UP SO EASILY?
I COULD NEVER DO THAT.
thud
wheeze
wheeze
I HATE IT WHEN PEOPLE JUST ACCEPT THE DIFFICULTIES IN THEIR LIVES
AND DON'T TRY TO DO ANYTHING ABOUT THEM.
WE'LL NEVER KNOW WHAT OUR FUTURE HOLDS.
AND SINCE WE CAN'T KNOW, I DON'T WANT TO JUST GIVE UP AND ACCEPT THINGS AS THEY ARE.
YOU HAVE TO DO WHATEVER YOU CAN DO.
I'LL KEEP GOING RIGHT UP UNTIL THE END.

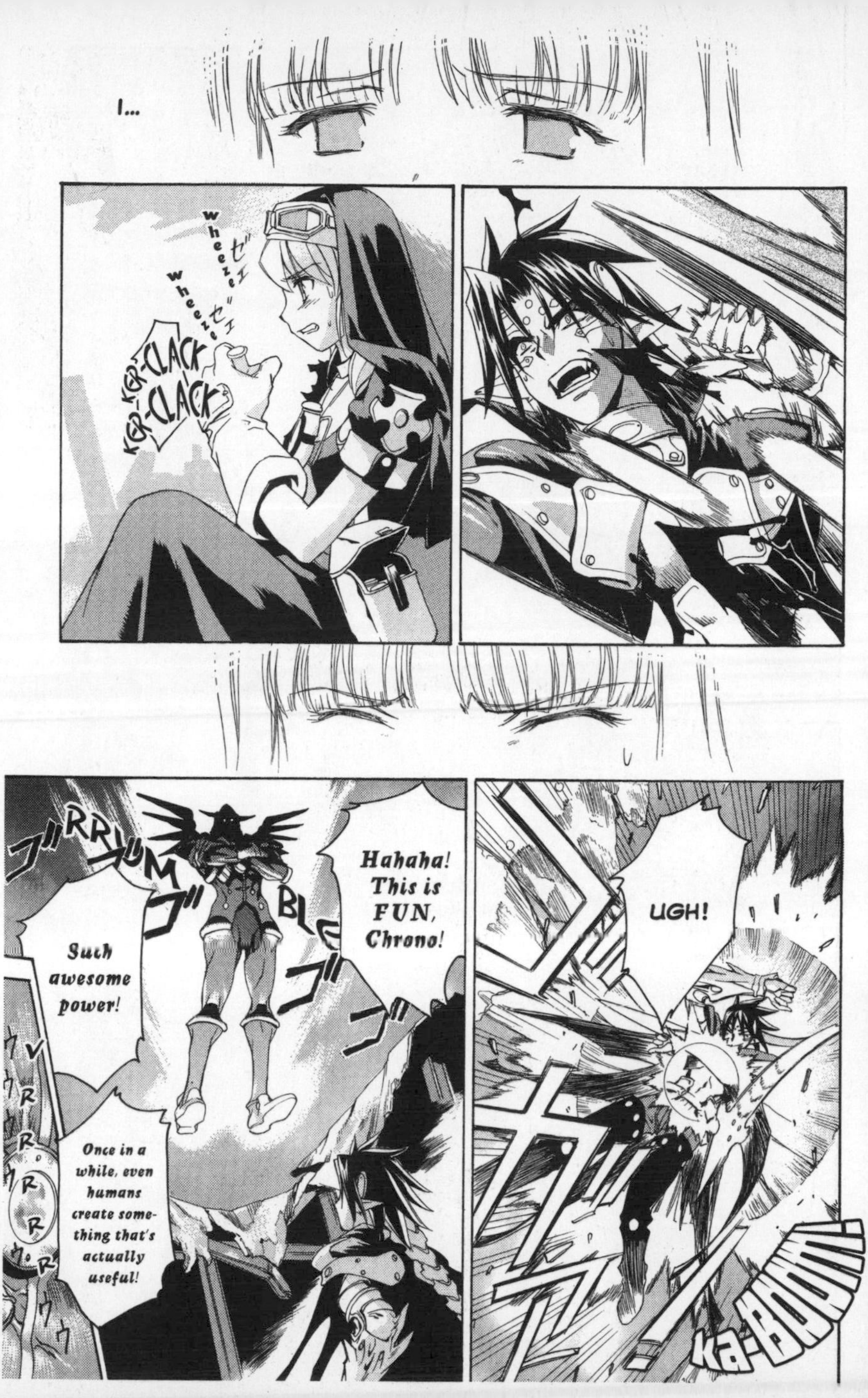
I...
wheeze
wheeze
KER-CLACK
KER-CLACK
UGH!
KA-BOOM
Hahaha! This is FUN, Chrono!
RRRUMM
Such awesome power!
Once in a while, even humans create something that's actually useful!
VRRRRR

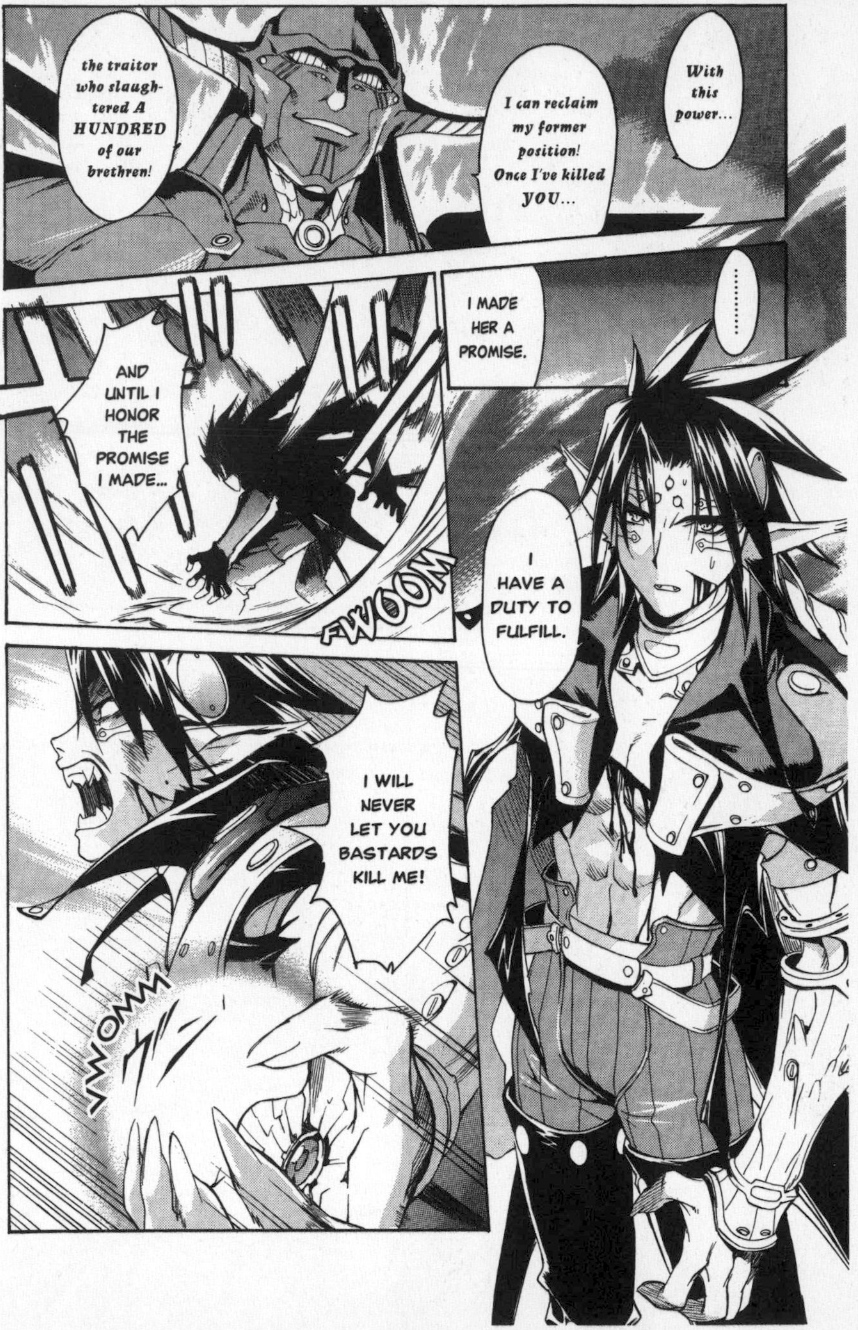
With this power...
I can reclaim my former position! Once I've killed YOU...
the traitor who slaughtered A HUNDRED of our brethren!
......
I MADE HER A PROMISE.
AND UNTIL I HONOR THE PROMISE I MADE...
FWOOM
I HAVE A DUTY TO FULFILL.
I WILL NEVER LET YOU BASTARDS KILL ME!
VWOMM

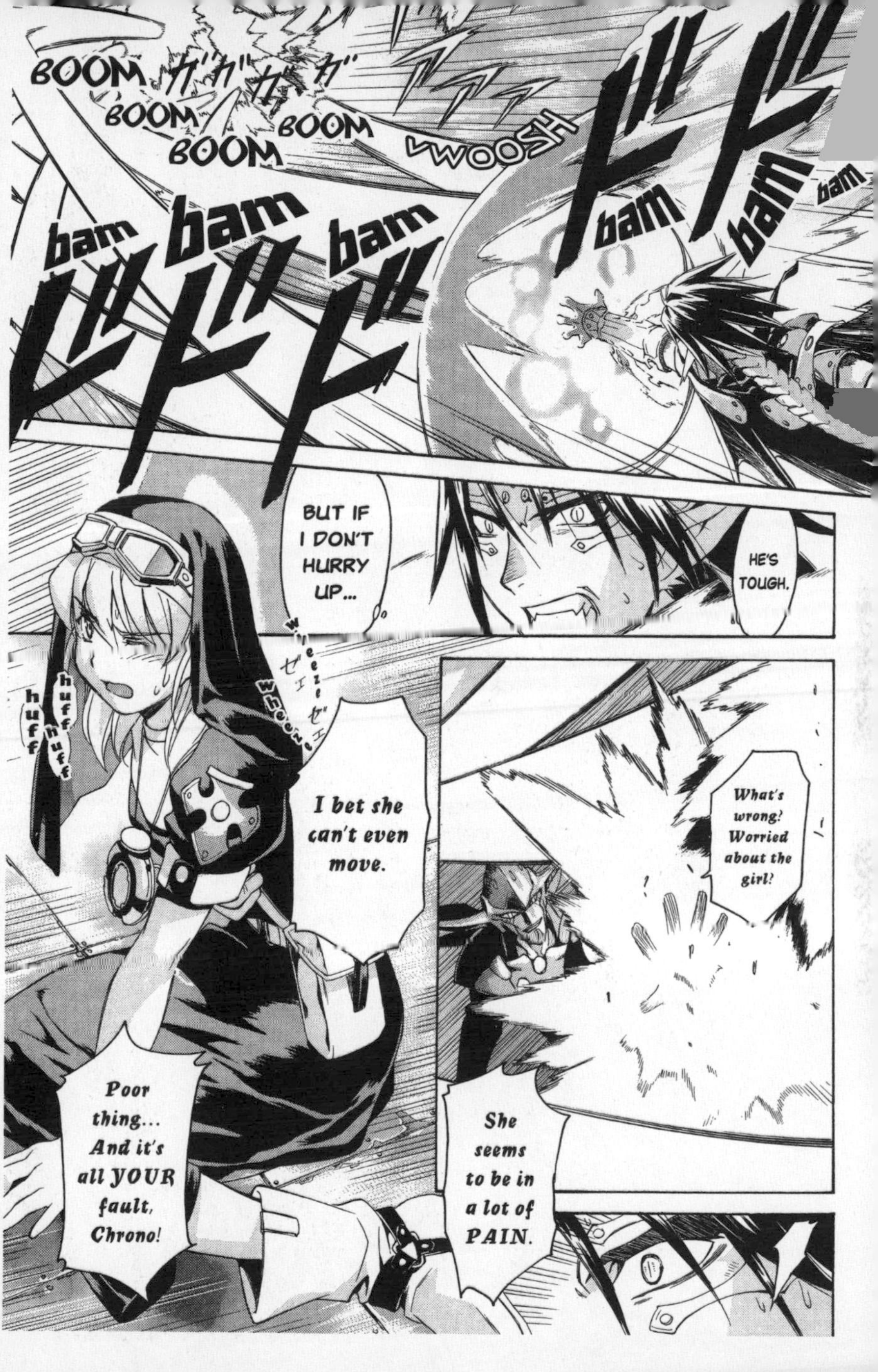
bam
bam
bam
bam
VWOOSH
BOOM
BOOM
BOOM
BOOM
bam
bam
bam
HE'S TOUGH.
BUT IF I DON'T HURRY UP...
What's wrong? Worried about the girl?
She seems to be in a lot of PAIN.
I bet she can't even move.
wheeze wheeze
huff huff huff
Poor thing... And it's all YOUR fault, Chrono!

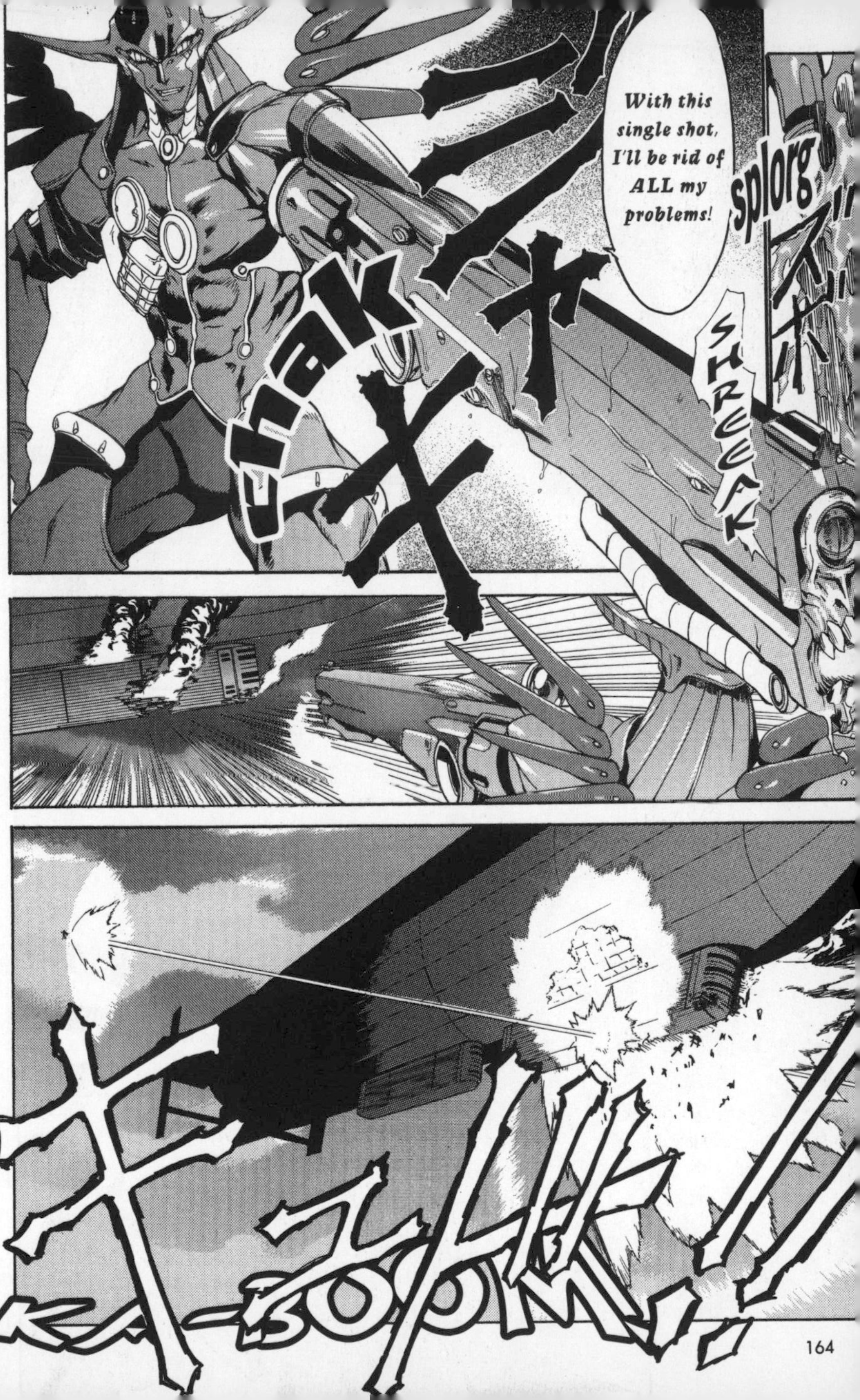
With this single shot, I'll be rid of ALL my problems!
splorg
SHRCCCK
chak
KA-BOOM!!

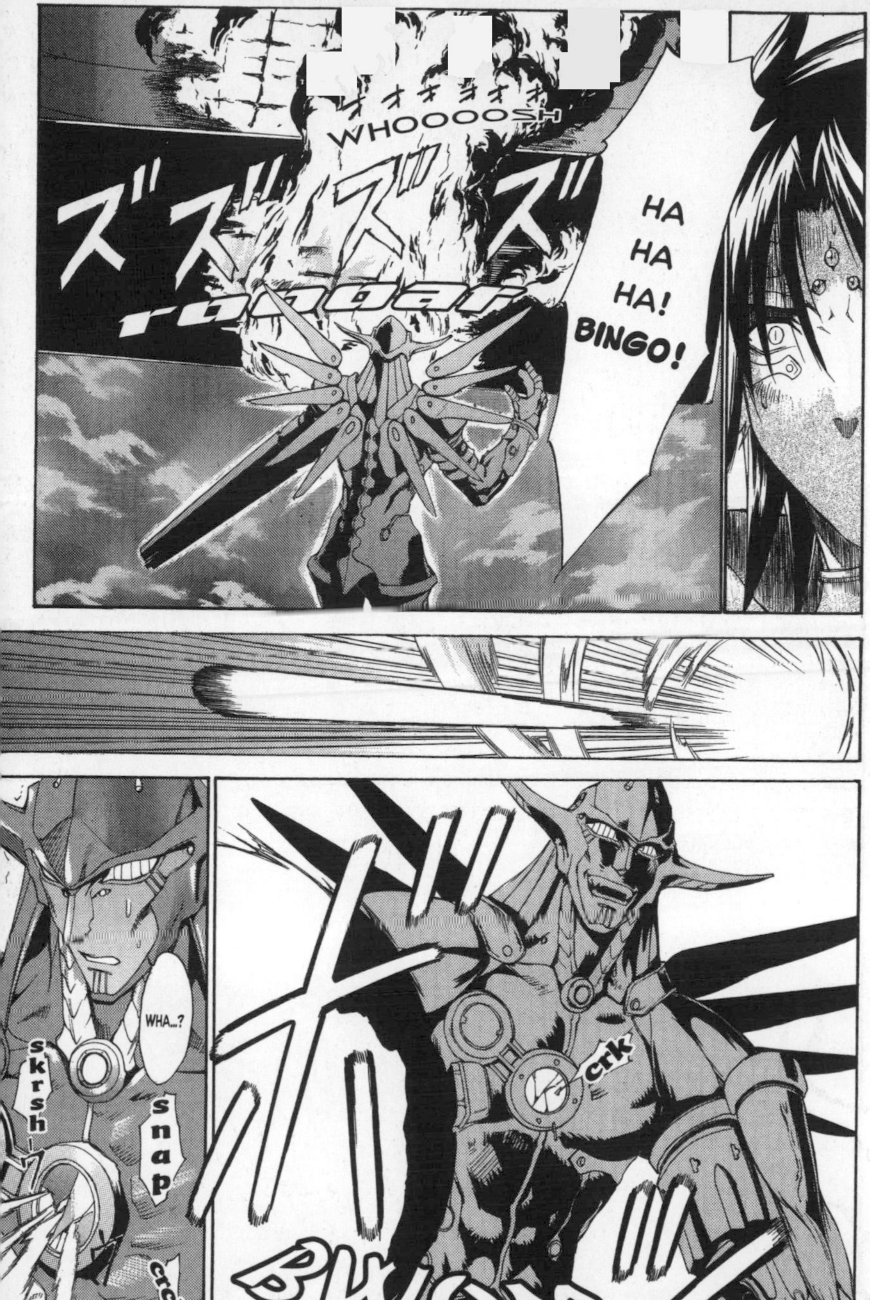
HA HA HA! BINGO!
ズズズ
WHOOOOSH
roooar
BWOM
crk
WHA...?
skrsh
snap
crck

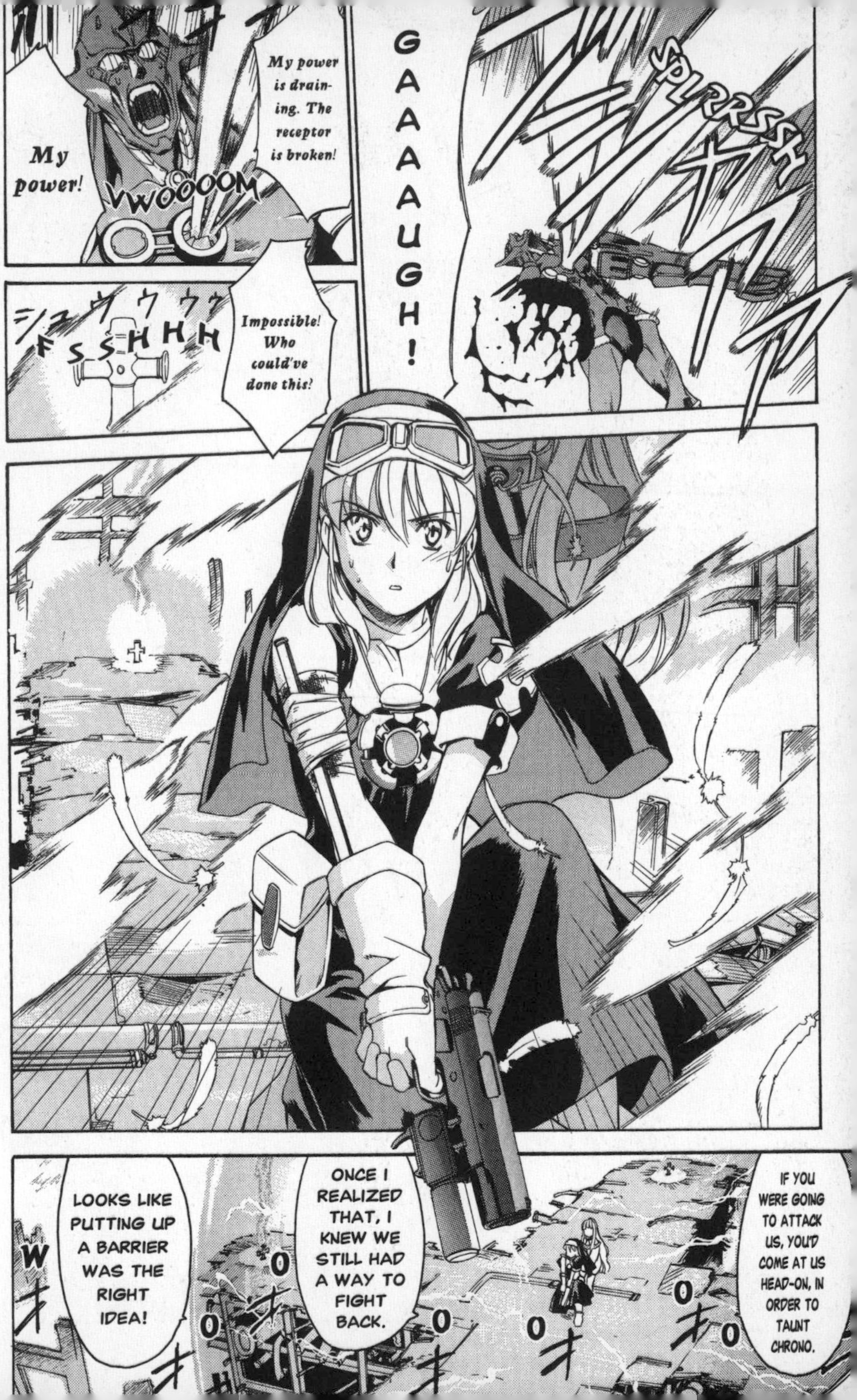
SPLRRSSH
GAAAAUGH!
My power is drain-ing. The receptor is broken!
My power!
VWOOOOM
FSSHHH
Impossible! Who could've done this?
IF YOU WERE GOING TO ATTACK US, YOU'D COME AT US HEAD-ON, IN ORDER TO TAUNT CHRONO.
ONCE I REALIZED THAT, I KNEW WE STILL HAD A WAY TO FIGHT BACK.
LOOKS LIKE PUTTING UP A BARRIER WAS THE RIGHT IDEA!

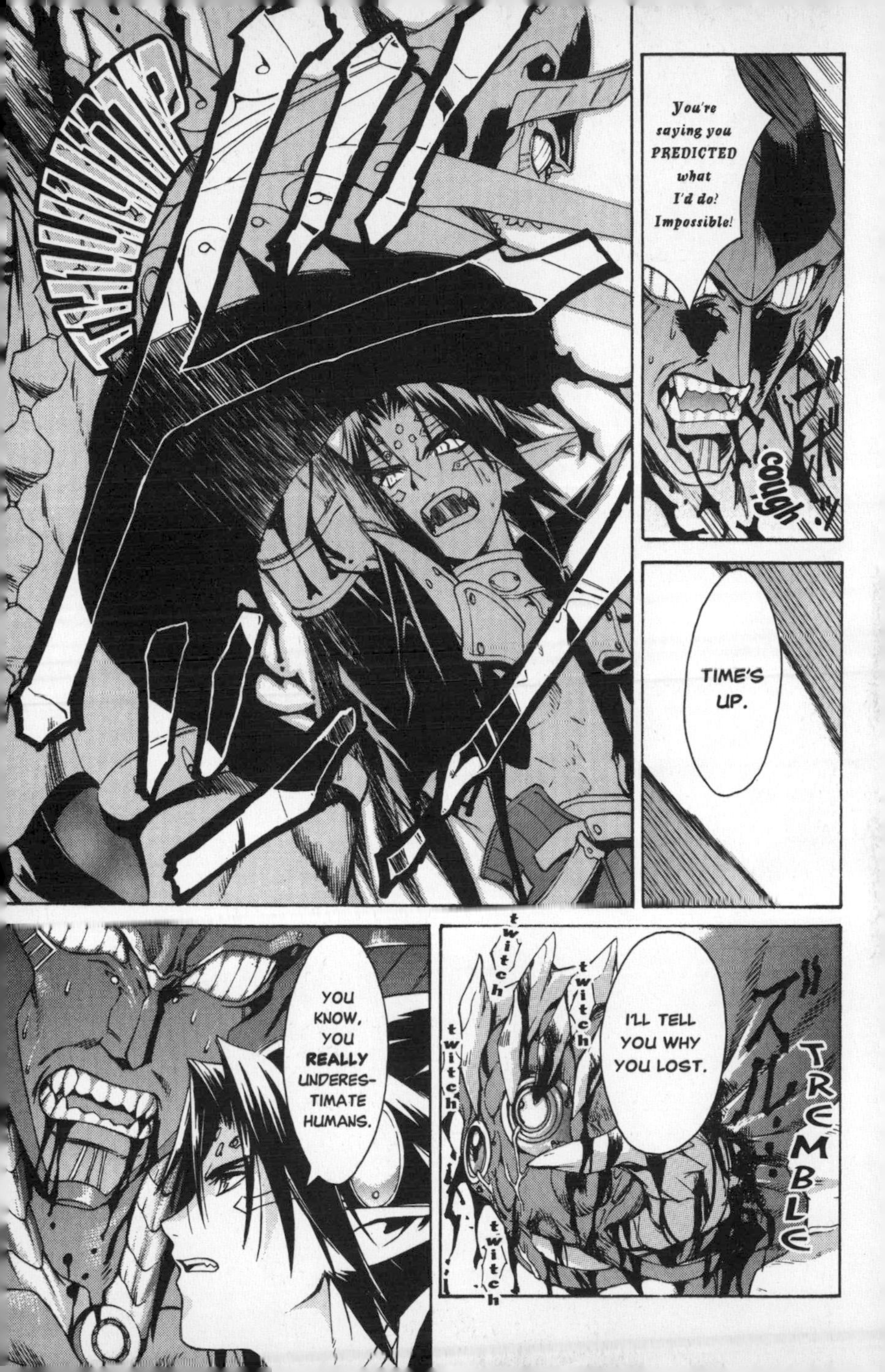
You're saying you PREDICTED what I'd do? Impossible!
cough
TIME'S UP.
twitch
twitch
twitch
twitch
I'LL TELL YOU WHY YOU LOST.
TREMBLE
YOU KNOW, YOU REALLY UNDERES-TIMATE HUMANS.

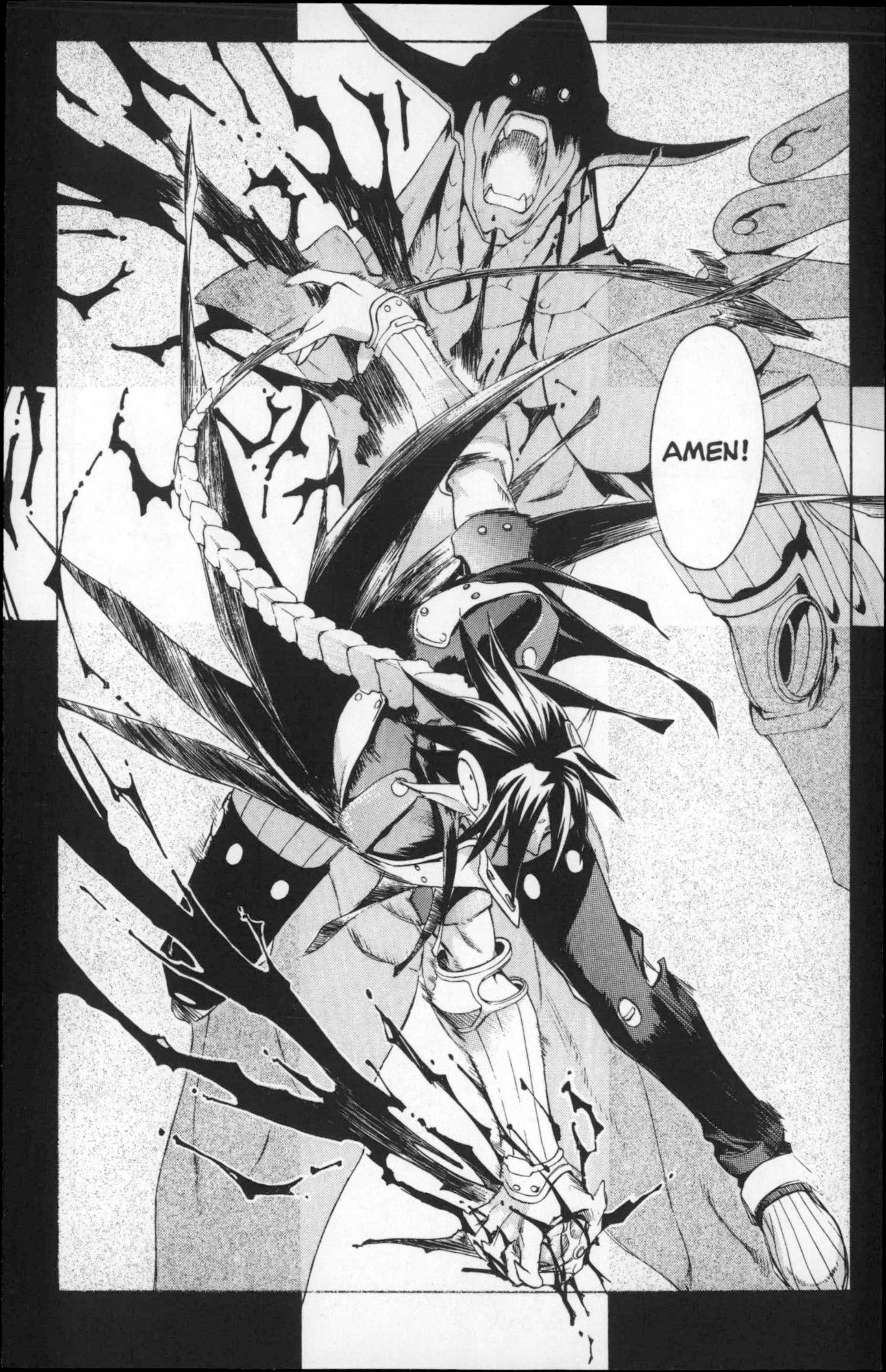
AMEN!

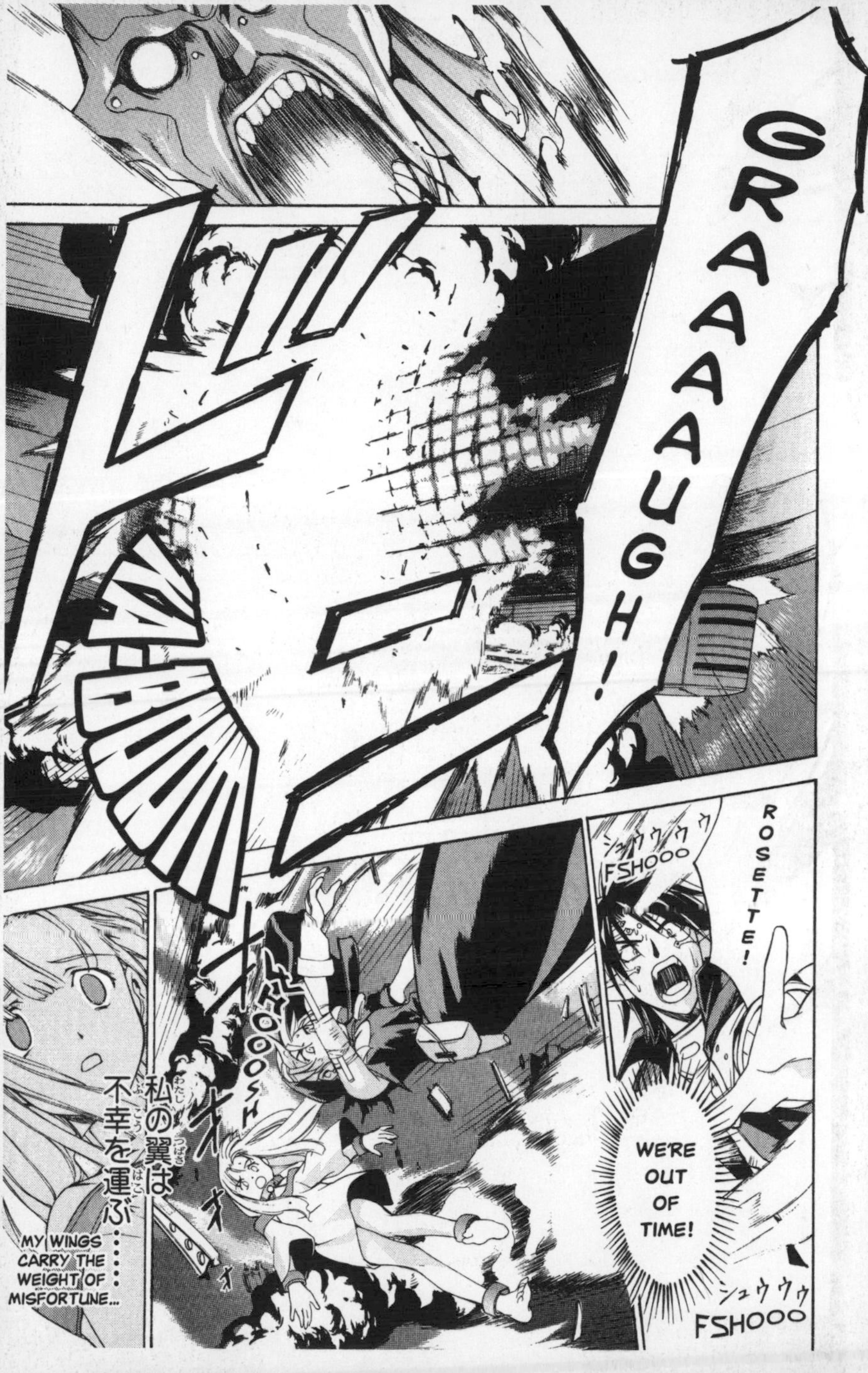
GRAAAAUGH!
ROSETTE!
シュウウウウ
FSHOOO
WE'RE OUT OF TIME!
WHOOOOSH
シュウウ
FSHOOO
私の翼は不幸を運ぶ……
MY WINGS CARRY THE WEIGHT OF MISFORTUNE...

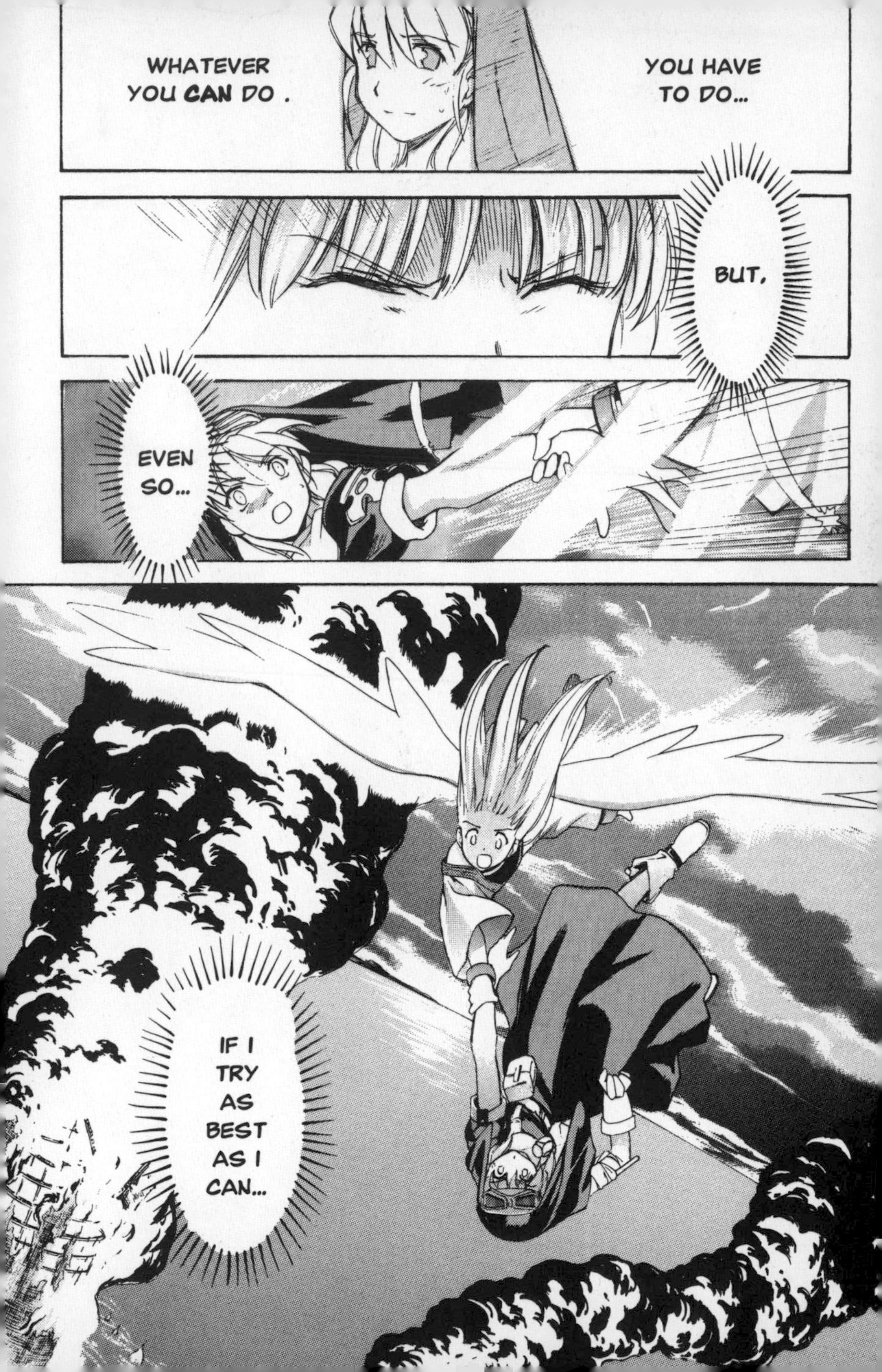
YOU HAVE TO DO...
WHATEVER YOU CAN DO .
BUT,
EVEN SO...
IF I TRY AS BEST AS I CAN...

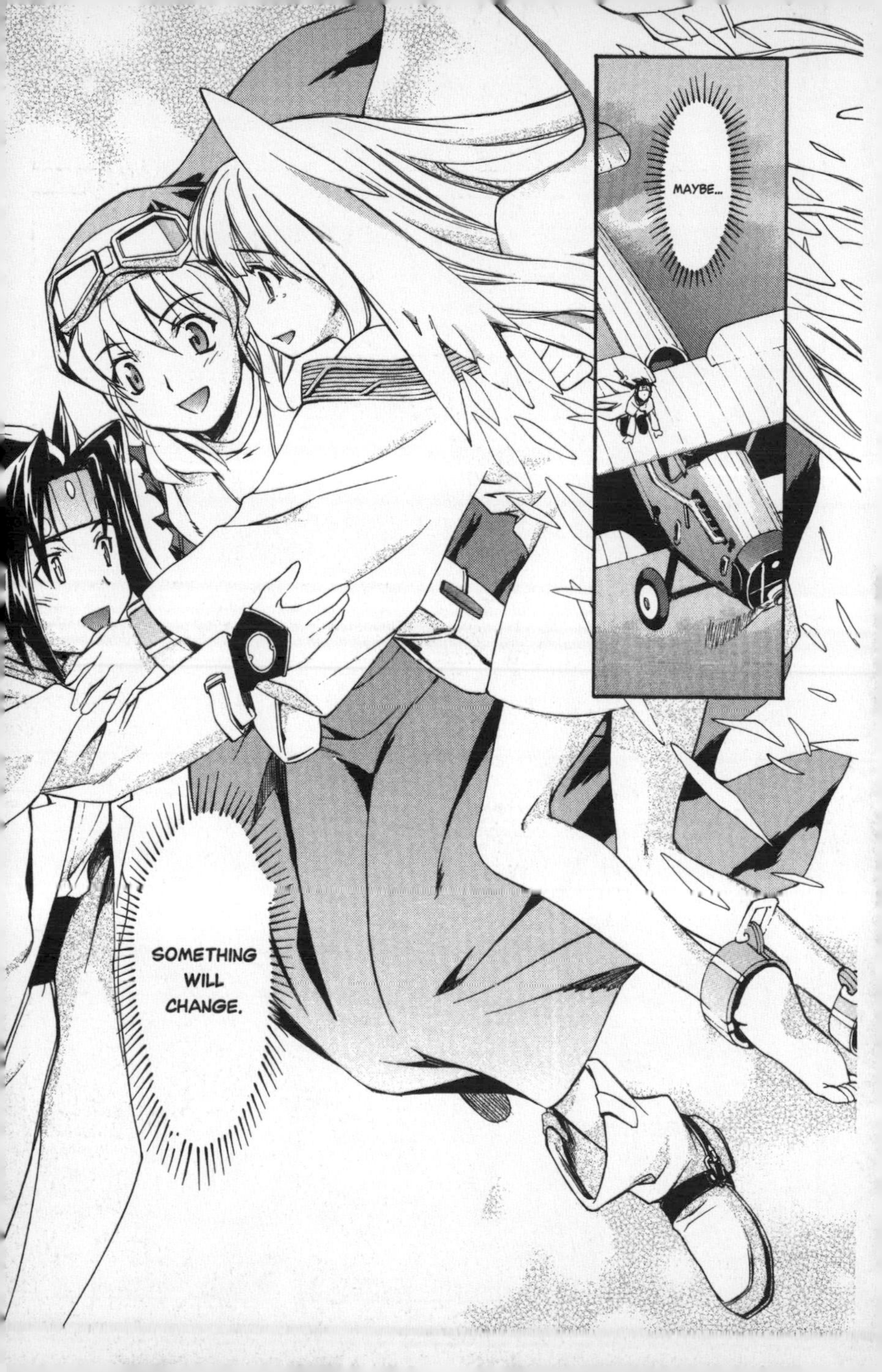
MAYBE...
SOMETHING WILL CHANGE.

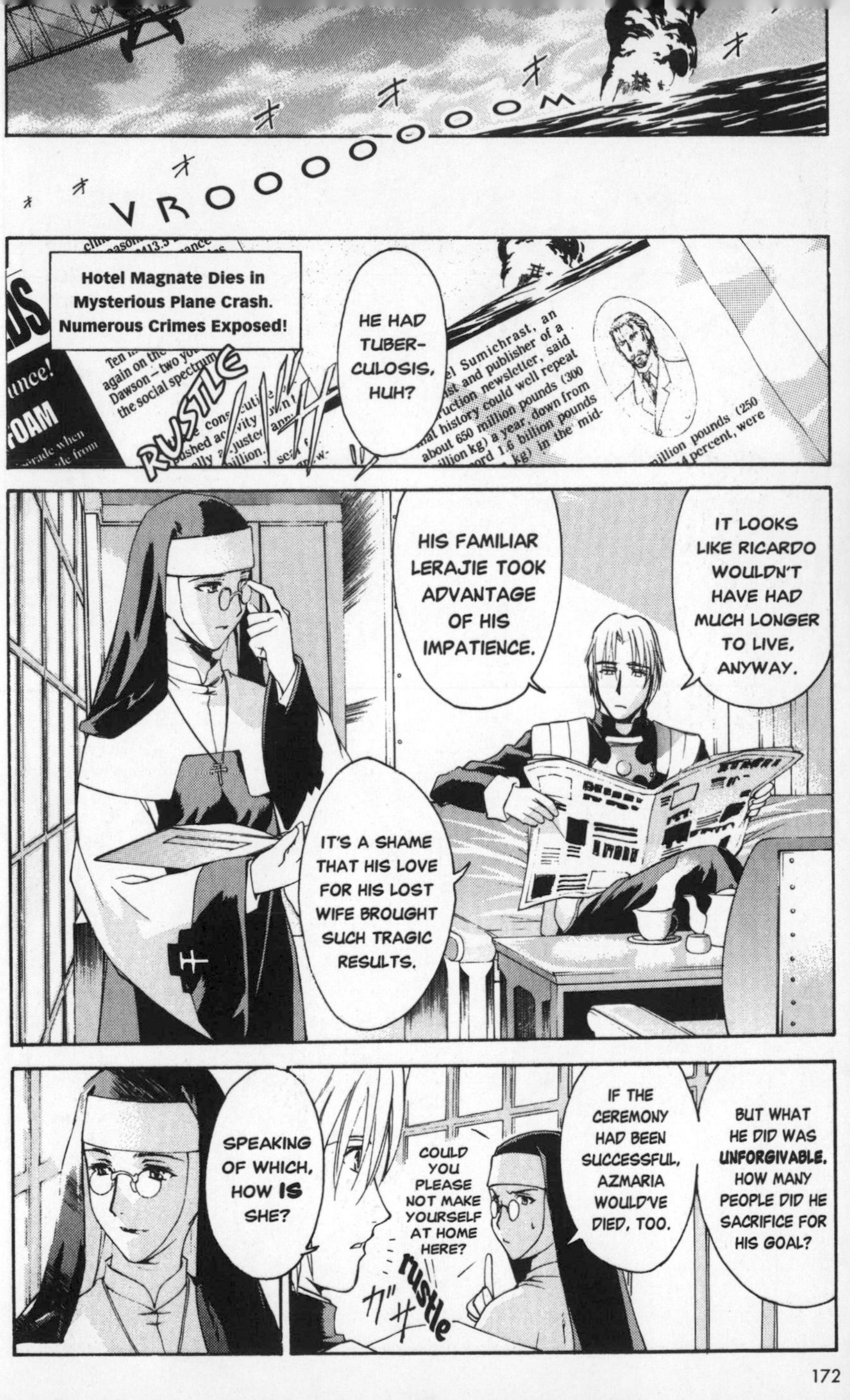
VROOOOOOOOM
HE HAD TUBER-CULOSIS, HUH?
Hotel Magnate Dies in Mysterious Plane Crash. Numerous Crimes Exposed!
RUSTLE
IT LOOKS LIKE RICARDO WOULDN'T HAVE HAD MUCH LONGER TO LIVE, ANYWAY.
HIS FAMILIAR LERAJIE TOOK ADVANTAGE OF HIS IMPATIENCE.
IT'S A SHAME THAT HIS LOVE FOR HIS LOST WIFE BROUGHT SUCH TRAGIC RESULTS.
BUT WHAT HE DID WAS **UNFORGIVABLE.** HOW MANY PEOPLE DID HE SACRIFICE FOR HIS GOAL?
IF THE CEREMONY HAD BEEN SUCCESSFUL, AZMARIA WOULD'VE DIED, TOO.
COULD YOU PLEASE NOT MAKE YOURSELF AT HOME HERE?
SPEAKING OF WHICH, HOW **IS** SHE?
rustle

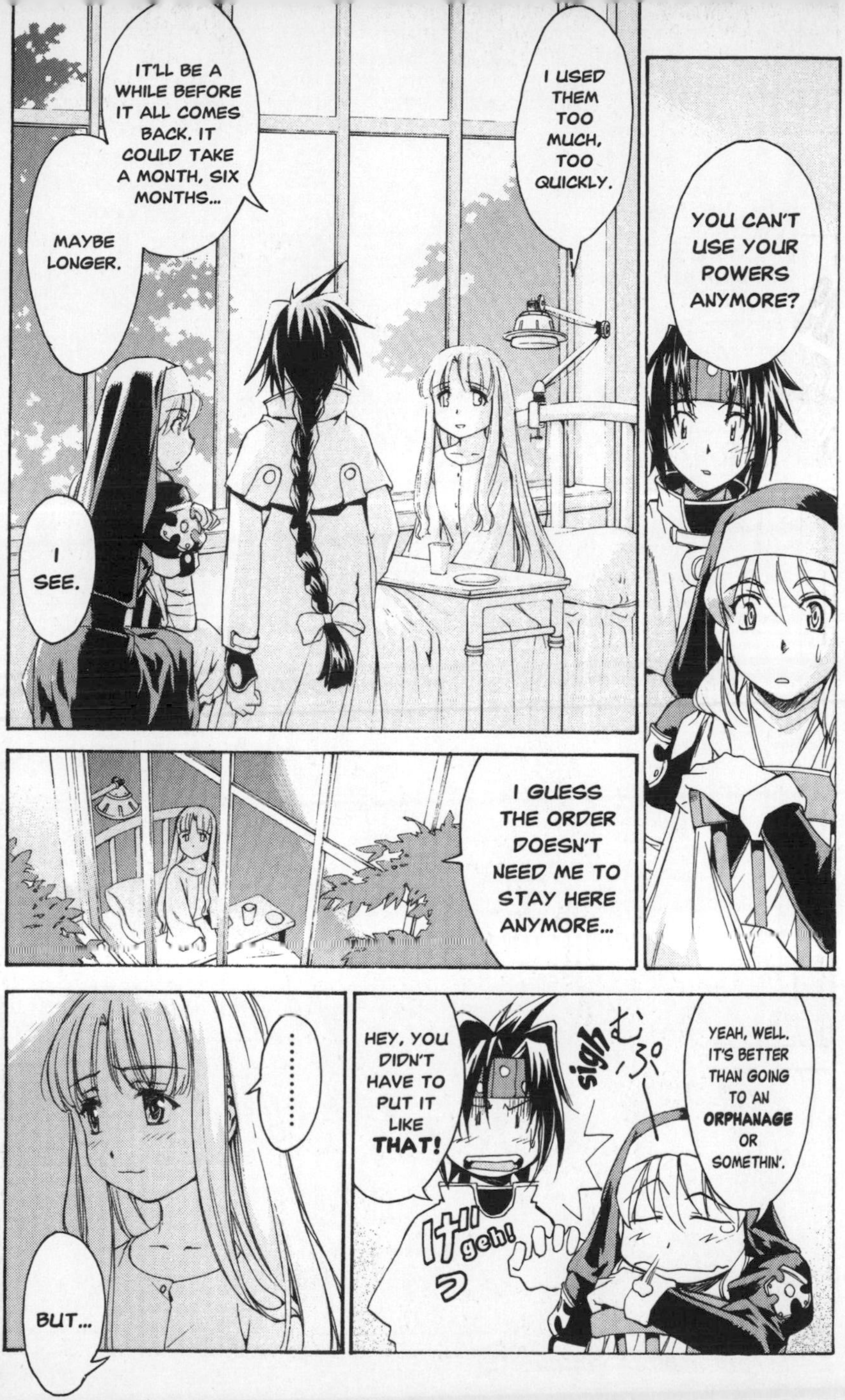
YOU CAN'T USE YOUR POWERS ANYMORE?
I USED THEM TOO MUCH, TOO QUICKLY.
IT'LL BE A WHILE BEFORE IT ALL COMES BACK. IT COULD TAKE A MONTH, SIX MONTHS...
MAYBE LONGER.
I SEE.
I GUESS THE ORDER DOESN'T NEED ME TO STAY HERE ANYMORE...
YEAH, WELL. IT'S BETTER THAN GOING TO AN ORPHANAGE OR SOMETHIN'.
sigh
HEY, YOU DIDN'T HAVE TO PUT IT LIKE THAT!
げっ
geh!
......
BUT...

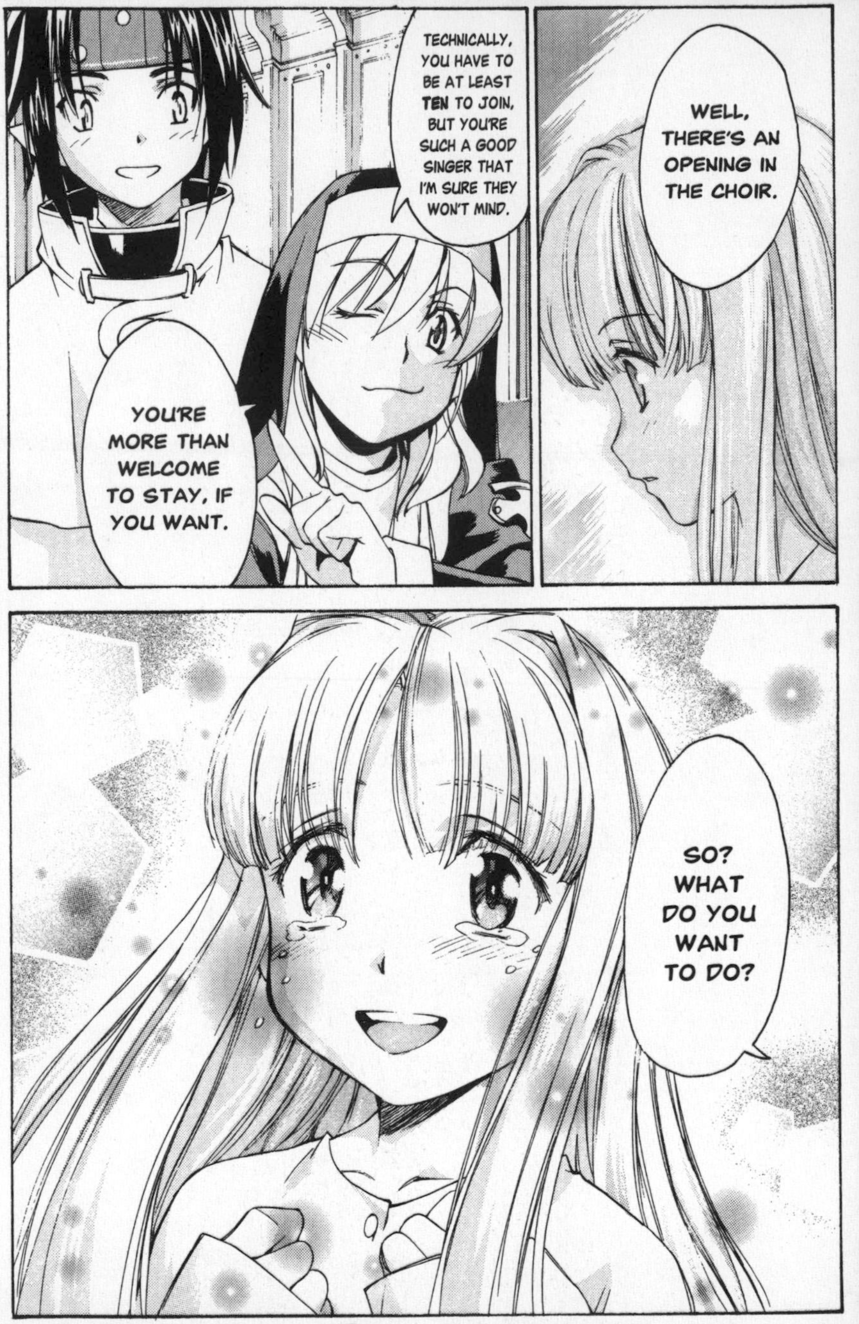
WELL, THERE'S AN OPENING IN THE CHOIR.
TECHNICALLY, YOU HAVE TO BE AT LEAST TEN TO JOIN, BUT YOU'RE SUCH A GOOD SINGER THAT I'M SURE THEY WON'T MIND.
YOU'RE MORE THAN WELCOME TO STAY, IF YOU WANT.
SO? WHAT DO YOU WANT TO DO?

To be continued in Volume 2

STAFF
DAISUKE MORIYAMA
TOKU NORI NAKANISHI
TETSUYA NAKATA
MASASHI KASHIWADA
ARUMI HIGASHI
UI SUZUKI

DESIGN
TADAO NAKAMURA (ARTEN)

EDITOR
AKIRA KAWASHIMA (COMIC DRAGON)
TAKESHI KURIHARA (COMIC DRAGON)
TAKESHI ASANO (DRAGON COMICS)
AKIHIKO NAKADA (DRAGON COMICS)

AFTERWORD My Dream Life in the Doghouse

THE "SOME DAY I'LL HAVE A REAL HOME" CHAPTER

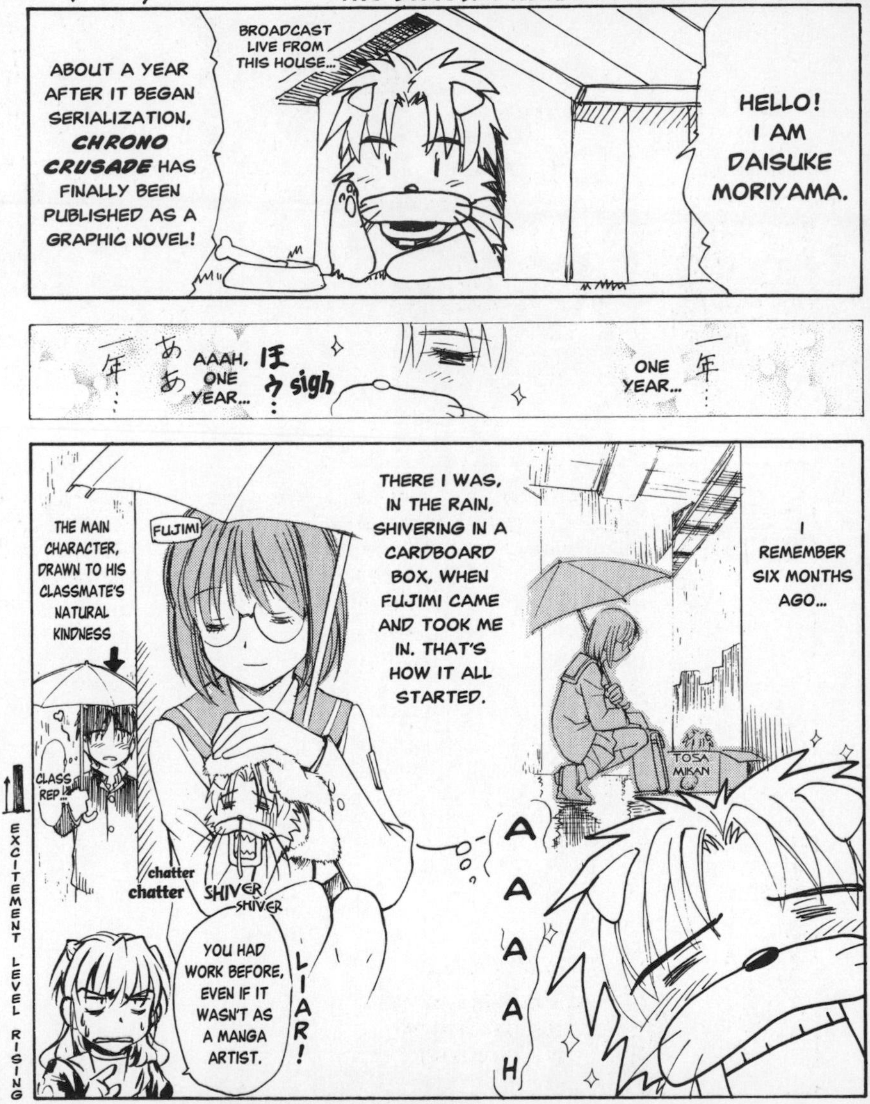
HELLO! I AM DAISUKE MORIYAMA.
BROADCAST LIVE FROM THIS HOUSE...
ABOUT A YEAR AFTER IT BEGAN SERIALIZATION, CHRONO CRUSADE HAS FINALLY BEEN PUBLISHED AS A GRAPHIC NOVEL!
一年…
ONE YEAR...
ほう… sigh
AAAH, ONE YEAR...
ああ
一年…
I REMEMBER SIX MONTHS AGO...
TOSA MIKAN
THERE I WAS, IN THE RAIN, SHIVERING IN A CARDBOARD BOX, WHEN FUJIMI CAME AND TOOK ME IN. THAT'S HOW IT ALL STARTED.
AAAAH
FUJIMI
THE MAIN CHARACTER, DRAWN TO HIS CLASSMATE'S NATURAL KINDNESS
CLASS REP...
chatter chatter
SHIVER SHIVER
LIAR!
YOU HAD WORK BEFORE, EVEN IF IT WASN'T AS A MANGA ARTIST.
EXCITEMENT LEVEL RISING

DOING THOSE "MONSTER COLLECTION" CARDS AND STUFF.

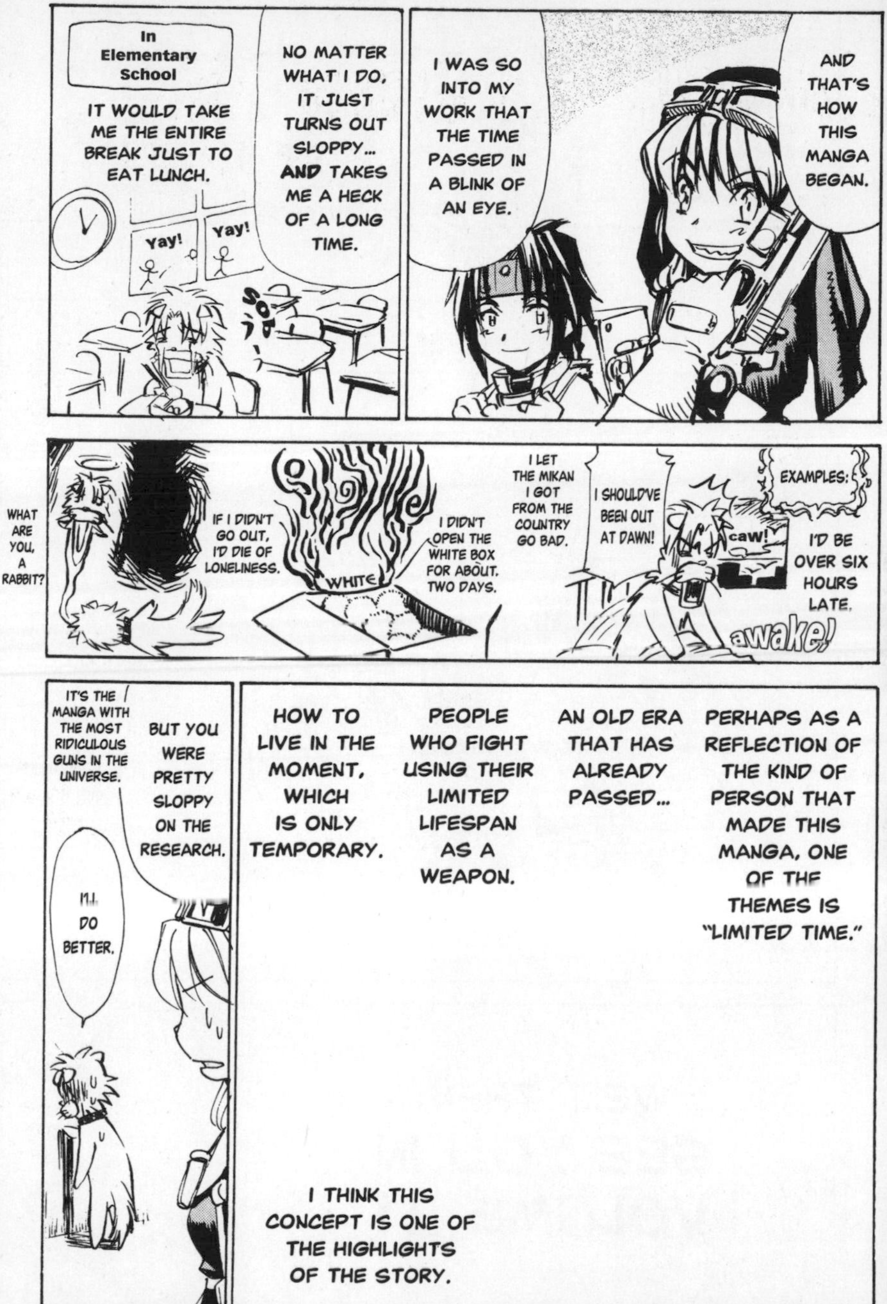
AND THAT'S HOW THIS MANGA BEGAN.
I WAS SO INTO MY WORK THAT THE TIME PASSED IN A BLINK OF AN EYE.
NO MATTER WHAT I DO, IT JUST TURNS OUT SLOPPY... AND TAKES ME A HECK OF A LONG TIME.
In Elementary School
IT WOULD TAKE ME THE ENTIRE BREAK JUST TO EAT LUNCH.
Yay!
Yay!
SOB
EXAMPLES:
I'D BE OVER SIX HOURS LATE.
awake!
caw!
I SHOULD'VE BEEN OUT AT DAWN!
I LET THE MIKAN I GOT FROM THE COUNTRY GO BAD.
I DIDN'T OPEN THE WHITE BOX FOR ABOUT. TWO DAYS.
WHITE
IF I DIDN'T GO OUT, I'D DIE OF LONELINESS.
WHAT ARE YOU, A RABBIT?
PERHAPS AS A REFLECTION OF THE KIND OF PERSON THAT MADE THIS MANGA, ONE OF THE THEMES IS "LIMITED TIME."
AN OLD ERA THAT HAS ALREADY PASSED...
PEOPLE WHO FIGHT USING THEIR LIMITED LIFESPAN AS A WEAPON.
HOW TO LIVE IN THE MOMENT, WHICH IS ONLY TEMPORARY.
I THINK THIS CONCEPT IS ONE OF THE HIGHLIGHTS OF THE STORY.
BUT YOU WERE PRETTY SLOPPY ON THE RESEARCH.
IT'S THE MANGA WITH THE MOST RIDICULOUS GUNS IN THE UNIVERSE.
I'LL DO BETTER.

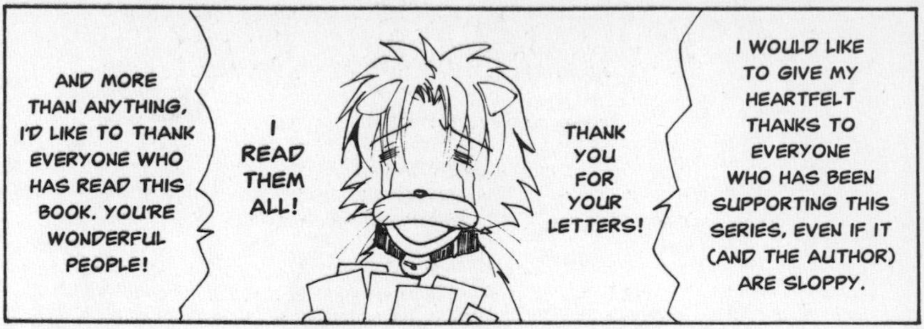
I WOULD LIKE TO GIVE MY HEARTFELT THANKS TO EVERYONE WHO HAS BEEN SUPPORTING THIS SERIES, EVEN IF IT (AND THE AUTHOR) ARE SLOPPY.
THANK YOU FOR YOUR LETTERS!
I READ THEM ALL!
AND MORE THAN ANYTHING, I'D LIKE TO THANK EVERYONE WHO HAS READ THIS BOOK. YOU'RE WONDERFUL PEOPLE!

Preview of the next volume

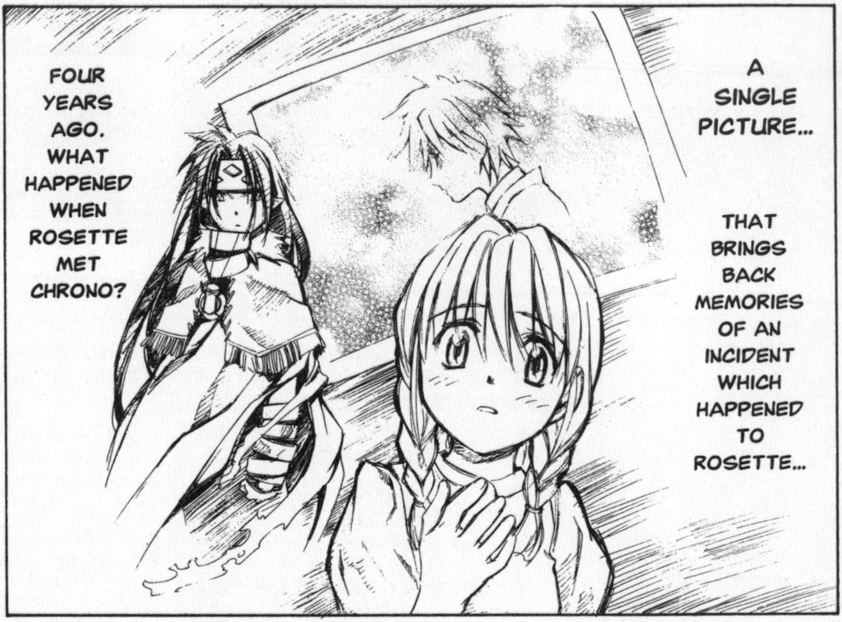
A SINGLE PICTURE...
THAT BRINGS BACK MEMORIES OF AN INCIDENT WHICH HAPPENED TO ROSETTE...
FOUR YEARS AGO. WHAT HAPPENED WHEN ROSETTE MET CHRONO?

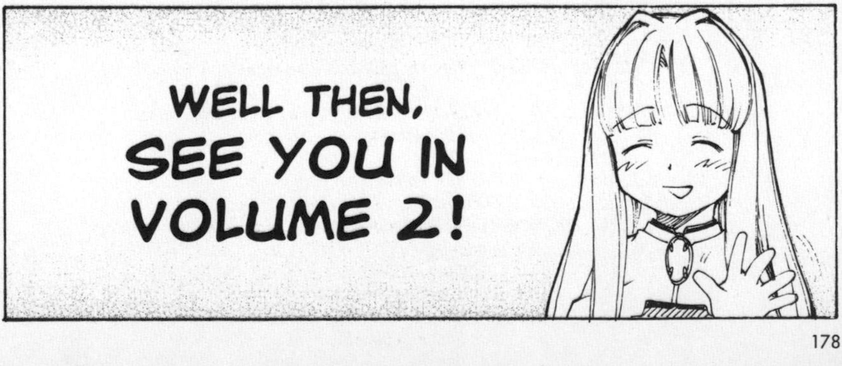
WELL THEN, SEE YOU IN VOLUME 2!

(Originally published as "CHRNO CRUSADE" in Japan.)

© 1999 DAISUKE MORIYAMA
Originally published in Japan in 1999 by KADOKAWA SHOTEN PUBLISHING CO., LTD., Tokyo.
English translation rights arranged with KADOKAWA SHOTEN PUBLISHING CO., LTD., Tokyo.

Translator **AMY FORSYTH**
Lead Translator/Translation Supervisor **JAVIER LOPEZ**
ADV Manga Translation Staff **KAY BERTRAND, BRENDAN FRAYNE, & EIKO McGREGOR**

Print Production/ Art Studio Manager **LISA PUCKETT**
Pre-press Manager **ERNIE ZUNIGA**
Art Production Manager **RYAN MASON**
Sr. Designer/Creative Manager **JORGE ALVARADO**
Graphic Designer/Group Leader **SCOTT SAVAGE**
Graphic Designer **HEATHER GARY**
Graphic Artists **SHANNA JENSCHKE, WINDI MARTIN, LISA RAPER, & GEORGE REYNOLDS**
Graphic Intern **MARK MEZA**

International Coordinator **TORU IWAKAMI**
International Coordinator **ATSUSHI KANBAYASHI**

Publishing Editor **SUSAN ITIN**
Assistant Editor **MARGARET SCHAROLD**
Editorial Assistant **VARSHA BHUCHAR**
Proofreader **SHERIDAN JACOBS**

Research/ Traffic Coordinator **MARSHA ARNOLD**

Executive VP, CFO, COO **KEVIN CORCORAN**

President, CEO & Publisher **JOHN LEDFORD**

Email: editor@adv-manga.com
www.adv-manga.com
www.advfilms.com

For sales and distribution inquiries please call 1.800.282.7202

 is a division of A.D. Vision, Inc.
10114 W. Sam Houston Parkway, Suite 200, Houston, Texas 77099

English text © 2004 published by A.D. Vision, Inc. under exclusive license.
ADV MANGA is a trademark of A.D. Vision, Inc.

ISBN: 1-4139-0084-4
First printing, May 2004
10 9 8 7 6 5 4 3 2 1
Printed in Canada

TRANSLATOR'S NOTES

Chrono Crusade Vol 01

PG. 28 **A Principatus Cross Barrier!**
Principatus is Latin for "rule" or "dominion." It is used here as a reference to the Principalities, the seventh ranking Order of angel. FYI, the Orders of angels (from high to low, according to their closeness to God) are: Seraphim, Cherubim, Thrones, Dominions, Virtues, Powers, Principalities, Archangels, and Angels.

PG. 30 **The Gospel**
Along with the English name for this type of ammunition is its Japanese one, which translates to "Bullet of the Good Word" (i.e. the Gospel).

PG. 44 **(1) Sacred Spirit**
The Japanese name for this translates to "Bullet of the Sacred Fire."

(2) Holy oil
Also called chrism, this is a mixture of oil and balsam used in various Church sacraments.

PG. 68 **Lerajie**
This war-loving spirit (or devil) is said to command thirty legions of his own. Traditionally, he appears in the guise of an archer, and has the handy ability to worsen the damage inflicted by arrows.

PG. 122 **The Second Prophecy**
Specifically, the prophecy stated that if Russia was not consecrated in the Virgin Mary's name and if regular communions were not begun, Russia would "spread her errors throughout the world, causing wars and persecutions of the Church." Proponents of the Fatima prophecy say this points to the spread of Communism.

PG. 124 **The Third Prophecy**
The Vatican finally released the full text (with commentary) of the Third Prophecy in 2000.

PG. 136 **Familiars**
A kind of spirit (or, in this case, demon) at the beck-and-call of its master.

PG. 140 **Geas**
A kind of binding spell.

PG. 148 **Running a fever**
More specifically, Chrono accused Rosette of running the kind of fever that accompanies teething in children.

PG. 176 **(1) Fujimi**
In a none-too-subtle allegory, Daisuke Moriyama is portraying himself as a stray dog taken in by Fujimi (the name of the company that originally published **Chrono Crusade** in Japan).

(2) Mikan
A kind of mandarin orange.

(3) "Monster Collection"
A card-based gaming system along the lines of ***Magic: The Gathering***.

THE ADVENTURE CONTINUES IN

CHRONO CRUSADE
VOL. 2

Vile creatures are flocking to America and infesting the city, leaving the Magdalan Order with no choice but to call on Sister Rosette, the one nun who can flatten demonic enemies and save the souls of their prey. This time, though, the gun-toting nun's past is resurfacing, beginning with flashbacks of a childhood spent in an orphanage, and more importantly, the introduction of her brother. Haunted by her memories, Sister Rosette is quick to overlook a more pressing matter—the demon Aion wants to make a deal with Chrono and it might be too tempting to refuse.

The entire cast of hard-hitting exorcists returns to wipe out another stain of evil upon the world in volume 2 of *Chrono Crusade.*

COMING IN AUGUST 2004 FROM ADV MANGA!

www.adv-manga.com

LETTER FROM THE ADV MANGA TRANSLATION STAFF

Dear Reader,

On behalf of the ADV Manga translation team, thank you for purchasing an ADV book. We are enthusiastic and committed to our work, and strive to carry our enthusiasm over into the book you hold in your hands.

Our goal is to retain the true spirit of the original Japanese book. While great care has been taken to render a true and accurate translation, some cultural or readability issues may require a line to be adapted for greater accessibility to our readers. At times, manga titles that include culturally-specific concepts will feature a "Translator's Notes" section, which explains noteworthy references to the original text.

We hope our commitment to a faithful translation is evident in every ADV book you purchase.

Sincerely,

Javier Lopez
Lead Translator

Eiko McGregor

Kay Bertrand

Brendan Frayne

Amy Forsyth

LETT~~T~~ER FROM THE EDITOR

Dear Reader,

Thank you for purchasing an ADV Manga book. We hope you enjoyed the thrilling adventures of Sister Rosette Christopher and her companion, Chrono, as they battle demons to save the world.

It is our sincere commitment in reproducing Asian comics and graphic novels to retain as much of the character of the original book as possible. From the right-to-left format of the Japanese books to the meaning of the story in the original language, the ADV Manga team is working hard to publish a quality book for our fans and readers. Write to us with your questions or comments, and tell us how you liked this and other ADV books. Be sure to visit our website at www.adv-manga.com and view the list of upcoming titles, sign up for special announcements, and fill out our survey.

The ADV Manga team of translators, designers, graphic artists, production managers, traffic managers, and editors hope you will buy more ADV books—there's a lot more in store from ADV Manga!

www.adv-manga.com

Publishing Editor
Susan B. Itin

Assistant Editor
Margaret Scharold

Editorial Assistant
Varsha Bhuchar

CHRONO✛CRUSADE
Vol. 2

DON'T MISS
THE FURTHER ADVENTURES
OF SISTER ROSETTE
AND CHRONO

Available August 2004

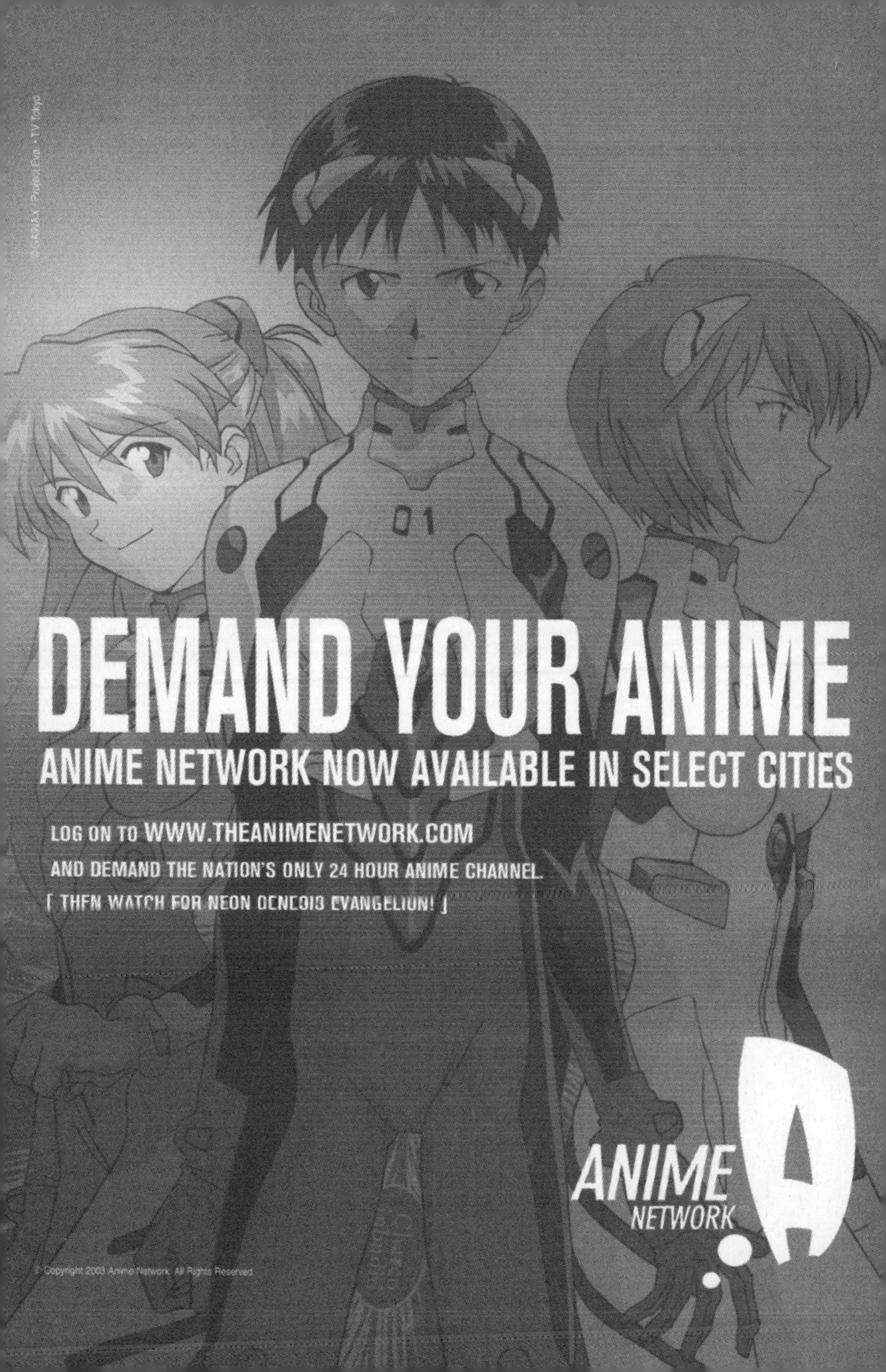
DEMAND YOUR ANIME
ANIME NETWORK NOW AVAILABLE IN SELECT CITIES
LOG ON TO WWW.THEANIMENETWORK.COM
AND DEMAND THE NATION'S ONLY 24 HOUR ANIME CHANNEL.
[THEN WATCH FOR NEON GENESIS EVANGELION!]
ANIME NETWORK
01
© GAINAX / Project Eva. • TV Tokyo
© Copyright 2003 Anime Network. All Rights Reserved.

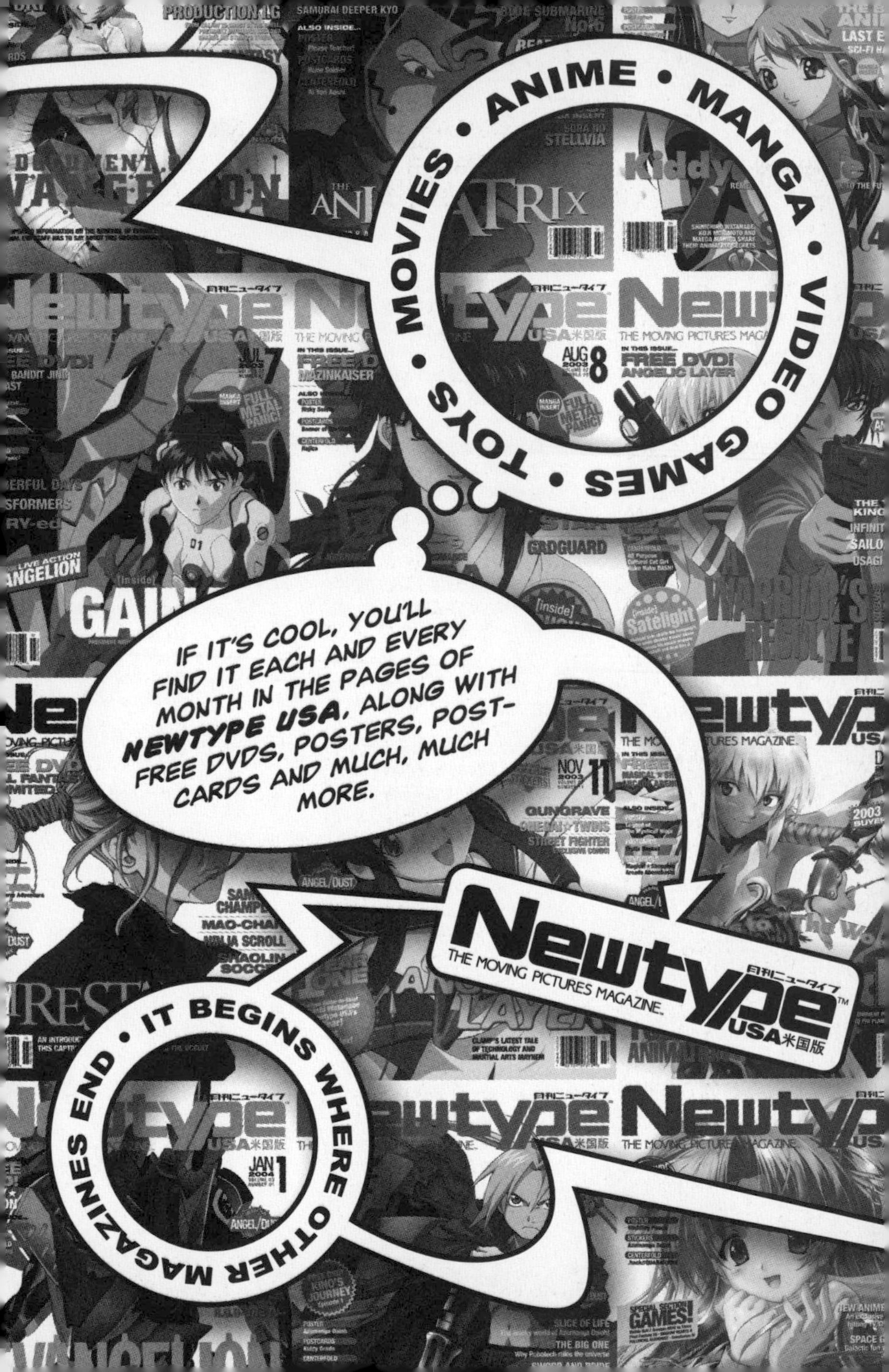
MOVIES • ANIME • MANGA • VIDEO GAMES • TOYS •
IF IT'S COOL, YOU'LL FIND IT EACH AND EVERY MONTH IN THE PAGES OF NEWTYPE USA, ALONG WITH FREE DVDS, POSTERS, POSTCARDS AND MUCH, MUCH MORE.
Newtype™ THE MOVING PICTURES MAGAZINE. 月刊ニュータイプ USA 米国版
IT BEGINS WHERE OTHER MAGAZINES END •